# Captive Selves, Captivating Others

Institutional Structures of Feeling

George E. Marcus, Sharon Traweek, Richard Handler,
and Vera Zolberg, Series Editors

# Captive Selves, Captivating Others

## The Politics and Poetics of Colonial American Captivity Narratives

### Pauline Turner Strong

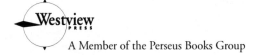

Westview PRESS
A Member of the Perseus Books Group

Institutional Structures of Feeling

Copyright © 1999 by Westview Press, A Member of the Perseus Books Group

Published in 1999 in the United States of America by Westview Press, 5500 Central Avenue, Boulder, Colorado 80301-2877, and in the United Kingdom by Westview Press, 12 Hid's Copse Road, Cumnor Hill, Oxford OX2 9JJ


Library of Congress Cataloging-in-Publication Data
Strong, Pauline Turner, 1953–
    Captive selves, captivating others : the politics and poetics of colonial American captivity narratives / Pauline Turner Strong.
        p.    cm.—(Institutional structures of feeling)
    Includes bibliographical references and index.
    ISBN 0-8133-1665-0 (hc) —ISBN 0-8133-1666-9 (pb)
    1. American prose literature—Colonial period, ca. 1600–1775—
History and criticism.    2. Indian captivities—Historiography.
3. Politics and literature—United States—History—17th century.
4. Politics and literature—United States—History—18th century.
5. Captivities in literature.    6. Indians in literature.
7. Narration (Rhetoric).    I. Title.    II. Series.

PS173.I6S78   1999
818'.10809358—dc21                                                              98-52413
                                                                                    CIP


The paper used in this publication meets the requirements of the American National Standard for Permanence of Paper for Printed Library Materials Z39.48-1984.

*PERSEUS*
**POD**
ON DEMAND         10        9        8        7        6        5        4        3        2        1

In memory of
D'Arcy McNickle
1904–1977
and
Alfonso Ortiz
1939–1997

and in honor of one of their enduring legacies—
the D'Arcy McNickle Center for the History of the American Indian,
at the Newberry Library

# Contents

# Maps and Figures

# Chronology of Events, 1576–1776

Shipwreck and captivity of Jonathan Dickinson (1696)

1702–1713     Second intercolonial war (Queen Anne's War, the
              American phase of the War of the Spanish
              Succession)

Captivity of John and Eunice Williams (1704)

1714          John Williams unsuccessfully attempts to redeem his
              daughter Eunice

1720          Narratives of Mary Rowlandson, Jonathan Dickinson,
              and John Williams reprinted

1723–1727     Hostilities in Maine and New Hampshire known
              variously as Grey Lock's War, Lord Dummer's War,
              or Lovewell's War

Captivity of Elizabeth Hanson (1724)

1730s–1740s   Religious revival known as the Great Awakening

Eunice Williams and her husband Arosen pay three
visits to Deerfield (1741–1744)

1744–1748     Third intercolonial war (King George's War, the
              American phase of the War of the Austrian
              Succession)

Captivity of Nehemiah How (1745) and John Norton
(1746)

Shipwreck and captivity of Briton Hammon (1747)

1754–1763     Fourth intercolonial war (the French and Indian War,
              the American phase of the Seven Years' War)

Captivity of Peter Williamson (1754), William and
Elizabeth Fleming (1755), Marie Le Roy and Barbara
Leininger (1755), Regina Leininger (1755), Robert
Eastburn (1756), Jean Lowry (1756), Thomas Brown
(1757), and John Maylem (1757)

1756          Seven Years' War begins in Europe with British
              declaration of war against France

1763          Seven Years' War ends with the Treaty of Paris

1763–1766     Pontiac's War

Captivity of Isaac Hollister (1763) and Charles Saunders
(1763)

1764–1765     Delawares and Shawnees release Regina Leininger and
              other captives to Col. Henry Bouquet

1766          Treaty concluded between Pontiac and Sir William
              Johnson

1770–1776     Numerous reprints of the narratives of Mary
              Rowlandson, Jonathan Dickinson, and John Williams
              appear

# Preface and Acknowledgments

Long ago John Aubrey, bibliographer extraordinaire at the Newberry Library, cautioned me against becoming captivated by the British colonial captivity narratives that I discuss in this book. Despite his warning my captivation has lasted for more than two decades, since I first read James Axtell's essay "The White Indians of Colonial America." In these years several excellent literary and ethnohistorical studies of captivity narratives have appeared, but none that analyze the entire set of colonial captivity narratives in light of current theories of colonial representation and practice. In aiming to do just that, I have considered not only all the narratives of captivity among Indians published in British North America but also the largely untold stories of Native Americans captured by British explorers and colonists. The more familiar captivity narratives of Capt. John Smith, gentlewoman Mary Rowlandson, and the Rev. John Williams appear in a new light when read alongside less familiar stories of captivity, particularly those concerning Native American captives. The "Captive Selves" of the title, then, are intentionally ambiguous, as are the "Captivating Others."

It is with equal measures of pleasure and embarrassment that I acknowledge the generosity of the many individuals and institutions that have contributed to the writing of this book. My interest in Anglo-American representations of Native Americans was inspired by the late Alfonso Ortiz of the University of New Mexico, and it was sustained at the University of Chicago by Raymond Fogelson and George Stocking. Their support as well as that of the late David Schneider was crucial in the early stages of this study, when research on American culture and history remained unusual, even suspect, in anthropology. The theoretical approach developed in this book is much indebted to my studies in philosophy at the Colorado College, where I also was introduced to the field of ethnohistory by Marianne Stoller. Much of my research was conducted at the D'Arcy McNickle Center for the History of the American Indian at the Newberry Library, where I benefited immensely from John Aubrey's expertise, the superb Edward E. Ayer Collection, and a lively, interdisciplinary community of scholars and writers. In addition to John Aubrey I want to thank Mary Druke Becker, Francis Jennings, Frederick Hoxie,

David Miller, Jacqueline Peterson, William Swagerty, and Helen Tanner
for facilitating my research at the Center. I am also grateful to Thomas
Buckley of the University of Massachusetts at Boston and to James and
Martha Davis of Harvard University for making it possible for me to
spend time in New England.

I am greatly indebted to those whose advice and criticism have made
this a better book and whose support and encouragement have been crucial to its completion. Eric Cheyfitz, Jean Comaroff, Raymond Fogelson,
Nancy Munn, Daniel Segal, George Stocking, and Barrik Van Winkle offered valuable critical comments on early drafts—only some of which I
have been able to take into account. Daniel Segal and Harry Liebersohn
gave me the opportunity to participate in an interdisciplinary conference
at the Claremont Colleges, where James Boon, Don Brenneis, Mary
Campbell, Derek Sayer, and Brackette Williams offered particularly help-
ful comments. James Lawrence, June Namias, and Kay Schaffer have
each shared unpublished work with me, and Professors Lawrence and
Namias organized stimulating interdisciplinary panels for the Western
Social Science Association and the Sixth Berkshire Conference on the History of Women. The annual meetings of the American Society for Ethnohistory facilitated my interaction with colonial historians, and I am especially grateful to James Axtell, Jean O'Brien, and Neal Salisbury for
welcoming me into the fold.

I also wish to acknowledge the extent to which this book builds upon
the work of scholars of history, literature, philosophy, religion, American
studies, women's studies, and cultural studies as well as anthropology.
Interdisciplinary research generates distinctive insights, but it also com-
pounds one's opportunities for error. I sincerely hope that the reader,
whatever his or her field, will find that the former outweigh the latter.

Support for the research on which the book is based was generously
provided by the National Science Foundation, the Danforth Foundation,
the Phillips Fund of the American Philosophical Society, and the D'Arcy
McNickle Center for the History of the American Indian at the Newberry
Library. The book was completed at the University of Texas at Austin,
where relatively uninterrupted time for writing was provided by a Summer Research Award and a Dean's Fellowship from the College of Liberal
Arts. The Department of Anthropology at Texas is an exceptionally stimulating and supportive environment. I am particularly grateful to my
graduate students for all they have taught me, and to James Brow, Joel
Sherzer, Kathleen Stewart, and Samuel Wilson for facilitating my writing
and influencing my thinking.

Given my theoretical debt to Raymond Williams, it is especially grati-
fying to be included in the Institutional Structures of Feeling series. I
thank series editor Richard Handler for his interest in the book, the edi-

torial and production staff at Westview for their patience, and Rebecca Ritke for thorough and insightful copyediting. Barrik Van Winkle generously assisted in the preparation of the maps, genealogy, and index, and the staff of the Newberry Library prepared most of the illustrations. The American Museum of Natural History and the Arizona Board of Regents have graciously permitted me to reprint material included in two previous publications ("Captive Images," Natural History 94 (12), December 1985, and "Captivity in White and Red," in Crossing Cultures: Essays in the Displacement of Western Civilization, ed. Daniel Segal, University of Arizona Press, 1992).

As much as I owe my teachers, colleagues, and students, my deepest gratitude is to my family. Although I have no doubt utilized it in unexpected ways, my upbringing in a family with strong Congregational and Quaker roots has strongly influenced this project. Hatsy, Nancy, and Martha Strong offered steadfast support and serve as models for gracefully combining a commitment to family, work, and community. Barrik Van Winkle put my work ahead of his own on many critical occasions, often at considerable sacrifice. Our daughters, Katie and Tina Van Winkle, cheerfully endured my captivity by this project and helped me maintain balance and perspective. Perhaps it is not entirely coincidental that their literary namesake, Rip Van Winkle, was thought by some of his acquaintances to have been "carried away by Indians."

Pauline Turner Strong<br>
Austin, Texas

# A Note on the Text

Decisions regarding whether or not to modernize language are commonly couched in terms familiar to anthropologists: They have to do with whether one wants to make a text (and its authors) more familiar or more strange, more transparent or more opaque. Because I have relied on a mixture of original and modernized sources, for consistency's sake I have generally followed modern conventions with regard to capitalization, spelling, and punctuation, with two notable exceptions: I have preserved italics when they indicate a quotation or are clearly used for emphasis, and I have quoted longer passages in the original version when I want to foreground their style. This is the case, for example, when I quote from Increase Mather and Cotton Mather, whose writing style evokes the spoken word.

Where there are several variants of Native American tribal, personal, and place names I have employed the form I consider most accurate, except in quotations, when I have retained the original form. Common variants are mentioned in the text or endnotes.

All dates are in modern notation.

# 1

## Introduction: Captivity As Convergent Practice and Selective Tradition

*Tradition is in practice the most evident expression of the dominant and hegemonic pressures and limits. It is always more than an inert historicized segment; indeed it is the most powerful practical means of incorporation. What we have to see is not just 'a tradition' but a* selective *tradition; an intentionally selective version of a shaping past and a pre-shaped present, which is then powerfully operative in the process of social and cultural definition and identification.*

—*Raymond Williams,* Marxism and Literature *(1977:115)*

In a selective tradition that dates to the seventeenth century, Anglo-American identity is represented as the product of struggles in and against the wild: struggles of a collective Self surrounded by a threatening but enticing wilderness, a Self that seeks to domesticate this wilderness as well as the savagery within itself, and that opposes itself to Others portrayed as savage, bestial, demonic, and seductive. Originally an outgrowth of the Puritan penchant for defining the individual and collective Self through opposition to presumably uncivil, ungodly Others, this remarkably resilient fabrication of identity took shape during the century of colonial wars preceding the American Revolution. In the course of extended struggles among English, French, Algonquian, Iroquoian, and other groups for control over northeastern North America,[1] a significant number of English colonists were taken captive by Native Americans. For the Puritan colonists of New England, who were continually searching for signs of the work of Providence in the world, these captivities came to epitomize the spiritual trial posed to the colonists by the American wilderness, its savage inhabitants, and perhaps most importantly, the savagery within themselves. By the mid-eighteenth century, colonists were representing the experience of captivity among Indians in a more

variegated fashion while continuing to find in captivity a compelling representation of an emerging American Self undergoing assault and transformation.

The most famous Anglo-American narrative of captivity among Indians, by Capt. John Smith, dates to his *Generall Historie* of 1624. Initially
more influential in the development of a selective tradition of captivity,
however, was a late seventeenth-century spiritual autobiography recounting the wilderness trials and redemption of a clergyman's wife,
Mary White Rowlandson, who was taken captive in 1676 during Metacom's War (or "King Philip's War"). Over the next half century the spiritual significance of captivity in the wilderness would be developed in a
corpus of widely disseminated narratives by or about Puritan and
Quaker captives, mainly women. Another dozen narratives of captivity
were published during the remaining decades of the colonial era, for the
most part during or immediately following the fourth intercolonial war
(or "French and Indian War"), of 1754–63.[2] In contrast to Puritan and
Quaker captivity narratives, mid-eighteenth-century narratives are often
secular accounts by male prisoners of war.

After Independence two dozen additional narratives by or about colonial captives were published, culminating in the unusual life history of
Dehewamis or Mary Jemison (1824), an adopted and thoroughly assimilated English captive among the Seneca. Meanwhile, from the late eighteenth century onward, post-Revolutionary captivity narratives, anthologies, visual representations of captivity, and completely fictional
accounts became common. Approximately two dozen fictional treatments of captivity, often based on John Smith's account of his rescue by
Pocahontas, preceded the publication in 1826 of James Fenimore
Cooper's classic *The Last of the Mohicans*.[3] Since Cooper, the captivity
theme has persisted in Anglo-American literature and popular culture as
a pervasive mode of representing a distinctively Euro-American identity.
The selective tradition of captivity has expanded from print to drama,
public sculpture, children's games, film, and television, remaining today
an implicit model for representations of threatening otherness.[4]

In sharp contrast to the dominant representation, captivity was practiced in both directions across the border between Native and colonial societies—a border that was considerably more fluid than it appears in
most historical representations. The practice of captivity in what Pratt
has called the "contact zone" (1992) has an extraordinarily complex history: one that extends back not only to the beginning of the European invasion of North America but beyond, since indigenous practices of captivity themselves were borderland phenomena. This book focuses on
only a portion of that history: captivity across the British–Native American borders during the two centuries between 1576 and 1776. These were

years of intensive exploration and colonial settlement, transformative interaction, and intermittent warfare, involving several indigenous wars of resistance[5] as well as four intercolonial wars between Britain and its indigenous allies, on the one hand, and France and its allies, on the other.

This book has three main aims: First, I analyze the representations of the collective Self and its significant Others that colonial Anglo-Americans developed in their accounts of captivity among Indians. Second, I attempt to demonstrate that captivity itself was a complex practice in which various indigenous and European traditions of mediation, redemption, and revitalization converged. Third, I explore the relationship between captivity as a historical practice and captivity as represented in what I call the *selective* or *hegemonic tradition of captivity*. I maintain that it is in large part through the suppression of the complexity of captivity as a practice—and particularly the suppression of the colonists' role as captors of Indians—that the selective tradition of captivity has gained its ideological force. In order to look closely at the relationship between colonial practice and representation I have confined my analysis to the years preceding the Revolutionary War.

Situating my study in the nexus of practice and representation has required me to bring together three scholarly traditions that are in themselves already interdisciplinary: ethnohistory, women's studies, and American cultural studies. The next section introduces my theoretical and methodological approach, and the one that follows it relates my approach to previous scholarship on the practice and representation of captivity. The introduction closes with a brief overview of the book, highlighting the central tales of captivity that will be told and retold. Readers who are more interested in the substance of the book than in its theoretical moorings and ambitions may wish to turn directly to the overview.

## Identity, Alterity, and the Process of Typification

> HERE LIES THE BODY
> OF LIEU[T] MEHUMAN HINSDELL
> DECD MAY YE 9TH 1736.
> IN THE 63D YEAR OF HIS
> AGE. WHO WAS THE FIRST
> MALE CHILD BORN IN THIS
> PLACE AND WAS TWICE CAPTIVATED
> BY THE INDIAN SALVAGES
>
> —*Tombstone in Deerfield, Massachusetts*
> *(formerly a Pocumtuck Indian town)*
> (Baker and Coleman 1925)

In American literary history the genre called, curiously enough, "Indian captivity narratives" has been considered the first indigenous literary tradition. That colonial literature appears in the scholarship as indigenously American indicates the extent to which captivity among Indians is part of an exclusionary and appropriative tradition. Indeed, Raymond Williams's definition of a hegemonic tradition may be taken as a condensation of the problematic that motivates this study. For Williams a tradition is a "radically selective" and "actively shaping force" that is "intended to connect with and ratify the present." It is, in particular, "powerfully operative in the process of social and cultural definition and identification" as well as exclusion (Williams 1977:115–116). If representations of captivity comprise a hegemonic tradition in this sense—as I attempt in this book to demonstrate—a critical analysis of this tradition must have at least four dimensions. It must (1) analyze the tradition's "shape" or structure, identifying the principles of selection that order this particular version of the past; (2) contextualize the tradition within a broader field of intercultural practice, revealing crucial elements that the tradition excludes or obscures; (3) locate the tradition socially, indicating the combination of position, perception, interest, and influence that have given the tradition its distinctive shape and connection to the present; and (4) relate the tradition, thus defined, to alternative traditions and to the ongoing process through which social and cultural identity, difference, and domination are constructed and contested. Considering all of these dimensions of the selective tradition of captivity requires a combination of textual and ethnohistorical analysis.

Williams's definition of tradition is a development and specification of one significant dimension of Antonio Gramsci's concept of cultural hegemony.[6] The captivity tradition may be considered what Williams calls an "element of a hegemony" (1977:111), insofar as it is part of the process through which a dominant social group legitimates its power by grounding it in a set of authoritative understandings. These understandings are taken for granted, and they permeate and structure lived experience. Alfred Schutz, a phenomenological theorist of the "natural attitude" of everyday experience, called such naturalized, taken-for-granted understandings "typifications"—a term I have adopted to refer to the conventional representations employed in the captivity tradition.[7] The two most significant typifications in this tradition are an oppositional pair that I call the Captive Self and the Captivating Other (the Captivating *Savage,* in colonial terminology).

A particularly revealing visual representation of these typifications, Horatio Greenough's *The Rescue* (see Figure 1.1), stood for a century at the east entrance to the U.S. Capitol Building, until its removal in 1958. In this monument to triumphant nationhood, a fully and archaically clothed

FIGURE 1.1 *The Rescue*, by Horatio Greenough, displayed at the east entrance to the U.S. Capitol Building between 1853 and 1958. SOURCE: Architect of the Capitol.

European male rescues a partially disrobed woman and her child from the uplifted tomahawk of a naked male Indian. Skillfully deploying oppositions in race, gender, civility, and rationality, Greenough's sculpture both depicts the vulnerability of European civilization in the American wilderness and legitimates the nation's use of force against savage Others.[8]

As we will see, the Captive Self, Captivating Other, and Noble Redeemer sculpted by Greenough are conventional representations thoroughly embodied in a hegemonic tradition—that is, they are *typifications*. I use this term rather than certain more common but less revealing alternatives—*images, stereotypes, figures, tropes*—in order to emphasize the relationship among analytical abstractions (my own Captive Self and Captivating Other), artistic or literary abstractions (Greenough's figures, for instance), and the socially constructed "natural attitude" or "habitus" (Bourdieu 1977) of lived experience. To explain: Schutz's concept of typification extends the Weberian notion of "ideal type" to the socially constructed "natural attitude" of lived experience. Although Weber himself was particularly interested in establishing the value and status of ideal types in social science, he considered the theorist's "ideal typical representations" or "conceptual constructs" more systematic, internally consistent, and consciously formulated versions of the "collective concepts" and "naturalistic prejudices" of everyday life.[9] Both common sense and theoretical concepts are abstractions in Hegel's sense—one-sided, simplified perspectives of the infinite complexity of the concrete, which accentuate certain situationally relevant aspects of experience. The Captive Self and Captivating Savage of my analysis, then, are second-order analytical typifications that synthesize and abstract from the various first-order typifications of colonial captives and Indian captors found in the captivity tradition, and that both constitute and reflect the lived experience of captivity.[10]

Schutz called attention to the need for studies of the typifications of those treated as Others because they do not participate in the same culturally constructed natural attitude.[11] One such study, explicitly based on Schutz, is Keith Basso's (1979) exemplary monograph on Western Apache typifications of "the Whiteman." Basso analyzes how Western Apache jokes typify or "epitomize" dominant Others by highlighting oppositions between Anglo-American and Apache behavior. Using the sociolinguistic concepts of structural opposition and poetic foregrounding, Basso demonstrates how Western Apache typifications of "the Whiteman" select behavioral elements for their contrast with those of the ideal Apache Self, distorting the selected elements so as to heighten the contrast.

This book, in a complementary fashion, considers two key typifications within the Anglo-American captivity tradition: the Captive Self and the Captivating Other. In addition to analyzing a hegemonic tradition of representation, I seek to illuminate the processes through which typifications are constructed, made authoritative, challenged, and transformed. In considering the conditions under which typifications are resisted, I draw on Gramsci's concept of alternative or oppositional hegemonies. These hegemonies challenge the dominant ideology, most often in derivative terms.[12] The complexity and dynamism of the concept "cultural hegemony" resides in its recognition of the importance of alternative or oppositional hegemonies, their dependence on the hegemonic, and their vulnerability to efforts to incorporate and diffuse them. When dealing with genuinely multicultural interactions such as those considered here, however, resistance and opposition draw on competing hegemonies that are far more radically alternative than in the situations of class conflict explored by Gramsci. In the British–Native American contact zone, various European, Iroquoian, and Algonquian traditions of captivity competed and to some extent converged.

In scholarship as in hegemonic representation, captivity has often been decontextualized such that it is viewed as a distinctively Indian practice rather than as a complex historical phenomenon affected in significant ways by European colonial discourses and practices. Recently, however, ethnohistorians have begun to demonstrate the extent to which northeastern Indian patterns of warfare, captivity, and diplomacy were transformed as they met the demographic, political, economic, and cultural challenges imposed by European colonial expansion. Ethnohistorians and other scholars are also beginning to acknowledge the extent to which Europeans used captivity as a strategy of colonial domination. As a result, those captivity practices coded as "Indian" in the hegemonic tradition are now being revealed as a "convergence" of multiple captivity practices, both indigenous and colonial.[13] Drawing upon Marshall Sahlins (1981) this convergence might be considered a "structure of the conjuncture," but I have found a more processual concept somewhat more useful: Richard White's "middle ground," defined as "the place in between: in between cultures, peoples, and in between empires and the nonstate world of villages," a place of partially shared meanings and practices born out of a search for "common meanings" and "cultural congruence" (1991:i, x, 85). I remain influenced, however, by Sahlins's emphasis on the power of elites to exploit the colonial encounter and manage its interpretation, as well as limitations upon that power.

My analysis, then, views captivity both as a middle ground of shared meanings and practices and as a hegemonic tradition. More precisely, it is the relationship between the middle ground and the hegemonic tradition that interests me: the complex relationship between captivity as a convergent historical practice and captivity narratives as a discourse of domination. Considering the relationship between representation and domination—colonial knowledge and colonial power—brings into play another stream of theoretical inspiration for this study: works by scholars such as Michel Foucault (1965, 1978, 1979, 1980) and Edward W. Said (1978) on the Western European construction and domination of Others.[14] Although a number of studies have presented the colonized Other as an "invention" or "projection" of European colonial powers, I aim to do justice to the extent to which the typification of the Other is a precipitate, as it were, of an intercultural encounter in which Native people as well as colonists were significant actors and interpreters.[15] I consider a problem of limited scope so that I can present a fine-grained analysis of "othering" as a symbolic, social, and historical process; and I situate my study in a colonial context, in which power relations were ambiguous and shifting, in order to consider hegemony-in-the-making—that is, collective identification and exclusion in the process of construction and contestation.[16]

Perhaps most significantly, in contrast to many analyses of the construction of cultural difference, and in line with the work of Michael Taussig on the play of mimesis and alterity (1993) and Eric Cheyfitz on imperialist metaphors (1997), my analysis of the selective tradition of captivity emphasizes how constructions of the Other are built not only on symbolic oppositions but also on continuities and resemblances. Uncovering the identification with Others that to some extent always accompanies the positing of difference is essential for understanding on what basis the cultural construction of difference is both fashioned and open to challenge.

The captivity tradition is a privileged arena for considering how identification with an Other underlies and complements even the most extreme opposition to that Other. To anticipate my argument, among indigenous peoples captivity is itself an incorporative, transformative operation upon Captive Others. On the other hand, Anglo-American captives often resisted identification with their captors with an urgency that reveals the force with which the possibility of "turning savage"—becoming other—was experienced. In the words of Roy Harvey Pearce, the intellectual historian whose analysis of "the image of the Indian" foreshadows many contemporary concerns with the cultural construction of otherness, the Indian "became important for the English mind, not for what he was in and of himself, but for what he showed civilized men they were not and must not be" (1965:5).[17] The Captivating Savage—understood in its figurative sense as well as in the archaic, literal sense used on colonial tombstones—not only defines but undermines, not only threatens but seduces, the Captive Self.

Both in quoting Pearce's passage about the "English mind" and in employing the term *Self* in a collective sense, I knowingly run the risk of appearing to revert to assumptions of cultural homogeneity that have been thoroughly criticized in anthropology, history, and literary studies alike. Let me stress that the Captive Self is not a psychological entity but a typification, a representation of collective identity—one that was constructed, challenged, and transformed through identifiable social processes. It is not isomorphic with any particular self, although as a hegemonic typification of identity it has played a role in shaping particular "structures of feeling" in American selves (to borrow a term from Raymond Williams that will be discussed in greater detail in Chapter 7) (1977:128–135).

The Captive Self is necessarily a relational aspect of identity: It requires a dominating Other, a Captor, who may indeed be "captivating" to those in his power.[18] A disclaimer is also in order with respect to the term *Other.* In this book I consistently use *the Other* not as a description of any particular individual or social group—a use I consider misguided—but as an analytic category referring to typifications through which and against which particular collective identities have been defined.[19] Although I am primarily concerned with the process through which the Captivating Savage was typified in colonial British America, several related constructions of alterity enter the analysis as well: seductive French idolaters, vulnerable women and children, the wilderness, the body, and (lurking behind and within all of these) the natural and demonic.

The reciprocal construction of identity and alterity among indigenous peoples will necessarily be sketched more lightly, as the colonial elite controlled the process of documentation. Still, certain key Others for indigenous people can be discerned: cannibal devourers, expansionist enemies, and sacrificial victims, all of whom at times coalesced in the Colonial Captive.[20]

## Scholarly Traditions of Captivity

*It is significant that much of the most accessible and influential work of the counter-hegemony is historical: the recovery of discarded areas, or the redress of selective and reductive interpretations. . . . This struggle for and against selective traditions is understandably a major part of all contemporary cultural activity.*

—*Raymond Williams*, Marxism and Literature
*(1977:116–117)*

Ever since the publication, in 1702, of *Magnalia Christi Americana*, Cotton Mather's massive providential history of New England, scholarly treatments of captivity have tended to be similar in literary form and ideological function to the narratives of captivity they interpret. Annotations on the most popular narratives, anthologies of captivities and "Indian atrocities," popular and scholarly histories, and even certain literary critiques replicate the typifications found within the narratives, reinscribing the captivity tradition within new genres directed at new audiences. In this section I survey fairly recent scholarship on captivity, which often seeks to challenge the typifications of the captivity tradition. Scholars achieve independence from the selective tradition to varying degrees, however, and some have unintentionally perpetuated typifications, often through insufficient attention to the cultural and historical contexts within which captivity occurred.[21]

Modern scholarly interpretations of captivity narratives fall under two main rubrics: literary or cultural history, and ethnohistory or social history. In the first category are two landmark works in American studies that deal in part with captivity among Indians, those of Richard Slotkin (1973) and Annette Kolodny (1984). These and other studies of what Robert F. Berkhofer, Jr. (1978) has called the "White Man's Indian" generally follow in the path of Roy Harvey Pearce's inquiry into how an Anglo-American identity has been defined in relationship to an imagined savagery. They do so, however, in two rather different ways, which following James Levernier and Hennig Cohen (1977) might be called "historical" and "typological." More historical studies follow Pearce's lead in tracing the development of the narratives as a historically variable set of genres. Typological studies, exemplified by Slotkin's *Regeneration Through Violence* (1973), analyze the content of the narratives at a mythic or archetypal level.[22]

Pearce's initial work on captivity narratives (Pearce 1947) outlines the development of several successive genres in which captivity has served as a vehicle for different cultural "functions" or "significances": religious confession (from 1682 to the early eighteenth century); political propaganda (in the early and the mid-eighteenth century); the expression of sensationalism and sensibility (from the mid-eighteenth century through the nineteenth century); and historical and ethnological knowledge (from the early nineteenth century to the present). Although there is much more overlap in what, following Jane Tompkins (1985), we might call the "cultural work" of the narratives, Pearce's schematic model has more or less withstood the test of time. It has been elaborated by Levernier and others in studies that are particularly strong on the role of captivity narratives as propaganda for Western expansion (Levernier and Cohen 1977; Levernier 1975; Derounian-Stodola and Levernier 1993). The religious significance of captivity narratives has received a great deal of study (most recently by Ebersole 1995), but sensationalism and sensibility have become more common scholarly foci (Burnham 1997, Ebersole 1995). Pearce himself turned his attention away from historical captivity narratives, focusing in subsequent works (1952a, 1957, 1965, 1969) on the "metaphysics of Indian-hating" as revealed in the classic American fiction of James Fenimore Cooper, Nathaniel Hawthorne, Henry David Thoreau, and Herman Melville (the latter of whom coined the striking phrase).[23]

Typological studies of captivity are best differentiated from historical studies by comparing the type of "meaning" being analyzed. Although

Pearce loosely defines "significance" or "function" as "what the narrative was for the readers for whom it was written" (1947:1), his model essentially involves the conscious aims of the narratives' authors and editors. Slotkin, in contrast, analyzes the narratives at a level he claims is grounded in the unconscious. As one of the earliest forms of a distinctly American mythology (or "structuring metaphor") of "regeneration through violence," captivity narratives are, in Slotkin's view, a cultural variation on the universal archetypal pattern of the heroic quest: The captive, at first (in the Puritan narratives) a heroine who resists and exorcises the threats of the wilderness and its inhabitants, is transformed by the late eighteenth century into a heroic hunter (prototypically Daniel Boone) who allows himself to be initiated into the mysteries of the wild. One need not share Slotkin's Jungian orientation to benefit from this analysis, as the structuring metaphor of regeneration can be understood also in more culturally and historically specific terms.

Slotkin, like Pearce, stresses the progressive secularization of the narratives, but he finds in the eighteenth-century narratives an increase in both the realism with which the captivity experience is portrayed and the degree of intimacy that obtains between captive and captor. Here Slotkin's analysis contrasts markedly with Pearce's, which emphasizes the highly propagandistic and sensationalistic qualities of the eighteenth-century narratives. The contrast can partly be explained by the fact that Slotkin takes into account an important group of narratives largely overlooked by Pearce: narratives written or dictated by adopted "white Indians" such as Mary Jemison and Alexander Henry, or by partly transculturated male captives such as James Smith and Daniel Boone. Like Cooper's Natty Bumppo (for whom they served as models), Smith, Boone, and others prized the wilderness skills and "natural" virtues they learned from—and then utilized against—their captors.

More significant than these differences in perspective and emphasis is the common tendency of both intellectual history and typological studies to focus on the *longue durée*, connecting captivity narratives to literary traditions such as "Indian-hating," the frontier hero, and the sentimental novel. The subtitles of two recent literary studies are revealing: *Puritan to Postmodern Images of Captivity* (Ebersole 1995) and *Captivity, Culture-Crossing, and White Womanhood from Mary Rowlandson to Patty Hearst* (Castiglia 1996). Although in their broad sweep these studies reveal a great deal about the persistence, pervasiveness, and flexibility of the selective tradition of captivity, they do not provide the detailed sociocultural and historical contextualization that is necessary for understanding relationships between captivity narratives as a literary tradition and captivity as a cultural practice.

The Native American context of captivity has been particularly neglected or distorted in literary studies. As Pearce later acknowledged (1974), his study of captivity narratives entirely neglected Indians as a cultural (as opposed to an ideological) reality; and Slotkin's broad generalizations about Indians resemble nothing so much as James Fenimore Cooper's. More ethnographically sensitive but still prone to overgeneralize across indigenous cultures is Richard VanDerBeets (1972b, 1984), who suggests how ritual practices such as the gauntlet contributed to the structure of captivity as an initiation. Similarly, the valuable feminist studies of Annette Kolodny (1981, 1984), Laurel Ulrich (1982), and June Namias (1993) are considerably more concerned with the perspectives and voices of the colonial women who were taken captive than with those of their captors. More recently, perceptive interpretations by Robert Breitwieser (1990), Gary L. Ebersole (1995), and Christopher Castiglia (1996) have been limited by inattention to Indian captors as cultural and historical beings. The most recent full-length literary study, Michelle Burnham's *Captivity and Sentiment* (1997), is a welcome exception to this general tendency, and suggests the power of an analysis that trains an equally sophisticated eye both on Native American captors and on their colonial captives.[24]

With this significant exception, literary studies of captivity narratives, whether historical or typological in nature, have largely abstracted the narratives from their indigenous contexts. In this respect, they replicate the decontextualization characteristic of the narratives themselves, and reproduce, if skeptically, the hegemonic typification of the Indian Captor. This is not a matter of intent, as the motivation for many of these studies is critical and counter-hegemonic. That is, these studies often seek not only to analyze the content of the literary tradition of captivity, but to challenge its authority. The difficulty that intellectual and literary historians have had in freeing themselves from captivity to the selective tradition is powerful testimony to its hegemonic nature, to the relationship between typification and decontextualization, and to the unfortunate effects of disciplinary specialization.

Anthropologists and ethnohistorians, in contrast, have tended to treat captivity narratives as documents revealing, if obscurely, the nature of native beliefs and practices, as well as intimate details of accommodation and conflict between native and immigrant peoples.[25] This strength regarding cultural and historical context, however, is rarely matched in the area of narrative analysis. Apart from the many editions of Henry Rowe Schoolcraft's anthology (e.g., 1978 [1851]), Lewis Henry Morgan's edition of Mary Jemison's narrative (Seaver 1978 [1856]), and Paul Radin's edition of John Tanner's narrative (Radin 1940), anthropological work on captivity narratives can be described as generally neglectful of the narra tives as texts, abstracting from them details that illuminate indigenous culture or the transformative process Hallowell (1963) called "transculturation."[26]

A new generation of ethnohistorical research on the assimilation of European captives was initiated by Axtell's provocative article "The White Indians of North America" (1975). Axtell culled ethnographic details from a large number of colonial narratives in order to analyze the attraction that Native American societies held for assimilated captives who resisted repatriation—an attraction that Axtell contrasts effectively with the generally unsuccessful assimilation of Indians into colonial society. Axtell's rather impressionistic conclusions regarding the extent to which non-Indian captives were successfully adopted into Indian society have been challenged by Vaughan and Richter (1980), who use the statistical techniques and concern for local detail characteristic of contemporary social history.[27] Also demonstrating the value of social history in the study of captivity narratives is Ulrich's study of feminine role definition in northern New England (Ulrich 1982), which emphasizes the symbolic importance of the (relatively few) female captives who violently resisted their captors.

The most satisfying of the recent studies of colonial captivity narratives follow Pearce's (1974) forward-looking program in melding literary and ethnohistorical approaches. In the introduction and annotations to their fine anthology, Vaughan and Clark (1981) place Puritan and Quaker narratives in the context of other contemporary genres and their characteristic modes of interpretation, Puritan social structure, and the course of British–Native American conflict. Recently Neal Salisbury (1997) issued an exemplary edition of Mary Rowlandson's narrative, reading it in the context of the available documentary evidence regarding Rowlandson's captors. And in very different ways John Demos (1994) and Evan Haefeli and Kevin Sweeney (1995) have demonstrated how fully it is possible to culturally and historically contextualize certain captivity narratives.[28] All of these recent works demonstrate the value of an integrative approach to analyzing the practice and representation of captivity in British North America.

### The Politics and Poetics of Captivity: An Overview

Although in numerical terms the captivity of English colonists among Indians pales in comparison to the abduction, imprisonment, and enslavement of Indians by the English, and indeed, to the captivity of Indians by Indians during the colonial period, only the relationship between the Indian Captor and the Colonial Captive is highlighted in the captivity literature. Chapter 2, "Indian Captives, English Captors, 1576–1622" and Chapter 3, "Captivity and Hostage-Exchange in Powhatan's Domain,

1607–1624," respond to this exclusion by addressing the captivity of Indians along the Atlantic seaboard in the early years of exploration and colonization. These chapters consider a Wampanoag representation of captivity among Europeans; colonial attempts to fashion informants, allies, and hostages through kidnapping; and the less frequent practice of hostage-exchange. Squanto and Pocahontas are the most famous of the Indian captives considered in these chapters, although they are rarely remembered as captives. Using these examples I examine Indian captives as subjects uninscribed in the hegemonic representation of captivity. I also analyze captivity as a particularly revealing context for exploring the relationships among power and knowledge, and conquest and resistance in the early colonial situation.

Chapter 3 also considers in some detail John Smith's account of his captivity among Pocahontas's people, the Powhatans. Chapter 4, "The Politics and Poetics of Captivity in New England, 1620–1682," turns northward, examining the convergence of indigenous and European captivity practices in the colonial northeast. I consider in greatest detail the practice of captivity during Metacom's War (1675–76), when for the first time a significant number of English colonists were held captive among indigenous peoples. A close reading of the captivity narrative of Mary White Rowlandson, a clergyman's wife taken captive by Metacom's allies, engenders a discussion of the relationship between two remarkable women—Rowlandson and her Indian "mistress," Wetamo—as well as the relationship between the practice and the representation of captivity more generally.

Chapter 5, "Seduction, Redemption, and the Typification of Captivity, 1675–1707," considers the process through which a hegemonic interpretation of captivity was forged by the Puritan clerical elite in the years that followed Metacom's War. The captivity narrative, which in Rowlandson's hands testified to the particularity of individual experience, became in the clergy's hands a testament to the collective vulnerability of the English in the American wilderness. A consideration of captivity in the works of three prominent clergymen—Increase Mather, Cotton Mather, and John Williams, himself a "redeemed captive"—reveals the process of typification through which individual experiences of captivity came to represent an entire society's relationship to pervasive savagery. At the same time, the experiences of John Williams's daughter Eunice, who chose to remain with her adoptive Mohawk family, indicates the presence of alternative interpretations of captivity.

Chapter 6, "Captive Ethnographers, 1699–1736," considers early eighteenth-century interpretations of captivity. In the narratives of Quaker captives Jonathan Dickinson and Elizabeth Hanson I trace the emergence of secular empiricism as well as a somewhat greater identification between captive and captor. Then, in the narrative of John Gyles—a fascinating, little known figure who served as a trader, translator, and diplomat on the Maine frontier after his release from captivity—I find a more thoroughly developed empirical concern with natural history beside a strong, proto-ethnographic interest in Indian "manners and customs."

The final chapter, "Captivity and Colonial Structures of Feeling, 1744–1776," explores continuities and transformations in the interpretation of captivity in the dozen narratives published during the third and fourth intercolonial wars. This is a diverse group of narratives in which secular empiricism and sentimentalism steadily gain ground as frameworks for interpretation. My consideration of the most influential of these narratives, Peter Williamson's, allows me to discuss a major transformation—from spiritual resignation to male heroism—in the structures of feeling expressed and produced in the selective tradition of captivity. Chapter 7 concludes with a survey of the ground covered by my analysis of the practice and representation of captivity over two centuries, and a brief glance at the role played by the selective tradition of captivity in early American nationalism—a topic foreshadowed in some of the book's illustrations, including *The Rescue.*

## Notes

1. The major conflicts during this period were Metacom's War (or King Philip's War) in 1675–76, four intercolonial ("French and Indian") wars waged intermittently between 1689 and 1763, and Pontiac's War (1763–64). The Chronology of Events lists these and other events related to colonial American captivity narratives.

2. The authors, titles, and publication histories of these narratives are listed in the Appendix.

3. See Strong (1992a:374–391) for the titles of captivity narratives published between 1776 and 1826. For recent analyses of these works, see Burnham 1997, Castiglia 1996, Ebersole 1995, and Namias 1993.

4. On captivity as a conceptual model for the present, see Castiglia 1996, Ebersole 1995, and Slotkin 1973. I have been influenced also by Jewett and Lawrence 1977 and by unpublished works of John Lawrence.

5. Indigenous wars of resistance include the resistance movements led by Opechancanough in Virginia in 1622 and 1644, Metacom's War of 1675–76 in New England, and Pontiac's War of 1763–64.

6. Although Gramsci developed the concept of cultural hegemony in connection with his analysis of the modern secular state, he applied the concept to certain precapitalist societies as well (1972:55–56, 264). His brief discussion of the attribution of barbarity or biological inferiority to southern Italians within the hegemonic discourse of the North is somewhat similar to my treatment of otherness in this book (Gramsci 1972:70–74). Bercovitch (1978) analyzes the hegemony of the Puritan elite; see also Lears (1985) and Denning (1986). Brow (1996) offers

a lucid discussion of the concept of hegemony; Strong (1996b) reviews Gramscian and other theoretical approaches to ethnohistory.

7. See Schutz (1964:226–273; 1973:3–47, 207–259, 260–286, 287–356). Williams (1977:101–103) brings Gramsci into relationship with Lukács's concept of typification, but this is not the sense in which I employ the term here. Although Schutz's use of *typification* does not highlight the structures of domination that make typifications authoritative, nor their nature as lived forms of domination and subordination, the concept is not incompatible with this Gramscian concern. I have previously used the concept in analyzing European explorers' typifications of Australian Aborigines (Strong 1986).

8. For captivity images in the U.S. Capitol Building, see Strong 1995. For the captive in nineteenth-century sculpture, see Kasson 1990.

9. The quoted terms are found in Weber 1968:3–62; 1949 (1904):191; and 1977:107.

10. Also relevant is the concept of "type" as used by Marshall Sahlins in analyzing the initial Hawaiian perception of Captain Cook. The British captain entered Hawaiian culture and history, writes Sahlins, as "an instance of a received category, the worldly token of a presupposed type" (1981:7). However, I have chosen to consider the Captive Self and Captivating Savage as "typifications" rather than "types" for two reasons. First, *typification* conveys more readily that these "received categories" are constructed, deployed, and transformed in practice—in other words, that they are a precipitate of a process of typification. Second, as a Puritan concept referring to Biblical precedents in reference to which events can be interpreted, *type* must be an object of the present analysis rather than a theoretical framing device.

11. See Schutz 1973:355–356; 1964:248–273.

12. See Williams 1977:108–114, 121–127.

13. Vaughan and Richter (1980:77) refer to a convergence of practices between the two major language families in the Northeast, the Iroquoians and the Algonquians. I extend the term to include, in addition, the convergence of these complex Native American practices with European practices. See also Haefeli and Sweeney 1995 and Salisbury 1997.

14. In addition to Foucault and Said, I have been particularly influenced by the lectures and writings of Bernard S. Cohn (1983, 1985, 1996), John Comaroff and Jean Comaroff (1992), Raymond D. Fogelson (1974, 1982, 1985, 1987, 1989), Stephen Greenblatt (1976, 1991), and George W. Stocking, Jr. (1968b, 1985, 1987, 1991, 1992).

15. On the Indian as a projection, see Pearce 1965, Salisbury 1972, and White 1976; on the Indian as an invention, see Berkhofer 1978 and 1988, Clifton 1990, Feest 1987, and O'Gorman 1961. Handler (1988), Hanson (1989), Hobsbawm and Ranger (1983), and Wagner (1975) have demonstrated the usefulness of the concept of "invention"; but for cautions regarding its ideological implications, see Linnekin 1991 and Strong 1991 and 1994. Among the important theoretical statements on Native Americans as actors and interpreters are Fogelson's (1974, 1989); Martin's (1987); and Ortiz's (1977). Krech 1991 and Strong 1996b are reviews of ethnohistorical scholarship in this vein.

16. I am indebted to Derek Sayer for suggesting the term *othering*, and to Jean Comaroff for *hegemony-in-the-making*. My thinking on the shifting grounds of collective identities and exclusions has been influenced by Chandler (1996, 1997), Dominguez (1986), Peterson and Brown (1985), Samuels (1999), and White (1991), and by feminist theories of multiple positioning (see Visweswaran 1997:613–614). It has been influenced even more by fictional accounts by métis, *mestizo*, and "mixed-blood" authors such as D'Arcy McNickle (1978 [1936], 1978, 1992). See also Strong 1997, Strong and Van Winkle 1995, and Kapchan and Strong 1999.

17. Winthrop Jordan discussed oppositional definitions of African Americans in similar terms: "In fearfully hoping to escape the animal within himself the white man debased the Negro" (1969:582).

18. The relationship between the Captivating Other and the Captive Self rather recalls Hegel's famous analysis of the dialectical relationship between Master and Slave (Hegel 1964 [1807]). See also Butler (1987) and Ricoeur (1970).

19. My studies of typifications of otherness lead me to object to the practice current in some ethnographic discourse and literature of using the term *Other* for one's interlocutors in ethnographic research. Our awareness that anthropology as a discipline has tended to construct Others for Western purposes and Western audiences is hardly reason to adopt a vocabulary of opposition and alienation to describe (and worse, to structure) our ethnographic encounters.

20. Scholars have paid less attention to the typifications of dominant Others than to those of the dominated; but see Basso (1979), Braroe (1975), Lipps (1966), Ortiz (1972), and Taussig (1980, 1993).

21. Derounian-Stodola and Levernier (1993) discuss the role of captivity in constructing a "usable past," and consider an exceptionally broad array of narratives in order to avoid replicating typifications. Scheckel (1998), which appeared when this book was in press, offers richly contextualized accounts of nineteenth-century representations of captivity. My understanding of the ideological importance of decontextualization and the critical importance of recontextualization derives especially from Johannes Fabian (1983) and George W. Stocking, Jr. (1987, 1991, 1992). The most glaring examples of decontextualization by scholars are anthologies directed to a general audience (e.g., Peckham 1954, Drimmer 1985 [1961]); but typifications are perpetuated in more serious scholarship as well, including the 111–volume series (1977–80) of facsimiles of captivity narratives compiled by Wilcomb E. Washburn, whose exegesis is limited to a single introductory volume (1983). The availability of the facsimiles has, however, facilitated a burst of excellent scholarship.

22. Levernier and Cohen's concise bibliographic essay (1977:277–278) is a good introduction to earlier literary studies of captivity; see also Ebersole 1995, Vaughan 1983, and Vaughan and Clark 1981. Baum (1993) offers a critique of typological interpretations.

23. Others who have analyzed the role of captivity in classic American literature include Barnett (1975), Castiglia (1996), Fiedler (1969), Lawrence (1964 [1923]), Seelye (1977), Slotkin (1973), and Zolla (1973).

24. Although focused on colonial literature more generally, Gordon M. Sayre's (1997) astute comparison of French and English representations of Native Americans is also exceptional.

25. Salisbury 1997, Vaughan and Clark 1981, and Vaughan 1983 include bibliographies of the ethnohistorical literature on captivity.

26. Hallowell's study is, unfortunately, neglected in recent studies of transculturation, including Pratt's influential work (1992). Among the earlier anthropological studies, in addition to Hallowell's, are Ackerknecht 1944, Barbeau 1950, Heard 1973, and Swanton 1926. Kroeber and Kroeber (1962) provide a rare textual analysis; like Vaughan and Clark's (1981) and Fierst's (1986, 1996) studies, it speaks to the value of interdisciplinary partnerships.

27. Most captives from colonial New England, Vaughan and Clark show, were ransomed in French Canada, where they often converted to Catholicism, married, and remained. Axtell (1985a) implicitly accepts and develops this point. Whatever their statistical frequency, however, one cannot overemphasize the symbolic significance of the transculturated captive.

28. Although not concerned with a colonial captivity narrative, the work of John Fierst and his colleagues on a long-awaited, annotated edition of John Tanner's narrative is also exemplary (Fierst 1986, 1996).

# 2

# Indian Captives, English Captors,
# 1576–1622

One of the few Indians known to American schoolchildren is Squanto, who brought seeds of maize to the starving Pilgrims and taught them how to cultivate it. The hospitality of Squanto and Native Americans more generally is commemorated each year at the Thanksgiving Day feast—a traditional practice that to Anglo-Americans represents salvation, peaceful communion, and the legitimate occupation of a plentiful land. A similar role in Anglo-American origin myths is played by Pocahontas, the "Indian princess" who represents salvation, communion, and colonial legitimacy in a distinctly feminine way. As John Smith's savior, a convert to Christianity, the mediator between her father Powhatan's chiefdom and the colonists at Jamestown, the wife of tobacco planter John Rolfe and the mother of his child, Pocahontas is an icon of the commingling of American and English "blood," the voluntary conversion of the American heathen to Christianity, and the rightful colonial appropriation of American abundance.[1]

Squanto and Pocahontas are all the more appropriate as legendary figures in hegemonic representations of American identity because both are tragic heroes—early personifications of the noble but vanishing Indian.[2] As Sanders has suggested, the romantic Pocahontas, like "austere New England's counterpart," the solitary Squanto, may be seen as a "quiet sacrificial victim to the earliest successful colonization efforts by Englishmen in America" (Sanders 1978:297). Indeed, neither Squanto nor Pocahontas lived long after ensuring the survival of the fledgling English colonies, Squanto dying in a lonely exile in his own land, Pocahontas aboard an English ship bound for Virginia.

Less well known, however, is another tragic dimension of the lives of Squanto and Pocahontas: Both were captives among the English before they became valuable allies. That Squanto and Pocahontas were prisoners as well as saviors and converts of the English is suppressed in the hegemonic representation not only because it is inconsistent with their personification of peaceful and voluntary acquiescence in the colonial project. The captivity of these two "savages" among the colonists subverts the dominant opposition in Anglo-American. representations of captivity in the New World: the opposition between the Colonial Captive and the Captivating Savage. Like the hegemonic legends of Squanto and Pocahontas, the dominant Anglo-American representation of captivity evokes a form of communion between Indians and colonists, but one that is involuntary, achieved through violence and generally repudiated. The captivity of colonists such as John Smith is utilized to justify violent conquest, whereas the captivity of Indians such as Pocahontas and Squanto, so instrumental to that very conquest, remains uninscribed.[3]

It is not only in the realm of popular legend that the captivity of indigenous peoples has been obscured. Although accounts by British and other European explorers and settlers frequently refer to the practice of taking Indian captives, until recently this has received little attention in colonial histories. A counter-hegemonic history of the Indian Captive and the Captivating Colonist has only begun to be written.[4] This chapter and the one that follows contribute to that effort by analyzing several early episodes in which English explorers took Indians captive as tokens, informants, or potential allies. Squanto and Pocahontas are only the most famous of these.

## European Devourers and Their Prey

In an intriguing legend of the Wampanoags—the Algonquian-speaking inhabitants of southeastern Massachusetts, Cape Cod, and the islands[5]— Europeans were first encountered riding a gigantic bird up the Taunton River, near the Wampanoag town of Pocasset (see Map 2.1). The newcomers seized several Wampanoags, holding them captive on the giant bird. Attacking the bird when it stopped at a spring for water, the Wampanoags managed to release its human prey despite the barrage of thunder and lightning with which the monstrous bird defended itself.

The only source for this revealing Native representation of a first encounter with Europeans is a skeletal fragment of local history collected in the early nineteenth century by a traveler who reported that "a brook, called White Man's Brook, has its name from this event" (Simmons 1986:70). With the exception of its reference to captivity, this legend resembles a number of northeastern Algonquian legends that assimilate European ships to the powerful Thunderbird of indigenous cosmologies. For example, in 1634 William Wood collected a Wampanoag account of that people's first encounter with Europeans, an account that predates

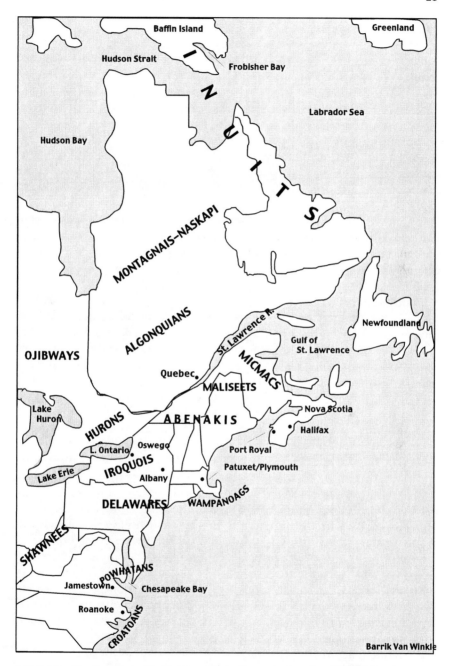

MAP 2.1   Northeastern North America in the seventeenth and eighteenth centuries, showing selected peoples, settlements, and sites of captivity.
SOURCE: Barrik Van Winkle.

large-scale English violence against the indigenous peoples of New England. The Wampanoags, Wood wrote, "took the first ship they saw for a walking island, the mast to be a tree, the sail white clouds, and the discharging of ordnance for lightning and thunder, which did much trouble them, but this thunder being over and this moving-island steadied with an anchor, they manned out their canoes to go and pick strawberries there" (Simmons 1986:66). This more idyllic version of the first encounter, like many other northeastern Indian tales of thundering birds or floating islands bearing European newcomers, presents the vessels as rich sources of material and spiritual wealth, since strawberries, like wampum and glass beads, were associated with physical and spiritual well-being.[6]

In contrast, the nineteenth-century thundering bird signifies the mortal dangers associated with the new source of wealth. Indeed, considering the nineteenth-century legend in the context of other northeastern Algonquian folklore reveals that it assimilates early encounters with Europeans to the most fearsome cultural model available of a kidnapper and human devourer. A huge cannibal bird figures prominently in Algonquian mythology across the Northeast.[7] The monster is described by nineteenth-century folklorist James Athearn Jones (1830), who grew up among Wampanoags, as "a great bird whose wings were the flight of an arrow wide, whose body was the length of ten Indian strides, and whose head when he stretched up his neck peered over the tall oak-woods" (quoted in Simmons 1986:189). In Wampanoag lore, the cannibal bird would carry away children in its talons to its nest on Nantucket or Martha's Vineyard, where it feasted upon them, dropping their bones in heaps on the ground below. Only the giant culture hero Maushop was a match for the cannibal bird. In Wampanoag tales dating in print to 1798 and persisting into the twentieth century, Maushop waded across the water to the predator's island home, where he killed him after a fierce battle. Relaxing with a pipe of pokeweed after killing the cannibal bird, Maushop is said to have created a thick fog. Although this powerful shaper of the indigenous world retreated from view upon the European arrival, Maushop was remembered by traditional Wampanoag people whenever a fog rolled in from the islands (Simmons 1986:172–234).

That Wampanoags would represent the earliest European invaders as kidnappers and potential devourers of their people is consistent with the accounts we have by European explorers, traders, and fishermen of their earliest forays along the eastern coast of North America. Following precedents reaching as far back as Columbus's kidnapping of ten Ciguayans (an Arawak people) from Hispaniola on his first voyage, European expeditions habitually abducted a few, and sometimes scores or hundreds, of the Native people they encountered, often luring them aboard ship with beads or other trade goods. Unlike the legendary Wampanoags rescued from the giant cannibal bird, most abducted Indians were forever lost to view.

Judging from accounts concerning the few captives who survived the journey overseas, the abductions had a variety of motivations aptly summarized by the Foucaultian expression "power/knowledge" (Foucault 1980). Through captivity Europeans fabricated human objects of knowledge and instruments of colonial power, a practice predating the pervasive diffusion of disciplinary practices that Foucault considers characteristic of modern Europe.[8] The majority of Indian captives were sold into slavery, a practice that began with Columbus and continued for several centuries. More central to the present concerns, however, are those Indian captives who were valued primarily as objects and possessors of knowledge rather than as instruments of physical labor. These were displayed in Europe as trophies or exotic curiosities, educated as translators and mediators, proselytized as model converts, utilized as guides, scrutinized by scholars, and captured for posterity in artistic representations. In turn, Indian captives turned their captivity to their own uses, sometimes managing to derive considerable power from a formally subordinate position.

Among the earliest visual and textual representations of New World peoples and artifacts are several portraits and accompanying descriptions of four Baffinland Inuits (or Eskimos) kidnapped by Martin Frobisher in 1576 and 1577, whom chronicler George Best described baldly as "new prey" and "tokens from thence" (Sturtevant and Quinn 1987:69–70).[9] In current parlance these captives might be considered "tokens of alterity," but in truth, Native American captives were seldom if ever treated as "sheerly other" (Mullaney 1983).[10] As an anonymous 1578 description of one of the Inuit captives put it, "They are not so completely awkward that they cannot learn and comprehend something: therefore it is hoped this new land will be well suitable to the kingdom" (Sturtevant and Quinn 1987:140).[11] Through controlling captives' bodies, isolating them from their communities, removing them from their familiar environments, and exposing them to demonstrations of European power and knowledge, explorers and colonizers attempted to turn their human prey not only into "tokens from thence" but also into valuable subjects—which required at least a minimal acknowledgment of their identity as sentient beings, if not as humans.

### Kidnapping Tokens and Informants: Frobisher's Inuit Captives

The first inhabitants of the New World to be displayed in England were three captives, possibly Micmacs, kidnapped from Newfoundland by Sebastian Cabot in 1498 (see Map 2.1). Although these captives were presented to the court of Henry VII, it was another three-quarters of a century before the details of a visit of New World captives to England were effectively captured for posterity. (The literalness of the expression in this instance should well give us pause, so well does it convey our dependence upon captive subjects for early ethnographic knowledge.) Among the few well-documented cases of captivity as a colonial practice are Martin Frobisher's kidnappings of four Inuits from Baffin Island during his search in 1576–1577 for precious metals and a westward passage.[12] The first Inuits that Frobisher's party encountered were a group of nineteen or twenty (one or two more than Frobisher's crew). The English retreated to the ship, prepared for battle, and then put a lone sailor on shore. The Inuits seem to have realized that the sailor was intended as a hostage, and in return an Inuit man boarded the ship. The Englishmen offered him food and drink as well as gifts from the store of mirrors, bells, and knives that they had brought for such occasions. After returning the Inuit to shore and taking the English hostage on board, the ship sailed off, Frobisher fearing an attack.

Subsequently, the English went on shore as a group, encountering a party of Inuits with whom they exchanged their "trifles" and "toys" for raw meat, fish, and skin garments. The English visited the Inuit settlement, where Frobisher again feared an attack and held his weapon at the throat of a hostage until he and his men returned safely to the ship. Even so, a second Inuit man boarded the ship voluntarily, receiving "many trifles of haberdash" to reward his courage.[13] Communicating through signs, the English understood him to be willing to serve as a guide westward, to what they hoped was a passage to India. Five sailors took the man ashore in the ship's boat, assuming he needed to get his kayak and equipment. The sailors then rowed the boat out of sight of the ship and into the realm of conjecture. Frobisher spent several days searching for the five sailors and for Inuits, hoping to kidnap hostages to exchange for his men as well as captives to carry back to England. As a promoter of the expedition, Michael Lok, put it, at this point in the expedition the captain was "oppressed with sorrow that he should return back again to his country bringing [not] any evidence or token of any place whereby to certify the world where he had been." Similarly, a second chronicler, George Best, reported that Frobisher, "desirous to bring some token from thence, of his being there, was greatly discontented, that he had not before apprehended some of them" (Stefansson 1938 [1578], 1:70–71).[14]

As the explorer's luck would have it, just as he was reluctantly preparing to sail homeward, a number of kayaks warily approached the ship. The captain responded by arming his vessel. Under these circumstances only the man who had previously served as a hostage was willing to approach the ship, and when even he showed some hesitation, Frobisher "enticed" him closer by ringing bells and throwing them, together with some clothing, into the sea. When the man reached for a bell, Frobisher grabbed his arm and pulled him and his kayak aboard. "Whereupon," reported Best, "when he found himself in captivity, for very choler and disdain he bit his tongue in twain within his mouth" (71). After two days of hoping in vain that the captive's companions would bring the English sailors in exchange, Frobisher disembarked "with this new prey (which was a sufficient witness of the captain's far and tedious travel towards the unknown parts of the world, as did well appear by this strange infidel, whose like was never seen, read, nor heard of before, and whose language was neither known nor understood of any)" (69).

While this chronicler, George Best, took the captive's unfamiliar language—doubly strange, perhaps, on account of his mutilated tongue—as witness to the captain's success in reaching an absolutely unknown part of the world,[15] one of the voyage's promoters, Michael Lok, likened the "sallow" color of the captive's skin to that of "the tawny Moors; [or r]ather to the Tartar Nation, whereof I think he was" (71–72). The promoter, predisposed to this interpretation of the man's provenance by virtue of his financial interest in the venture, repeatedly called him the "strange man of Cathay."[16] In this case, as in others we shall consider, whether the captive was considered a token of the familiar, the unfamiliar, or both—whether he was identified with the known, opposed as absolutely other, or placed somewhere in between—varied markedly according to the social position and interests of the interpreter.

The Inuit captive survived in England only about a fortnight, apparently perishing, like so many captives, of one of the European diseases to which New World peoples had no immunity. During his brief tenure as evidence and token, the captive posed in native and in English costume for portraits intended for the Queen and Frobisher's backers, the Cathay Company.[17] For an idea of the captive's treatment in England we may turn to the Company's financial records, where in addition to expenses for medical care and supplies, there is a payment to a surgeon "for opening of the Indian man, and [em]balming him dead, preserved to have him sent back again into his country." This plan for some reason was abandoned, as a subsequent charge is for "burying the tartar Indian man in Saint Olave's churchyard." Before the burial his "image"—either his face or his entire body—was preserved for continued scrutiny, as there are charges "for making a mold of hard earth of the tartar man['s] image to be cast in wax" (72–75).

While Frobisher did not take the unfortunate captive's body when he led a mining expedition to Baffin Island the following year, he did take a portrait with him, which was shown to an Inuit man captured on that expedition. The circumstances of the second capture resemble those of the first, the captive being "enticed" within grabbing distance by trade goods. Or, in the curious wording of Dionysus Settle, a member of the expedition whose chronicle of the voyage circulated widely throughout Europe, "Our General, desirous to allure them unto him by fair means, caused knives and other things, to be preferred unto them" (Settle 1979 [1577]:209–10).[18] This time the Inuits were understandably more hesitant to approach the English than previously, but finally they were willing to set down hunting bows and other goods in exchange for metal goods such as pins and knives. Following this wary exchange, Frobisher and the ship's master attempted to seize two men, "bring them aboard, with intent, to bestow certain toys and apparel upon the one, and so to dismiss him with all arguments of courtesy, and retain the other for an interpreter" (Best 1938 [1578]:59). One wonders whether Frobisher was surprised that the captives distrusted his "fair means" and did not submit to him long enough to experience his "courtesy."[19] They broke loose and a fight ensued, in the course of which Frobisher was wounded and one Inuit was tackled and captured. (The captive, Kalicho, later died of the injuries he incurred in the fight.)

When the explorers subsequently discovered an abandoned winter settlement, they brought the captive ashore "to declare the use of such things as we saw," noted Best. The captive "stayed himself alone behind the company, and did set up five small sticks round in a circle, one by another, with one small bone placed just in the midst of all." At first fearing witchcraft, the English finally conjectured that he intended that "thereby his countrymen should understand, that for our five men which they betrayed the last year . . . he was taken and kept prisoner." Afterward, when he was shown "the picture of his countryman, which the last year was brought into England," the captive

> was upon the sudden much amazed thereat, and beholding advisedly the same with silence a good while, as though he would strain courtesy whether should begin the speech (for he thought him no doubt a lively creature) at length, began to question with him, as with his companion, and finding him dumb and mute, seemed to suspect him, as one disdainful, and would with a little help have grown into choler at the matter until at last by feeling and handling, he found him but a deceiving picture. And then with great noise and cries, ceased not wondering, thinking that we could make men live or die at our pleasure. (65)

This extraordinary intercultural communication by signs that each interlocutor had reason to interpret as the equivalent of witchcraft culminated in what the English considered a confession regarding their own countrymen's plight:

> And thereupon calling the matter to his remembrance, he gave us plainly to understand by signs, that he had knowledge of the taking of our five men the last year, and confessing the manner of each thing, numbered the five men upon his five fingers, and pointed unto a boat in our ship, which was like unto that wherein our men were betrayed. And when we made him signs, that they were slain and eaten, he earnestly denied, and made signs to the contrary. (65–66)

However plain or transparent the captive's signs might have been,[20] subsequent events left the English convinced that the five lost sailors had indeed been slain and eaten. While searching through a deserted summer settlement the English found articles of clothing they assumed belonged to the five men. Frobisher left a letter for "our poor captive countrymen," according to Best, and "glasses, points, and other of our toys" for the Inuits, intending later to return "that he might by force or policy, entrap or entice the people to some friendly conference." As one might suspect from the reference to force and entrapment here, no friendly conference ensued. Rather, thirty or forty Englishmen pursued and attacked some sixteen or eighteen Inuits, both sides armed with bows and arrows. The Inuits wounded one Englishmen but lost five or six lives. Three of these, wounded in the fray, leapt off a cliff, reported Best, lest "their enemies should receive glory or prey off their dead carcasses, for they supposed us likely to be Cannibals, or eaters of man's flesh."[21] The very desperation of the Inuits, together with the discovery of English clothing and Frobisher's letter among their possessions, were taken as evidence "that we had already heard the last news of our men, which the last year were betrayed of these people. And considering also their ravenous and bloody disposition, in eating any kind of raw flesh or carrion, howsoever stinking, it is to be thought, that they had slain and devoured our men" (67–69).[22]

Two women were unable to avoid capture, "one being old and ugly . . . the other being young and encumbered with a sucking child at her back." The former, an "old wretch, whom divers of our sailors supposed to be either a devil, or a witch, had her buskins plucked off, to see if she were cloven footed, and for her ugly hue and deformity, we let her go" (Sturtevant and Quinn 1987:77). Relieved to be rid of the ugly if not demonic "wretch," they retained the mother and child, delighted to have, in Best's words, "a woman captive for the comfort of our man" (1938 [1578]:69). The woman was brought to the man and they were eagerly observed by the English. As Best described it, in a passage worth quoting at length,

At their first encountering, they beheld each the other very wistfully a good space, without speech or word uttered, with great change of color and countenance, as though it seemed, the grief and disdain of their captivity had taken away the use of their tongues and utterance. The woman at the first very suddenly, as though she disdained or regarded not the man, turned away, and began to sing, as though she minded another matter. But being again brought together, the man broke up the silence first, and with stern and staid countenance, began to tell a long solemn tale to the woman, whereunto she gave good hearing, and interrupted him nothing, till he had finished, and afterwards, being grown into more familiar acquaintance by speech, were turned together, so that (I think) the one would hardly have lived, without the comfort of the other.

And, for so much as we could perceive, albeit they lived continually together, yet did they never use as man and wife, though the woman spared not to do all necessary things that appertained to a good housewife indifferently for them both, as in making clean their cabin, and every other thing that appertained to his ease: for when he was seasick, she would make him clean, she would kill and flea the dogs for their eating, and dress his meat. Only I think it worth the noting, the continence of them both, for the man would never shift himself, except he had first caused the woman to depart out of his cabin, and they both were most shamefast, lest any of their privie parts should be discovered, either of themselves, or any other body. (69–70)

Despite the Inuits' modesty, the Englishmen's surveillance of their captive subjects was more satisfying than Frobisher's attempt to employ them as instruments in his quest for his lost men. Although the captain tried to communicate through Kalicho his desire to exchange hostages, the only outcome of his endeavors was an appreciation among the English for the kindness of Kalicho and his countrymen toward each other. The captives and their comrades on shore were equally unsuccessful in their attempts to arrange an escape or exchange. Stymied in his attempts to retrieve his sailors, Frobisher regretfully embarked for home with a load of fool's gold and his three tokens of the unknown.

In England the three Inuits attracted considerable attention for the two months they survived. The captives were known by the Inuit terms with which they addressed one another: Kalicho (a proper name, also spelled *Calichough*), Arnaaq ("woman"), and Nutaaq ("young new thing").[23] English observers marveled at Kalicho's skills with his kayak and his bow, Arnaaq's improbable method of nursing the baby perched on her back; their diet of raw fish, meat, and entrails; their odor, unpleasant to the English; and their use of English phrases, including "farewell" and "God give you good morrow." All three had their portraits painted in native dress, Nutaaq tucked inside his mother's parka (see Figure 2.1).[24]

FIGURE 2.1    Portraits of Kalicho, Arnaaq, and baby Nutaaq, Frobisher's captive Inuits, by John White. Watercolor drawings, 1577. SOURCE: Paul Hulton, *America 1585: The Complete Drawings of John White.* © 1984 University of North Carolina Press. Color plates © the British Museum, British Museum Press. Reprinted by permission.

Arnaaq distinguished herself not only as a "housewife" but as an assertive nurse, taking charge of her baby's wounded arm and blocking a bloodletting operation on Kalicho. Dying of complications from a broken rib, Kalicho sang a song on his deathbed "just like the swans," reported his doctor, "who foresee what good there is in death, and die happily with a song. I had scarcely left him when he moved from life to death, forcing out as his last words, given in our language, 'God be with you'" (Dodding 1979 [1577]:217).

Though considered a heathen, Kalicho was buried in consecrated ground. At his doctor's insistence, Arnaaq was present throughout the burial. Anxious to convince Arnaaq that the English did not engage in human sacrifice or cannibalism—a practice he thought "had become deeply rooted among them"—the doctor had human bones disinterred for her to inspect. "But that woman," he wrote, "either excelled all our people in decorum and stoicism or else was far outstripped in human sensitivity by the wild animals themselves. For she was not in any way disturbed by his death, and, as far as we gathered from her expression, it did not distress her." Her reaction to Kalicho's death seemed to confirm what the doctor and others had long conjectured: "that she had regarded him with an astonishing degree of contempt, and that although they used to sleep in one and the same bed, yet nothing had occurred between them apart from conversation, his embrace having been abhorrent to her" (218). Arnaaq died four days later and was buried in the same churchyard as Kalicho. Their son Nutaaq died soon afterward and was buried in the same churchyard as Frobisher's first captive.

The doctor's postmortem report indicates with some eloquence the ambiguous status of the Inuit captives as objects of knowledge and tokens of exploration. Dr. Dodding searched for ways to explain behavior that struck him as anomalous, uncertain whether to consider the captives extraordinarily bestial or extraordinarily social beings. Kalicho sang like a swan but spoke like an Englishman upon his deathbed; Arnaaq either exceeded the English in "decorum and stoicism" or showed less human sensitivity than the beasts; together the couple violated all English expectations regarding physical relations between the sexes. Interestingly, Dodding's uncertainty stopped short of questioning the captives' preference for human flesh, a supposition that, to paraphrase the doctor, had become deeply rooted among the English. It is also significant that the doctor was particularly disturbed by Arnaaq, finding nothing more shocking than the "astonishing degree of contempt" with which she treated Kalicho. Given that this statement occurs in the context of a discussion of their continence and that other observers remarked upon Arnaaq's solicitude toward her injured companion, it may be that the lack of sexual relations between the pair indicated to the doctor a threatening undermining of expected patterns of dominance and submission.

However great Dodding's own human sensitivity, he reported that he was deeply grieved "not so much by the death of the man himself as because the great hope of seeing him which our most gracious Queen had entertained had now slipped through her fingers, as it were, for a second time." Kalicho's death caused this specialist in physiology to reflect upon the gallantry of the explorers and to predict that "consequently we may retain these nerves and life-blood of kingdom and state (which is how the theorists appositely describe economic resources) as easily as we have sought them out." From the body politic Dodding's reflections turned to the theological implication of Kalicho's inability to save himself from death. "If the libation-vessels of incantation-makers, begged-for effigies, vacuous rituals and magic charms had been of any avail in overcoming disease," he concluded, "this man Calichoughe (for that was his name) would, while he was still alive, have hacked it off quivering like a hydra-head and then thrown it away. For nobody was more practised than he in this art, and (unless I am mistaken) nobody trusted more deeply in those very superstitions; he made an incantation for every time his pain abated" (217–218).

In the doctor's report one clearly sees Kalicho and Arnaaq being transposed from complex and ambiguous individuals into typifications supporting the claims of Christianity and the Crown. In death as in captivity, Kalicho and Arnaaq were valued primarily as tokens of exploration—tokens of English knowledge and power—and as objects verifying English beliefs about their superiority over the heathen. A similar movement from the complexity and ambiguity of the concrete to abstract typification can be traced in the visual and textual representations of the captives that were soon disseminated throughout Europe. As Sturtevant and Quinn note: "Kalicho, Arnaaq, and Nutaaq must be almost unique as known, named individuals whose portraits ended as typifying whole populations. By way of the woodcut in the French version of [Dionysus] Settle['s account] they entered the set of costume types of exotic peoples, almost endlessly copied" (1987:119, n. 16). The movement from particular existences within their Inuit bands into captivity, portraits, and finally, collections of exotic costumes is one of progressive loss, abstraction, typification, and assimilation to European categories.

It is also a movement in which we can discern resistance—resistance to capture, to domination, and to typification alike. Whether seized off of Baffin Island, confined together on Frobisher's ship, observed on board and in English society, or consigned to the care of English doctors, Kalicho and Arnaaq struggled to retain the particularity of their existence, fighting against attempts to objectify, control, and make spectacles of them. They adapted Inuit norms of conduct to the restricted and demeaning conditions of their captivity, Kalicho fulfilling the roles of hunter, go-between, and perhaps shaman as well as he could; Arnaaq caring for her baby and Kalicho as she thought appropriate and resisting intervention; both maintaining proper decorum with respect to their bodies. They attended carefully to English norms of polite behavior even while being confronted with such threatening practices as portraiture, bloodletting, and exhumation, as well as signs of cannibalism (for how else were the captives to interpret English signs referring to the eating of the lost sailors?).

That which they resisted in captivity, however, they were powerless to resist after death. Their bodies and clothing, captured in paintings and reproduced in woodcuts, were reduced to typifications of the exotic and picturesque, with nearly all references to their historical particularity or the conditions of their captivity extinguished.[25] These representations made their way to the Queen's court, onto broadsides, into costume books, and thence onto maps and into public spectacles. Their behavior, captured in print and widely reproduced in colonial literature, became the basis for ethnological and historical interpretation, including the present chapter. Yet the power and knowledge they conferred upon their captors were limited, partly because they refused to be "known"—refraining from displays of sexuality and emotion, discarding the will to live, perhaps, or even severing a tongue. Given Frobisher's desire to "catch informants"—as the caption to a sixteenth-century woodcut of Kalicho puts it—the "tartar man's" biting of his tongue comes through as an eloquent, if perhaps involuntary, denial of his captor's will.[26]

## Capturing Allies and Enemies:
## Tisquantum, Alias Squanto

Similar themes of capture, typification, and resistance emerge in the case of a subsequent captive, Squanto, who survived some eight years after his initial abduction. Although he was more successfully fashioned into an informant and an ally, Squanto might have more successfully resisted colonial domination than the hegemonic typification acknowledges.

The Wampanoag known to his compatriots as Tisquantum was one of the few Indian captives whose allegiance was won through the dubious strategy of abduction.[27] Tisquantum was among twenty-seven natives of the Wampanoag towns of Patuxet and Nauset who were treacherously kidnapped in 1614 by shipmaster John Hunt against the orders of his commander, who was none other than Captain John Smith (see Map 2.1). These Wampanoags were taken to the slave market at Málaga, Spain, where some, at least, were claimed as apprentices by the Church.

Three years after his abduction Tisquantum found himself in London serving the treasurer of the Newfoundland Company, John Slaney. He accompanied Slaney to Newfoundland, where he encountered Capt. Thomas Dermer, a member of the expedition to New England that had kidnapped Tisquantum. Dermer, now working directly for Ferdinando Gorges, who had sponsored John Smith's expedition to New England, introduced Tisquantum to his employer. Gorges, the commander of Plymouth Harbor and the foremost promoter of colonization in North America, had attempted to use Indian captives to promote various colonization schemes since 1605, when explorer George Waymouth turned over to him three of the five Abenakis he had abducted from Maine.

The abductions that Gorges encouraged were useful propaganda in England but created lasting enmity against the English among coastal Algonquians. Like pathogens and trade goods, tales of European treachery preceded explorers into presumably "virgin" territory. One of the most disastrous abductions was Edward Harlow's seizure in 1611 of six natives, including Epenow (or Epanew), the *sachem* (chief) of Martha's Vineyard. Gorges pinned his colonial ambitions upon Epenow, who learned English well, impressed would-be financiers with his noble bearing, and told intriguing tales of gold in New England. Epenow proved disappointing, however, when his docility evaporated upon his return to Martha's Vineyard in 1614. After escaping from the gold-seeking expedition he had engineered as a ticket home, Epenow became the foremost leader of Wampanoag resistance to the English. Like many other escaped captives, Epenow turned the knowledge he had gained during captivity against those who had abducted him.

Tisquantum proved more enduringly useful to the English than did Epenow, in part because his interests happened to coincide more closely with those of his captors. By the time Tisquantum managed to return home in 1619, accompanying Thomas Dermer on a fishing and trading expedition, his native village was completely deserted. During Tisquantum's absence the Indians of Patuxet had nearly been annihilated by a European disease to which they had no immunity. The epidemic, which claimed seventy-five to ninety percent of the coastal Algonquians living from southern Maine to Cape Cod, opened prime agricultural land to European settlement.[28] Tisquantum, bereft of kin and lacking any power base with which to oppose the English, threw in his lot with his captors, at least for the time being. He facilitated contacts between Dermer's party and the leadership of several Wampanoag towns, proving himself an able diplomat. Tisquantum's diplomatic success, together with his resilience, has suggested to ethnohistorians that he had attained the status of *pniese:* that is, through an arduous vision quest he had attracted the spiritual aid of the deity Abbomocho (or Hobbomok) and become an influential counselor and powerful warrior.[29] But Tisquantum's efforts to forge an alliance between the English and the semiautonomous Wampanoag settlements did not prevail over the hostility created by earlier English visitors. Tisquantum was captured once again, this time by Gorges's former captive and protégé, Epenow.

Tisquantum was soon transferred into the hands of Massasoit (later known as Ousamequin), the paramount sachem of Pokanoket.[30] Once the largest and most powerful of the Wampanoag villages, Pokanoket had been severely weakened by the epidemic, Massasoit being forced into a tributary relationship to his inland enemies, the Narragansetts. Soon after Massasoit took control of Tisquantum, the Pilgrims arrived on Cape Cod, establishing Plymouth on the abandoned site of Patuxet. The besieged Massasoit explored the possibility of an alliance with the Plymouth colony, sending as emissaries an Abenaki sachem named Samoset (himself probably a former captive of the English) and his captive, Tisquan-

tum.[31] The latter won his freedom from the Pokanokets through successfully negotiating a treaty with Plymouth. Living on the site of his ancestral home as an interpreter and intermediary for Massasoit, Tisquantum
helped Plymouth extend its influence over several Wampanoag towns,
ensuring the English settlers a reliable supply of maize and pelts. He also
taught the colonists how to gather native foods and cultivate maize, planting it in hills fertilized with whole fish. Curiously (but consistent with the
complexity of colonial–indigenous cultural exchanges), the use of fish as
fertilizer might not have been an indigenous Algonquian practice but a
product of Tisquantum's exile in Newfoundland.[32]

Then, as now, a prominent symbol of alliance between natives and
colonists, Tisquantum managed to construct a place for himself in the
middle ground between Wampanoag and English society. However,
given the opposition to English colonization among a portion of the indigenous population, as well as rampant factionalism among the
colonists at Plymouth, Tisquantum's position was never secure.[33] Further, it appears that Massasoit never fully trusted his former captive, for
he sent two other emissaries to Plymouth, a man named Tokamahamon,
and the *pniese* Hobbomok, named for his spiritual ally. But Massasoit and
these two emissaries seem to have been dependent upon Tisquantum's
skills as an interpreter, however little they trusted his intentions. On
many occasions Squanto accompanied one or both of the emissaries on
diplomatic missions.

One such mission involved reclaiming an English boy named John
Billington from the Wampanoag town of Nauset, where he had been
taken after becoming lost in the woods. It was perhaps no coincidence
that on the way there, at the town of Cummaquid, the English party
was approached by an old woman who, an anonymous narrative reports,

> could not behold us without breaking forth into great passion, weeping and
> crying excessively. We demanding the reason of it, they told us she had three
> sons who, when Master Hunt was in these parts, went aboard his ship to
> trade with him, and he carried them captives into Spain (for Squanto at that
> time was carried away also) by which means she was deprived of the com-
> fort of her children in her old age.

The English, who found this "very grievous," told them

> we were sorry that any Englishman should give them that offense, that
> Hunt was a bad man, and that all the English that heard of it condemned
> him for the same; but for us, we would not offer them any such injury
> though it would gain us all the skins in the country.

They concluded the interview by giving her "some small trifles, which somewhat appeased her" (Heath 1963 [1622]:70).

That this unsettling incident occurred as the colonists were trying to retrieve the lost Billington boy is intriguing given the common practice across the northeast for bereaved families to control the fate of captives. A further indication that the boy may have been treated as a captive is that when Tisquantum, through conferring with Aspinet, the sachem of Nauset, managed to get the boy returned to his people, he was "behung with beads." The English, understanding the goodwill signified by the wampum, presented knives to the sachem and to the man who had cared for the boy.[34]

Soon after the happy resolution of this affair, Tisquantum, Tokamahamon, and Hobbomok were captured by the head sachem of Pocasset, Corbitant, who was a leading opponent of Massasoit's alliance with the English. Tisquantum's value as an interpreter is indicated by Corbitant's boast that without Tisquantum the colonists would "lose their tongue" (74). Hobbomok managed to escape to the English, and the forces of Capt. Miles Standish rushed to rescue Tokamahamon and Tisquantum. The latter, upon being rescued from this, his third captivity, began to move ever more boldly to turn his relationship with the English to his own political ends. Proclaiming that he had special powers deriving from his association with the colonists, Tisquantum sought tribute from those desiring his protection and began to advise the English without conferring with Massasoit. Notably, when the Narragansett sachem Canonicus sent a rattlesnake skin filled with arrows to Plymouth, Tisquantum took it upon himself to counsel William Bradford to return the skin filled with powder and shot.

His bid for independent power having aroused the enmity of Massasoit, Tisquantum was forced to seek protection from his English patrons, who continued, despite considerable pressure from the paramount sachem, to consider Tisquantum a "special instrument sent of God for their good beyond their expectation" (Bradford 1953:81). In 1622, half a year after Massasoit demanded Tisquantum's head and hands from Governor Bradford, the colonists' godsend suddenly sickened and died of a mysterious ailment that Bradford called an "Indian fever." Branded a traitor and perhaps the victim of witchcraft, on his deathbed Tisquantum asked Bradford "to pray for him that he might go to the Englishmen's God in Heaven; and bequeathed sundry of his things to sundry of his English friends as remembrances of his love" (114). The isolated and defeated Tisquantum had ultimately accepted his captors' claims upon him, acknowledging as a last resort the power of their God.

Captive, refugee, interpreter, teacher, aspiring political leader, exile, convert, traitor: As all of these, Tisquantum may indeed be taken as a symbol of colonial interaction; but contrary to the hegemonic Squanto, Tisquantum embodies colonial interaction in its concrete complexity and resistance to typification. Unlike Squanto, the historical Tisquantum was no simple interpreter, teacher, diplomat, or convert, though he was all of those; no simple captive, though he was a captive thrice over; no simple instrument of conquest, though he was indeed such an instrument; and no simple object of knowledge—whether for captor, colonist, rival political leader, or ethnohistorian. Tisquantum resisted what captivity would make of him, and resists what historical interpretation would make of him as well. What did Tisquantum himself make of his situation? What was his own project? What kind of new world did he envision? What was his sense of identity, his source of strength, and his ultimate vulnerability?

Recent suggestions that Tisquantum was a *pniese*—his name referring to the relationship he established with a source of spiritual power through a vision quest—have provided a fruitful way of approaching these questions, a way of piecing together yet leaving open his story. More generally, conceiving of Tisquantum as a powerful and knowing subject sheds light on the complex relations that may obtain between power and knowledge, domination and representation, control of the body and regimentation of the mind. Tisquantum was a captive who was so useful to his captors—colonists and natives alike—that they were profoundly dependent upon him; so docile that three times he earned his freedom; so disciplined that he was powerful. The English believed that their God had sent them his instrument in Tisquantum; he may have believed, in turn, that his gods had sent him the English.

It might be objected that Tisquantum the resister is as much a romantic typification as Squanto the savior.[35] Indeed, it is only part of his story, but an important part—crucial for understanding Tisquantum's survival and for understanding the challenge that he and his fellow captives offered to their captors. Tisquantum, Epenow, and the Inuit captives had sources of strength and sources of vision beyond the ken and beyond the reach of their captors. Frobisher's captives might be put under surveillance for signs of witchcraft, cannibalism, treachery, or sexual depravity, but they had the strength to resist what their captors would make of them with the paltry means at hand. The sachem Epenow might impress the English nobility with his noble bearing and his knowledge of their language, but they could not impress him with the superiority of their vision or the inevitability of their claims on his homeland.

Similarly, the English had mixed results in bringing two Carolina Algonquians, Manteo and Wanchese, to London as tokens of their reconnaissance mission of 1584 to Roanoke. Thomas Hariot, the scientist on Sir Walter Raleigh's expedition there the following year, prepared himself for the trip by studying the Carolina Algonquian language with Manteo and Wanchese. In turn, he groomed them to serve as interpreters, informants, and converts by teaching them English. Manteo, a Croatoan, performed his role quite to the colonists' satisfaction, but Wanchese, who hailed from Roanoke itself, became hostile toward the colonists.[36]

The French and Spanish had similar problems with the captives they groomed as instruments of conquest. Domagaya and Taignoagny, two Iroquoian boys kidnapped by Cartier in 1534, returned from two years in France knowledgeable enough to serve as interpreters but also to suspect French intentions toward their people. Initially more impressed but in the end more violently resistant was a young Algonquian of chiefly rank abducted from Chesapeake Bay during a Spanish reconnaissance and slaving expedition in 1561. The captive was taken to Havana, where he was baptized under the name of his godfather, Don Luis de Velasco, the Viceroy of New Spain. In 1570, after traveling to Spain, where he was received by Philip II, educated by the Jesuits, and confirmed in the Christian faith, Don Luis agreed to lead a party of Jesuit missionaries headed by Juan Bautista de Segura to his homeland. The Jesuits expected Don Luis to serve as a priceless instrument of conversion; instead, after moving away from the mission and being denounced for polygyny by the Jesuits, he led an attack on the mission, in which all the priests were killed. Only a Spanish altar boy was spared.[37]

Upon such stories is built a prominent typification—that of the Treacherous Savage.[38] Unlike Don Luis, Wanchese, Epenow, and others remembered as traitors to the kidnappers who had trusted them to recognize and further European superiority, Tisquantum and the Inuit captives ultimately found their options all but closed, Tisquantum converting to Christianity and the Inuits submitting to the capture of their images in portraits. Still, their resistance to complete co-optation was significant and gives us cause, in turn, to view the relationship between power and knowledge with subtlety. To do justice to the complexity of the colonial encounter, we must resist assertions about power and knowledge and about self and other that dichotomize between a knowing, dominating Self and an Other who is either known and dominated or falsely known and treacherous.

### Notes

1. Green (1988:588) discusses "Pocahontas Saving Capt. John Smith" and "Squanto Helping the Pilgrims" as national legends currently "spread primarily through print in educational institutions and reinforced by visualization." For Pocahontas, also see the analysis by Feest (1987:5), who interprets her story as an "origin myth of white America." For Squanto, see the work of Humins (1987), who attributes the more recent spread of the myth in schools to Willison (1945). It

is curious that Hirsch's list of "What Literate Americans Know" (1987:152–215), which might be taken as an indication of the hegemonic representation of Indians within a particular segment of American culture, omits Squanto. Pocahontas, however, is one of the few women included on this list of literate Americans' "core knowledge." Captivity is involved in several entries: John Smith, Daniel Boone, James Fenimore Cooper's *The Last of the Mohicans*, and "dime novels." This is discussed further in Strong 1992b:81–82, n. 1.

2. On the vanishing Indian, see O'Brien n.d., Berkhofer 1988, Fiedler 1988, and Marsden and Nachbar 1988. The entire section on "Conceptual Relations" in Washburn 1988 (522–616) provides a basic introduction to European representations of Indians, as does Berkhofer 1978.

3. Strong develops this point in a critique of the most recent hegemonic representation of Pocahontas, the Disney animated feature (Strong 1996a).

4. As Feest notes, "The history of Indian visits to Europe and European reactions to them still remains to be written" (Feest 1987:614). This is perhaps even truer of Indians who visited Europe against their will. Early exceptions to the scholarly neglect of Indian captives are Lauber 1970 [1913] and Foreman 1943 (xvii–33). More recent scholarship on Indian captives includes works by Axtell (1981, 1985b, 1988), Dickason (1984:203–229), Feest (ed., 1987), Hemming (1978), Kawashima (1989), Salisbury (1981, 1982a, 1997), Snell (1972), Sweet and Nash (1981), and Wood (1989).

5. *Wampanoag*, a general term used since the latter half of the seventeenth century, refers to a closely related group of Massachusett-speaking peoples who lived in a number of semiautonomous villages at the time of the first European explorations of New England. Contemporary Wampanoags include the inhabitants of Mashpee, on Cape Cod, and Gay Head, on Martha's Vineyard. Their recent court battles for tribal recognition demonstrate—in a context quite removed from captivity—the hegemony of Anglo-American constructions of history and corporate identity (Campisi 1991; Clifford 1988a; Simmons 1986:10–36, 257–270). Map 4.1 shows Wampanoag territory in some detail.

6. For "floating islands," see especially Hamell 1987 and Miller and Hamell 1986. Axtell (1988:155; 273, n. 21) stresses the retrospective nature of mystical images of European ships, contrasting them with "pragmatic" trading behaviors. However, as Sahlins (1981, 1985) has shown, even the most "pragmatic" trading relationship is symbolically coded, and even the most esoteric symbolic system is transformed in practice.

7. Morrison (1979) discusses a similar Abenaki cannibal giant, Kiwakwe—better known as Windigo. Although not a bird, this giant resembled the cannibal bird in that it epitomized an asocial state and could only be overcome by a culture hero (such as Gluskabe or Nanabush), a shaman, or an exceedingly generous person. Fogelson (1980) discusses Windigo's Cherokee counterpart.

8. Foucault (1979) briefly mentions but does not explore colonial practices as an important site of disciplinary practice. Burnham (1997:151–155) discusses Foucault as a theorist of captivity.

9. Sturtevant quotes from Best 1938 [1578]. Even earlier than the representations of Inuits were those of the Tupinamba of Brazil, deriving in part from the captivity narrative of Hans Staden. For the Staden captivity and its far-reaching

influence on subsequent representations of Indians, see Hemming 1978 and Sturtevant 1976. Bucher 1981 offers a structural analysis of de Bry's illustrations of Tupinambas.

10. Mullaney (1983) briefly discusses two of Frobisher's Inuit captives in his analysis of "the spectacle of the Other" in the late Renaissance.

11. This is Sturtevant and Quinn's translation of the German text of a woodcut printed in Strasbourg.

12. The Baffin Islanders are part of the broad group traditionally known as Central Eskimos. The English word *Eskimo* derives from a pejorative Algonquian term meaning "raw meat eater," and *Inuit* is the preferred term in the Eastern Arctic. Today the native inhabitants of Baffin Island call themselves *Nuntatsiaqmiut* ("people of the beautiful land") (Kemp 1984:475). See Kemp 1984 and Damas 1984 for historical and ethnographic summaries.

13. Axtell (1988:144–181) provides a valuable discussion of the sixteenth-century trade of European "trifles" for goods that Indians considered equally plentiful and commonplace.

14. My description of Frobisher's first voyage closely follows the excellent account by Sturtevant and Quinn (1987:68–76). There were three chronicles of the expedition: a laconic eyewitness account by Christopher Hall, the ship's master, first published by Hakluyt (Hall 1598–1600); Lok's account, unpublished until the nineteenth century (Lok 1867); and the account by George Best, who accompanied Frobisher on his second and third voyages but not his first (Best 1578). All were reprinted in Stefansson 1938. See also Sturtevant and Quinn 1987:114, n. 4.

15. On linguistic evidence of discovery, see Greenblatt 1976. The man's severed tongue apparently did not prevent him from providing a seventeen-item vocabulary, mainly referring to body parts and clothing, as recorded in Hall's account (Hall 1938 [1598–1600], 1:154). See also Stefansson 1938, 2:233–236.

16. Despite reports of the absolute strangeness of this captive, he was not the first Inuit in Europe. A woman and child captured by Basque or Breton fishermen, probably in Labrador, were exhibited in Antwerp and the Hague a decade earlier (in 1567). But the 1577 broadside failed to have as much influence as visual and textual representations of Frobisher's captives, perhaps because the captivity occurred outside the course of colonial expansion.

17. The one extant portrait, featuring carefully depicted native dress on a manikin-like figure, is reproduced in Sturtevant and Quinn 1987 (74, fig. 2).

18. In describing Frobisher's second voyage I rely on the journals of Settle (1979 [1577]) and Best (1938 [1578]:52–79) as well as on Sturtevant and Quinn 1987:76–84. Settle's chronicle was the first piece of American exploration literature to be translated and circulated widely in Europe. Both Settle's and Best's accounts include ethnographic sketches of the Baffinland Inuits, largely based on direct observation of the captives, and both were included in Hakluyt's collection of travel literature (Sturtevant and Quinn 1987:77, 98, 114–115).

19. The facile transpositions between fair means and foul, courtesy and kidnapping, and bestowing gifts and using them as enticements in these and other accounts of Frobisher are consistent with Greenblatt's analysis of the mobile Renaissance self and its improvisation of power (Greenblatt 1980). However, Frobisher seems to have had a limited repertoire of enticements, lacking the sophis-

tication (or "empathy," in Greenblatt's interpretation) that allowed Columbus to fill his ship with Arawak captives who thought they were being piloted to heaven by their gods.

20. See Greenblatt 1976 for a useful explanation of the distinction between transparent and opaque interpretations of signs.

21. Best's ability to use attributions of cannibalism reflexively—to represent the English as cannibalistic Others in the eyes of the Inuits—is an intriguing twist on the representation of cannibalistic Others. A similar reflexive projection of cannibalism motivated the bizarre exhumation of English bones discussed below.

22. Sturtevant and Quinn suggest that Frobisher and his crew might have been influenced by *Mandeville's Travels* (a copy of which was carried on board their ship) as well as by a diet that struck the English as bestial. Mandeville told of "a great isle" off the east coast of Asia near the country of Prester John, "wherein dwell people as great as giants of twenty-eight or thirty feet of length . . . and they have no clothing but beasts' skins that hang on them, and they eat no bread but flesh raw, and they drink milk, and they have no houses, and they eat gladlier flesh of men than [any] other" (Sturtevant and Quinn 1987:115, n. 7; cf. 77, 80). Cannibalism was a standard feature in early descriptions of New World peoples, including a broadside describing an Inuit woman and girl captured a decade earlier and exhibited in Amsterdam and the Hague. A German broadside of 1577 reporting the exhibition of this "wild woman" and her daughter emphasized "cannibalism, gigantism, paganism, and promiscuity" alongside a remarkably accurate woodcut of a tattooed woman and her daughter in sealskin clothing (Sturtevant and Quinn 1987:65, fig. 1; 61–68). The woman's husband is described formulaically as a man "12 feet tall [who] had in 12 days killed 12 people with his own hands, Frenchmen and Portuguese, in order to eat them, for they like to eat no flesh better than human flesh" (130). For analyses of European representations of cannibalism in the New World, see Cheyfitz 1997; Greenblatt 1976; Hulme 1992; Sturtevant 1976; Taussig 1987; and White 1976. For colonial representations of cannibalism elsewhere, see the debate between Marshall Sahlins (1981, 1983, 1985, 1996) and Ganath Obeyesekere (1992a, 1992b); also see Schaffer n.d.

23. For translations, see Stefansson 1938, 2:235–236; and Sturtevant and Quinn 1987:115–116, n. 8.

24. A highly skilled Flemish portraitist named Cornelis Ketel, who had painted Frobisher's first Inuit captive, was commissioned for the official portraits of Kalicho, Arnaaq, and Nutaaq. Figure 2.1 shows John White's watercolor drawings. Sturtevant and Quinn (1987:88, 97, 108) suggest that White might have been a member of Frobisher's second expedition, citing his detailed and accurate portrayal of the fight during which Arnaaq and Nutaaq were captured. See also Hulton 1984 and Cheshire, Waldron, Quinn, and Quinn 1980.

25. An exception to the decontextualization of the representations are two paintings indicating moments of capture (Sturtevant and Quinn 1987:74, fig. 2b; 86, fig. 7; 110, fig. 12a).

26. "Master Frobisher pursued them," the caption to the 1578 woodcut relates, referring to a party of Inuits fleeing in their kayak, "so that he could catch some of them for informants" (Sturtevant and Quinn 1987:139).

27. My discussion of Tisquantum relies on the somewhat contrasting analyses by Salisbury (1981, 1982a), Humins (1987), and Sanders (1978), as well as on primary sources, including the anonymous "Mourt's Relation" (Heath 1963 [1622]) and William Bradford's journal (Bradford 1953). Humins debunks Tisquantum's heroic status; Sanders presents him as a sacrificial victim to English colonization; and Salisbury presents him as an example of survival through accommodation.

28. The disease that caused this epidemic has not been identified with certainty, but it might have been hepatitis (Spiess and Spiess 1987; see also Cook 1973b, 1976), typhus, or bubonic plague (Crosby 1978). The region's population was further ravaged by a smallpox epidemic in 1633.

29. See Salisbury 1981. Simmons has suggested that Tisquantum's name refers to a vision he had of a god (presumably Squant, the wife of the culture hero Maushop, slayer of the cannibal bird). The *pniese*, like the more familiar *powwow*, was a kind of shaman (see Simmons 1986:37–64).

30. Salwen (1978) and Rountree (1989) compare Wampanoag political organization under Massasoit to the more developed Algonquian chiefdom in Virginia under Powhatan. In both cases, centralization was probably a response to European trade, diseases, and colonization.

31. Samoset may have been one of the Abenakis whom George Waymouth abducted in 1605 and presented to Gorges (Salisbury 1982a:90–92; 266, n. 15). But his familiarity with the English language and English customs also might have been due to the frequent visits of English fishermen to his home on Monhegan Island in Maine (Sanders 1978:301).

32. Ceci (1975, 1990) and Nanepashemet (1993) discuss the origin of the practice of using fish as fertilizer. Tisquantum's cultural hybridity has become "paradigmatic" for James Clifford, who has coined the phrase *Squanto effect* to refer to uncanny travel conjunctures (Clifford 1997:18; 1988b:17).

33. Sanders (1978) treats Tisquantum's isolation as a result of rivalry between colonists loyal to Gorges and Bradford (and thus to their protégé, Tisquantum) and the Separatists, led by Edward Winslow (whose own favored emissary was Hobbomok). Shuffleton (1976) also discusses Tisquantum and Hobbomok.

34. The incident is recounted as part of the anonymous *Mourt's Relation* (Heath 1963:69–72). The connection drawn here between the old woman and the boy is my own speculation, but see also Sanders's account of Tisquantum's influence in retrieving the boy (1978:308–311).

35. Abu-Lughod (1990) criticizes a romantic approach to resistance, suggesting instead that resistance be taken as a diagnostic of domination.

36. See Cheyfitz 1997:175–213; Kupperman 1984; Fausz 1977:197–200; and Feest 1978a.

37. For the French example, see Trigger 1985:125, and for the Spanish, see Barbour 1970:4–5; Brindenbaugh 1980:10–33; and Swagerty 1981:743–755. Both examples are discussed further in Chapter 3.

38. See Hulme 1992:137–173; Kupperman 1977 and 1980; and Sheehan 1980.

# 3

# Captivity and Hostage-Exchange in Powhatan's Domain, 1607–1624

### A Christian for a Savage:
### The Middle Ground of Hostage-Exchange

As Frobisher's initial contact with the Baffinland Inuits demonstrates, Europeans took captives not only in order to fashion informants and allies but also to obtain hostages who might be used as instruments of diplomacy. Europeans employed hostages to ensure the safety of other Europeans who were in indigenous hands, to bargain for political concessions, and more rarely, to cement alliances. Similar uses of hostages were known in indigenous societies, as Massasoit's capture of Tisquantum attests. The political use of hostages and the reciprocal exchange of hostages, then, were forms of mediation between societies with which both Europeans and indigenous peoples were familiar. However, because considerable variation existed in conventions regarding hostages and in the extent to which conventions were followed, there was ample room for misunderstandings and hostility to arise. Particularly objectionable to Native Americans were European violations of reciprocity in the training of interpreters and mediators—that is, their attempts to fashion such individuals asymmetrically through capture rather than reciprocally through hostage-exchange.

In comparison to the English and the Iberians, the French more often obtained consent before transporting Indians across the ocean, hoping to win over persons of influence to the cause of the Crown and the Church. The most notorious exception, Cartier's kidnapping of Domagaya and Taignoagny in 1534, is revealing in its conspicuous breach of indigenous expectations. These two boys were the teenage sons or matrilateral nephews of Donnacona, the headman of the St. Lawrence Iroquoian village of Stadacona (at the site of Quebec) (see Map 2.1). No doubt the Stadaconans, like other Iroquoians, would have understood Cartier's motivations for training interpreters, but they would have expected him to exchange French boys for the Stadaconans, following a traditional pattern of creating kinship ties between trading partners through temporary child-exchange. Indeed, the headman of the nearby Iroquoian village of Achelacy presented Cartier with two of his children as a token of alliance, and Donnacona himself entrusted the explorer with several children on his next visit. Cartier, however, failed to reciprocate. Quite to the contrary, because he wished to impress his King with the Iroquoians' knowledge of precious metals (probably native copper), at the conclusion of his second trip Cartier abducted Donnacona himself, two additional headmen, and the two interpreters. Neither these captives nor the children were ever seen again in Stadacona. By 1541, when Cartier established a short-lived settlement west of Stadacona, only one of the captives remained alive. She was not allowed to return to her people, lest she reveal the sad fate of her fellow captives. Though Cartier tried to convince the Stadaconans that their leaders and relatives were safe and happy in France, his abductions had extinguished all goodwill, and his colony was doomed. By the time a permanent French settlement was established on the site, Stadacona had been abandoned.[1]

Although the English were more prone to kidnap potential interpreters and intermediaries than to train them through apprenticeship or hostage-exchange, there are a few significant instances of such exchanges between English and indigenous peoples in the earliest years of colonization. The earliest recorded exchange of English for Indian persons occurred in 1531, when William Hawkins of Plymouth exchanged his townsman Martin Cockeram for a Brazilian *cacique* (chief). The cacique spent one year in England, where he had an audience with Henry VIII. Although the Brazilian died on the return voyage, the English hostage was yielded up to his people.[2] Frobisher's brief hostage-exchange with the Baffinland Inuits occurred a half century later.

More significant politically was an exchange in 1608 between Powhatan, paramount chief *(mamanatowick)* over Tsenacomoco, an Algonquian chiefdom in tidewater Virginia, and Capt. Christopher Newport, the one-armed former privateer who served as the first president of the Council of the Royal Virginia Company's colony at Jamestown (see Map 3.1).[3] Wishing to train an interpreter, Newport presented to Powhatan as his "son" a thirteen-year-old youth named, appropriately enough, Thomas Savage. In return Powhatan offered to Newport his adviser, or *caucorouse*, Namontack, whom Capt. John Smith described as "one of a shrewd, subtle capacity" (Smith 1986 [1612], 1:216).[4] According to Powhatan diplomatic practices this exchange of "sons" was expected to seal an alliance and develop knowledgeable interpreters and mediators. Namontack accompanied Newport to London, where he received a royal welcome as the son of Powhatan, the "King of Virginia." Unfortunately

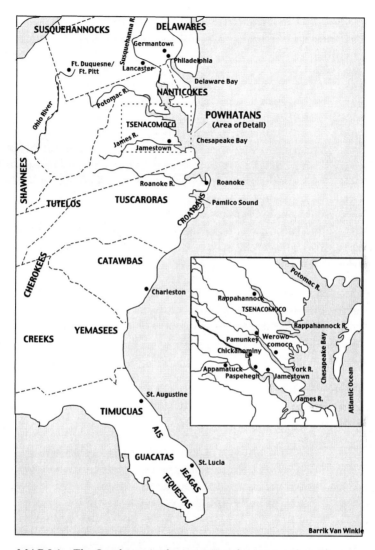

MAP 3.1   The Southeast in the seventeenth century, showing selected peoples, settlements, and sites of captivity. SOURCE: Barrik Van Winkle.

for Powhatan, however, Namontack's experience and shrewdness were of limited use, as he was killed in a brawl some two years later. Young Tom Savage, for his part, established a close relationship with the ma-manatowick, learned the Powhatan language, and served the colony for years as an interpreter.

The atmosphere of goodwill and reciprocity signified by Newport's and Powhatan's "exchange of a Christian for a Salvage" (1:216) quickly turned to distrust and hostility, and there were no further long-term exchanges of hostages. Still, certain colonists found it attractive to live in native villages, where food and women were considerably more plentiful than in Jamestown. This development was of great concern to colonial leaders, who were suspicious of Englishmen who established relations with Indians, including Thomas Savage and eventually John Smith himself.

In contrast to the English policy, Powhatan's was to accumulate as much knowledge as possible about the strangers on his land through the strategic placement of trusted intermediaries. The most beloved of his many daughters, Pocahontas, played this role from the time of her initial encounter with John Smith in December 1607 until her death in England nine years later. When Pocahontas and her husband, the English colonist John Rolfe, traveled to London, Powhatan included in her entourage his son-in-law Uttamatomakkin, a *quioccosuk* (high priest) as well as a trusted adviser. Like Pocahontas, Uttamatomakkin achieved considerable prominence in London. He was sought out by Samuel Purchas, who recorded his conversations with "Tomocomo" regarding Powhatan religion in his *Pilgrimage* (Purchas 1617), a collection of travel and colonial accounts focused in particular on comparative religious beliefs and practices.[5] In dramatic contrast to the transculturated Pocahontas, Uttamatomakkin appeared in his native dress, demonstrated Powhatan dances and rituals, and was little impressed by the sights and personages of London. Purchas and John Smith reported condescendingly that to his chagrin, Uttamatomakkin was unable to carry out two of his missions for Powhatan: He could neither "number the people" by carving notches on a stick nor get John Smith to show him the English God. "Concerning God," Smith admitted to the Queen, "I told him the best I could" (Smith 1986 [1624], 2:261). The priest retained faith in his own deities, claiming that the god Okeus had warned the Powhatan priests about the *tassantasses*, or strangers, who would arrive from over the sea. He advised Purchas to confine his proselytizing to the younger Powhatans in the entourage, as he was too old to learn.

Unlike Powhatan's advisers Namontack and Uttamatomakkin, the youthful Pocahontas adopted the English God and "civilized" demeanor. In her own time and in her own society, as in ours, Pocahontas personified the possibility of a voluntary and peaceful union between indigenous and colonial societies in North America. But given the nature of marriage in seventeenth-century English society and the conditions under which Pocahontas was transformed into Lady Rebecca Rolfe, it is more accurate to view Pocahontas as a personification of the subordination of indigenous to colonial peoples. Indeed, as we explore the context of violence in which her incorporation by the English was embedded, it becomes clear that Pocahontas is a double embodiment of indigenous subordination and submission to colonial authority. Not only did she submit herself to the authority of Rolfe, his Church, and his King, but she was a key instrument in the submission of her entire people to the English. And contrary to hegemonic representations of Pocahontas acting upon her own free will, it was as a captive of the English that Pocahontas was converted to Christianity and accepted the hand of John Rolfe. Abducted by the English and held hostage for a year in an attempt to force her father to capitulate to colonial demands, Pocahontas served as a valuable and a docile instrument of colonial conquest in Virginia. This is not to deny that Pocahontas welcomed her conversion and her marriage, whatever her reasons, but to begin to place her compliance within a broader cultural and political context.[6]

As savior, informant, captive, wife, and mother, Pocahontas embodies the complexity of the relationships among captivity, knowledge, and power in early colonial Virginia. To appreciate her significance fully, we must locate Pocahontas's captivity and assimilation within a lengthy series of abductions in the Chesapeake Bay area. To the south, on the Carolina Banks (the site of Roanoke), abductions date as far back as 1524, when Verrazano snatched a child from its mother's arms. The recorded history of abductions in what was to become Powhatan's tidewater domain began in 1561, nearly half a century before the founding of Jamestown, with the capture of an Algonquian of chiefly status baptized as Don Luis. Although his precise parentage remains uncertain, we know that Don Luis was the son of a *werowance* (chief) whose territory was near Werowocomoco, which would later serve as the seat of Powhatan's chiefdom. It was in this territory, across the York River and downstream from Werowocomoco, that Don Luis helped both to establish and to destroy a short-lived Jesuit mission. Scholars have speculated that Don Luis was closely related to Powhatan and his close kinsman Opechancanough, werowance over the powerful Pamunkeys, for Don Luis is supposed to have joined his brothers on the Pamunkey River after leaving the mission.[7] Whatever the precise relationship among Don Luis, Opechancanough, and Powhatan, the latter would have been a young man at the time of the Spanish incursion, and might have participated in the attack on the mission Don Luis led in 1571. The young Powhatan certainly would have known of, if not witnessed, the revenge wreaked by the Spanish the following year upon fourteen Algonquian captives, including two chiefs, who after receiving Christian baptism were hung from the ship's riggings in full view of their compatriots.

The English settlement at Roanoke in 1585 and the precipitous violence toward the Algonquian people of the area that led to the destruction of the colony would also have been well known to Powhatan. To compound Powhatan's uneasiness about the European intruders, a Spanish ship searching for Roanoke in 1588 had paid a visit to Chesapeake Bay and kidnapped one of Powhatan's own people. Finally, shortly before the settlement of Jamestown, a European vessel had docked at the Powhatan village of Rappahannock, responding to the town's hospitality by killing their werowance and taking several captives.[8]

## The Captivity and Transformation of John Smith

Powhatan and his people had enough experience with the people they called *tassantasses* to view with both interest and trepidation the landing of more than one hundred Englishmen (all males) on the James River in spring 1607. Initially the mamanatowick kept his distance, employing subordinate werowances to assess the strangers and perhaps to drive them off through diplomatic or military means. The Virginia colonists were feasted by the chiefs of several towns, who traded with them, tried to learn their intentions, and warned them away from Powhatan's domains. They were also attacked unsuccessfully by the Paspaheghs, upon whose hunting grounds they had settled. John Smith, a well-traveled adventurer and soldier of fortune, quickly assumed control of exploration and trade in Powhatan territory. Some six months after the founding of Jamestown, in December 1607, Smith was captured during his first reconnaissance mission into the heart of Pamunkey territory upstream from Jamestown (see Figure 3.1).[9] The Pamunkeys, the most skilled warriors of his chiefdom, killed three Englishmen during the attack and lost two of their own men. Smith, identified by his Chickahominy guide as an English werowance, was spared and brought before the Pamunkey werowance Opechancanough. One of Powhatan's "brothers" (probably the son of his mother's sister), Opechancanough served as Powhatan's "outside" or war chief.[10]

Smith's successive accounts of his captivity have received extensive critical scrutiny, both as autobiographical and as proto-ethnographic texts. My reading of Smith's accounts focuses first on Smith's strategies as a captive and interpreter of captivity. I then turn a more ethnographic gaze upon Smith's texts in order to consider the extent to which Powhatan strategies can be discerned in what Peter Hulme, in his analysis of colonial discourse, calls the "disjunction between the discursive and the experiential" (Hulme 1992:129). This interpretive strategy allows further consideration of the gap between Smith's and Powhatan's understandings of the obligations each incurred as a result of Smith's captivity.

After what Smith interpreted as a victory dance around him, he was examined by Opechancanough regarding the recent murder and abductions at Rappahannock and then submitted to three days of a ceremony, the meaning of which, he believed, was to divine whether his intentions toward them were for good or ill. In the midst of the ceremony the priests laid down a circle of meal surrounded by two circles of corn kernels, and then placed a stick between each pair of kernels. "The circle of meal signified their country," Smith surmised, "the circles of corn the bounds of the sea, and the sticks his country" (Smith 1986 [1624], 2:113).

FIGURE 3.1  "King Powhatan commands Capt. Smith to be slain; his daughter Pocahontas begs his life." Detail, *A Description of Part of the Adventures of Captain Smith in Virginia*; engraving by Robert Vaughan. SOURCE: *The Generall Historie of Virginia, New-England, and the Summer Isles* (London, 1624). (Courtesy of the Newberry Library, Chicago.)

Smith was then marched to Rappahannock itself, where he was absolved of the murder and abductions, thanks to his notably short stature. "Expecting . . . every hour to be put to one death or other" (Smith 1986 [1624], 2:151), Smith took a cue, it seems, from the Roanoke colonist Thomas Hariot, a mathematician and astronomer. He showed Opechancanough his compass, "describing by my best means the use thereof, whereat he so amazedly admired, as he suffered me to proceed in a discourse of the roundness of the earth, the course of the sun, moon, stars, and planets." When Smith went on to discuss "the greatness of the land and sea, the diversity of nations, variety of complexions, and how we were to them Antipodes, and many other such like matters," he reports, "they all stood as amazed with admiration" (2:147).[11] Perhaps most amazing to the modern reader is what Smith was able to accomplish with his rudimentary knowledge of the Powhatan language, which was confined mainly to trading jargon if the words and phrases included in his *Map of Virginia* are any clue. (Among the more complicated—and intriguing—entries is *Kekaten pokahontas patiaquagh ningh tanks manotyens neer mowchick rawrenock audowgh*: "Bid Pokahontas bring hither two little baskets, and I will give her white beads to make her a chain" (Smith 1986 [1612], 1:137).

In an era that highly valued eloquence, Smith's account stressed his rhetorical skills.[12] He also improvised upon the disparity between Powhatan and English systems of inscribing signs, contriving to send news of a planned attack on the fort at Jamestown in a letter, and predicting to his Pamunkey messengers what the recipients of his letter would do upon opening it. In the letter Smith gave a list of things that the men at the fort should provide so as "to affright the messengers." As he had predicted, the messengers returned to Werowocomoco with the items he wished, apparently "to the wonder of them all that heard it, that he could either divine, or the paper could speak" (Smith 1986 [1624], 2:148–149).[13]

By Smith's own admission, the Pamunkeys succeeded in their own attempts to amaze Smith. Most dramatically, they made their captive undergo three days of "the most strange and fearful conjurations," presided over by "a great grim fellow" who was "as ugly as the devil" and pronounced invocations over him in "a hellish voice" (1986 [1624], 2:149–150). Smith gathered that the purpose of the ceremony was to learn whether he "intended them well or no." The conjuration was interspersed with sumptuous feasts from which his hosts abstained, leading Smith to fear that he was being fattened for the slaughter. "So fat they fed me," he wrote, "that I much doubted [feared] they intended to have sacrificed me to the Quiyoughquosick [*quioccosuk*], which is a superior power they worship; a more uglier thing cannot be described" (1986 [1608], 2:59).[14]

After several weeks of mutual attempts to amaze, frighten, divine, and conjure the other, Smith was brought to Werowocomoco for his first audience with the mamanatowick. Dressed in a raccoon robe and chains of pearls, Powhatan reclined on an elevated throne, surrounded by an impressive retinue of priests, advisers, and young women, each wearing a chain of white shells or pearls. The mamanatowick greeted him "with such a grave and majestical countenance," reported Smith, "as drew me into admiration to see such state in a naked savage" (Smith 1986 [1608], 2:53). The people acknowledged the captive's arrival with "a great shout," and in preparation for a feast two women, one of whom he recognized as the "Queen of Appamatuck," brought him water and feathers to use in washing and drying his hands.[15] After this royal welcome and a feast Powhatan held "a long consultation" with his advisers, during which Smith believed his fate was decided (see Figure 3.1). As he described the subsequent events in his *Generall Historie of Virginia, New England, and the Summer Isles*:

> Two great stones were brought before Powhatan: then as many as could laid hands on him, dragged him to them, and thereon laid his head, and being ready with their clubs, to beat out his brains, Pocahontas, the King's dearest daughter, when no entreaty could prevail, got his head in her arms, and laid her own upon his to save him from death: whereat the Emperor was contented he should live to make him hatchets, and her bells, beads, and copper. (Smith 1986 [1624], 2:151)

This reprieve was followed, two days later, by a ritual in which Powhatan, disguised in "the most fearful manner," appearing "more like a devil then a man," and accompanied by "some two hundred more as black as himself, "told him now they were friends, and presently he should go to Jamestown, to send him two great guns, and a grindstone, for which he would give him the Country of Capahowasic, and forever esteem him as his son Nantaquoud." Smith agreed to the terms in order to secure his release but never took up residence at Capahowasic, a nearby town downstream on the James River. Neither did the Englishman find it necessary to supply Powhatan with cannons, since the mamanatowick's messengers, once confronted with transporting the hefty weapons to Werowocomoco, were content with the grindstone and lesser gifts Smith disparaged as "toys" (Smith 1986 [1624], 2:151).

John Smith construed his captivity as one in which he was examined and absolved, "amazedly admired," threatened with death and saved, and given land in exchange for English goods. Establishing himself as simultaneously guiltless, wondrous, redeemed, and legitimated, Smith emerged from captivity as a prototypical resourceful traveler. Small wonder that his captivity came to serve Virginia, the Confederacy, and the United States as what Doris Sommer (1991) calls a "foundational romance." But to understand the extent to which this foundational romance is a selective tradition, we must consider what it overlooks or suppresses. We might do this best by looking closely at the relationship established during the captivity between Smith and Pocahontas, as well as the subsequent events in the latter's life.

Smith was certain that he owed his life to the "compassionate pitifull heart" of Pocahontas, as he declared in a letter of 1616 introducing her to Queen Anne.[16] After some weeks "fatting amongst those savage courtiers," wrote Smith, "at the minute of my execution" Pocahontas

> hazarded the beating out of her own brains to save mine, and not only that, but so prevailed with her father, that I was safely conducted to Jamestown, where I found about eight and thirty miserable poor and sick creatures, to keep possession of all those large territories of Virginia, such was the weakness of this poor Commonwealth, as had the savages not fed us, we directly had starved. (Smith 1986 [1624], 2:258–259)

Smith's account of the fragility of the colony is no exaggeration, and matters were only somewhat improved by the arrival, immediately after Smith's return, of a ship bearing Capt. Newport, Powhatan's adviser Namontack, eighty additional colonists, and a supply of provisions. More crucial to Jamestown's survival was the food Powhatan provided every four or five days, which, wrote Smith to the Queen, "was commonly brought us by this Lady Pocahontas," only some ten years old at the time.

> Notwithstanding all these passages when inconstant Fortune turned our peace to war, this tender virgin would still not spare to dare to visit us, and by her our jars [dissensions] have been often appeased, and our wants still supplied. Were it the policy of her father thus to employ her, or the ordinance of God thus to make her his instrument, or her extraordinary affection to our Nation, I know not. . . . Jamestown with her wild train she as freely frequented, as her father's habitation; and during the time of two or three years, she next under God, was still the instrument to preserve this Colony from death, famine and utter confusion. (Smith 1986 [1624], 2:259)

However Pocahontas's loyalty is explained, there is no doubt that she served at least as the proximate instrument of the colony's salvation for the nearly two years between Smith's release from captivity in January 1608 and his departure for England. Yet Smith's contention that Pocahontas also served as the instrument of his own personal preservation from death has been unconvincing to many scholars since the seventeenth century.[17] One reason for skepticism is that rescue from captivity by an enamored princess is a conventional motif in European travel narratives, one that had already appeared in North American travel literature (in the sixteenth-century Portuguese explorer Juan Ortiz's account of his decade-long captivity among the Timucuas of Florida) and would later be featured in Smith's account of his release from an earlier episode of captivity and slavery in Turkey (Smith 1986 [1630], 3:184–203).[18]

Another cause for doubt is the lack of independent testimony regarding the events at Werowocomoco. Indeed, with the exception of his letter to Queen Anne in 1616, Smith himself was silent regarding any attempt to execute him until 1624, after Pocahontas had married John Rolfe, become famous in England as a convert to Christian civility, and tragically died.[19] In the earliest extant account of the captivity—a letter that was edited and published as *A True Relation* without Smith's permission—the events at Werowocomoco lack drama altogether. Although Smith confessed that he feared becoming a sacrificial victim when he was among the Pamunkeys, there is no mention of a threatened execution at Werowocomoco, and Pocahontas is simply described as "nonpareil," or without equal (as Shakespeare's Miranda would soon be described).[20] Smith's interaction with Powhatan is confined to feasting and polite conversation regarding Smith's intentions, Powhatan's domains, and their common enemies.

The clear implication of *A True Relation* is that Smith's own cunning—particularly his representations of English intentions and English power in terms that Powhatan would respect—won him his freedom and Powhatan's friendship. During his interview with the mamanatowick, Smith portrayed the English as temporary visitors to Tsenacomoco, claiming that his party had traveled upriver because his "father," Captain Newport, wished to avenge the death of his "child" at the hands of Powhatan's enemies, the Monocans (a Siouan-speaking people to the west). Newport became "King of all the waters" in Smith's hands, and of such greatness that the mamanatowick "admired, and not a little feared" him. The happy outcome of their discussion was that Powhatan "desired me to forsake Paspahegh, and to live with him upon his river, [in] a country called Capahowasic. He promised to give me corn, venison, or what I wanted to feed us; hatchets and copper we should make him; and none should disturb us" (Smith 1986, [1608] 1:57).

Setting aside for a moment Smith's later claim to have been rescued from execution, there is a significant amount of agreement between Smith's two major published versions of his audience with Powhatan. Most generally, both the 1608 and the 1624 accounts feature an attempt by the mamanatowick to subordinate Smith to himself, offering his protection over English life in exchange for tribute payments of metal goods and other valuables. Indeed, the terms Powhatan set for his captive's freedom appear entirely consistent with what is known of Powhatan's expectations of other subordinated polities. Nor is Powhatan's attempt to encompass the English and assert control over their manufactures in-

compatible with Smith's account of his rescue from execution by Pocahontas. Understanding Pocahontas's actions as coordinated with her father's and political rather than romantic in motivation allows us to posit
an interpretation of John Smith's captivity that demonstrates just how
thoroughly Smith and his people were incorporated into Tsenacomoco,
and just how thoroughly they violated Powhatan's expectations of tribute and loyalty.

Like Peter Hulme (1992) and especially Frederic Gleach (1997), I consider Smith's account of his near execution and salvation not as a fabrication but as Smith's culture-bound and self-serving interpretation of a
series of Powhatan rituals designed to transform strangers into relatives, allies, and trading partners.[21] That Smith's account of 1624 is authentic can neither be proven nor conclusively denied. But it "rings
true"—at least provisionally true—given what we know of subsequent
relations between Powhatan and Pocahontas, on the one hand, and
Smith and the other English colonists, on the other. It also has powerful
resonances with what scholars have otherwise been able to reconstruct
of the Powhatan chiefdom and of eastern Algonquian societies more
generally.

In this light, each of Smith's three accounts of his captivity and release
may be considered not as relatively authentic or relatively fabricated, but
as distinct moments in what Greenblatt (1980) has called "self-fashioning." In 1608 Smith (or his editor) had good reason to omit a near execution and rescue by an Indian maiden because such an event was incompatible with the Royal Virginia Company's attempt, against great odds,
to fashion the colonists as competent and autonomous during the tenu-
ous early years of colonization. In 1616, in contrast, Smith had reason to
use Pocahontas's visit to England as a pretext for fashioning himself before his Queen as a loyal, courageous, and self-sacrificing subject. By this
time Smith's colonial ambitions had turned to New England, where he
had led one fishing, trading, and surveying expedition (the very voyage
on which Tisquantum was kidnapped, though not by Smith himself). He
had since made two abortive attempts, sponsored by Ferdinando Gorges,
to establish a colony in New England. Finally, by 1624, two years after
Powhatan's successor, Opechancanough, led a deadly war of resistance,
both Powhatan and Opechancanough had gained reputations for treachery, whereas the tragically deceased Pocahontas represented the lost opportunity for amity between natives and colonists in Virginia. These di-
chotomous, gender-coded representations of the Virginia Algonquians,
promulgated by Samuel Purchas, among others, provided a symbolic
field within which Smith could continue to fashion himself as a colonial
hero.[22]

That Smith wished thus to fashion himself in his *Generall Historie* is evident in his introduction to the captivity episode, although he takes an alternative path toward that end:

> Six or seven weeks those barbarians kept him prisoner, many strange triumphs and conjurations they made of him, yet he so demeaned himself amongst them, as he not only diverted them from surprising the fort, but procured his own liberty, and got himself and his company such estimation amongst them, that those salvages admired him more than their own Quiyouckosucks [priests]. (Smith 1986 [1624], 2:146)

Here, as in his account of 1608, Smith begins by presenting himself as a successful pragmatist, one who ensured his freedom and the safety of his compatriots through his demeanor. But the consequence of Smith's pragmatism, particularly his effort to fabricate himself as a diviner, is that the Powhatans perceived Smith as more admirable than their own priests (or did he mean their deity, since the word applies to both?). In fashioning himself as a bearer of supernatural power Smith intriguingly resembles Capt. Cook and Cortez.[23] It would seem, however, that the supernatural mode of heroism constructed here is not entirely compatible with Smith's role as passive victim in the execution-and-rescue tale. In giving a romantic reading to Pocahontas's actions, however, Smith only underscores his superiority—at least in her estimation. Subsequently, Smith presents himself as spurning any sexual relationship with Pocahontas, again underscoring (for his English audience) his heroic status.[24]

Proceeding under the assumption that Pocahontas did indeed place her body between Smith's head and an executioner's club, and that Smith treated this event both in terms of his own cultural categories and his successive projects of self-fabrication, let us now attempt to substitute Powhatan meanings for Smith's "fictions of translation" (Cheyfitz 1997).[25] From Smith's own testimony it appears that the decision to spare Smith's life was made in council by Powhatan's priests and advisers. Far from defying her father in response to her own emotions, then, Pocahontas seems to have been enacting some kind of transformative ceremony upon his orders. Like the arduous Powhatan male initiation rite known as the *huskanaw* and similar rites of passage known across North America and worldwide, it would seem that the transformative ritual performed on Smith entailed symbolic death and rebirth. That is, during the ritual the English commoner symbolically died and was reborn: as some kind of relative to Powhatan and Pocahontas, as a subordinate werowance, as an allied priest, or most likely, as a combination or transformation of all these roles.[26]

As we have seen, Smith described two ritual events at Werowocomoco: the execution and rescue scene, and two days later, a religious ceremony that seems to have completed Smith's rite of passage from captive to kindred, ally, and provider of valuables. With regard to the alleged execution attempt, we know from Smith himself, a subsequent English captive named Henry Spelman, and a few other English observers that in Powhatan's chiefdom both disobedient subjects and male war captives were subject to execution. Murderers and thieves were executed by clubbing and burning. The high priest Uttamatomakkin told Samuel Purchas that he had personally executed a subject found guilty of stealing from the English. In Spelman's account of the execution of the male accomplices to an infanticide, the execution was preceded by the severing of the victims' scalplocks—presumably the seat of their souls—which were hung in front of the temple. The victims' bones were broken by clubs and then, still alive, the victims were thrown on a fire (Spelman 1910 [1613?]:cxi). Prior to reporting his own rescue from execution, Smith noted that Powhatan presided over several forms of execution, sometimes causing "the heads of them that offend him to be laid upon the altar or sacrificing stone, [while] one with clubs beats out their brains" (Smith 1986 [1612], 1:174–175; cf. Smith 1986 [1624], 2:127). Whatever the extent of the clubbing, victims' bodies were generally consumed by flames. In contrast, the honorable disposition of bodies consisted of burial for commoners and scaffold burial for the elite, whose bones were preserved in the temple.[27]

In contrast to domestic offenders, male war captives were tortured to death. The agents of torture were either the town's women or a male executioner. The victim's body, stripped and tied to a tree or stake, was gradually cut away and burned in his full sight. An honorable warrior would meet this torture with proclamations of his bravery and predictions of the revenge his relatives would take upon his captors. Only upon being disemboweled would the victim be released from his pain. Contrary to John Smith's fears that he might be sacrificed and eaten, however, ritual cannibalism was not practiced among the Powhatans. The victim's body and entrails were entirely consumed by flames, except for certain portions, particularly the scalp, that were dried as trophies. The scalps of executed captives, like those of enemy warriors killed on the battlefield, would be placed in the temple.[28]

Captive women, children, and werowances, on the other hand, were often adopted and placed in the service of the mamanatowick or one of his subordinate werowances. This was simultaneously an insult to the enemy and a way to increase the chiefdom's relative strength. Given Smith's reception as an enemy werowance and Powhatan's acknowledgment of Smith as his son, it is not unlikely that Smith was submitted not to an attempted execution but to an adoption ritual. Although there is no record of an adoption ceremony to compare to Smith's account, we do know of another rite of passage: the *huskanaw*, an initiation rite for boys who had already distinguished themselves in hunting or warfare. The initiates would be abducted by male elders, during which women would mourn the initiates' "death." The abduction was followed by violent beatings in the form of a gauntlet, repeated ingestion of an intoxicating potion (perhaps made of jimsonweed), and confinement in the woods. When the boys returned after several months, profoundly disoriented, they were expected to show no memory of their previous life. Freed of their previous attachments, prejudices, and fears, they were considered reborn and "consecrate[d] . . . to the service of their God," as Robert Beverley interpreted the ritual in 1705 (Axtell 1981:47). If they successfully completed this rite of passage, the initiates became appropriate candidates for the powerful roles of adviser, priest, diviner, or werowance. If a boy did not survive the rite, according to Smith, he was considered a sacrifice to the god Okeus.[29]

There is strong evidence that John Smith was treated during his captivity as an enemy werowance who might be usefully incorporated into Powhatan's domain. As such he was saved from the fate of one of his companions on the trip into Pamunkey territory, George Cassen, who, Smith reported, was tied to a tree, cut at the joints, skinned at the head and face, disemboweled, and burned (Smith 1986 [1612]:175). Smith, in contrast, was turned over to Opechancanough, who consulted his priests and advisers as well as the bereaved leaders of Rappahannock, and then conducted some kind of divinatory or incorporative ritual before turning Smith over to Powhatan.[30] The mamanatowick, in turn, consulted his priests and advisers, who must have concluded that it would be advisable to preserve Smith's life in order to contribute to the strength of the chiefdom. This interpretation is strongly indicated by the terms Powhatan set for Smith's release: Smith "should live to make him hatchets, and her [Pocahontas] bells, beads, and copper." In exchange for the valuables of metal and glass that Smith could provide, Powhatan would treat him as an adopted son and subordinate werowance, providing him with what he desired and needed most: land and sustenance.

This theory of Smith's transformation suggests that Smith's adoption and subordination alike were signified in the ritual execution. Clubbing a victim's head upon a stone "altar" was not the usual way of executing male war captives, but instead a form of punishment for the mamanatowick's own subjects. This particular way of threatening execution, then, already signified that Smith was no longer to be considered an outsider, but rather as a dependent of Powhatan. Smith, that is, was no longer sovereign over his own life, but dependent upon the goodwill of the mamanatowick. Due to his trespass into Pamunkey territory, Smith had no reason to count on that goodwill, as the clubs raised over his head indicated. At this juncture, however, the mamanatowick's daughter placed her own head upon his, joining her fate to the captive's. As we have seen, Powhatan women played an important role in torturing captives; here, in contrast, Pocahontas and two other high-ranking women played prominent roles in what appears to be the adoption of an enemy who would otherwise be tortured and killed. Two women of chiefly rank had already indicated Smith's status as a valued guest in their provision of water and feathers, the latter a sign of high rank. The repetitive feasting is similarly indicative of Smith's valued status. Pocahontas, for her part, signified in her transformative embrace the adoption of Smith, at the same time that the raised clubs signified his subordination under Powhatan.

If this interpretation is correct, the ritual execution was neatly constructed to convey a complex and interrelated set of messages and enact a complex set of transformations. Powhatan himself presided over a ceremony in which those close to him signified various aspects of the captive's new relationship to Powhatan. Smith would not immediately assume his new status, however. Two days later a blackened, disguised, and fearsome Powhatan took a more active role in a second ritual, one similar in tone to the rituals Smith had already undergone when under Opechancanough's control. During this ritual Powhatan told Smith that he would "forever esteem him as his son Nantaquoud" and proposed that Smith set up residence at the nearby town of Capahowasic. Here, it seems, Powhatan was ritually completing and explicating the relationship that Pocahontas's embrace had initiated—a kinship relationship with far-reaching social, economic, and political implications.

The kinship relationship the mamanatowick established with Smith, however, may be less fixed than Powhatan's words suggest. Powhatan would seem to have placed the English werowance in a position equivalent to that of his son (and Pocahontas's brother) Nantaquoud—who was, according to Smith, "the most manliest, comeliest, boldest spirit I ever saw in a savage" (Smith 1986 [1624], 2:258).[31] Shedding doubt on this interpretation, however, is Pocahontas's insistence on addressing Smith as "father" when she met with him in London. She explained, "You did promise Powhatan what was yours should be his, and he the like to you; you called him father, being in his land a stranger, and by the same reason so must I do you . . . , and you shall call me child, and so I will be for ever and ever your countryman" (Barbour 1964:331).

Son to Powhatan, therefore brother to Pocahontas in Tsenacomoco, where he was a stranger; father and countryman to Pocahontas in London, where she was a stranger: Smith was adopted, it seems, in a way that was situational and strongly inflected by his status as countryman or stranger, insider or outsider. The adoption ceremony was something of a naturalization ceremony as well, but with hierarchical ramifications expressed through the relationship between generations. However situational and hierarchical the adoptive relationship might be, however, it was enduring ("for ever and ever," as Pocahontas reminded Smith) as well as reciprocal ("what was yours should be his, and he the like to you").

Perhaps most central to the relationship Powhatan established with Smith was the exchange of valuables. At the conclusion of each of the two ritual transformations at Werowocomoco and as the condition of his captive's release, Powhatan demanded a tribute payment from the English, offering land and sustenance in return. In each case, the mamanatowick's specific demands are revealing: in the first case, "the Emperor was contented he should live to make him hatchets, and her bells, beads, and copper"; in the second, Powhatan requested two cannons and a grindstone. These exchanges appear to be an ingenious adaptation of the Powhatan tribute, alliance, and gender systems to the nascent colonial situation. To begin with, copper and shell beads were among the valuables exacted as tribute by the mamanatowick and his subordinate werowances, along with maize, game, and certain other foodstuffs. Unlike other forms of tribute, copper and shell beads were considered spiritually potent and were generally obtained through foreign trade (shell beads coming from Algonquian groups to the north such as the Nanticoke, copper perhaps from as far away as the Great Lakes). In demanding copper ornaments, metal weapons, and glass beads, then, Powhatan was attempting to control and domesticate his supply of exotic valuables. He was construing his relationship with Smith not as equal trade partners but as sovereign to dependent, authority to subordinate, provider of life to provider of tribute, controller of land to maker of valuables. To this extent the relationship was constructed entirely upon traditional lines, for controlling trade and wealth was key to Powhatan's rule. Metal weapons served as particularly attractive alternatives to tribute payments of copper; Venetian glass beads as substitutes for *peak* or shell beads; metal bells as substitutes for native copper ornaments.[32]

Powhatan, then, was fashioning Smith and his countrymen as artisans in such a way that he emphasized and exploited the dependency of the English upon him for protection, sustenance, and life itself (as the threatened execution demonstrated). The mamanatowick was not only applying but creatively adapting indigenous patterns of hierarchy to the particular strengths and weaknesses of the Jamestown colonists: So valuable were European manufactures and so inept were the colonists at providing for their own sustenance that Powhatan was willing to provide them with the very foodstuffs that he ordinarily exacted as tribute. Thus, though Powhatan confirmed his sovereignty over life by threatening and then preserving Smith's life, and confirmed his sovereignty over land by exacting tribute from Smith, he was also willing to support the lives of Smith and his countrymen through gifts of maize and game. In doing so Powhatan may have been treating Smith less as a relative and subordinate werowance than as an allied priest. The mamanatowick and his subordinate werowances customarily attempted to attract powerful diviners into an alliance by offering them sustenance, in return employing the priests' powers at prophecy and supernatural mediation to enhance their own prestige and authority.[33] Smith, it seems, had succeeded in his strategy of inspiring awe through his demonstrations of European technology, cosmology, and writing. Powhatan wished to draw Smith away from Paspahegh territory and into his own domain in order to draw upon his supernatural powers as well as to appropriate European glass and metal goods, themselves tokens of both material and spiritual wealth.

Powhatan, it seems, combined several native models in his ritual transformation of Smith: Beginning as a captive werowance, Smith took on the roles of kinsman, tribute-paying artisan, and power-enhancing priest. Still another set of Powhatan meanings were embedded in the two ritual transformations of Smith. All of the European valuables Powhatan requested, like his own offers of deer and maize, were not only inflected with prestige but were highly gender-coded. Thus, the exchange Powhatan proposed was modeled not only after Powhatan patterns of chiefly dominance over subordinates and the reciprocity between chief and priest but also after the reciprocity between men and women. As in most Eastern Woodland societies with mixed economies, male hunters in Virginia provided venison and other game in exchange for the maize and other produce grown, gathered, and processed by women. Powhatan, then, offered the essential male and female foodstuffs to Smith. In return, he requested metal weapons, which would enhance the prestige and ease the labor of his high-ranking male warriors, together with copper, beads, bells, and a grindstone, which would enhance the prestige and ease the labor of Pocahontas and other high-ranking Powhatan women. The exchange Powhatan proposed, then, involved the giving of foodstuffs that he had exacted as tribute from lower-ranking Powhatan men and women in exchange for artifacts that would further differentiate male and female members of chiefly lineages from commoners.[34] Powhatan forged an extremely complex set of relations with the English—one akin to Mauss's "total prestation" (Mauss 1954 [1925])—in the terms he set for Smith's release.

Both the gendered nature of the exchange and the great importance Powhatan accorded to his relationship with the English is underscored by his choice of Pocahontas to serve as his primary emissary to Jamestown. Powhatan's daughter became a familiar and welcome figure in the colony: a young, joyful, even "wanton" presence (as the English translated her name), and moreover, the very personification of salvation.[35] In describing his return from captivity Smith wrote that his "relation of the plenty he had seen, especially at Werowocomoco, and of the state and bounty of Powhatan (which until that time was unknown) so revived their dead spirits (especially the love of Pocahontas) as all men's fear was abandoned." In this context "the love of Pocahontas" refers to her delivery, every four or five days, of "so much provision, that saved many of their lives, that else for all this had starved with hunger" (Smith 1986 [1624], 2:152). On more than one occasion the very survival of Jamestown depended on Pocahontas's goodwill. The love of Pocahontas for Smith and his people remained constant even when her father determined that the colony was a threat to his chiefdom's survival and forbade all contact between his people and the English. Indeed, until the end of her life Pocahontas acted as though she and Smith, in particular, were bound together with enduring ties of affection and obligation. In sum, even if one were inclined to consider her rescue of Smith at Werowocomoco as entirely the Englishman's fabrication, the story is an apt one that dramatically encapsulates Jamestown's dependence upon Pocahontas in the early years of colonization.

If Powhatan had hoped to encompass English power within his own through the relationship he established with Smith, he was soon disappointed. Once free from captivity Smith set aside his strategy of fashioning himself in terms of indigenous categories and expectations. He did not move to Capahowasic as Powhatan requested at his release and repeatedly thereafter, but remained at Jamestown. As far as he lets on, he refrained from any sexual relationships with native women, even after witnessing a "Virginia masque" of thirty naked young "nymphs," dancing and "falling into their infernal passions" and finally "most tediously crying, Love you not me? love you not me?" (Smith 1986 [1624], 2:183). Most consequentially, Smith violated the terms of exchange that Powhatan proposed. More than any other colonist, Smith was intent on maintaining a monopoly on English weapons and establishing an exploitative trading relationship that would provide desperately needed food supplies for a minimal amount of English manufactures. Most notably, Smith exploited the great value the chiefly lineages placed on blue Venetian glass beads. He was convinced that he, personally, had made of them such a precious commodity that "none darest wear any of them but their great kings, their wives, and children" (2:156–157). Smith reported Powhatan's strong aversion to his mercantile approach to exchange, noting after one episode of "trucking" that Powhatan, "seeming to despise the nature of a merchant, did scorn to sell, but we freely should give [to] him, and he liberally would requite us" (Smith 1986 [1608], 1:71, 77).

Nothing could have been farther from Powhatan's expectations nor more discordant with Powhatan's generosity and noble status than Smith's style of commerce. However, the mamanatowick had never intended to confine his strategy of encompassment to his relationship with Smith. He insisted upon meeting directly, and at his own seat of power, with the leader he considered his direct counterpart, Capt. Christopher Newport. In the weeks after Newport's arrival in Jamestown, Powhatan designated half of the provisions he supplied for Smith, and half for Smith's "father," the "great werowance" (Smith 1986 [1608], 1:61). It was at their first meeting that Newport presented Powhatan with Tom Savage, "a child of his, in full assurance of our loves," as Smith told Powhatan, receiving the adviser Namontack in exchange. When John Smith informed Powhatan of Newport's plans to leave his "child" with him, also offering to use English weapons to subjugate his Monacan enemies, Powhatan responded with an exuberant oration that clarified, if any doubt remained, the nature of the relationship with the English he had meant to establish during Smith's captivity. "He proclaimed me a werowance of Powhatan," reported Smith, "and that all his subjects should so esteem us, and no man account us strangers nor Paspaheghans, but Powhatans, and that the corn, women, and country should be to us as to his own people" (1:67). Powhatan clearly envisioned an enduring alliance that featured an exchange of English technological and military strength for land, corn, and women.[36]

Newport, unlike Smith, was willing to meet Powhatan's expectation of an exchange of English weapons for Powhatan maize. Smith sharply criticized Newport's more open trade policy as well as his acquiescence in the Royal Virginia Company's orders to crown the mamanatowick and present him with an English bed and basin. Powhatan resisted the ritual, refusing to bow his head to be crowned despite Namontack's urging, and afterward, according to Smith, his pride and officiousness toward the English only increased.[37] Relations certainly deteriorated from about that time onward, perhaps less because the coronation ceremony confirmed his pride than because it, together with increasingly onerous demands for corn, aroused his suspicion. Powhatan began to refuse the incessant English demands and ordered his subordinates to do likewise. When Smith succeeded Newport as president of the Council, he resorted anew to "breeding awe and dread," as Purchas would later put it approvingly.[38] Most momentously, Smith forced Opechancanough at gunpoint to promise a continued supply of grain. At the same time as he stepped up demands upon the native population, Smith took advantage of his post as president to reverse Newport's policy of supplying his trading partners with English arms. Powhatan responded by ordering his people to steal English weapons and metal tools, theft being considered a capital offense within the chiefdom but a daring achievement against enemies. When seven Powhatans attempted to steal his own sword, Smith responded brutally, imprisoning the thieves, beating and whipping them, and threatening them, "first with the rack, then with muskets," and finally, "caus[ing] them all [to] believe, by several volleys of shot [that] one of their companions was shot to death, because they would not confess their intents and [the] plotters of those villainies" (Smith 1986 [1608], 1:89, 93; Smith 1986 [1624], 2:159). He released the prisoners only in response to personal entreaties from Powhatan and Opechancanough, the first delivered by Pocahontas.

The last time Smith saw Pocahontas in her native land was in October 1609, shortly before he was forced by an accidental injury and political rivalry to return to London. By this time Pocahontas had moved with her father to his inland stronghold, Orapaks. Hearing of plans for a surprise attack upon the English, Pocahontas stole away to warn Smith, no doubt at some risk to herself. Smith departed for England almost immediately thereafter, without contacting Pocahontas, and the severely strained relations between the English and the Powhatans soon broke into open warfare. During this period, which contemporary chronicles refer to as "the starving time," the colonists raided Powhatan stores of corn as well as Indian burial sites. Some resorted to necrophagy and cannibalism, including one man who confessed under torture to salting and eating his own wife. Others ran away, but they could no longer count on receiving hospitality among the Powhatans. One group of Englishmen seeking food were found slain, their mouths stuffed full of corn bread.[39]

## The Captivity and Typification of Pocahontas

In Smith's absence there were few colonists who had any expertise in dealing with the Powhatans. Tom Savage, the young interpreter, was one; another was Henry Spelman, the disinherited nephew of Sir Henry Spelman, a prominent antiquarian. Smith had left Spelman among the Powhatans in October 1609, only about two weeks after the lad's arrival in the colony and entirely against his will. As Spelman told his tale, he was "sold" to Powhatan's son Tanx-Powhatan ("Little Powhatan") for control over a Powhatan town's resources. Smith left shortly thereafter for London, and Spelman lived in various native villages over the following year, serving Powhatan as an intermediary. At first he was not anxious to return to Jamestown because food was considerably more plentiful in Algonquian villages; but he escaped from Powhatan's retreat at Orapaks after witnessing the torture and execution of an English officer, John Ratcliffe, who had embarked on a desperate quest for corn. Aided in his escape by Pocahontas, if we are to believe John Smith, Spelman took refuge among the somewhat autonomous Potomacs, ignoring Powhatan's orders to return. In September 1610, Spelman was ransomed from his Potomac protectors for a payment of copper by Capt. Samuel Argall, who had come seeking trade. The chance encounter with Spelman was fortuitous for Argall as well, for Spelman facilitated a successful trade. The freed captive made his way to London, where he recounted his experiences to Samuel Purchas as well as in an unpublished, semiliterate narrative (Spelman 1910 [1613?]). He later returned to Virginia, serving as a military officer and interpreter until 1623, when in the midst of Opechancanough's war of resistance he was killed while attempting to trade for corn among his former Potomac protectors.[40]

The same captain who ransomed Spelman was responsible for kidnapping Pocahontas in April 1613, after four years of hostilities between Jamestown and Powhatan's Tsenacomoco. Argall was admiral of a ship that had brought a new governor, a new, more militant charter, additional settlers, and vital supplies to Virginia just in time to rescue the colony from abandonment.[41] Within a few months the strengthened colony had completely destroyed two Algonquian towns, including nearby Paspahegh, and established plantations on the land of two other Algonquian villages. Towns and cornfields were burned; women and children—including a Paspahegh *weroansqua* (female chief) and her children—were brutally murdered. In this violent and polarized environment Argall made several attempts to trade in towns that were marginal to Powhatan's influence.

On one momentous trading expedition to a Potomac village, Argall learned of Pocahontas's presence there. He promptly brewed a scheme to take her hostage, hoping thus to assure Powhatan's submission. With a copper kettle Argall bribed a minor Potomac werowance, Iapassus, and his wife to entice Pocahontas, then a young married woman of eighteen or nineteen, onto Argall's boat. A narrative of 1615 by colonist Ralph Hamor justifies the kidnapping as a response to Powhatan's "treachery" in murdering Englishmen, and characterizes Pocahontas's reaction as "pensive and discontented" (Robertson 1996:565). Capt. Argall demanded as a ransom the return of eight English prisoners and Powhatan's store of captured English weapons. During three months of silence on Powhatan's part, his daughter was lodged at the new English settlement of Henrico, with Anglican minister Alexander Whitaker, who began instructing her in his faith. Finally, the mamanatowick returned seven prisoners, each carrying a broken gun. Powhatan claimed that all of the captured weapons had been broken or stolen from him, but he promised supplies of corn and a renewed alliance in return for his daughter. The English insisted that Powhatan meet Argall's original conditions.

The new settlement of Henrico was located upriver on the James, in the heart of Powhatan's chiefdom. With the conquest of this area, achieved with the strength of three hundred additional settlers against fierce Powhatan opposition, the tide had turned decisively against Powhatan. He had retreated far into Pamunkey territory, where the English launched a devastating attack in February 1614. Perceiving the opportunity to press the English advantage, Sir Thomas Dale, then in command of the colony, sailed up the James River with Pocahontas, offering to return her to Powhatan in exchange for his submission. During negotiations over her release she declared publicly that, as Dale put it, "if her father had loved her, he would not value her less than old swords, pieces, or axes: wherefore she should still dwell with the English men, who loved her" (Barbour 1970:126). Powhatan acquiesced to her wish, asking Dale to treat her as his own daughter.

One member of Dale's delegation was John Rolfe, a planter at Henrico experimenting with the cultivation of West Indian tobacco. By this time Rolfe, a widower, was tortured by his love for a woman he described in a letter to Dale as "an unbelieving creature, namely Pocahontas" (Barbour 1970:248). Rolfe conquered his ambivalence by resolving to work toward her conversion and civility, and obtained consent to marry Pocahontas from both Powhatan and Dale, whom Powhatan had appointed her English "father."[42] Along with his permission, the broken mamanatowick granted his consent to a peace treaty that made him subject to the English Crown.

Thus, in the spring of 1614, a year after her capture, Pocahontas was baptized as Rebecca (see Figure 3.2) and married to John Rolfe, in the presence of Opechancanough and two of Powhatan's sons. Rev. Whitaker baptized Pocahontas under a Biblical name aptly chosen to convey the epic character of the marriage, for Rebecca, upon leaving her people to marry Abraham's son Isaac, was told, "Two nations are in thy womb, and two manner of people shall be separated from thy bowels; and one people shall be stronger than the other people; and the older shall serve the younger" (Genesis 25:23).[43] In Pocahontas's marriage to Rolfe, Powhatan saw his own strategy gone awry: His daughter's abduction, conversion, and marriage signified the subordination of her people to the English rather than the realization of his dream that Smith's people should become Powhatan's subordinates.

The English, for their part, saw in Pocahontas's conversion and marriage a confirmation of the convergence of their capitalist and missionary enterprises. Since the charter of 1609 had been enacted, the colony had been dedicated officially to "the conversion of the natives" (Fausz

FIGURE 3.2 *The Baptism of Pocahontas at Jamestown, Virginia,* by John Gadsby Chapman, 1840, in the U.S. Capitol Rotunda. John Rolfe is shown to the right of Pocahontas; behind him are her brother, sister (seated), and Opechancanough. Source: Architect of the Capitol.

1977:265), a goal expected to reap temporal as well as spiritual rewards for the English. As the Council advertised to potential supporters at home in 1610, the colonists "by way of merchandising and trade, do buy of them the pearls of earth, and sell to them the pearls of heaven" (Nash 1972:210).[44] Governor Gates, however, had been instructed to pursue the goal of conversion not only through trade but through militant action. Specifically, he was ordered to use force, if necessary, to "procure from them some convenient number of their children to be brought up in your language and manners." Gates was advised that the children of werowances, in particular, should be educated so that "their people will easily obey you and become in time civil and Christian" (Fausz 1977:265–266). Even the extermination of priests and werowances was condoned as a means toward this goal. Throughout the war, the Virginia Company justified its brutal aggression against Powhatan—including the murders of the Paspahegh werowance Wowinchopunk, his "queen," and her children; the burning of villages and cornfields; and the desecration of temples—by promising that victory would be followed by mass conversion. Rev. Whitaker himself, the agent of Pocahontas's conversion, wrote that once the English "were masters of their country, and they stood in fear of us . . . it [would be] an easy matter to make them willingly to forsake the devil [and] to embrace the faith of Jesus Christ" (287).[45]

On the basis of its commitment to militant proselytization the Virginia Company received monetary support from prominent clergymen as well as from a broad segment of the public. The conversion and marriage of Pocahontas was publicized in England as the first fruit of this policy. King James approved Company plans, spearheaded by Samuel Purchas and Alexander Whitaker, to erect a school and college at Henrico for "the training up of the children of those Infidels in true Religion, moral virtue and civility and for other godly uses" (Fausz 1977:294). As a fund-raising device the Virginia Company brought the Rolfe family, which by then included a young son, to London in 1616. Rebecca Rolfe, the main attraction, was accompanied by about a dozen Powhatan attendants, including her sister Matachanna and Matachanna's husband, the high priest Uttamatomakkin. Lady Rebecca was displayed at court and sat for an official engraving by Simon Van de Passe (see Figure 3.3) Both she and Uttamatomakkin were seated in the place of honor next to King James I at Ben Jonson's masque in celebration of Twelfth Night.[46] Like Uttamatomakkin, Pocahontas had an interview with Samuel Purchas, who found her "Christian sincerity" a welcome contrast to the stubborn blasphemy of the high priest (Mossiker 1976:260).

By all reports Pocahontas was delighted with her reception in London, although she sharply chided John Smith for neglecting her. Like so many

FIGURE 3.3 *Matoaka, Alias Rebecca, Daughter to the Mighty Prince Powhatan, Emperor of Virginia,* by Simon Van de Passe, 1616. SOURCE: John Smith, *The Generall Historie of Virginia, New-England, and the Summer Isles* (London, 1624). (Courtesy of the Newberry Library, Chicago.)

Native American visitors to Europe, however, she became ill with a pulmonary infection and retreated into the country. She was in poor health when her ship, piloted by Capt. Argall, embarked for Virginia. She disembarked and died at Gravesend. After burying "Mrs. Rebecca Rolfe . . . a Virginia Lady born," her husband returned to the colony to oversee the expansion of the tobacco industry, leaving their son, Thomas, to be raised in England. The boy did not see Virginia until the late 1630s, and in 1641 he found it necessary to petition the governor to see his relatives Matachanna and Opechancanough, who as Powhatan's successor had tried and failed to expel the English by force in 1622. By 1644, when the aged Opechancanough led a second war of resistance, Thomas Rolfe was an officer in the colonial militia.

Pocahontas truly was "nonpareil," and her "love" was exceptional as well as essential to the survival of the first successful English colony in America. Her marriage and conversion occurred within a context of militant colonial expansion, and within five years of her death any thought of alliance was banished by Opechancanough's violent resistance to English rule. Rhetoric hardened, an exterminationist policy was implemented, plans to establish a school at Henrico were set aside, and relations between Christians and "savages" were outlawed. Within the Rolfe family itself can be discerned the limits of Pocahontas's love: Her husband pioneered the plantation economy that proved a fatal threat to the Algonquian's mixed subsistence economy; her kinsman Opechancanough led a desperate war of resistance against her adopted people; and her son Thomas, after meeting her sister and Opechancanough, became an officer in the force responsible for bringing Opechancanough to his final defeat.

After Opechancanough's revolt, Pocahontas came to embody, for Samuel Purchas among others, what Leslie Fiedler (1969) called a "vision of love and reconciliation between the races whose actual history is oppression and hate." But it was not until the late eighteenth century, when hopes for peaceful alliance between European and indigenous peoples had largely been consigned to the realm of myth, that "the love of Pocahontas" began to take a central place in American historical memory. Her captivity largely forgotten, Pocahontas was fashioned into the royal savior and ancestress of the English in America, particularly in the South. By the first half of the nineteenth century, Pocahontas's rescue of one Englishman, and to a lesser extent her marriage to another, was firmly enshrined in American popular culture, so much so that for some she became the subject of parody.[47]

A different transformation of the Pocahontas story was wrought in the late nineteenth century by Pocahontas's Pamunkey descendants, who utilized their relationship to Pocahontas to mark their distinctive cultural identity. Countering the hegemonic forces that have attempted to define them as individual "persons of color" and to deprive them of the land, rights, and history they hold as "tribal Indians," since the 1880s Pamunkeys have represented themselves in pageants, artifacts, and naming patterns as the rightful heirs of Pocahontas (understood not as a captive but as a princess and savior). Some might view this ironically, as an assertion of distinctive cultural identity in terms that are largely hegemonic (thus "inauthentic"), but somewhat like Christian Feest (1987) I regard the Pamunkeys' reappropriation of the Pocahontas legend as a form of resistance to a historical memory that would confine them to the past and define Pocahontas as "the mother of us all" (Young 1962).

## Captivity, Conquest, and Resistance

John Smith, not knowing whether to attribute his good fortune to Powhatan, God, or Pocahontas's personal attachment to the English, presented Pocahontas to his Queen as "next under God . . . the instrument to preserve this colony from death, famine and utter confusion" (Smith 1986 [1624], 2:259). Although Smith was referring to Pocahontas's generosity toward himself and his countrymen, she was equally an instrument of colonial conquest in her role as captive, convert, and affine of the English. She became a primary instrument both for breaking Powhatan's resistance and raising support in England for the Virginia colony. Pocahontas's contemporary, Tisquantum—abducted one year after Pocahontas and present in London by 1617, the year of her death—received similar praise from his patron, William Bradford. Considerably more confident regarding divine intervention in history, Bradford characterized Tisquantum as a "special instrument sent of God for their good beyond their expectation" (Bradford 1953:114).

Tisquantum, originally captured for his value as a slave, managed to fashion himself into an indispensable translator and mediator. Pocahontas, taken hostage in order to extort political concessions from Powhatan, fashioned herself into a Christian lady and yet remained true enough to Powhatan values to be able to reprimand John Smith for his neglect of the reciprocal obligations of kinship. Both were valuable as instruments of conquest precisely because they were not merely instruments: They had the ability to create and inhabit a middle ground between their native Algonquian worlds and that of the English.

In the cases of Pocahontas and Tisquantum, captivity proved an effective way of fashioning a fairly docile instrument of conquest. More often, however, Indian captives resisted those who would make them instruments of conquest, escaping captivity through suicide, like some of Arnaaq's contemporaries; or like Don Luis, Wanchese, and Epenow, employing the knowledge gained through captivity to engage in active resistance. Whether relatively docile or resistant, an Indian captive was subject to a powerful process of typification, one that accelerated after his or her death. Captured once again—this time, in visual imagery and ethnographic accounts—the Inuit captives live on in the representational system of their captors. Similarly, Squanto and Pocahontas live on more prominently in historical narratives and sentimental performances as well as in visual imagery. Neither is remembered as a captive but as a savior, intermediary, and ally in a process known as colonization rather than conquest.

Even so, these Inuit and Algonquian captives retain the ability to capture our imagination and complexify the hegemonic typification of captivity. As we trace the development of a typification in which Indians come to exclusively play the role of Captor, it is essential to remember the captivities that are not inscribed in the selective tradition—the Indian captives taken by Columbus, Cartier, Cabot, Frobisher, Waymouth, Hunt, Harlow, Argall, and others. This is particularly important as we turn to representations of captivity in Puritan New England, where the Captive Self and Captivating Other are more thoroughly polarized than in Virginia.

## Notes

1. For discussions of this incident see Dickason 1984:163–175, 210–211; Trigger 1976:182–200, 129–134; and Trigger 1985:130–135. Trigger and Pendergast 1978 summarizes what is known of the St. Lawrence Iroquois. Map 4.1 shows their territory in some detail.

2. This incident is discussed by Dickason (1984:208) and Hemming (1978:11, 532).

3. *Tsenacomoco* (also spelled *Tsenacommacah*) probably means "densely inhabited land" (according to Feest 1966:69, citing Gerard 1904). Feest 1990, Rountree 1989, and Gleach 1997 are recent authoritative sources on Powhatan's polity; Rountree compares it to Massasoit's chiefdom to the north (1989:140–152, passim). See also Feest 1966 and 1978b and Salwen 1978. Some scholars continue to follow Thomas Jefferson and James Mooney in characterizing the Powhatan polity as a "confederacy" or "confederation," although Mooney's notion of a confederacy "founded on conquest and despotic personal authority" offers a contradiction in terms and understates the importance of Powhatan's advisers and priests (1907:136). Like Fausz (1977), Gleach (1997), Potter (1989), Rountree (1989), and Turner (1985), I consider the thirty-odd ranked, kin-ordered towns under the rule of Powhatan and a hereditary elite closer to Sahlins's (1968) definition of a chiefdom. The degree of expansion and centralization effected by Powhatan was unprecedented along the Atlantic coast and was undoubtedly influenced by the European presence in the area (in addition to the sources cited above, see Swagerty 1981). On the terminological debate, see Gleach 1997:24; and Cheyfitz 1997:217–218, n. 9.

4. *Caucorouse* (sometimes spelled *cockarouse*) is the Powhatan variant of the Algonquian term from which the English word *caucus* was derived (Gleach 1997:207–208, n. 3).

5. Purchas's *Pilgrimage* is now rare, and references to Uttamatomakkin (and positive accounts of Indians more generally) are largely omitted from the more readily available *Pilgrimes* (Purchas 1625), published after Opechancanough's deadly revolt of 1622. See Mossiker 1976:259–263; Rountree 1989:131–139 and passim; and for a general discussion of Purchas's comparative studies of religion, Boon 1982:154–177.

6. Rountree suggests that Pocahontas—who was not a member of Powhatan's matrilineage and thus not a potential *weroansqua*, or female chief—might have been attracted by her status as a "princess" in English society (1989:112–113). The most scholarly biography of Pocahontas is Barbour's (1970); see also Mossiker 1976 and Woodward 1976. The Pocahontas myth is treated by Dearborn (1986), Feest (1987), Fiedler (1969), Green (1975), Hubbell (1957), Scheckel (1998), Strong (1996a), and Young (1962), and especially by Tilton (1994).

7. *Werowance* (also *weroance*) has been variously translated as "he who is rich," "he who is of influence," and "he who is wise" (Feest 1966:71; Gleach 1997:28–35; Potter 1989:152). These are all appropriate descriptions of the basis of the werowance's authority. Brindenbaugh's (1980) identification of Don Luis with Opechancanough would require Opechancanough to have been nearly one hundred years old when he was captured and killed by the English in 1646; and Brindenbaugh's assumption that Opechancanough acquired his political sophistication from the Jesuits seriously underestimates the strengths of indigenous Algonquian leaders. See also Fausz 1977:56–58, passim; Feest 1966; Lewis and Loomie 1953; Swagerty 1981:743–755; and Gleach 1997:90–97, 142–143. The latter provides a hypothetical kinship diagram.

8. See Axtell 1988:187; Barbour 1970:1–7; and Kupperman 1984:137–140. Recent scholars have cast doubt on earlier claims that Powhatan might have killed the survivors of the "lost colony" at Roanoke; see Gleach 1997:104.

9. For knowledge of Smith's capture we are dependent on two autobiographical accounts: *A True Relation* (Smith 1986 [1608], 1:45–61), a letter that was edited and published without his permission; and the expanded account in *The Generall Historie of Virginia* (1986 [1624], 2:145–153). Smith's editor, Phillip L. Barbour, provides extensive annotations and a comparison of the two versions (Barbour 1986, 2:9–15). See also Kupperman 1988.

10. The Chickahominies were an Algonquian group generally allied with Powhatan but not subordinate to him; they were governed by a council rather than a werowance (Gleach 1997:26; Potter 1989:154). Although Opechancanough is commonly identified as Powhatan's brother or half brother, this relation is not particularly meaningful in a society where chiefly descent was matrilineal. My identification of Opechancanough's role and his relationship to Powhatan follows Gleach's (1997). See also Feest 1966; and for a division between peace and war chiefs elsewhere in the Southeast, Fogelson 1977; Gearing 1958 and 1962; and Hudson 1976.

11. On Hariot and Smith, see Barbour 1986, 1:102, n. 101; Quinn 1955, 1:375–376; and Sanders 1978:274–278. Greenblatt (1988:21–65) gives a provocative account of Hariot's encounter with Algonquian religion.

12. For the Powhatan language, for which Smith himself would became a key source, see Gerard 1904, and Goddard 1978:70–77. See Cheyfitz 1997 on eloquence as a recurrent colonial figure; and Greenblatt 1976 and 1991 on Elizabethan assumptions regarding linguistic transparency. Hariot's language study with Manteo and Wanchese, among other examples, suggests that we must think of linguistic colonialism in more than the two dimensions Greenblatt highlights, as important as those dimensions are: Colonial power was furthered not only by those who considered Indian languages nonexistent or transparent but also by those who considered Indian languages opaque and who subordinated themselves at least temporarily to Indian teachers in order to learn their languages. Because of the study of Indian languages by early linguists such as Hariot, and more significantly, by missionaries such as John Eliot and various French Jesuits, our knowledge of extinct Indian languages (and thus of Indian "realities") is not quite as bleak as Greenblatt suggests (1976:576). Cheyfitz offers a somewhat similar critique of Greenblatt (Cheyfitz 1997:104–110).

13. In regard to John Smith's actions as an "improvisation of power" I am drawing upon Greenblatt, who means by this phrase "the ability both to capitalize on the unforeseen and to transform given materials into one's own scenario" (Greenblatt 1980:227). See also Hulme 1992:153–156; and Sayre 1997:49–78. The latter contrasts Smith's and Champlain's uses of power in relations with Native Americans. Note that Powhatan demonstrates a similar improvisatory ability in the use he makes of his English captive. On writing as a form of power, see also Anderson 1983, Goody 1977, and Todorov 1982. Cheyfitz (1997:104–110) critiques both Greenblatt and Todorov.

14. Both minor Powhatan deities and Powhatan priests were called *quioccosuk* (sg. *quioccos*). However, Smith seems to be referring here to the major Powhatan deity Okeus, or Oke (Rountree 1989:131–136; Feest 1966; Gleach 1997:30–43). Purchas's *Pilgrimage* (1613) includes an edited version of Smith's account of the divination (Barbour 1986, 2:9–15; 104, n. 141).

15. Although there were hereditary female rulers known as *weroansqua* among the Virginia Algonquians, Rountree (1989) believes that this particular "queen" was, rather, the wife of the werowance of Appamatuck. The sister of that werowance was the weroansqua of a nearby town.

16. Smith wrote the letter in 1616, but we know it only from the abstract he published in his *Generall Historie* (1986 [1624]:258–262).

17. The first skepticism expressed in print was in a biographical entry by Thomas Fuller (1662, 2:275–276, quoted in Barbour 1986, 1:lxiii). A more influential critic was Smith's nineteenth-century editor, Charles Deane (1866:38–40); see Barbour 1986, 1:lxii–lxiv; Morse 1935; and Tilton 1994.

18. Barbour discusses the controversy over Smith's use of the "enamored Moslem princess" motif and defends Smith (1986, 1:lxx–lxxi; 3:125–136). See also Hulme 1992, Morse 1935, and Smith 1953. Ortiz, the commander of a relief party seeking Panfilo de Narvaez, reported that he had twice been saved from sacrifice through the intercession of his captor's daughter. He was rescued by DeSoto, and his captivity tale appears in an anonymous narrative by a member of that expedition (*The True Relation of the Gentleman of Elvas . . .* , 1557). Smith might well have been familiar with Ortiz's account, as an English translation was published

in Hakluyt's *Virginia Richly Valued* (1609). It is reprinted in Levernier and Cohen's anthology (1977:3–11).

19. Pocahontas's "rescue" is included in the published version of Smith's letter to Queen Anne (Smith 1986 [1624], 2:258–260), but as the original of 1616 has not been preserved, we cannot be certain of its contents. Still, the letter reads very much as if it were written prior to 1622.

20. Cheyfitz (1997) and Hulme (1992) offer insightful analyses of *The Tempest*. For the comparison of Miranda and Pocahontas, see Cheyfitz 1997:171.

21. See Barbour 1964; 1970:23–27; and 1986, 1:5–15, 2:31; Fausz 1977; and Gleach 1994, 1996, and 1997. Rountree (1989:121–122) finds insufficient ethnographic support for a political interpretation of the execution and rescue scene, but Gleach's consideration is much more complete.

22. For the shift in representations of Virginia Algonquians after 1622, see Fausz 1977 and 1981; Gleach 1997; Kupperman 1977 and 1980; Nash 1972; and Sheehan 1980. Hulme (1997:170) discusses representations of Pocahontas and Uttamatomakkin as offering a similarly gendered splitting of Virginia Algonquians into noble and ignoble variants. (See Figure 3.2, in which Uttamatomakkin is glowering in the right foreground.)

23. See Sahlins 1981, 1985, and 1996; and Todorov 1982. Obeyesekere (1992a, 1992b) offers a critique of Sahlins.

24. In Part II of his *Map of Virginia* (1612), which *The Generall Historie* expands upon, Smith wrote that the Powhatans "admired him as a demi-God" (1986 [1612], 2:146, n. 3). This comment is illuminated by Gleach's discussion of the spiritual power of werowances, on the one hand, and Cheyfitz's analysis of the "technology of eloquence," on the other (Gleach 1997:32–43; Cheyfitz 1997:78–79, passim). With regard to Smith's self-fashioning sexually, compare Sahlins (1981, 1985) on Capt. Cook. The intimations of romance in Smith's writings and other sources have been exploited to the fullest in Anglo-American literature since the late eighteenth century (see Tilton 1994).

25. The interpretation offered here is also, inevitably, a fiction of translation, but one that is aimed at contesting the exclusions of the dominant fiction.

26. The classic work on rites of passage is Van Gennep (1960 [1908]). For the *huskanaw*, see Gleach 1997:38–39 and Rountree 1989:80–84; and for a reprint of Robert Beverley's account of 1705, see Axtell 1981:46–49. There are similarities between this rite and the one that Tisquantum would have undergone to become a *pniese*; see Axtell 1981:44 and Simmons 1986:37–64.

27. On burial, see Rountree 1989:116–117. Smith described clubbing as a form of capital punishment as early as 1612, in the context of a discussion of the extent of Powhatan's power (Smith 1986 [1612], 1:175; 1986 [1624], 2:127). This is one case in which Smith serves as a primary source for a more culturally sensitive reading of his own narrative. My interpretive strategy here can best be described as reading some of Smith's representations against others; the ethnographic realities thus extracted are no more than partial and provisional.

28. See Rountree 1989:84 and Smith 1986 [1612], 1:175.

29. See Axtell 1981:46–49 and Rountree 1989:80–82, 121.

30. Gleach (1997:113–115), suggesting a parallel with the Delaware Big House ceremony, offers an elegant interpretation of the ceremony at Pamunkey as a

world renewal ritual that mimetically incorporated Smith and his people into Powhatan's domain.

31. Nantaquoud was also known as Nantaquaus (Barbour 1986, 2:51, n. 4).

32. On shell, copper, and other forms of tribute, see Feest 1966; Gleach 1997; Miller and Hamell 1986; Potter 1989; and Rountree 1989:71–73, 111.

33. See Rountree 1989:142–145, passim.

34. The analysis of the gendered and ranked dimensions of Powhatan's demands are influenced by Sahlins's analysis (1981, 1985) of exchanges of valuables in Hawaii.

35. Pocahontas was known to the English by her nickname rather than as Matoaka, the name she gave as hers upon her baptism. Strachey reported the meaning of Pocahontas's nickname. This, together with his report of a young, naked Pocahontas doing cartwheels in Jamestown, is exploited to the fullest in John Barth's *The Sot-weed Factor* (1980 [1960]). See Tilton 1994:179–180.

36. This statement appeared in Smith's *True Relation* of 1608, in the context of a discussion about the exchange of hostages rather than about Smith's release from captivity.

37. Cheyfitz (1997:59–61) discusses the coronation ritual as an imperialist "translation"—in other words, an imposition of English notions of sovereignty.

38. Purchas contrasted Smith with Newport, who sought "to grace with offices of humanity, those which are graceless." Rather, like children and beasts, Indians should be treated "with severe gentleness and gentle severity, which may breed in them loving awe, or awfull love, at least a just dread toward us" (Purchas 1625, 18:497–498, quoted in Pennington 1966:23).

39. This was the same party whose leader, Capt. Ratcliffe (alias John Sicklemore), was tortured and executed in the presence of Henry Spelman. Chronicler George Percy rightly considered the act a sign of "contempt and scorn," likening it to the treatment meted out to a Spaniard whose throat was filled with molten gold (Sheehan 1980:150); see also Gleach's discussion of the spirit of irony in Powhatan warfare (1997:47–54).

40. John Smith's confused account of Spelman is found in the fourth book of *The Generall Historie*. According to Smith, "Pocahontas the King's daughter saved a boy called Henry Spilman, that lived many years after, by her means, amongst the Patawomekes" (1986 [1624] 2:232–236, 257, 304, 320–321). Spelman himself wrote, "I shifted for myself and got to the Patoaomeckes country." As Henry Spelman was treated as a prisoner after Smith's departure to England, his semi-literate *Relation* is of interest as perhaps the first Anglo-American captivity narrative, although unpublished until recently.

41. See Fausz 1977:252–285.

42. For Rolfe's ambivalence and resolve, see his remarkable letter to Dale (Barbour 1970:247–252).

43. Hulme (1997:145–146) quotes from the Geneva Bible [1560]. Tilton's extensive discussion of Chapman's *The Baptism of Pocahontas* (see Figure 3.2) also considers other visual images produced in the eighteenth and nineteenth centuries; see also Scheckel (1998).

44. Purchas would later give classic expression to this sentiment, writing, "God in wisdom having enriched the savage countries, that those riches might be at-

tractive for Christian suitors, which there may sow spirituals and reap temporals" (Nash 1972:210).

45. The policy of militant conversion has inspired impassioned critiques from contemporary scholars. Morgan caustically wrote: "If you were a colonist..., you killed the Indians, tortured them, burned their villages, burned their cornfields. It proved your superiority in spite of your failures" (1975:90). Cheyfitz calls militant conversion "an example of the need for violence being simultaneously acknowledged and ignored (rationalized) in the process of colonization" (1997:63–64), whereas Hulme describes it as "a massive effort of repression whereby the violent dispossession of the native Americans is rewritten as a crusade against the unregenerate savage, the guilt of conquest being transferred from usurper to usurped: as from Prospero to Caliban" (1992:168). The selective tradition of captivity is precisely such a transference mechanism.

46. Robertson's "Pocahontas at the Masque" (1996) also analyzes tensions in the engraving between her posture, visage, and gaze, on the one hand, and European conventions of dress and portraiture, on the other.

47. For eighteenth- and nineteenth-century representations of Pocahontas, see Tilton 1994 and Scheckel 1998.

# 4

## The Politics and Poetics of Captivity in New England, 1620–1682

As we can see from the cases of Tisquantum, Pocahontas, and the Stada-conan Iroquois, both the captivity of enemies and the exchange of hostages among allies were significant indigenous practices among the Algonquian and the Iroquoian peoples of the Eastern Woodlands. Both captivity and hostage-exchange varied across indigenous groups, over time, and from situation to situation. Nevertheless, it is useful to distinguish between the two practices in a more general way. Hostage-exchange involved a poetics and politics of reciprocity, whereas captivity enacted a poetics and politics of incorporation in which captives or their symbolic equivalents—scalps, wampum, and other soul-infused substances—served to enhance the power of a leader, a war party, a lineage, or an entire polity. Both captives and hostages could be used as "statements" about sovereignty; however, the poetics of reciprocity was aimed at accomplishing diplomatic objectives such as alliance and subordination, whereas the poetics of incorporation was geared more toward internal political goals such as retaliation, recruitment, and revitalization. Still, reciprocity and incorporation were not mutually exclusive processes, and many captives inhabited an ambiguous space in which various forms of exchange and incorporation remained open possibilities—possibilities they might help to realize, sometimes unwittingly, through their own actions.[1]

Indigenous captivity practices were affected in complex ways by the presence of colonial captives, captors, and mediators—all of whom had their own ways of interpreting, utilizing, and responding to captivity. This chapter views seventeenth-century captivity practices in the Northeast as a complex conjuncture of indigenous and European forms, focusing in particular upon the intercultural politics and poetics of Mary Rowlandson's captivity during the hostilities of 1675–76 that are commonly known as King Philip's War. In Rowlandson's influential account of her experiences, *The Soveraignty and Goodness of God* (1682), captivity is interpreted within a colonial rather than an indigenous poetics. The colonial poetics, as we will see, revitalizes and establishes the sovereignty of the Captive Self rather than that of the Captivating Other.

## Indigenous and Convergent Captivity Practices

Chapter 3 offered several examples of captivity and hostage-exchange in coastal Algonquian societies: Tisquantum's abduction by two Wampanoag sachems, Epenow and Corbitant, who opposed an alliance with Europeans; the Nausets' release of John Billington, decked with strings of wampum; the peaceful exchange of Powhatan's adviser Namontack for Captain Newport's "son," Tom Savage; John Smith's exchange of Henry Spelman, against Spelman's will, for English control over some of Powhatan's resources; and the captivity of John Smith and several less fortunate Englishmen among the Powhatans. These examples indicate a wide range of coastal Algonquian captivity and hostage-exchange practices. In contrast to the better-known captivity practices of northern Iroquians, coastal Algonquian practices appear to have been somewhat more embedded in a poetics of reciprocity than in a poetics of incorporation.[2]

In both captivity and hostage-exchange, leaders of coastal Algonquian polities asserted power over an Other's body in order to enhance their position vis-à-vis the polity of that Other. The forms in which power was asserted varied according to the situation, ranging from peaceful exchange to forcible abduction; from divination to instruction; from bodily adornment to mutilation; and from integration to subordination to destruction. The political aims of captivity varied as well, as the various Powhatan examples attest. Hostage-exchange was practiced in order to forge or cement a political alliance and to train knowledgeable intermediaries, as in the exchange of Namontack for Tom Savage. Abduction might be employed toward similar ends, as in John Smith's case, but asymmetrically subordinating the captive's group to that of the captor. Both abduction and hostage-exchange might be utilized in an attempt to fashion enduring kinship ties through adoption or marriage, together with the many forms of reciprocity that kinship entailed. This is evident in the relationships Powhatan and Pocahontas attempted to establish with John Smith and later with John Rolfe. Abduction and hostage-exchange might also be used in an attempt to gain knowledge about the captive's group, exemplified in the divination ceremony performed over Smith. Finally, as in the cases of Smith's countrymen George Cassen and John Ratcliffe, abduction, torture, and execution were occasionally utilized in order to assert sovereignty over or retaliate against a political rival.

Captives were most often obtained through raiding an enemy village, and like scalps or enemy heads, were taken home as war trophies. Captives who proved weak, dangerous, or troublesome on the homeward journey might be killed, typically with a "knock on the head" by a tomahawk. Sometimes a captive was tomahawked as an object lesson for other captives; even the threat of the tomahawk served as an effective means of controlling captives. Torture was rare but not unknown among Algonquians, and verbal taunting was common. Coastal Algonquians generally exchanged captives for some kind of economic or political advantage, incorporated them as kin, or held them in a state of subordination or servitude.[3] The release of captives in exchange for valuables, pledges of peace, political subordination, tribute payments, or other captives was especially common among Algonquians. This was understood by Europeans as analogous to their own use of captives to extract ransom payments or political concessions, and a convergence of Algonquian and European practices soon developed.

Coastal Algonquians sometimes attempted to obtain a captive's release with a gift of wampum, as Dutch traders observed in the early 1620s. Strings and belts of wampum—purple and white beads made from the quahog clam shell—were worn as signs of chiefly wealth, power, and prestige. They were also exchanged as "total prestations" (Mauss 1954 [1925]) to establish goodwill among persons, social groups, and those spiritual forces Hallowell (1976b [1960]) has called "other-than-human persons." European colonists tended to interpret such prestations as impersonal, commodified "ransom payments," as when, in 1622, Jacob Elekens demanded one hundred forty fathoms of wampum (more than eight hundred feet) for the release of a captive Pequot sachem, Tatobem. In time, Algonquians themselves came to solicit currency or trade goods as ransom payments for European captives.[4]

The use of wampum in transactions involving captives is only one of the many ways in which Algonquian captivity practices involved beliefs about spiritual beings and forces. The divination ritual to which John Smith was submitted, for example, probably involved examining his soul in order to determine how he should be treated. Scalping or beheading of dead enemies was practiced in order to obtain a physical manifestation of the soul. The use of enemy scalps or heads in ceremonies both asserted power over, and derived power from, the enemy's "dream soul," which was located in the head. In Virginia, scalps of enemies would be taken to the temple and offered as a sacrifice to the god Okeus. The remainder of the body was not customarily eaten, as John Smith feared, but consumed by fire.[5]

Contrary to colonial beliefs, ritual cannibalism was not an indigenous practice among Algonquians (except, perhaps, as revenge against Iroquoians). Algonquians despised and feared anyone suspected of eating human flesh, attributing such practices to asocial monsters such as Gulloua, the giant cannibal bird, or the more famous Windigo.[6] In contrast, northern Iroquoians institutionalized the practice of incorporating an enemy's power through ritual ingestion. Just as the Powhatans offered scalps as a sacrifice to Okeus, so too Iroquoians conceptualized the ritual ingestion of soul-infused portions of the captive's body as a sacrificial act. Consistent with the pronounced matrilineality of Iroquoian society, clan matrons played a prominent role in deciding the fate of captives. Often they chose to incorporate the power of the captive's soul not through the ingestion of flesh but through adopting the captive into their lineage as a replacement for a deceased relative.[7]

It would not be an exaggeration to state that seizing captives was often the primary goal of Iroquoian warfare. An Iroquois woman whose grief remained unassuaged after a series of condolence rituals (involving, most centrally, prestations of wampum) might initiate what has been aptly characterized as a "mourning war" (Smith 1951). She would assert her influence upon the sons of her brothers (or equivalent male relatives) to "set up the war kettle," that is, to send out a war party. The warriors would raid the village or camp of an enemy group in order to obtain one or more captives to present to their *agadoni*, the women of their father's clan.[8] The status of these captives was ambiguous until clarified by ritual action, and their fate was contingent upon a variety of circumstances, including their own deportment. Upon the war party's return a captive would be submitted to a variety of rituals in order to revitalize the lineage and "dry its tears." To begin with, the mourners would vent their rage against the captives as they were forced to "run the gauntlet," that is, to run between two parallel lines of villagers who administered physical and verbal abuse. Next the captives would be divided among bereaved lineages, if necessary, and incorporated through adoption. Women and children would most often be welcomed as valuable additions to a bereaved lineage, their cultural identity being transformed through an astute mixture of inducements and punishments.[9] An adolescent or adult male, expected to be less malleable and compliant, was more likely to be tortured and sacrificed.

During the prolonged torture rituals the captive's status as an adopted member of the matrilineage would be underscored through repeatedly addressing him as "sister's son." He was expected to face his pain courageously, mocking or cursing his tormentors, who would try to goad him on to ever more impressive displays of bravery. Women took an active part in the proceedings—which, insofar as they served as an arena for avenging the death of kindred, may have constituted a female equivalent of battle.[10] Following torture a captive would be sacrificed at dawn to Agreskwe, the spiritual power associated with the sun, who was thought to be responsible for success in warfare. After a lethal blow to the captive's head, his heart would be removed, the body eviscerated and dismembered, and the flesh prepared in the "war kettle." Portions of the body were offered to Agreskwe, followed by collective consumption, particularly of his soul-infused heart and blood. As the first captive of the year was designated to be sacrificed, this practice might best be understood as a "first fruits" ceremony, a captive being the first fruit of warfare. During years in which no captives were obtained, the obligation to Agreskwe might be met by sacrificing a bear, one of the many examples of the close identification of bears with humans across the Northeast and Subarctic.[11]

The adoption of a captive filled the vacant social position left by the deceased and also was thought to replenish the spiritual power of the lineage. Similarly, ritually ingesting the heart and blood of a captive was a way of revitalizing a lineage, especially when the captive had exhibited uncommon strength and bravery under torture. In the absence of a captive, a bereaved lineage might be revitalized through performing an adoption ceremony over a dead enemy's scalplock. Each of these forms of revitalization involved the incorporation of alien "soul-substance." As the seat of the victim's "breath soul" (in the case of the scalp) or "flesh soul" (in the case of the heart and blood), these bodily substances were metonymical representations of human life. Wampum, on the other hand, was a metaphor of the soul by virtue of sharing its reflective quality. (The shells may also have represented, metonymically, the transformative power of the sea.)[12] The acceptance of wampum—like the performance of a scalp ceremony, the ingestion of a heart or blood, or the adoption of a captive—was a ritual of incorporation and revitalization, one that restored life and power to a bereaved lineage.[13]

The poetic equivalence among captives, bears, scalps, hearts, blood, and wampum, on the one hand, and the acts of ingestion, adoption, and prestation, on the other, lent considerable flexibility to this set of incorporative practices—a flexibility that facilitated their adaptation to a wide variety of personal, social, and historical circumstances. Historical adaptations are particularly well documented for Iroquoians, whose warfare and captivity practices changed significantly in response to the European invasion. The major colonial source on Iroquoian captivity, the *Jesuit Relations*, documents events in the mid-seventeenth century, when warfare and captivity reached an unprecedented intensity, largely in response to the European presence. In contrast to colonial warfare, indigenous conflicts were limited in scale, in large part due to the goal of taking captives without sustaining casualties (since any additional casualties among the raiding party would require the mounting of still another raid). Following sustained contact with Europeans in the 1620s, however, Iroquoian peoples suffered a demographic crisis of unparalleled proportions. This dramatically intensified the Iroquoian search for captives to revitalize their lineages.[14]

The serious decrease in population that Iroquoian villages suffered in the early and mid-seventeenth century had a number of related causes: devastating European epidemics; depletion of fur-bearing animals due to trade with Europeans; an intensification of warfare from the 1640s through the 1670s due to the introduction of firearms and the struggle to control the colonial fur trade; and the emigration of large numbers of Iroquoians to mission villages in Canada or fur-trading sites to the west. Increasingly, Iroquoians adopted non-Iroquoian captives: By the 1660s, according to French missionary estimates, foreigners outnumbered natives in many Iroquois villages. Even so, massive adoptions could not offset Iroquoian losses to disease, Christian missions, and warfare—losses augmented by serious conflicts with the French after 1674. In the early eighteenth century the Five Nations of Iroquois (including the Mohawks, Oneidas, Onondagas, Cayugas, and Senecas) turned increasingly to peacefully incorporating weak or remnant Indian groups, such as the Susquehannocks, Tutelos, and most notably, the Tuscaroras (after which the league became known as the Six Nations).

A significant proportion of the captives or refugees adopted by Iroquoians were Algonquians—a factor that might have contributed to the convergence of Iroquoian and Algonquian captivity practices in the seventeenth and eighteenth centuries. Algonquians adopted some of the incorporative Iroqouian rituals that were previously foreign to them; in turn, Iroquoians may have adopted from the Algonquians a more exchange-oriented approach to captivity, which proved particularly compatible with the practices of warfare and diplomacy that Europeans imported to America. Notably, late seventeenth- and eighteenth-century Algonquian and Iroquoian war parties took captives, heads, and scalps in order to fulfill the conditions of alliance imposed by French and English colonial officials as well as to obtain from them ransom or bounty payments. When they chose to keep European captives among themselves, their treatment of those captives was sometimes influenced by European patterns of servitude, with which Native people became familiar through personal experience. At the same time, the indigenous allies of the English or the French insisted on utilizing captives, refugees, and scalps in indigenous (if syncretic) ways, adopting captives or refugees to replenish their numbers and offering captives and scalps as sacrifices to spiritual forces.[15]

Always diverse and flexible, indigenous captivity practices were transformed in significant ways by the colonial invasion. In their intercultural scope, expanded scale, and responsiveness to demographic, political, and economic changes, captivity practices in the colonial era were part of the extraordinarily complex conjuncture of practices and meanings that constitute what Richard White (1991) has called the "middle ground."[16] As we shall see, colonial representations of captivity highlight an extremely selective set of these practices and meanings, presenting colonists as the vulnerable victims of Captivating Others and erasing colonists' role as Captors of indigenous people.

## Metacom's War, Wetamo's Grievances, and the Captivity of Mary Rowlandson

The first time in the course of English colonization that a significant number of colonists were taken captive by Native peoples was in 1675–76, during the conflict known as King Philip's or Metacom's War.[17] New Englanders recorded only one instance of captivity among Algonquians prior to that time: In 1637, two "English maids" were seized during an attack that the Pequots launched against the new settlement of Wethersfield, Connecticut, as a protest against English expansion and treaty violations (see Map 4.1). Although the girls were ransomed by Dutch traders, hostilities between the Pequots and the colonists of Connecticut rapidly intensified, culminating in the infamous destruction of the Pequots' fortified village on the Mystic River. During the raid, between three hundred and seven hundred inhabitants of the village were burned alive or shot while attempting to escape. The survivors were hunted down by colonial forces and their Mohegan allies, who were offered a bounty payment for severed Pequot heads.

During the next several months, most of the Pequot refugees were captured and either executed or enslaved. At least four hundred Pequots were distributed to English colonists or their Mohegan and Narragansett allies. A smaller number, including fifteen boys and two women, were shipped into slavery in the West Indies. Those distributed among Mohegans and Narragansetts were not enslaved, as Roger Williams explained in a petition, but "as they say is their general custom," would be "used kindly, have houses and goods and fields given them: because they voluntarily choose to come in to them and if not received will to the enemy or turn wild Irish themselves" (Jennings 1975:226).[18] Nevertheless, the English counted the adopted Pequots as slaves and required the Mohegans and Narragansetts to pay an annual tribute for each.[19]

The two captive maids from Wethersfield were a recurring figure in one of several competing Puritan accounts of the war, *Newes from Amer-*

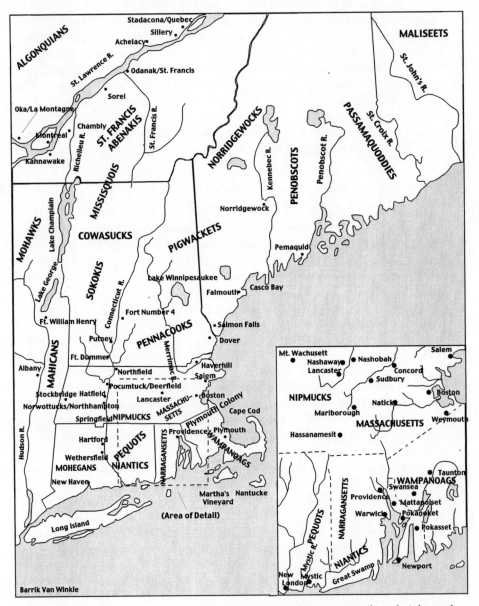

MAP 4.1   New England and southeastern Canada in the seventeenth and eighteenth centuries, showing selected peoples, settlements, and sites of captivity. SOURCE: Barrik Van Winkle.

*ica* (1837 [1638]) by Captain John Underhill, the leader of colonial Massachusetts forces in the attack on the Pequots, and a follower of antinomian Anne Hutchinson. Underhill reported that the girls were returned unharmed, although the eldest, about sixteen years of age, "told us that they did solicit her to uncleanness." Underhill's account not only initiated the persistent literary trope of the sexually threatened captive (for which there is no reliable evidence in the colonial period) but also, in comparing the "two maids captives" to "captive Israel," prefigured subsequent Puritan captivity narratives such as Mary Rowlandson's. The girls, according to Underhill, considered their captivity an expression of "God's just displeasure to them, that had lived under so prudent means of grace as they did, and had been so ungrateful toward God, and slighted the means" (Slotkin 1973:74–75). Further extending the figure of "captive Israel" in a more unorthodox, antinomian direction, Underhill concluded that "the greater the captivities be of His servants, the contentions amongst His churches, the clearer God's presence is amongst His, to pick and cull them out of the fire" (Seelye 1977:209). In other words, captivity, like sectarian controversy, was a purifying trial.[20]

Four decades later, following the next major English–Algonquian conflict over land and political sovereignty, the Puritan poetics of captivity—a poetics of trial and redemption—would be more fully fleshed out. Metacom's war of resistance to colonial expansion pitted a collection of Pokanoket, Pocasset, Narragansett, and Nipmuc forces against the United Colonies (Massachusetts Bay, Connecticut, Plymouth, and New Haven) and their Christian Indian allies. Dubbed "King Philip" by the English, Metacom was the sachem of Pokanoket, and the son of Plymouth's staunch ally Massasoit. In defeating Metacom's forces in 1676, the English put an end to effective Algonquian resistance in southern New England. To be sure, the price of victory was high: More than a dozen towns on the western frontier were destroyed; approximately 2,500 colonists were killed (5 percent of the population); and forty-two colonists were captured by Metacom's forces and his allies. But the cost of the war to the Algonquians of southern New England was greater still. By the end of the year-long struggle approximately five thousand (40 percent) had lost their lives, and those who survived were captives of one kind or another: slaves, indentured servants, refugees, or residents of closely supervised "praying towns." The Algonquians who had formerly coexisted with the English as neighbors and trading partners were now decisively subordinated or exiled.[21]

Although Puritan ministers Increase Mather and William Hubbard included references to captives in their contesting histories of the war years, it was the spiritual autobiography of a ransomed captive, Mary White Rowlandson, that offered the most compelling and authoritative interpretation of captivity as a redemptive trial in the American "wilderness."[22] *The Soveraignty and Goodness of God, Together, With the Faithfulness of His Promises Displayed; Being a Narrative of the Captivity and Restoration of Mrs. Mary Rowlandson* appeared in 1682, six years after the close of Metacom's War (see Figure 4.1). The most prominent colonial captive of the war, Mary White Rowlandson was the wife of the pastor of Lancaster, Massachusetts, and the daughter of one of the town's leading families. Several of Rowlandson's captors were prominent allies of Metacom, and they recognized her as an exceptional prize. Ransomed by Nipmuc and English mediators after nearly twelve weeks of captivity, Mary Rowlandson reflected in writing upon the transformative experience she had undergone, adapting the Puritan conversion narrative to her experience of captivity among Nipmucs, Narragansetts, Pokanokets, and Pocassets. Advertised in the first American edition of *Pilgrim's Progress* as "pathetically written, with her own hand," Mary Rowlandson's masterful narrative went through four editions in 1682 (printed in Boston, London, and twice in Cambridge), and some forty other editions and issues in succeeding centuries. The second of only four works by women to be published in seventeenth-century New England (and the first by a living author), Mary Rowlandson's captivity narrative is among the most influential and enduring works of colonial literature.[23]

Because Puritan hermeneutics led her to consider the most mundane occurrences as signs of the workings of Providence, Mary Rowlandson left a vivid and detailed record of her experiences as a captive. The immediacy of her account, together with Rowlandson's placement among major Algonquian actors, allows an unusually thorough examination of the persons and events involved in her captivity. There is some irony in this, as it is largely through abstracting the captivity from its political context and portraying it within a spiritual framework that the narrative gains its ideological effect. Resisting this abstraction, my reading seeks to resituate the narrative within the struggle for political sovereignty that remains largely uninscribed. At the same time, I aim not to lose sight of Rowlandson's own struggle for survival, meaning, and a voice in patriarchal society.[24]

Mary Rowlandson and her three children were captured on February 20, 1676, along with twenty other inhabitants of Lancaster, which then numbered about fifty families. A dozen residents of Lancaster were killed in the attack, and several others died while in captivity, including Rowlandson's six-year-old daughter, Sarah. Local Nipmucs as well as Pokanokets, Pocassets, and Narragansetts took part in the attack, the first of several raids on frontier towns following a devastating English attack on the "Great Swamp Fort," the main Narragansett stronghold. Although the Nipmucs of nearby Nashaway had maintained generally peaceful re-

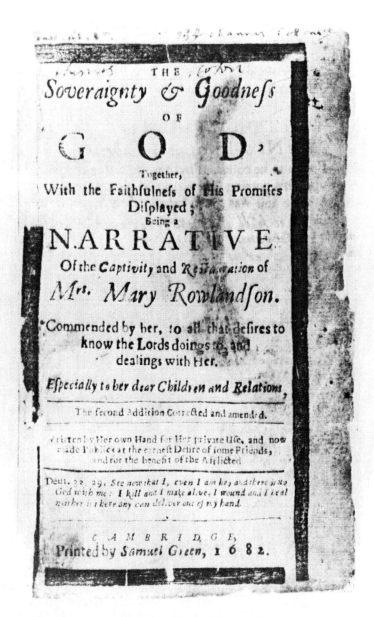

FIGURE 4.1   Title page from *The Soveraignty and Goodness of God,*
by Mary Rowlandson (Cambridge, 1682). (Courtesy of the Edward
E. Ayer Collection, the Newberry Library, Chicago.)

lations with the English for the first two decades of Lancaster's existence, there had been increasing conflicts in recent years as the townspeople became less dependent on the fur trade and more intent upon expanding their farming and grazing lands. Relations had deteriorated also with the Nipmuc Christians of the neighboring praying town of Nashobah, who by the time of the attack had been incarcerated on Deer Island in Boston Harbor.[25]

Soon after her capture the forty-year-old Mrs. Rowlandson was "sold," she reports, to a Narragansett sachem named Quanopin (or Quinnipin), whom she called "master" for the twelve weeks of her captivity. A prominent member of the leading Narragansett patrilineage, Quanopin played a central role in negotiations with the colonies and ranked along with Canonchet (his patrilateral parallel cousin) and Pessicus (his father's brother) as a leading war chief (see Figure 4.2). Quanopin, a close ally of Metacom, was married to the widow of Metacom's brother Wamsutta.[26]

Unfortunately, there are no further details regarding Quanopin's acquisition of Mary Rowlandson, although she reports that her older daughter, Mary, was "sold" for a gun (Rowlandson 1997:75). Perhaps Rowlandson's original captor received some kind of valuable for turning her over to Quanopin, but Rowlandson's perception of herself as a "servant" to be bought and sold misses an important aspect of the indigenous meaning of her captivity. Quanopin's acquisition of Mary Rowlandson is reminiscent of the control that Opechancanough and Powhatan established over John Smith, and suggests that because of her status as a gentlewoman Rowlandson was turned over to Quanopin as a political hostage. Although her captors highly valued her skills in sewing and knitting—skills she employed industriously and fairly autonomously throughout her captivity—Rowlandson was especially prized for her exchange value.[27]

Mary Rowlandson thought highly of Quanopin, calling him "the best friend that I had of an Indian, both in cold and in hunger," but she despised and dreaded his third wife, Wetamo (spelled *Wettimore* in the narrative and *Weetamoo* elsewhere).[28] Rowlandson portrays Wetamo as a "severe and proud dame" who took delight in tormenting her (86, 96). Although she realized that Quanopin was a "saggamore" or sachem (75), Rowlandson betrays no knowledge that Wetamo was herself a hereditary sachem. Wetamo, sachem of the recently abandoned town of Pocasset, was one of several "squaw sachems" or female chiefs who came into prominence during Metacom's War. Also known as "sunksquaws," squaw sachems could attain a position of authority either as the widow of a sachem, or like Wetamo, through descent within a high-ranking lineage.[29] Like their male counterparts, female sachems governed their villages mainly through persuasion and the control of resources, regulating

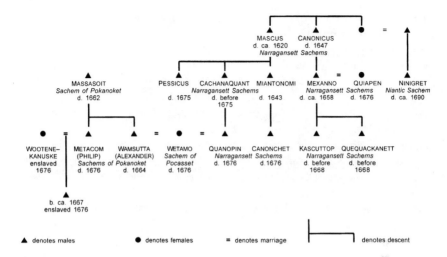

FIGURE 4.2   Genealogy of Metacom, Wetamo, and other seventeenth-century sachems.

internal matters such as the production of food, the distribution of resources, and the resolution of disputes. Both male and female sachems established alliances with other villages through diplomacy, trade, tribute, and marriage (exemplified in Wetamo's and Quanopin's alliance). During times of hostility leadership might pass to another leader with demonstrated proficiency in warfare, but some sachems also served as war chiefs. This was apparently the case with Wetamo, who reportedly commanded three hundred warriors at the outbreak of the war and was greatly feared by the English.[30]

Wetamo and Quanopin each had ample reason to join Metacom in his war of resistance against the English. Metacom had succeeded his brother, Wamsutta or Alexander, as sachem of the village of Pokanoket, in 1664.[31] At this time the sturdy alliance that their father Massasoit had maintained with Plymouth from 1621 until his death in 1662 was already endangered. The alliance had survived intact for nearly four decades—years that witnessed the establishment of Massachusetts Bay, Connecticut, New Haven, and dissident Providence; the near extermination of the Pequots in 1637; and English treachery leading to the execution in 1643 of the Narragansett sachem Miantonomi, Quanopin's father's brother. But relations between Plymouth and Pokanoket became severely strained following the Restoration of 1660, when Plymouth had to defend its land claims before Charles II in the face of competing claims from the other English colonies. After Massasoit's death in 1662, Plymouth applied increasing pressure on Pokanoket to recognize the colony's claim to exclusive control over its lands.

One expression of strained relations was the seizure at gunpoint of Massasoit's successor, Wamsutta, who was forced to march to Plymouth to answer for his land dealings with Plymouth's rival, Providence, whose royal charter of 1663 encompassed Pokanoket. Wamsutta, already sick, died immediately after this episode, leaving as his widow the squaw sachem of Pocasset, who assumed the new name Wetamo to mark her change in status. Metacom, succeeding his brother as sachem of Pokanoket, faced a Plymouth determined to encroach upon both his authority and his people's land. In 1667 Plymouth established a new town, Swansea, on land claimed both by Metacom and the colony of Providence. Metacom protested, only to see Swansea expand. Four years later, after armed Pokanoket warriors marched on Swansea to demonstrate their displeasure with English territorial expansion, Metacom was forced to subject himself formally to colonial authority—signaling a significant loss of sovereignty for a people who heretofore had considered themselves subject only to the king of England. Rumors of a conspiracy against the colonists had surfaced periodically since Wamsutta's brief tenure, and more than a decade of mounting tension climaxed in the murder, in March 1675, of Metacom's interpreter, a Christian Indian named John Sassamon, who had accused Metacom of conspiracy. Three allies of Metacom were hanged for the murder in June 1675. Soon thereafter Pokanoket warriors attacked the town of Swansea, and Metacom's War was under way. Among the early attacks was an August raid by Nashaway Nipmucs on Mary Rowlandson's town of Lancaster, which left seven colonists dead.[32]

Wetamo, who controlled lands that several of the colonies coveted, was one of Metacom's earliest and most valuable supporters.[33] Not only was she suspicious about Wamsutta's death, but the Pocasset people had a history of opposition to the English dating to the 1620s, when the sachem Corbitant (possibly Wetamo's father) had taken Tisquantum captive. Wetamo parted with her second husband, the sachem Petananuet (or Benjamin), over his allegiance to the English, and supplied provisions and forces for the surprise attacks on frontier villages that became the hallmark of the war.[34] At the end of June, Wetamo allowed Metacom and his forces to hide along with her own people in the Pocasset cedar swamp. Like other swamps, this one was considered the home of powerful spirits and served as a traditional place of refuge. This time, however, the swamp provided only a brief respite, as all were driven out by colonial forces at the end of July. Metacom and Wetamo then parted company, the Pocasset sachem and her people taking refuge among the Narragansetts, most of whom were attempting to maintain neutrality. Within the next few months Wetamo married the Narragansett sachem Quanopin.[35]

Offering refuge to the Pocassets turned out to be disastrous for the Narragansetts. Shortly before the main body of Pocassets arrived among the Narragansetts, on July 15, 1675, the United Colonies had coerced four obscure Narragansetts to promise that refugees would be handed over for a bounty payment of two "coats" (or lengths of woolen trading cloth) per captive. In the same agreement the colonies offered a bounty of one coat for each enemy head; twenty coats for Metacom's head; and forty if Metacom were delivered alive. About three weeks later, on August 5, a Rhode Island trader reported mixed results to the Governor of Connecticut, John Winthrop, Jr.:

> The Narragansetts have been out, three hundred of them, brought me in seven heads of the enemy, also [are] now come home, and with them at least one hundred men, women, and children of Wettamore's, the Pocasset Sachem squaw, and her with them. She is kind to Sucquauch [Pessicus, Quanopin's father's brother] and he desires all favor for her that can be. (Updike 1937:110)

The Narragansett warriors received seven coats as a bounty payment for the enemy heads, but Wetamo and her people were not handed over to the English. Disappointed in the results of their offer, Connecticut and Massachusetts soon extended the bounty to colonial soldiers, offering for each enemy head or scalp a payment of thirty shillings, approximately three times the bounty offered to the Narragansetts.[36]

The spurious agreement of July 15 was confirmed on October 18 by the Narragansett sachem Canonchet and three members of his council but later was repudiated by Canonchet, the only one of the four with the authority to negotiate with the colonies. Although eager to maintain neutrality, Canonchet was reluctant to surrender the Pocassets, knowing from bitter experience that refugees could expect harsh treatment from the colonists. Not only had the Pequot refugees been enslaved or indentured, but in 1643 the English demanded that the Narragansett sachem Miantonomi be executed while captive among the Mohegans, despite the payment of a ransom. Indeed, at the same time that the English were pressing the Narragansetts to surrender the Pocasset refugees, they were confirming the Narragansetts' worst fears by selling several hundred Algonquian captives to slave traders headed for Spain and the West Indies, retaining an additional hundred as domestic slaves.[37] The majority of the enslaved prisoners were at peace when they were captured or had voluntarily surrendered.

The Narragansetts' protection of the Pocassets became the rationale for a massive colonial attack on the Narragansett stronghold in December. In this attack, known to the English as the Great Swamp Fight, from three to six hundred Narragansetts were killed, including large numbers of women and children. This attack forced the majority of the Narragansetts into the hostilities: Together with the Pocassets, the surviving Narragansetts fled westward and took refuge among the Nipmucs, allying themselves with Shoshanim (or Sam Sachem) of Nashaway and other sachems hostile to the English.[38]

When Mary Rowlandson was captured in the first of the raids following the Great Swamp Fight, her husband Joseph was in Boston seeking aid, alarmed by the warning of a Nipmuc Christian, James Quanapohit of Nashaway. Quanapohit had agreed to spy on Metacom's forces for the English, together with another Nipmuc Christian, Job Kattananit, who was eager to learn the fate of his own three children, who had been captured by Metacom's forces from the praying town of Hassanamesit. In return for their loyalty, both informers were returned to Deer Island in Boston harbor, where since October some five hundred Massachusett and Nipmuc Christians had been incarcerated under brutal conditions. Although their suffering on Deer Island and the distrust of the English had alienated some converts, others remained loyal to the English, including Tom Dublet (or Nepanet) of the praying town of Nashobah. Dublet, along with about sixty other inhabitants of Nashobah, had been living peacefully in Concord under the supervision of English attorney John Hoar when Capt. Samuel Moseley, a notorious Indian hater, forced them to march to Deer Island. Even so, Dublet agreed to undertake three missions on behalf of Mary Rowlandson, accompanied on the second trip by another displaced resident of Nashobah named Peter Conway (or Tatiquinea). On the third and final trip John Hoar himself accompanied the Nipmuc mediators, and together they obtained Mary Rowlandson's release—negotiating not with Metacom or Quanopin but with Shoshanim and the other Nipmuc sachems with whom they had taken refuge.[39]

Rowlandson's narrative recounts the arrival of the Christian Indian emissaries, whom she called "Tom and Peter," at Mt. Wachusett, where the Nipmucs, Narragansetts, Pokanokets, and Pocassets were then camped (see Figure 4.3): "Though they were Indians, I got them by the hand and burst out into tears" (Rowlandson 1997:97). The captive was redeemed in May 1676, for a price she herself suggested—twenty pounds, delivered partly in the form of trading cloth. Rowlandson's son and her surviving daughter were returned the following month, Joseph for a ransom payment and Mary "free of cost" (110). As their home and village had been destroyed, the reunited Rowlandson family was dependent upon others for lodging until the following spring, when Joseph Rowlandson was called to a new pulpit in Wethersfield, Con-

FIGURE 4.3    Woodcut of Mary Rowlandson with Tom Dublet (Nepanet) and Peter Conway (Tatiquinea). SOURCE: *A Narrative of the Captivity, Sufferings, and Removes of Mrs. Mary Rowlandson* (Boston, 1771). (Courtesy of the Edward E. Ayer Collection, the Newberry Library, Chicago.)

necticut. He died the following year, and in 1679 Mary married a wealthy Wethersfield landowner, Samuel Talcott. When *The Soveraignty and Goodness of God* appeared in print three years later, the author, now known as Mary Talcott, had achieved some distance from the dreadful events of 1676.[40]

The months following Mary Rowlandson's release were disastrous for Metacom, Quanopin, and Wetamo. Quanopin assumed leadership over the Narragansetts in June after his father's brother, Pessicus, was killed by Mohawks (Canonchet having already been captured, shot, and beheaded by Indian allies of the English, including a band of Narragansetts). Quanopin held this position only briefly, however, as he was captured in mid-July. The following month Quanopin, the Nipmuc sachem Shoshanim, and one of the latter's brothers were court-martialed and publicly hanged for treason against the king of England—a sentence that presumed the very subordination that Metacom's forces were resisting. Wetamo's forces had dwindled throughout the spring as English attacks increased; they were dispersed altogether during the summer.

In August Wetamo and her three dozen remaining followers were ambushed while trying to return to their home at Pocasset. As Boston minister Increase Mather told the tale in the entry for August 6 of his *Brief History of the War with the Indians in New-England*:

Only the *Squaw-Sachem of Pocasset,* who was next unto *Philip* in respect of the mischief that hath been done, and the blood that hath been shed in this War, escaped alone; but not long after some of *Taunton* finding an Indian Squaw in *Metapoiset* newly dead, cut off her head, and it happened to be *Weetamoo,* i.e. *Squaw-Sachem* her *head.* When it was set upon a pole in *Taunton,* the Indians who were prisoners there, knew it presently, and made a most horrible and diabolical Lamentation, crying out that it was their Queens head. Now here it is to be observed, that God himself by his own hand, brought this enemy to destruction. For in that place, where the last year, she furnished *Philip* with Canoes for his men, she herself could not meet with a Canoe, but venturing over the River upon a Raft, that broke under her, so that she was drowned, just before the English found her. Surely *Philip's* turn will be next. (Mather 1978 [1676]:137–138)

Mather quickly saw his prophecy fulfilled. Within six days Metacom's wife and young son were captured, and the demoralized sachem himself was killed by a Pocasset deserter named Alderman. Col. Benjamin Church, the English commander, ordered that because Metacom "had caused many an Englishman's body to lie unburied and rot above ground, that not one of his bones should be buried" (1975:156). Church's Indian executioner decapitated and quartered Metacom's body, the punishment accorded to domestic traitors. Metacom's head and hands were given to Alderman so he could collect a bounty; his jaw would later be disengaged from his skull by Increase Mather's son Cotton, a youth at the time. Just as Wetamo's head was displayed on a pole at the scene of her death, Metacom's was displayed in Plymouth, remaining for twenty years a grisly emblem of King Philip's "treason" against the colony.

As in the case of Wetamo, the elder Mather interpreted the significance of Metacom's death and punishment through a poetics that traced (and left traces) of spatial and temporal correspondences between past and present, body and spirit, sign and meaning.[41] His *Brief History* observes:

Thus when Philip had made an end to deal treacherously, his own Subjects dealt treacherously with him. This Wo was brought upon him that spoyled when he was not spoyled. And in that very place where he first contrived and began his mischief, was he taken and destroyed, and there was he (Like as Agag was hewed in pieces before the Lord) cut into four quarters, and is now hanged up as a monument of revenging Justice. (Mather 1978 [1699]:139)

For Mather it was especially significant that Metacom's head arrived in Plymouth on a day that had previously been set aside for thanksgiving. "Thus did God break the head of that Leviathan," he wrote, "and give it to be meat to the people inhabiting the wilderness" (Mather 1978 [1699]:139). Identifying Metacom with Satan in his guise as a monstrous sea serpent and Metacom's death with the deliverance of Israel as foretold by Isaiah, Mather further envisioned the sachem as a sacrifice that would nourish God's people in the wilderness. The dismembered body of the Pokanoket sachem signified not only his decapitated and dispersed body politic but also his domain, which would soon be divided among the English and provide them with "meat."

Many of Metacom's captains and warriors were executed in August and September, and armed resistance soon abated, although Algonquian attacks upon the western and northern frontiers continued into 1678. The colonies sold at least one thousand Algonquian prisoners and refugees in West Indian and Iberian slave markets, including Metacom's wife Wootonekanuske and their nine-year-old son. The son's enslavement caused considerable debate among the Puritan clerics, some of whom cited scriptural precedents in recommending that the boy receive the presumably harsher punishment of execution for his father's "treason."[42]

Hundreds of other New England Algonquians were sold to colonists as slaves or indentured servants, including fifteen to Capt. Samuel Moseley and thirteen to slave trader James Whitcomb, in whose house the Rowlandson family resided after Mary's return from captivity. Numerous Algonquian children—whose parents had been killed in the war or executed, or whose "relations seemed willing"—were placed in English homes, under the condition that they be "religiously educated & taught to read the English tongue" (Salisbury 1997:142–144). Adult survivors who were able to establish their loyalty were settled in four closely supervised praying towns, one of which was overseen by Wetamo's former husband, Petananuet (now called Ben Sachem). Others managed to retreat to relatively isolated enclaves, especially on Cape Cod, Martha's Vineyard, and Nantucket. A few were restored to positions of relatively high visibility in colonial society, notably James Printer, who before the war had served for sixteen years as an apprentice to Cambridge printer Samuel Green, Sr. Forced into the hostilities when the praying town of Hassanamesit was attacked by Metacom's forces, Printer served as a scribe for the Nipmuc sachems during the negotiations over Mary Rowlandson's release. Successful in his bid for a pardon, Printer returned to work for Green, and was responsible for composing the type for the second and third editions of Rowlandson's narrative—in which, ironically, he appears as a leading example of praying Indians' "treachery."[43]

But James Printer was exceptional. Of the Algonquians who were not killed in the war, executed, enslaved, indentured, or confined to praying towns, the majority took refuge with other Native peoples in what Evan Haefeli and Kevin Sweeney (1995) have called an "Algonquian diaspora."

Various groups in northern New England that became known as "Abenakis" took them in, as did French missions such as St. Francis (primarily Abenaki) and Kahnawake (primarily Mohawk). Pokanoket, Pocasset, Narragansett, and Nipmuc lands, now cleared of their native inhabitants, were distributed to soldiers and sold to colonists. Benjamin Church, Metacom's nemesis, developed lands in both Pokanoket and Pocasset in the decade following the war.[44]

### Wilderness Trials: A Gentlewoman's Conversion Narrative

Increase Mather's interpretation of the deaths of Wetamo and Metacom is one example of how New England Puritans discerned the hand of Providence in both the Algonquian challenge to New England's sovereignty and in their defeat. Providential interpretations of the war were developed in fast-day sermons, histories, and most compellingly, in Mary Rowlandson's *Soveraignty and Goodness of God*, which interprets her hardships while in captivity as a personal spiritual trial and opportunity for redemption. Although it is largely consistent with Increase Mather's interpretation of the war, Rowlandson's spiritual autobiography speaks in a distinctly personal voice and with the authority of experience—indeed, of an experience so "astonishing" that it sometimes threatened to exceed the totalizing capacity of Puritan hermeneutics (Rowlandson 1997:82, 112).[45]

From the first sentence Rowlandson's narrative records a seemingly unprovoked assault upon her town, home, family, and friends.[46] The immediacy of Rowlandson's prose draws the reader into her experience of "the dolefullest day" and "the dolefullest night that ever mine eyes saw." She tells of the burning of her house (which served as one of Lancaster's garrison houses), the wounding of her young daughter, Sarah, as well as herself, and the death of her sister, nephew, and brother-in-law, capturing the chaos in a vivid summation: "Thus were we butchered by those merciless Heathen, standing amazed, with the blood running down to our heels" (see Figure 4.4). Although she had always thought she would rather die than be taken by those "ravenous beasts," Rowlandson writes that "when it came to the trial my mind changed" (68–70).

Rowlandson figures her captivity as a series of twenty "removes . . . up and down the wilderness"—a landscape that she, echoing other Puritan writers, describes as "vast and howling" or "vast and desolate" (70–71, 80). As Hambrick-Stowe (1982) noted, Rowlandson's "removes" are reminiscent of John Bunyan's account in *Pilgrim's Progress* (1678) of Christian's pilgrimage "through the wilderness of this world." But as Neal Salisbury has pointed out, they are also reminiscent of the historical experience of many a New England Puritan, including Rowlandson

FIGURE 4.4   Woodcut of the burning of the garrison house at Lancaster. SOURCE: *A Narrative of the Captivity, Sufferings, and Removes of Mrs. Mary Rowlandson* (Boston, 1771). (Courtesy of the Edward E. Ayer Collection, the Newberry Library, Chicago.)

herself, whose "entire life was punctuated by removes from one place to another"—from Somerset county, England, to Wenham, Massachusetts, to the inland settlement of Lancaster, and finally, after her captivity, to Wethersfield (Salisbury 1997:7). Rowlandson's figure of the "remove" combines these physical and spiritual meanings, coupling a description of her removal from the comforts, supports, and maternal responsibilities of her familiar life with observations on her parallel spiritual journey and transformation. The attack caught her at a time of "carelessness" and complacency, Rowlandson confesses, when she was almost wishing for God to submit her to a trial that would test and strengthen her faith (Rowlandson 1997:74). "Affliction I wanted and affliction I had, full measure," she reflects, seeing her captivity as a trial analogous to the Biblical captivities of God's chosen people (112). When she succumbed to tears shortly after crossing the Connecticut River in a canoe, Rowlandson recalled the first verse of Psalm 137: "By the rivers of Babylon, there we sat down; yea, we wept when we remembered Zion" (82).[47]

In captivity Rowlandson found herself stripped of the comforts of domestic and community life; isolated from her family and the supports of Christian existence; reduced to what she considered a near-bestial state, exemplified by her "wolfish" appetite; and "enslaved" by a "master" and, worse, a "mistress" who themselves served the Devil. Most poignantly, she endured the suffering and death of six-year-old Sarah from a bullet wound as well as separation from her surviving children, fourteen-year-old Joseph and ten-year-old Mary. "All was gone (except my life)," she laments, "and I knew not but the next moment that might go too" (71). In these extremities Rowlandson learned that even the Bible—her "guide by day," her "pillow by night"—could cease to comfort her if God so willed it. She found that she "could not sit still . . . but kept walking from one place to another," going "up and down mourning and lamenting" (90, 76, 84).[48]

Like Job returned to the naked human condition of isolation and vulnerability, Rowlandson at last abandoned all pride and vanity, acknowledging her utter dependence upon God's power. Upon recounting a brief reunion with her son, Joseph, she reflects:

> We had Husbands and Father, and Children, and Sisters, and Friends, and Relations, and House, and Home, and many Comforts of Life, but now we may say as Job, *Naked came I out of my Mothers Womb, and naked shall I return. The Lord gave, and the Lord hath taken away, Blessed be the Name of the Lord.* (81–82)

When at last Rowlandson was "sold" to her husband (88), she felt herself to be spiritually as well as physically redeemed. Although she recorded being redeemed from captivity in exchange for a ransom payment of silver coins and cloth, it is rather as "the redeemed of the Lord" that she writes. Comparing her ordeal to Daniel's in the lion's den, she invokes Psalm 107: "Oh give thanks unto the Lord for He is good, for his mercy endureth forever. Let the Redeemed of the Lord say so, whom He hath redeemed from the hand of the Enemy" (107).

Rowlandson's narrative bears witness to the spiritual trials and opportunities for redemption constituted by her radical displacement from her home, family, and accustomed social role. Seeking to read every experience as evidence of the work of Providence, Rowlandson portrays her captors as instruments of God whose actions, whether abusive or merciful, were ultimately oriented to her own spiritual condition rather than to Algonquian values, grievances, or interests. Although she views herself as an economic asset to Quanopin and Wetamo—both because of the substantial ransom payment she would bring and her highly valued handiwork—she fails to acknowledge any other motives her captors might have for holding her. Echoing her contemporaries, Rowlandson characterizes her captors, particularly when they act collectively, as bestial and diabolical Others: They are "wild beasts of the forest," "bears bereft of their whelps," "ravenous wolves," "a company of hell-hounds," "black creatures in the night, which made the place a lively resemblance of hell" (39, 68–71, 105). Inhuman as they might be, however, her captors were not simply satisfying their animal appetites; rather, they were serving God as a "scourge to His people" (105). Likewise, when they treated her with compassion and generosity, they were restrained in their "savageness and brutishness" by God's hand (71).

Puritan hermeneutics provided a totalizing poetics within which the unfamiliar complexity of her captors' actions and motivations could be reduced to an instrumentality in which they entirely lacked rationality, morality, or agency. Even so, Rowlandson's narrative demonstrates a pragmatic, if limited, familiarity with the cultural world and individual variability of her captors—one that, to some extent, appears to date back to her interactions with Nipmucs prior to her captivity. Rowlandson uses quite readily such Algonquian words as *wigwam, wampum, squaw, papoose, sagamore* (a local variant of *sachem*), *powwow* (ritual shaman), *sannup* (husband), *samp* (corn porridge), *nux* (yes), and *matchit* (bad). She describes a pre-battle divination ceremony and a celebratory feast with an attention to detail that gives her accounts ethnographic value even today.[49] She secured her survival by finding protectors and engaging in numerous economic exchanges.[50] Although she repeats conventional typifications of Indian brutality, she also offers somewhat nuanced characterizations of particular individuals, including Metacom. Even the individuals who are not described sympathetically are sometimes identified by name: Among the captors Rowlandson most despised are former Nipmuc residents of praying towns, including James Printer. Characteristically, however, Rowlandson offers no worldly reason for the hostility of Christian Nipmucs. Whether they hailed from the praying towns of Nashobah and Hassanamesit or the English town of Marlborough, Christian Nipmucs found themselves caught between the colonists and Metacom's forces and subject to the suspicions of both.[51]

Neither does Rowlandson offer any worldly motivation for the antagonism of Wetamo, whom she describes as threatening, taunting, and striking her, and depriving her of food, fire, shelter, and the solace of the

Bible. Most distressing of all to Rowlandson was her sense that Wetamo
and her compatriots acted in a completely unpredictable and arbitrary
fashion.[52] Rowlandson was eager to please the Indians she called "master" and "mistress," offering them gifts and once even inviting them to a
dinner of bear and peas. But she found that "sometimes I met with
favour, and sometimes with nothing but frowns" (85). Unable to anticipate whether her actions would bring approval or punishment, Rowlandson considered her captors "unstable and like mad men." She attributes her own disorientation entirely to her captors' sins: "There was little
more trust to them than to the master they served" (97). That devious
master was, of course, Satan, "him who was a liar from the beginning"
(89).

Besides being cruel and inconstant, Rowlandson considered Wetamo
to be ludicrously vain. She describes her mistress as "bestowing every
day in dressing herself neat as much time as any of the gentry of the land:
powdering her hair, and painting her face, going with necklaces, with
jewels in her ears, and bracelets upon her hands." Once Wetamo was
dressed, Rowlandson reports, "her work was to make girdles of *wampom*
and beads" (97). Wetamo and Quanopin wore wampum belts and necklaces at a dance during the night of the negotiations that led to Rowlandson's release. Rowlandson describes the dance as

> carried on by eight of them, four *Men* and four *Squaws*; My master and mis-
> triss being two. He was dressed in his Holland shirt, with great Laces sewed
> at the tail of it; he had his silver Buttons, his white Stockins, his Garters were
> hung round with Shillings, and he had Girdles of *Wampom upon his Head and
> shoulders*. She had a Kersey Coat, and covered with Girdles of *Wampom* from
> the Loins and upward: her armes, from her elbows to her hands were cov-
> ered with Bracelets; there were handfulls of Neck-laces about her neck, and
> severall sorts of Jewels in her Ears. She had fine red Stockins and white
> Shoos, her hair powdered and her face painted Red, that was alwayes before
> Black. And all the Dancers were after the same manner. There were two oth-
> ers singing and knocking on a Kettle for their musick. . . . They held on till it
> was almost night, throwing out *Wampom* to the standers-by. (103)

Rowlandson can not be expected to realize that this was a "give-away"
ceremony in which Wetamo, Quanopin, and others of chiefly status were
demonstrating their wealth (through displays of wampum and trade
goods), their generosity (through gifts of wampum), and their goodwill
and desire for peace (through wearing red face paint instead of black).[53]
But she hardly could have missed Wetamo's elevated status. Nor could
she have been unaware, at least by the time she wrote her narrative, that
her mistress was the very squaw sachem whom Increase Mather de-

scribed as "next unto Philip in respect of the mischief that hath been done." The narrative, however, completely fails to acknowledge We-tamo's status and authority, just as Rowlandson herself sometimes did while in captivity—refusing, for example, to follow an order to hand over a piece of her apron for a child's loincloth. Not acknowledging We-tamo's authority as either her mistress or her people's sachem, Rowland-son interprets all signs of Wetamo's elevated status as personal vanity, pride, and "insolence" (86). Ultimately, all were signs not of Wetamo's authority but of her subservience to that diabolical master, Satan.[54]

It is notable that foremost among Wetamo's sins in Rowlandson's eyes were her pride and vanity—two of the very sins for which Rowlandson chastises herself. Indeed, Rowlandson came to believe that the captivity experience was God's way of bringing her own pride and vanity to her attention. "The Lord hath showed me the vanity of these outward things," she wrote in closing the narrative, quoting from Ecclesiastes. "That they are the *Vanity of vanities, and vexation of spirit;* that they are but a shadow, a blast, a bubble, and things of no continuance" (112) Although Rowlandson does not acknowledge it explicitly, Wetamo served her cap-tive not only as God's scourge but as a spiritual object lesson—possible only because of the qualities Wetamo shared with her captor. Paradoxi-cally, it was through identifying with what she saw as her captor's faults that Rowlandson gained the self-knowledge and strength to further dif-ferentiate herself from her captor and from Satan—that is, to be spiritu-ally redeemed.

Contrasting sharply with Rowlandson's antipathy toward Wetamo was her gratefulness for the kindnesses of her master. Quanopin often protected Rowlandson from his wife's antagonism, and he reassured the captive that she would eventually be returned to her husband for a ran-som payment.[55] Rowlandson also remarks upon the kindness of Meta-com himself, and marvels at the respect the other men showed her, de-claring emphatically, "I have been in the midst of those roaring Lions, and Salvage Bears, that feared neither God, nor Man, nor the Devil, by night and day, alone and in company: sleeping all sorts together, and yet not one of them ever offered me the least abuse of unchastity to me, in word or action" (107). Instead of finding this an occasion to question the typification of these men as "roaring lions and savage bears," however, she seizes the opportunity to defend her own reputation and magnify God's power. "Though some are ready to say, I speak it for my own credit," she writes in response to rumors that her chastity had been vio-lated, "*I speak it in the presence of God, and to His glory*" (107).[56]

Rowlandson also notes with gratitude the many "common mercies" she experienced at the hands of "strangers," often involving the provi-sion of food, clothing, or shelter, sometimes but not always in exchange for a handmade shirt, shift, cap, or stockings. Early in her captivity she was given a Bible; she also notes several times when someone facilitated a visit with her children. But such benign interactions, like her captors' chastity, do not lead Rowlandson to cast doubt upon the assumption that she was in the hands of Satan's servants. Rather, they confirmed her belief in the "sovereignty and goodness of God." Although God had ample reason "to cut the thread of my life, and cast me out of his presence forever," she notes, "as he wounded me with one hand, so he healed me with the other" (74). If Wetamo was a scourge wielded by one hand, then Quanopin, Metacom, and others were instruments wielded by the other. Just as God utilized her captors' depravity in order to enable Rowlandson to recognize and examine her own failings, so God restrained it in order to insure the possibility of His chosen servant's redemption.

The vivid and differentiated details of Rowlandson's descriptions, however, supplement and potentially subvert the providential interpretation she offers.[57] Only in abstract generalizations, or when committing or celebrating acts of violence, do Rowlandson's captors resemble Increase Mather's diabolical Weetamoo and treacherous Philip. More often Rowlandson's captors appear quite human in scale, understandable in terms of the same qualities she would (and did) apply to herself and other Puritans: mercy, kindness, and restraint as well as pride, insolence, and deviousness. Even though Rowlandson interprets these qualities in the self-serving terms of providential hermeneutics, the concrete "particularizing" of these virtues and vices is a movement in the direction of humanizing her captors. The contrast she draws between being "hemmed in with the merciless and cruel Heathen" during captivity and "with pitiful, tender-hearted and compassionate Christians" upon her return is subverted not only by the implication that Rowlandson felt equally confined by the Christians but also by the examples she herself provides of tender and compassionate actions on the part of her captors (108).

To "particularize" and interpret experience is the imperative of the spiritual autobiography. Apart from certain passages near the close of the narrative that enumerate the offenses of praying Indians (98–100), or as in a jeremiad, censure her society's shortcomings (104–107), Rowlandson's narrative focuses upon the condition of her own body and soul under adversity.[58] Her interpretations are closely intertwined with the course of the events she relates, and her references to Biblical precedents or "types"—Babylon, Job, Daniel, and Rebecca, among others—are in the context of her need for comfort or insight at particular times. Although Scripture was essential in sustaining her, in true nonconformist fashion the narrative presents experience as the sine qua non of knowledge. "Mine eyes have seen it" (69, 111) is the leitmotif of the narrative, which stresses how much one takes for granted—about oneself, others, the material world, and God—until one is utterly removed from everyday experience.

In reflecting upon her captivity Mary Rowlandson emphasizes the transformative nature of what she experienced as isolation, nakedness, and vulnerability—all classic characteristics of what Victor Turner (1967) has called the liminal stage of a pilgrimage or rite of passage. Having partaken of the "wine of astonishment," Rowlandson resembled neither her past self nor those surrounding her upon her return. "When others are sleeping mine eyes are weeping," she reports, her mind full of "the thoughts of these things in the particulars of them" (Rowlandson 1997:111, 112). Telling her tale serves an act of reincorporation, an attempt to fit her transformed self and the "particulars" of her experience into the redemptive structure her society offered.[59] Granted, the particulars do not all fit readily into a providential hermeneutics, leading to the "double-voicedness" and uncanny "excess" that have perhaps been as central to the narrative's enduring appeal as its strong interpretive frame. But it was those particulars that could be publicly narrated that would be most influential upon the subsequent development of "Indian captivity" as a selective tradition.

## Captivity, Servitude, and Authority

The creative blend of experience and interpretation found in Mary Rowlandson's narrative makes it an exceptional captivity narrative, just as Mary Rowlandson, a minister's wife, was an exceptional captive.[60] In contrast to Rowlandson's first-person interpretation of captivity, the narratives of other New England captives published over the next several decades were written or "improved" by prominent clergymen, including Increase Mather, Cotton Mather, and John Williams, a frontier minister related by marriage to the Mathers who was himself taken captive in 1704. In "improving" the narratives of captives, just as in "improving" land, Puritans sought to make a "profitable" use of the resources at their disposal.[61] As Chapter 5 argues, clerical "improvements" tended to subordinate the particulars of experience to totalizing interpretation, presenting captivity less as a personal spiritual trial than as a divine rebuke to an unregenerate society. With the instructive exception of two Quaker narratives published in Philadelphia—those of Jonathan Dickinson and Elizabeth Hanson—the accounts of captivity published for half a century after Rowlandson's appear less as spiritual autobiographies than as jeremiads—a form that explicitly reinforced clerical authority.

Even Rowlandson's narrative—internally free of overt clerical "improvements"—is framed by clerical interpretations. Preceded by a "Preface to the Reader" signed "Per Amicum" (Latin, meaning "by a friend"), the narrative is followed in early editions by an outline of the last sermon Mary's husband Joseph Rowlandson preached before his death.[62] The preface, written in a baroque style that contrasts strongly with Rowlandson's "plain style," was most likely written by Increase Mather, who helped Joseph Rowlandson obtain Mary's ransom and whose church provided a home for the family after Mary's release. Mather's *Brief History of the War with the Indians in New-England* (1676) speaks of the attack on Lancaster in a similar fashion to that found in the preface to Rowlandson's narrative, and his *Essay for the Recording of Illustrious Providences* (1684) contains the next published narrative of a captive, Quentin Stockwell. Given his interest in captivity and his connections to the Rowlandsons, it is likely that Mather not only wrote the preface to Rowlandson's narrative but also facilitated its publication.[63]

For the thirty years since Anne Hutchinson's banishment for challenging clerical authority, women had been restrained from speaking in public. Only a handful of women had even been allowed to confess their faith (Mary Rowlandson's mother, Joan White, was among them), and a posthumously published volume of poetry by Anne Bradstreet was the only work by a woman that had appeared in print in New England.[64] Therefore the preface to Rowlandson's narrative had to offer a powerful justification, and it does so by introducing the author through her relationship to "that reverend servant of God, Mr. Joseph Rowlandson." In sharp contrast to the narrative itself, the preface presents the attack on Lancaster through the eyes of Mr. Rowlandson, who returned home after seeking aid for the defense of Lancaster only to find his own house consumed by fire and his "precious yokefellow, and dear children, wounded and captivated . . . by these cruel and barbarous savages." The catastrophe that befell the Rowlandson family is described as particularly "solemn and remarkable" because it occurred to "God's precious ones," who drank "as deep as others, of the cup of common calamity." Mary Rowlandson, "that worthy and precious Gentlewoman, the dear consort of the said Reverend Mr. Rowlandson," was the Lord's "precious servant, and hand maid," one of "his dear ones, that are as the apple of his eye, as the signet upon His hand, the delight of his eyes, and the object of his tenderest care." But her "affliction and deliverance" were all the more of public concern "by how much nearer this gentlewoman stood related to that faithful servant of God, whose capacity and employment was public in the house of God, and his name on that account of a very sweet savor in the churches of Christ" (Rowlandson 1997:64–66).

The preface, in short, defines the narrative's author exclusively by her relationship to her deceased husband (for she is never named) and justifies the publication—the making public—of her experiences by virtue of her marriage to a legitimate spokesman of Puritan society. Even so, Mary

Rowlandson's character needed protection, and the preface dwells on her modesty and piety, assuring the reader, as does the title page, that the narrative was written for "her private use, and now made public at the earnest desire of some friends, and for the benefit of the afflicted" (Rowlandson 1997:62). The narrative is commended not as a record of spiritual trial and redemption but rather for "particularizing" instances of divine providence in outward events. The preface summarizes the particular knowledge the narrative imparts:

> As none knows what it is to fight and pursue such an enemy as this, but they that have fought and pursued them: so none can imagine what it is to be captivated, and enslaved to such atheistical, proud, wild, cruel, barbarous, brutish (in one word) diabolical creatures as these, the worst of the heathen; nor what difficulties, hardships, hazards, sorrows, anxieties, and perplexities do unavoidably wait upon such a condition, but those that have tried it. (67)

Rowlandson's narrative is here reduced to an example of sufferings among a generalized diabolical enemy. The "particularizing" nature of Rowlandson's interpretive strategy—her imaginative correlation of her inner and outward "removes"—as well as Rowlandson's "particularizing" descriptions of individual captors recede from view.

As it went public, then, the narrative's significance flowed outward—an intimation of the direction in which a selective tradition of captivity would develop. The clergy, preaching to an unregenerate, unredeemed society, would "improve" upon the experiences of captives in the form of the socially oriented jeremiad, not the more personally centered spiritual autobiography. As it happens, the sermon by Joseph Rowlandson that is affixed in outline form to Mary's narrative is itself a jeremiad, delivered in preparation for a public fast day in 1678. Discussing "The Possibility of God's Forsaking a people, That have been near and dear to him" (Rowlandson 1997:152–164), Joseph Rowlandson warned that divine abandonment, the most fearful of judgments, was indeed possible, even imminent, unless the colonists stopped forsaking God. To illustrate his point Rowlandson made use of a common Puritan trope: the proper relationship of a wife to her husband exemplifies the Saint's relationship to God.[65] Like the faithful wife, who retains good and respectful thoughts toward her husband, even in his absence, the Saint remains faithful to God even when seemingly forsaken. The sinner who forsakes God in this situation is like an adulteress; the sinner who, in response, is utterly forsaken by God is like a widow.

Although we cannot know for certain how Joseph Rowlandson developed his sermon, when this text is juxtaposed to the captivity narrative,

Mary Rowlandson emerges as doubly faithful in her captivity: to her husband in his absence, and to God, who seemingly had forsaken her. Interestingly enough, the juxtaposition of narrative and sermon does not present Mary Rowlandson as faithful to her children as well as to her husband and God. Rowlandson's solicitude for her children, especially the wounded Sarah, has no place in the trope of the faithful wife.

As Chapter 5 reveals, these correspondences between the faithful wife, the faithful Saint, and the faithful captive would be developed by Cotton Mather in an influential typification of captivity. Unlike Mary Rowlandson, who was able to maintain and strengthen her faith when removed from the influence of her husband and the clergy, Mather's female captives would personify spiritual vulnerability and faithlessness. This representation of the captive would be developed further in the narrative of John Williams, whose own daughter Eunice came to personify the captive's—and New England's—vulnerability to the double seductions of savagery and Catholicism. In asserting increased control over the interpretation of captivity, Cotton Mather and John Williams would treat what Rowlandson called the "captive-condition" or "wilderness-condition" as a metaphor of collective vulnerability and degeneration. In doing so, they would once again abstract captivity from its political context of colonial conquest and resistance—and also, increasingly, from the particularity, complexity, and ambiguity of the captive's experience. "Improving" upon the experience of captives in an attempt to reinforce clerical and patriarchal authority, Mather and Williams would produce increasingly polarized representations of the relationship between Captive Self and Captivating Other.

### Notes

1. My attention to the poetics and politics of each of these processes is indebted to remarks by Jean Comaroff and Kathleen Stewart, and evokes the work of Clifford and Marcus (1986), Karp and Lavine (1991), and Stallybrass and White (1986). The distinction I draw between the poetics of reciprocity and that of incorporation is somewhat similar to Sayre's distinction between an "economy of exchange" and an "economy of vengeance" (1997:248–304). The latter category, however, is narrower than my "poetics of incorporation."

2. My discussion of Algonquian captivity practices and beliefs remains speculative, as they are less well documented than those of Iroquoians; but see Axtell 1981; Axtell and Sturtevant 1980; Bragdon 1996; Haefeli and Sweeney 1995; Richter 1983; and Salisbury 1982a, 1987, and 1997. My treatment of the convergence of Algonquian and Iroquoian practices builds on the work of Trigger (1978) and of Vaughan and Richter (1980) and utilizes the distributional studies of Flannery (1939), Knowles (1940), and M. Smith (1951).

3. Roger Williams (1973 [1643]) noted "obscure and meane" persons without kinship ties among the Narragansetts, and there are other examples of captives

who are treated more as subordinated outsiders than as kin (Bragdon 1996:47, 169; see also Haefeli and Sweeney 1995:16; and Prins 1996:111). This subordinate status is poorly understood, but translating it into the Western concepts of "servant" and, especially, "slave" is misleading, for reasons discussed in Cheyfitz 1997 and Strong n.d.a.

4. Sources on wampum include Bragdon 1996, Ceci 1986, McBride 1994, Salisbury 1982a, and Speck 1919; and especially Hamell 1983 and 1987, and Miller and Hamell 1986.

5. On Algonquian soul concepts, see Bragdon 1996, Fogelson 1985, Hultkrantz 1953, and Simmons 1970. For scalping and beheading, see also Axtell 1981:16–35, 207–41; Axtell and Sturtevant 1980; Flannery 1939; and Friederici 1985 [1907].

6. Fogelson (1980), Morrison (1979, 1984), and Simmons (1986) discuss Algonquian monsters. Human-eating monsters also appear in Iroquoian mythology; these include Hiawatha, who was reformed and turned toward peace when he saw the face of Deganawidah reflected in a pot of water (Arens 1979, Wallace 1969).

7. My summary of Iroquoian patterns of warfare, captivity, and condolence privileges the Five Nations and is based on Abler 1980 and 1992; Abler and Logan 1988; Axtell 1975 and 1981; Beauchamp 1975 [1907]; Fenton 1971, 1978, and 1985; Goddard 1984; Jennings 1984 and 1988; Richter 1983 and 1992; Richter and Merrell 1987; Shoemaker 1995b; Snyderman 1948; Starna 1991; Tooker 1978; and Wallace 1969. Among Hurons, according to Trigger (1969, 1976), captured women and children were generally tortured and killed immediately; headmen were more important in decisionmaking and torture rituals; and captives were given a farewell feast to fulfill their desires before death. Cherokees practiced both the adoption and the torture of war captives, but not human sacrifice (Hudson 1976, Perdue 1979).

8. Although clan affiliation was matrilineal among the Iroquois, relations to one's father's clan were especially significant in mourning rituals, which entailed relations of reciprocity between clans related by marriage (Fenton 1978, Richter and Merrell 1987).

9. For vivid examples and a pathbreaking analysis of the socialization of captives, see Axtell 1981:168–206.

10. The ritual emphasis upon bringing captives into the "clearing"—the camp or village—and burning (or "cooking") them with fire or boiling water may mark torture as a female domain in contrast to the male domain of hunting and warfare in the forest (see Fogelson 1971, 1977, and 1980). Trigger (1969, 1976) suggests that colonial accounts overemphasize the role of women in torture because it so horrified Europeans.

11. Hultkrantz (1953) argues that ritual cannibalism did not involve a conception of psychophagy (soul-eating), but see Fogelson 1985. Abler (1980) and Sahlins (1983) defend the reality of ritual cannibalism against Arens (1979) and other skeptics; see also Jaenen 1976; Axtell 1981:168–206; and Shoemaker 1995b. Sources on bear symbolism include Fenton 1978, Goddard 1984, Hallowell 1926, and Speck 1945.

12. The classic semiotic discussion of metaphor and metonymy is that by Jakobson (1960). The Iroquoian distinction between "breath" and "flesh" souls

may parallel the Algonquian distinction between "dream" and "clear" souls, also located in the head and heart, respectively (Bragdon 1996, Simmons 1970). It is possible that the matrilineal nature of the flesh soul was one motivation for the participation of women in torture rituals (Fogelson 1977, 1985, 1990; Hultkrantz 1953). Other souls resided in the liver and bone (two in the bone, according to Trigger 1969), but it is unclear whether these souls figured in captivity practices.

13. Wallace (1969) offers an interpretation of incorporation similar to mine, whereas Abler (1980) attributes this interpretation's appeal to its resonance with Christian beliefs regarding the Eucharist. But see Shoemaker's (1995b) discussion of how Jesuits and Iroquois converts may have conceptualized the parallel between ritual torture and cannibalism, on the one hand, and the Eucharist, on the other.

14. Following Richter (1983), I stress transformations following the European invasion; for prehistoric transformations in the intensity of warfare and of ritual cannibalism, see Abler and Logan 1988, and Trigger 1976.

15. Axtell (1981:16–35, 207–241) documents the indigenous provenance and colonial adoption of scalping; Prins (1996:119–120) summarizes the Abenaki adoption of Iroquoian practices of warfare and diplomacy. For a further discussion of slavery and servitude in Native North America, see Strong n.d.a.

16. Haefeli and Sweeney (1995) extend the definition of *middle ground* to include warfare and captivity practices in New England; see also Salisbury 1997.

17. I refer to the conflict as Metacom's War because in resisting English rule the Pokanoket sachem was repudiating his identity as "King Philip"—an identity the English used to execute him for treason. For another view, see Lepore 1998.

18. Williams's use of the term "wild Irish" is an interesting example of the English conflation of Irish and Indian "savagery." See Canny 1973, Jennings 1975, and Muldoon 1975.

19. Although a few Algonquians were enslaved in the seventeenth century for theft, the Pequot War marked New England's first entry into extensive Indian slavery. The extent of Indian slavery is difficult to document: S. F. Cook (1973a) suggests that as many as fifteen hundred Pequots were integrated into other tribes, but no more than four hundred appear in colonial records. See also Brasser 1971:74; Jennings 1975:223–226; Lauber 1970 [1913]:1–31; Salisbury 1982a:222; Vaughan 1979:148, 341; and Washburn 1978:90, 92.

20. Typifications to the contrary, there are no eyewitness accounts of sexual assault on female captives in this period. Indeed, sexual relations of any kind were forbidden from the time warriors left their villages until their return. Normal sexual activities were resumed only after rituals of purification. Beyond this, sexual assault was considered a heinous offense under any circumstances (Calloway 1992). Sources on the Wethersfield captives include Jennings (1975:202–227), Seelye (1977:206–211), and Kibbey (1986:92–120); Kibbey explores the relationship between Puritan prejudices against women and those against Indians. The figure of *Judæa capta* is discussed in Chapter 5; also see Kolodny 1984:12–28.

21. On mortality figures see Salisbury 1997:1; Vaughan 1979:320; and Washburn 1978:90. Vaughan and Richter (1980:49, 91) have provided a list and statistical analysis of colonial captives taken by Algonquians during the war. See

O'Brien 1997 and Salisbury 1997 for relations between Algonquians and English colonists before and after the war.

22. For Puritan histories of the war, see Lepore 1998, Salisbury 1997, Slotkin 1973, and Slotkin and Folsom 1978. On spiritual autobiographies as a genre, see Caldwell 1983, Ebersole 1995, Hambrick-Stowe 1982, Shea 1968, and Watkins 1972.

23. See the Appendix for the publication history and popularity of Rowlandson's narrative; also see Derounian 1988, Diebold 1972, Mott 1947, Salisbury 1997, and Vail 1949. Rowlandson 1977 [1682] is a facsimile of the fourth (London) edition. Of the available annotated editions, Salisbury's (1997) edition of the second, Cambridge edition (the earliest extant version) is the most completely annotated. Other useful modern editions include the two edited by Diebold (Diebold 1972, Rowlandson 1975) as well as the volumes edited by Lang (Rowlandson 1990); Slotkin and Folsom (Rowlandson 1978); and Vaughan and Clark (Rowlandson 1981).

24. There is now a rich and varied body of criticism on Rowlandson's narrative, offering discursive, phenomenological, feminist, postcolonial, and ethnohistorical perspectives in addition to the traditional, typological interpretations of intellectual history. Nevertheless, most scholars in the fields of literary criticism and the history of religion continue to view Rowlandson's narrative chiefly in its Puritan context. Salisbury's treatment (1997) is exemplary in its balanced and nuanced presentation of the complex cultural borderland in which Rowlandson's captivity was situated.

25. See Salisbury 1997 for Lancaster's relations with local Nipmucs as well as the Nipmuc role in the war.

26. All five of the Eastern Algonquian languages spoken in southern New England are extinct (Salwen 1978, Goddard 1978), and the spellings of Algonquian names are inconsistent in the literature. I have generally chosen the simplest or most common variants. Similarly inconsistent are the genealogies of leaders, due to English confusion regarding Algonquian social structure and naming practices as well as to difficulties in translation. For the Narragansetts I follow Chapin 1931, Simmons 1978, and Simmons and Aubin 1975. The latter provides an elegant discussion of Narragansett kinship, in which tribal affiliation and political authority appear to have been inherited patrilineally, whereas membership in an exogamous descent group was inherited matrilineally. See also Bragdon's more general account (1996:140–168).

27. There is little evidence that Rowlandson's captors intended to adopt her, although she was taunted ("What, will you love English men still?") in response to her plea to spend the first night of her captivity in a deserted farmhouse nearby rather than in her captors' camp (Rowlandson 1997:71).

28. *Weetamoo*, favored by Increase Mather, has become the most common form, but like many English renderings of Indian personal and place-names, it has a somewhat demeaning effect. Rowlandson's spelling is closer to other, earlier variants: William Hubbard's *Wetamore*, Benjamin Church's *Weetamore*, Josiah Winslow and Thomas Hinkley's *Weetamoe*, and *Wetamo*, found in a deed of 1673 (Church 1865 [1716]:41; Pulsifer and Shurtleff 1855–61, 12:242; Drake 1832:346). I have used the latter for its simplicity, its dignity, and its approximation to my best

guess, following Goddard and Bragdon (1988), as to a phonemic transcription: *wetômá* ('e' pronounced as in *he*, 'á' as in *father*, and 'ô' the same as 'á' but nasalized). Speck (1928:67) offers the translation "lodge keeper," which seems consistent with the forms *wetomomun* (we dwell with forever) and *weetomau* (she dwelt with), found in John Eliot's Bible (Goddard and Bragdon 1988:738).

29. Grumet (1980) called attention to Algonquian "sunksquaws"—the latter word being an Anglicization of the Narragansett plural noun *sauncksquûaog* (queens; sg. *saunks*). I have used the alternative Anglicization *squaw sachem* because Wetamo was known to English colonists as the "squaw sachem of Pocasset." Juxtaposing *squaw* to *sachem* helps to destabilize the derogatory connotation that has become attached to *squaw*, which is an Anglicization of the word for "woman" in many Algonquian languages (Green 1975, Shoemaker 1995a). See also Bragdon (1996), who translates the Algonquian forms as "queen sachems," "sachem women," and "women sachems," with the first two phrases also referring to sachems' wives.

30. If the report that Wetamo's forces numbered three hundred is accurate, this is quite a significant number in view of the estimated twenty-nine hundred Algonquians allied with Metacom, five hundred of whom were Wampanoag (Cook 1973a). It is interesting that war hero Benjamin Church greatly downplays Wetamo's significance, perhaps because his stature as a war hero was not enhanced by having a female antagonist. Another squaw sachem, Awashonks, was his friend and ally (Church 1978 [1716], Plane 1996).

31. The classical names *Alexander* and *Philip* were assigned by the English at Wamsutta's request upon the death of their father. For English-Algonquian relations before and during Metacom's War, see Jennings 1975, Leach 1958, Salisbury 1982a and 1997, Vaughan 1979, Washburn 1978, and Slotkin and Folsom 1978. The latter contains reprints of and extensive comments on contemporary accounts of the war, including those by Rowlandson, Increase Mather, and Benjamin Church.

32. Salisbury has reprinted a colonial document in which Metacom's grievances are expressed (1997:115–118). For Sassamon, see Anderson 1994, Drake 1995, Jennings 1975, and Lepore 1994.

33. Wetamo's rights to land, independent of her marriage to Alexander, are demonstrated by various deeds through which Alexander sold land he had acquired from her, as well as by complaints by Wetamo (known earlier as Tatapanum or Namumpum) that Alexander had alienated her lands without permission (Drake 1880:187; Rhode Island Historical Society 1970:188–189; Pulsifer and Shurtleff 1855–61, 4:8, 17, 186).

34. Regarding Corbitant and his relationship to Wetamo, see Bradford 1953:88–89; Drake 1834:27–30; Heath 1963 [1622]:73–76; Salisbury 1982a:119–124; Speck 1928:69; and Vaughan 1979:75–76. Wetamo was married to Petananuet by at least June 27, 1673, when they were listed as husband and wife on a land document (Pulsifer and Shurtleff 1855–61, 12:242).

35. On the spiritual significance of swamps, see Bragdon 1996 and Hamell 1987. Wetamo and Quanopin were married before the Great Swamp Fight of December 21, 1675, judging from the garbled account of N[athaniel] S[altonstall] (Lincoln 1966 [1913]:53, 55).

36. See the Council of Connecticut's letter of August 8, 1675 (Connecticut Historical Society 1932:18). Regarding the bounty, see Axtell 1981:223 and Leach 1958:61.

37. The number of enslaved Indians is difficult to ascertain, but see Lauber 1970 [1913]:253–604.

38. Providence, allied to the Narragansetts and excluded from the United Colonies, sharply criticized the attack. The figure of three hundred Indian casualties at the Great Swamp Fight is Cook's conservative estimate (1973a:15–17). On the justification for the attack, and the Narragansett belief that the agreements of July 15 and October 18 were not binding, see Drake 1834, 3:41; Jennings 1975:298–312; Leach 1958:56–77, 112–119; Rhode Island Historical Society 1835:169; and Simmons 1978.

39. For the involvement of Shoshanim and other Nipmucs in Metacom's War, see Salisbury 1997. For Christian Indians, see Axtell 1981 and 1985b, O'Brien 1997, Pulsipher 1996, Salisbury 1974 and 1997, and Simmons 1979, all of which provide references to earlier works. Connecticut utilized Christian Indian allies throughout the war; but Massachusetts abandoned the practice at an early date, due to public opposition. Capt. Samuel Moseley, the officer who took the Nashobah Indians to Deer Island, is also notorious for having ordered that an Indian woman who was captured near Hatfield be torn to pieces by dogs. See Diebold 1972:65–67, 75, 83–87, 94–95; Drake 1997; Gookin 1972 [1836]:450, 472–474, 488–491, 495–497, 507–508; Johnson 1977; Leach 1958:150–152, 179–180; Leach 1961:352–363; Vaughan 1979:318–319; and Vaughan and Clark 1981:61.

40. Biographical sources on Rowlandson include Greene 1985, Leach 1961, and Salisbury 1997.

41. On Cotton Mather, see Silverman's biography (1984:20). Jennings (1975:146–170) compares public brutality among Indians and Europeans; see also Axtell 1981:16–35, 207–41; and Axtell and Sturtevant 1980. My interpretation of Mather's poetics of dismemberment is influenced by Foucault's discussions (1973, 1979) of the premodern episteme and of drawing and quartering as a public spectacle.

42. Cook's estimate of one thousand Algonquians sold into foreign slavery is conservative. Cook includes in this number about four hundred who surrendered near the end of the war expecting lenient treatment (1973a:11–22). Rhode Island allowed the indenture but not the enslavement of war refugees. On Indian slavery and indenture after Metacom's War, see Drake 1997; Kawashima 1969; Koehler 1979; Lauber 1970 [1913]:125–130, 138–152; Leach 1958:224–228; O'Brien 1997; Diebold 1972:80–81, 89; Sainsbury 1975:378–393; and Salisbury 1997. The latter includes valuable primary documents.

43. Regarding James Printer, see Lepore 1998 and Salisbury 1997. For the survival and contemporary resurgence of those Algonquians who remained in enclaves or returned to New England, see Baron, Hood, and Izard 1996; Calloway 1997; Lepore 1998; O'Brien 1997; Weinstein 1986 and 1994; and Weinstein-Farson 1989.

44. In 1686, Plymouth allotted a tract of 120 acres to Petananuet and other Pocassets at Freetown. In 1707 this land was supplemented by other lands belonging to Benjamin Church. By 1907, all these lands were individually owned,

and the Pocassets had dispersed. See Church 1975:38; Conkey, Boissevain, and Goddard 1978; Drake 1834, 3:3; Pulsifer and Shurtleff 1855–61, 5:210, 215; Slotkin 1973:157–179; and Speck 1928:80–81.

45. Providential hermeneutics is discussed by Bercovitch (1972, 1978), Ebersole (1995), Kibbey (1986), Lowance (1980), Miller (1953), Murdock (1942, 1949, 1955), Orians (1970), Slotkin (1973), Slotkin and Folsom (1978), Stout (1986), and Vaughan and Clark (1981). In contrast to earlier scholars' focus on typology, contemporary critics stress the uncanny "excess" in Rowlandson's experience. See Burnham 1997, Castiglia 1996, Derounian 1987, Fitzpatrick 1991, and Toulouse 1992b.

46. So compelling is Rowlandson's opening that many commentaries (e.g., Kolodny 1993 and Lang 1990) begin by echoing her words—an interpretive move that might unintentionally reinforce the ideological effect of the narrative.

47. For Babylon, see Kolodny 1984:19–22, more generally a pathbreaking account of Rowlandson's (and other captives') relationship to the landscape. For the Puritan interpretation of affliction, see Fitzpatrick 1991; for Rowlandson's redemptive journey, see Stanford 1976; and for her use of the Bible, especially the Psalms, see Downing 1980–81, Ebersole 1995, Henwood 1997, and Minter 1973.

48. On Rowlandson's mourning, see Breitwieser 1990 and Derounian 1987; on extremity as an existential condition, see Ebersole 1995. These perceptive discussions of mourning and extremity would be enhanced by attention, as well, to the sufferings of Rowlandson's captors (see Strong 1992c).

49. Simmons (1986:51–52) and Bragdon (1996) have reprinted and commented on Rowlandson's description of the divination ceremony; see also Simmons 1976.

50. Many critics, including Breitwieser (1990), Derounian (1987), Henwood (1997), Namias (1993), and Ulrich (1982), interpret Rowlandson as first and foremost a survivor.

51. Salisbury (1997) interprets Rowlandson's animosity toward praying Indians as an intervention—remarkable for a woman—in post–Revolutionary War debates over the treatment of the Algonquians remaining in New England.

52. On the captive's experience of captors as unpredictable, unreadable, or mendacious, see Sewell 1993 and Toulouse 1992b.

53. Give-away ceremonies are found throughout North America, most famously in the potlatch of the Northwest Coast, but also in contemporary pow-wows. For Algonquian ritual symbolism see Bragdon 1996:222–229 and Simmons 1986:45–46.

54. Toulouse (1992b) and Davis (1992) discuss the challenge posed by Wetamo—more than by her male counterparts—to Rowlandson's sense of appropriate servitude.

55. The disparity between the treatment Rowlandson received from Wetamo, on the one hand, and Quanopin, on the other, is striking. An intriguing possibility is that Wetamo's hostility toward Mary Rowlandson, so distinct from Quanopin's and Metacom's protectiveness, involved the rights of a female lineage head over the fate of captives. When Mary Rowlandson was held captive, Metacom, Quanopin, and Wetamo were all displaced sachems, struggling desperately to rid their homeland of the English intruders or at least to push back the borders of English settlement. All had lost relatives, and all had themselves been

"removed" from their towns, to use Mary Rowlandson's language. Under these conditions, it appears that Wetamo, on the one hand, and Quanopin and Metacom, on the other, may have been taking alternative, gender-coded stances toward their captive: Wetamo, seeking revenge through physical and verbal abuse; Quanopin and Metacom, remaining more interested in Rowlandson's political and economic value. Tempting as this interpretation is, however, it is probably at least as significant that Wetamo and her people had long opposed the English, whereas Quanopin was of the once-neutral Narragansetts, who had experienced a satisfying relationship with Roger Williams's Providence.

56. See Toulouse 1992b for a discussion of this passage, and Diebold 1972 and Salisbury 1997:43 for the rumors Rowlandson faced at her return.

57. Many contemporary critics stress the ambiguous or double-voiced nature of Rowlandson's narrative, but interpretations differ. Somewhat like Ebersole (1995), Henwood (1997), and Toulouse (1992a, 1992b), and influenced by Stewart (1996), I find ambiguity—what Chambers (1991) calls "room for maneuver"— within Puritan hermeneutics. Another kind of doubleness is discussed below: the tension between Rowlandson's narrative and its clerical framing. On this see Breitwieser 1990, Castiglia 1996, Fitzpatrick 1991, Logan 1993, and Smith-Rosenberg 1993.

58. Immediately prior to recounting her ransom and homecoming, Rowlandson lists, as in the numbered "reasons" of a Puritan sermon, examples of "the wonderful providence of God in preserving the Heathen for further affliction to our poor country," an affliction provoked by "our perverse and evil carriages in the sight of the Lord." Also like a sermon, the narrative closes with a summarizing lesson or "use" that encapsulates the general moral meaning of her sufferings: "The Lord hath showed me the vanity of these outward things ... [and] that we must rely on God himself and our whole dependence must be upon Him" (Rowlandson 1997:75).

59. Sewell (1993), building upon Asad (1986) and Pratt (1986), compares Rowlandson's narrative to an ethnography that achieves mastery through translation. Somewhat similarly, Logan (1993) argues that the narrative was aimed at restoring Rowlandson's precaptivity status in Puritan society.

60. *The Sovereignty and Goodness of God* has until recently been considered archetypal; see Pearce 1947 and 1965, and Slotkin 1973.

61. The *Oxford English Dictionary* defines this archaic sense of "improvement" as the "profitable spiritual application of a text or incident" (1971, 1:1393).

62. Salisbury (1997) conveniently reprints the preface and sermon; but to get a full sense of the framing effect of the preface and sermon, one must turn to the fourth edition, available in facsimile (Rowlandson 1977).

63. The publisher of the first edition of Rowlandson's narrative, Samuel Green, Jr., was a protégé of Increase Mather, and later, of Cotton Mather; the second and third editions were printed by Green's father, Samuel Green, Sr. Two years later, the junior Green published Increase Mather's *Essay for the Recording of Illustrious Providences* (Hall 1988:136, 173).

64. For Joan White, see Dunn 1980 and Salisbury 1997. For limitations imposed on Puritan women's self-expression or "authorship," see Koehler 1980, Logan 1993, and Smith-Rosenberg 1993.

65. Congruences between Puritan imagery of the ideal woman and the regenerate sinner are discussed in Dunn 1980, Kolodny 1984, Masson 1976, Moran 1980, Porterfield 1992, and Ulrich 1980 and 1982. Regarding Puritan patriarchy more generally, see E. M. Cook 1976, Demos 1970, Kibbey 1986, Koehler 1980, Morgan 1966, and Norton 1996.

# 5

## Seduction, Redemption, and the Typification of Captivity, 1675–1707

During the first month of Metacom's War the magistrates of Massachu-setts Bay, as was their custom in times of crisis, proclaimed a day of pub-lic humility, fasting, and prayer. The magistrates' proclamation inter-preted the hostilities as a sign of God's displeasure with a number of collective failings. Among these were complacency, vanity, and pride—the very faults that Mary Rowlandson would subsequently discover in herself. According to the magistrates, the English colonists were being punished, first, for their "great unthankfullness for, and manifold abuses of our wonderfull peace, and the blessings of it in this good land which the Lord hath given us," and second, for their "inordinate affection [for], and sinful conformity to this present evil vain world." Lastly, God was punishing them for "abiding very much unreformed, notwithstanding all warnings, and chastisements." These sins had provoked God "to stir up many adversaries against us, not only abroad, but also at our own door (causing the heathen in this wilderness to be as thorns in our sides, who have formerly been, and might still be a wall unto us therein; and others also to become a scourge unto us)" (Mather 1978 [1676]:102–103).

Increase Mather, whose influence on the magistrates' pronouncement is evident, included the text in his Brief History of the War with the Indians in New-England, a volume concerned with documenting in detail the events and providential significance of Metacom's War.[1] In the course of his history Mather occasionally refers to captivity, suggesting that it was those most prone to captivity—the frontier settlers—who best exempli-fied the prevalent sins of complacency, pride, and worldliness. After all, they were living among heathen and often like heathen, far from the "in-stituted ordinances" of church and town. Mather singled out for com-mentary the sufferings of the Wakely family of Casco Bay, Maine (see Map 4.1). Though "esteemed a godly man," old John Wakely "would

sometimes say with tears, that he believed God was angry with him, because although he came into New England for the Gospel's sake, yet he
had left another place in this country, where there was a church of Christ,
which he once was in communion with, and had lived many years in a
plantation where was no church, nor instituted worship" (99). Wakely's
death and the captivity of his family, suggests Mather, was punishment
for seeking a life outside the bounds of clerical authority.

Mather's other extended comment on captivity in his Brief History concerns the providential escape of an unnamed "Captive Negro," who revealed to the English Metacom's plan to launch an attack against the town
of Taunton. "There was a special providence in that Negro's escape,"
Mather observes, "for he, having lived many years near to the Indians, understood their language, and having heard them tell one another what
their designs were, he acquainted the English therewith" (Mather 1978
[1676]:132). The pragmatic value of acculturation was more easily acknowledged in the case of the "Captive Negro" than in the case of an English captive, for whom "Indianization" was the supreme threat. Not until
1736, with the publication of John Gyles's captivity narrative, would the
experience of an acculturated captive be more fully explored in print.

Increase Mather subsequently indicated a special interest in the providential meaning of captivity both in his support for the publication of
Mary Rowlandson's narrative, and two years later, in his inclusion of
"The Relation of a Captive" in his Essay for the Recording of Illustrious
Providences (1684).[2] Mather had asked other clergymen to send him any
accounts of providential occurrences that came to their attention, and he
included Quentin (or Quintin) Stockwell's first-person narrative among
accounts of storms, shipwrecks, apparitions, and acts of witchcraft. In
contrast to his treatment of Rowlandson's narrative, Mather offered
Stockwell's account with only minimal exegesis. This underscores the extent to which Mather's framing of Rowlandson's narrative was predi-
cated upon her gender; for Stockwell's secular account of captivity
would otherwise seem to demand considerably more clerical "improvement" than that of the pastor's wife.

Quentin Stockwell was among the first of many captives taken from
Deerfield, then the northernmost English settlement in the Connecticut
Valley. Originally called Pocumtuck, the English settlement was established in 1670 on the site of an Algonquian village with the same name,
which had been destroyed by Mohawks six years previously. The English
were forced to abandon Pocumtuck during Metacom's War, after which
Algonquians returned to farm the fertile clearing, which was also prized
as an interethnic meeting place. By September 1677, however, a party of
English men and boys, including Stockwell, were attempting to reclaim
and rebuild the English town, which they christened Deerfield. The En-

glish were captured by a party of Pocumtucks and their former southerly neighbors, the Norwottucks. The war party tortured and killed the English settlers' leader, Sergeant John Plympton, and together with a group of Wachusetts, marched Stockwell and about forty other captives from Deerfield and nearby Hatfield to the village near Sorel, Canada, where they had taken refuge. A starving and frostbitten Stockwell was exchanged to a Frenchman for fourteen beaver and eventually was redeemed along with the other captives from Deerfield and Hatfield (except for the three who had been killed). A ransom payment of nearly three hundred pounds was raised and brought to Canada by Benjamin Waite and Stephen Jennings, whose families were among the captives. Each of these two men had a child among the ransomed that had been born in captivity, aptly named Canada Waite and Captivity Jennings.[3]

Stockwell's account of what Mather called his "Captivity and Redemption" begins, like Rowlandson's narrative, with a seemingly unprovoked attack: "In the year 1677, September 19, between sunset and dark, the Indians came upon us" (I. Mather 1981 [1684]:80). Also like Rowlandson, Stockwell portrays his captors as individuals, distinguishing between the kind and judicious Ashpelon, the chief, and his own main master (one of three), whom he described as "the very worst of all the company" (81). But Stockwell does not play upon the spiritual significance of "captivity" and "redemption," quote Biblical passages, examine himself for shortcomings, or explicitly attribute to Providence his deliverance from torture, hunger, exhaustion, and frostbite. Rather, he gives considerable attention to human virtues: his own ingenuity and diplomatic skills, the solidarity of his fellow captives, and the kindness and influence of certain Algonquians and French commoners. Stockwell demonstrates enough practical knowledge of his captors' ways to attach plausible motivations to their actions—whether they were binding the captives at night (until they were "out of our knowledge" of the land), making "strange noises as of wolves and owls" (as signals to each other), or threatening to "knock" him "on the head" (because he appeared unfit to travel) (81–82). A tale of physical survival rather than spiritual redemption, Stockwell's narrative receives a providential interpretation only by virtue of being juxtaposed to other "illustrious providences" in Mather's compilation. Although not entirely secular (Stockwell reports praying for game and giving thanks at meals, at his captors' request), the account is unique among seventeenth-century English captivity narratives, foreshadowing one turn this selective tradition would take after the influence of clerical hermeneutics had waned.[4]

Both Rowlandson's and Stockwell's narratives were published during the hiatus between Metacom's War and the explosion of intercolonial hostilities in 1689. The captivity narratives of the harrowing 1690s were subjected to a much more intrusive and extensive clerical "improvement" at the hands of Increase Mather's son, Cotton. The younger Mather, who succeeded his father as the dominant interpreter of captivity and of colonial warfare more generally, was not content with offering his providential interpretation through editorial framing devices. Instead, he heavily edited the captivity narratives he published, usually offering them as third-person accounts.

Of all interpreters of captivity, Cotton Mather most clearly attempted to establish a hegemonic typification. After considering the development of that typification in Cotton Mather's own writings, this chapter turns to the captivity narrative of his cousin's husband, John Williams, another clerical interpreter of captivity who was able to combine the captive's voice of experience with the minister's voice of authority.

## To Live Like Heathen: The Two Hannahs

In the years following Metacom's War, Puritan clergymen were inordinately concerned with what they perceived as their flock's increasing faithlessness and worldliness. Church membership in New England was declining, and the lands conquered in Metacom's War were enticing ever more settlers away from the authoritarian confines of the established towns. Compounding New England's troubles were two devastating fires in Boston and a smallpox epidemic. Meeting in 1679 under the leadership of Increase Mather to consider spiritual degeneracy, a Reforming Synod deplored the colonists' "insatiable desire after land, and worldly accommodations, yea as to forsake churches and ordinances, and to live like Heathen, only so that they might have elbow-room enough in the world" (Hambrick-Stowe 1982:256–265).[5]

The clergy feared that frontier settlers were succumbing to what missionary John Eliot called "wilderness temptations" (Nash 1982:102), willingly abandoning the lawful and godly order of Puritan settlements to embrace the individualistic anarchy presumably characteristic of heathen life. One significant manifestation of this anarchy was the lack of hierarchical relations taken to be natural and ordained by God: the subordination of women to their husbands, children to their parents, servants to their masters, and laity to the clergy. Such a subordination of the weak, wild, passionate, and spiritually vulnerable to their "natural" masters, who were considered stronger, more reasonable, and more godly, was central to the Puritan construction of domestic and civic order. Just such notions of the natural subordination of wife to husband were at the base of Joseph Rowlandson's sermon when he used the proper marital relationship as a model for the saints' submission to God. Similar notions of the natural vulnerability of women and children would be called into play in the hegemonic typification of captivity developed by Cotton Mather and John Williams. Whereas for Mary Rowlandson captivity constituted a wilderness trial, in the clerical typification captivity came to take on, more specifically, the character of a wilderness seduction.

The temptation of vacated, cleared farmland—what Jennings (1975) has aptly called "widowed land"—attracted an increasing number of English settlers to the western and northern frontiers in the decades following Metacom's War. The new, widely scattered English settlements in the Connecticut River Valley, New Hampshire, and Maine were vulnerable to intermittent attacks by Algonquians and Iroquoians from across the Canadian border—some of them refugees from southern New England, many of them converts to Catholicism and allied to France. Hostilities intensified from 1689 through 1697 (the first intercolonial war, or King William's War) and again from 1702 through 1713 (the second intercolonial war, or Queen Anne's War), when England and France were engaged in power struggles in Europe and related contests for colonial dominance in North America.[6] During these two early intercolonial wars, some six hundred captives were taken from English frontier settlements by parties of Canadian Indians led by French officers—what Cotton Mather called "half Indianized French and half Frenchified Indians" (1981 [1702]:136). Though some of these captives were adopted (mainly children) or tortured to death (mainly adult males), most were sold to French citizens as servants or ransomed to French officials. The French, like the English, offered a bounty for enemy scalps, European as well as Indian, but they paid more for captives, owing to their desire to increase the European population. A large number of captives remained in Canada and converted to Catholicism, although many were eventually returned to the English in negotiated settlements.[7]

In the context of their anxiety over the colonies' spiritual vulnerability, Puritan clergymen interpreted the intercolonial wars as battles against the seductiveness of heathenism and Catholicism alike, and they employed captivity to signify a redemptive experience less for individual captives than for the community as a whole. Captivities were seen at once as signs of God's displeasure with the English for their collective unfaithfulness and as God's means of evoking a renewed allegiance to the covenant. The notion that captivity was a punishment for collective degeneration or "backsliding" rather than a personal spiritual trial was articulated most forcefully in the captivity narratives Cotton Mather published in the course of more than two decades.

Mather succeeded his father as the most prominent divine of his generation.[8] A prolific and exuberant writer, Mather defined in authoritative, compelling terms the meaning of the dreaded experience he called "Indian captivity" (143)—an odd and curiously long-lived phrase that constructs a parallel between the New World captivities and Israel's "Baby-lonian captivity." For Mather, as for John Underhill a half century earlier, Judæa capta (captive Israel) provided the Biblical "type" through which the significance of captivity among Indians, the "antitype," could be un-derstood.[9] In numerous sermons and histories published between 1692 and 1714, Cotton Mather related and "improved upon" the sufferings of those who were submitted to this, "the worst captivity in the world" (138). Many of Mather's captivities were incorporated in 1702 into his magnum opus, Magnalia Christi Americana, a massive chronicle of "the wondrous works of Christ in America."[10]

Cotton Mather's works on captivity include a number of brief, grue-some accounts of infanticide and torture—decontextualized, sensational-ized anecdotes that presaged the anthologies of atrocities published in the late eighteenth and nineteenth centuries.[11] But he is most notable for developing an influential typification of the female captive, who person-ified for Mather the collective vulnerability of the dispersed and degen-erate population both to physical and to spiritual onslaughts. The most extensive captivity narrative in his writings, that of Hannah Swarton, tells of Swarton's experiences after she was seized in 1690 by Abenaki al-lies of the French.[12] As Swarton's ten months of captivity among Catholic Abenakis were followed by more than four years as a servant in a French household, her experiences exemplified for Mather the double threat posed to New England by the "bloody, popish, and pagan enemies" on the northern frontier (C. Mather 1977 [1697]:12). First published by Mather in 1697 as an appendix to a fast-day sermon, Humiliations Follow'd with Deliverances (see Figure 5.1), Swarton's narrative was reprinted in slightly revised form in volume 6 of Mather's Magnalia (1702).[13]

"The Narrative of Hannah Swarton," like that of Mary Rowlandson, is a first-person account of spiritual trial and redemption—an unusual de-parture from Cotton Mather's practice of retelling captives' tales in his own voice. But the sins Hannah Swarton ascribes to herself are strikingly similar to those preoccupying Mather and other clergymen. Prompted by her Indian mistress, who suggested that her captivity was a punishment for her sins, Swarton confesses that she and her husband had "turned our backs upon God's ordinances to get this world's goods," leaving "the public worship and ordinances of God . . . to remove to the north part of Casco Bay, where there was no church, or minister of the Gospel." This, Swarton admits, "we did for large accommodations in the world, thereby exposing our children, to be bred ignorantly like Indians, and our selves to forget what we had been formerly instructed in." In response to her in-ordinate desire for worldly goods, Swarton concludes, "God hath stripped me of these things" (C. Mather 1981 [1702]:150–151). As a divine rebuke, Swarton's captivity, the death of her husband and child, and her

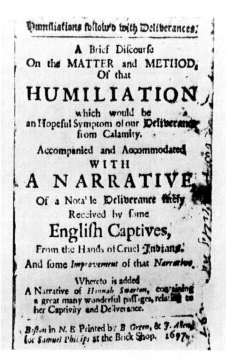

FIGURE 5.1  Title page from Humiliations Follow'd with Deliverances, by Cotton Mather (Boston, 1697). (Courtesy of the Edward E. Ayer Collection, the Newberry Library, Chicago.)

separation from three other children became instructive, exaggerated versions of the independence that she herself had sought on the frontier; her material deprivations became instructive reversals of her search for "this world's goods" and "large accommodations"; and the spiritual temptations of French Catholicism became instructive, involuntary exaggerations of the temptations she had deliberately courted by moving to the frontier.

Hannah Swarton, like Mary Rowlandson, represents "Indian captivity" as a profoundly threatening separation from all that had sustained her. She figures this isolation, however, not as "removal"—for she had already voluntarily "removed" herself to remote Casco Bay prior to her captivity—but as a process of being "stripped," like Job (19:9–10), and "bereaved" of what was dear to her. "I was now bereaved of husband, children, friends, neighbors, house, estate, bread, clothes, or lodging suitable," she lamented, "and my very life did hang daily in doubt" (C. Mather 1981 [1702]:151). This last phrase echoes Mather's sermon, which describes all New England as deserving to "have our lives continually hanging in doubt" under the enemy's "furious tyrannies" (C. Mather

1977 [1697]:12). No doubt it was partly as an exemplification of this state that Mather appended Swarton's narrative to his sermon.

To have her life "hang daily in doubt" meant, for Swarton, "being continually in danger of being killed by the Indians, or pined to death with famine, or tired to death with hard traveling, or pinched with cold till I died in the winter season" (C. Mather 1981 [1702]:151). As she was "hurried up and down the wilderness" Swarton suffered "for want of clothing, being put by them into an Indian dress with a slight blanket, no stockings, and but one pair of Indian shoes, and of their leather stockings for the winter" (see Figure 5.2). As she struggled through the snow, her "sores bled so that as I travelled I might be tracked by my blood that I left behind me on the snow."[14] Although this vivid image seems to prefigure her subsequent desire (in the relative comfort of Canada) to "suffer for Christ," in the wilderness Swarton was preoccupied with "how to preserve myself in danger and supply myself in the want that was present." Unlike Rowlandson, she "had not time or leisure so composedly to consider of the great concernments of my soul, as I should have done, neither had I any Bible, or good book to look into, or Christian friend to be my counsellor in these distresses" (149, 151–152). She reports sustaining herself with remembered passages from the Psalms and the books of John, Jeremiah, and Job; but it was only after being ransomed in Quebec that she turned attention to her soul.

Whereas Mary Rowlandson considered her physical and spiritual life directly correlated, and therefore scrutinized the details of everyday experience for their spiritual significance, Hannah Swarton considers separately and sequentially the state of what, following theological usage, she calls her "outward man" and "inward man."[15] Swarton's ordeal is almost described as two successive captivities: first, a struggle for self-preservation in the wilderness, followed by "the affliction of my captivity among the papists" (C. Mather 1981 [1702]:156). After being ransomed to a French official's wife, Swarton experienced "a great and comfortable change as to my outward man in my freedom from my former hardships and hardhearted oppressors." But this was accompanied by "a greater snare and trouble to my soul and danger to my inward man" (153). It is her "captivity among the papists" that provides the context for Swarton's spiritual trial and conversion, and with one exception this spiritual trial is situated entirely in Canada rather than in the wilderness.

The exception is a crucial one, however, for it involves Swarton's relationship to her Indian mistress, who "had been bred by the English at Black Point," or Scarborough, Maine, and was "now married to a Canada Indian, and turned papist." Considerably more pious than her captive, it was Swarton's mistress who first suggested to her "that God delivered us into their hands, to punish us for our sins." Although the mistress may have been thinking of other kinds of sins (the colonists' Reformed religion, for example, or their "insatiable desire for land"), her suggestion provides the occasion for Swarton's reflections regarding her worldliness. The mistress also told Swarton "that had the English been as careful to instruct her in our religion as the French were to instruct her in theirs, she might have been of our religion" (C. Mather 1981 [1702]:150). Like Wetamo, who exhibits the vanity Rowlandson sought to repudiate, this unnamed but cosmopolitan mistress serves as an object lesson, exemplifying the piety Swarton and many of the English lack—albeit a Catholic piety.

Despite Swarton's relatively lengthy captivity among the Abenakis (ten months compared to Rowlandson's three), she reveals little further knowledge of her captors or their way of life. They remain nameless and largely featureless "Indians." Swarton's French mistress is somewhat more thoroughly characterized, although Swarton's overriding preoccupation in the Canadian portion of the narrative is with her efforts to resist conversion to a religion she considered idolatrous. After refusing to attend mass any longer, she falls into "the very pit of despair," fearing that she was "not fit to suffer for the true religion, and for Christ"—that, in fact, she "had no interest in Him" (C. Mather 1981 [1702]:155). While reading Scripture in this state she experienced the inexpressible "ravishing comfort" of the Lord's Spirit, repented of her sins, and prayed to return to New England, "that the works of God might be made manifest." Endeavoring with a fellow captive, Margaret Stilson, "to return to God with all our hearts," Swarton prayed toward Christ just as Solomon (in 2 Chron. 6:36–39) had urged captive Jews to "pray towards the temple" (C. Mather 1981 [1702]:157). Convinced that God had heard their prayers, she and Stilson were among twenty-two captives redeemed in 1695, along with her youngest son. She left two children behind in Canada, whom she never saw again. French records show that her daughter, Mary, married an Irishman and became a naturalized Canadian.

Much shorter than The Soveraignty and Goodness of God, Hannah Swarton's narrative is neither as detailed nor as artfully constructed. Both its level of abstraction and the closeness of Swarton's rendering of her sins to clerical concerns suggest that Cotton Mather asserted a strong influence upon the narrative. A similar conclusion might be drawn from the copious and precise scriptural references and theological argumentation—unexpected in a woman who admits to having forgotten much of her Christian upbringing. These features of the narrative have led several scholars (most recently, Lorrayne Carroll [1996]) to attribute authorship of the text to Mather rather than to Swarton. But with only one exception—a reference to "hardhearted oppressors"—the Swarton narrative lacks the typifying epithets characteristic of Mather's descriptions of Indians.[16] Swarton's captors are most often called, rather neutrally, "our en-emies," "the Indians," "my Indian master and mistress," or simply "they." Indeed, when Swarton speaks of her hunger, she often refers to herself and her captors inclusively: "We had no corn or bread but some-times groundnuts, acorns, purslain, hogweed, weeds, roots, and some-times dogs' flesh. . . . We had no success at hunting save that one bear was killed, which I had part of. . . . And fish if we could catch it." She also refers inclusively to herself and her mistress when they are left alone on an island: "They left us no food from Sabbath-day morning till the next Saturday, save that we had a bladder (of moose I think) which was well filled with maggots; and we boiled it and drank the broth, but the blad-der was so tough we could not eat it." Sent by her mistress to seek help (one of several instances revealing the freedom of movement she was granted), Swarton "espied a canoe and by signs invited them to come to shore. It proved to be some squaws who, understanding our wants, one of them gave me a roasted eel which I ate and it seemed unto me the most savory food I ever tasted before" (C. Mather 1981 [1702]:149–150).

A second indication of Swarton's authorship of the narrative, as Eber-sole (1995:77–88) argues convincingly, is its resemblance to conversion narratives composed for public confession. To attribute the narrative to a regenerate Swarton does not, of course, imply that Cotton Mather re-frained from "improving" it to his satisfaction, constructing Hannah Swarton as the exemplary captive for a "backsliding" generation. But it does suggest that Swarton participated in this orthodox fashioning of herself, coauthoring an interpretation of her captivity that emphasizes contemporary preoccupations with the "backsliding" and "Indianiza-tion" of frontier settlers.[17] The narrative demonstrates the extent to which a providential interpretation of captivity extended to church members as well as the clerical elite—in other words, the breadth of the clergy's he-gemony.

Even so, Swarton's narrative, like Rowlandson's, exceeds and subverts the typifications of the vulnerable Captive and threatening Captor that Mather attempts to construct. For the captive is not so very vulnerable, the captor not so very threatening. Like Rowlandson and Stockwell, Swarton managed to survive an ordeal in which "her very life did hang daily in doubt." She learned to travel long distances in the snow with heavy burdens on her back, to eat food she formerly would have spurned, and to convey her hunger by signs to strange Indians in a canoe. She learned to think of herself and her mistress, at least occasion-ally, as "we." The mistress, who had "been bred by the English" but "turned papist," gives spiritual lessons to her captive, who with her hus-band had "turned our backs upon God's ordinances, . . . exposing our children, to be bred ignorantly like Indians." All in all, Swarton's narra-

FIGURE 5.2    Hannah Swarton and her Abenaki mistress, as depicted in a
nineteenth-century edition of Swarton's narrative. SOURCE: The Casco Captive, 3d
ed. (Massachusetts Sabbath School Society, 1837). (Courtesy of the Edward E.
Ayer Collection, the Newberry Library, Chicago.)

tive suggests how captivity often took place not in the context of complete estrangement but on a middle ground in which captors and captives had previous experience with each other's societies—and with
"turning" from one to the other.

A very different but equally complex blend of identification and opposition, mimesis and alterity, is found in the second captivity narrative
Mather included in Humiliations Follow'd with Deliverances—in this case,
within the sermon proper. Mather's sermon, delivered in Boston before a
general fast, was intended to inspire repentance in the congregation.[18] In
order to "quicken humiliation" Mather asked his listeners to consider the
most humiliating circumstance God had brought upon them—that is,
captivity among a "barbarous adversary." This Mather presented as a
contemporary antitype of Judæa capta, captive Israel. First, he described
Roman coins commemorating the conquest of Israel, which pictured "a
silent woman sitting upon the ground, and leaning against a palm tree,
with this inscription: JUDÆA CAPTA." Then, Americanizing this image,
he lamented, "Alas, if poor New England were to be shown upon her old
coin, we might show her leaning against her thunderstruck pine tree,
desolate, sitting upon the ground" (C. Mather 1977 [1697]:31, 33).[19] Right

there in the congregation, he announced, were three persons who exemplified the desolation of captivity. Hannah Swarton was not among these former captives, but another Hannah was: Hannah Emerson Dustan, who would become the most famous if least exemplary of Mather's captives. Dustan's tale hardly conformed to the image of.a desolate and passive New England, but Mather "improved" it in order to make it serve his call for collective humility and repentance.

Some months previously, a week after Hannah Dustan had given birth, her home in Haverhill, New Hampshire was attacked by Abenakis mounting one of the last raids of the first intercolonial war. Hannah's husband John Dustan escaped with seven of their children, leaving his wife, their infant, and a widowed nurse and midwife, Mary Corliss Neff, "in the care of Divine Providence" (C. Mather 1981 [1702]:162). After seeing "the raging dragons rifle all that they could carry away and set the house on fire," Dustan and Neff were led away by their Abenaki captors, who, "ere they had gone many steps . . . dashed out the brains of the infant against a tree." Other captives were tomahawked to death when they tired on the journey, but Dustan's and Neff's sighs were heard by God, who "gave them to find unexpected favor from the master who laid claim unto them" (163). Despite Dustan's weakened condition, the two captives marched about one hundred fifty miles, halfway to the "rendezvous of savages, which they call a town," where they expected to be "stripped and scourged" and forced to "run the gauntlet." Dustan, resolving "to imitate the action of Jael" (who had hammered a tent spike into the head of Israel's enemy, Sisera), found an opportunity one night when her captors were sleeping soundly.[20] She awakened Neff and Samuel Lennardson, a captive English youth traveling with them, and convinced them to help her attack "their sleeping oppressors." They succeeded in killing all but two of them (a woman and child) with their own hatchets. The victims "bowed, they fell, they lay down"; in Mather's telling, echoing the Song of Deborah (Judges 5:27). "At their feet they bowed, they fell where they bowed; there they fell down dead" (C. Mather 1981 [1702]:164).

Hannah Dustan had accomplished a deed that Quentin Stockwell contemplated but abandoned when his "heart failed" him (I. Mather 1981 [1684]:80). Remaining on the scene, she and her companions turned to "cutting off the scalps of the ten wretches." They had hoped to bring one sleeping child with them—presumably for adoption—but the child awoke and "scuttled away from the devastation." At the time of Mather's sermon, Dustan, Neff, and Lennardson were in Boston to collect a bounty from the General Court of Massachusetts, which (although the law authorizing bounties had expired) had awarded them fifty pounds for the scalps of two men, two women, and six children. Additionally, the governor of Maryland sent "a very generous token of his favor," and their personal friends offered "many presents of congratulation" (C. Mather 1981 [1702]:164).

Cotton Mather, so quick to deplore the "Indianization" of frontier colonists, voiced no criticism of the scalping, an act the colonists had adopted from Indians and associated strongly with savagery. He borrowed Dustan's voice to justify the murders themselves: "Being where she had not her own life secured by any law unto her, she thought she was not forbidden by any law to take away the life of the murderers by whom her child had been butchered" (164). Characteristically, Mather employed formulaic typifications to dehumanize Dustan's victims: They are "raging dragons," "formidable savages," "furious tawnies," and "those whose tender mercies are cruelties" (162–164).[21]

There is one significant exception to Mather's negative typifications, however: He describes these same captors as an "Indian family" that put many a "prayerless" English family to "shame." Indeed, Mather reports that Dustan's master gave his captive a lesson in spiritual resignation, asking her: "What need you trouble yourself? If your God will have you delivered, you shall be so." This assessment appealed to Mather, who agreed, "And it seems our God would have it so to be" (C. Mather 1981 [1702]:163). Although this moment of theological discussion may have been entirely fabricated by Mather—who clearly relished the trope of the pious Indian—it fits with what we happen to know of Dustan's master. Just as Hannah Swarton's mistress had abundant previous experience with the English, so too did Dustan's master: He had been a servant in Joseph and Mary Rowlandson's household in Lancaster prior to Metacom's War. Dustan's master, like many displaced natives of southern New England, presumably had taken refuge among the Abenakis after the war.[22]

In comparing Hannah Dustan to the Hebrew heroine Jael, Mather justified Dustan's violence as not only an act of personal revenge and self-protection but as a defense of her beleaguered society as a whole. Nevertheless, Mather's uncharacteristic description of the captors as an "Indian family" gives a sense that Dustan's violence may have remained unsettling. Perhaps her violence against the Indian family was too similar to that directed against Dustan's infant: Tomahawking, scalping, and dashing infants against trees fell under the same sign of savagery.[23] Or perhaps Dustan's violence was too reminiscent of her sister Elizabeth Emerson's act of infanticide four years previously—which Mather would have remembered because he delivered the execution sermon.[24] At any rate, a captivity tale that would initially seem to offer Mather clearly polarized captors and captives offered him, instead, a tangle of resemblances. In raising the tomahawk, and perhaps especially in scalping her victims, Dustan imitated not only Jael but also an Indian warrior; in showing his captives "unexpected favor" and counseling spiritual resignation, Dustan's master imitated Christ. Here the Captor was as vulnerable as the Captive, the Captive as threatening as the Captor.

Whatever caused Mather to disrupt his own typification by referring to the "Indian family," he managed to assert discursive control over Dustan by emphasizing her pride, complacency, and spiritual vulnerability.[25] He admonished Dustan and her companions to guard against undue pride, cautioning them not to think that their deliverance was testimony to their righteousness. They must "make a right use of the deliverance," he insisted, for mercies, like judgments, should humble a person and lead to repentance. Mather warned them, "You are not now the slaves of Indians, as you were a few days ago; but if you continue unhumbled, in your sins, you will be the slaves of devils; and, let me tell you, a slavery to devils, to be in their hands, is worse than to be in the hands of Indians!" (C. Mather 1977 [1697]:47–50). No doubt it was as an example of the desired humility that Mather appended to the sermon upon its publication the narrative of the more humble, more vulnerable, more repentant Hannah Swarton. Despite Mather's direct warning, Dustan would not publicly repent until "the eleventh hour," in 1724, when she expressed thankfulness for her captivity, calling it "the comfortablest time that ever I had: in my affliction God made his word comfortable" (Derounian-Stodola and Levernier 1993:135).[26]

Mather repeated Dustan's story in his providential histories, Decennium Luctuosum (1699) and Magnalia (1702),[27] and her deed remained legendary in New England long after Mather lost his influence (see Figure 5.3).[28] But the correspondence between Dustan's "notable exploit" (C. Mather 1702, 7:90) and Mather's typification of captivity was awkward at best, and this may be one of the reasons why he refrained from referring to any captive in particular when he next set out to offer an authoritative interpretation of captivity.

## Texts Written in Blood: Cotton Mather and the Production of Meaning

When the first intercolonial war finally ended, Cotton Mather broke with the precedent his father had established of interpreting particular captivities as illustrations of Providence. He offered, instead, an abstract typification of captivity that claimed its authority from his own clerical stature rather than from the experience of any specific captive (although it invokes recollections of many). This powerful typification appeared in "Observable Things," a fast-day sermon delivered in 1697 to mark the end of the war. Mather's estimation of the importance of this sermon is indicated

DUSTIN STATUE.—FIRST DRAFT.

FIGURE 5.3    Hannah Dustan Memorial Statue, Haverhill, New Hampshire, dedicated June 17, 1874. Pen-and-ink drawing of statue designed by Charles A. Andrews, William Andrews, Andrew Orsolini, and James Murray. SOURCE: The Heroism of Hannah Dustan, by Robert B. Caverly (Boston, 1874). (Courtesy of the Harry Ransom Humanities Research Center, University of Texas at Austin.)

by its placement at the conclusion of both his history of a "melancholy decade" of war, Decennium Luctuosum (1699), and his Magnalia.[29]

Mather's bid for interpretive hegemony appears at the outset of the sermon, when he introduces his text as follows.

The Judgments of God, under which we have been Languishing for Ten years together, are a sort of Book put into our Hands; a Book indeed all written in Blood; a Book yet full of Divine Lessons for us. But can every man Read this

Terrible Book? No, Methinks. . . . It will certainly be a work, well becoming a
Minister of the Gospel . . . to take this Book, and help you, as well as we can,
to Spell the Divine Lessons contained in it.

    Christians, let us now do a work, for which the Great God hath given us
that Warrant, and that Command, in Psalm CVII.43.

    Who is Wise, and will observe these Things?

(C. Mather 1978 [1699]:201–202)

Mather uses his Biblical text, part of the closing verse of Psalm 107, as a
refrain that both introduces his various interpretations of history and legitimates his authority as an interpreter of the first intercolonial war. In
using this verse Mather invokes the entire psalm, which begins:

> O give thanks unto the Lord for he is good,
> For his mercy endureth for ever.
> Let the redeemed of the Lord say so,
> Whom he hath redeemed from the hand of the enemy.

The familiar psalm, also quoted by Mary Rowlandson, expresses thanksgiving for God's deliverance of wanderers in the wilderness and of imper-
iled seafarers as well as captives. Subsequent verses, which Mather especially stresses in his jeremiad, observe that God has often turned "a fruitful
land into barrenness, For [on account of] the wickedness of them which
dwell therein." The psalm closes, "Who so is wise and will observe these
things, Even they shall understand the loving kindness of God."

    Mather, then, chose for the text of his jeremiad a classic example of
providential history: one that presents all events in history, both afflictions and deliverances, as "marvellous dispensations of the Divine Providence, towards the children of men," in Mather's words, and that provided ample opportunity for drawing correspondences between the
history of Israel on the one hand and the sufferings and deliverance of
New England on the other. Mather went so far in drawing correspondences between his text and events in New England as to call the first intercolonial war a book written in blood—a book that could only be
spelled out by one who was wise, that is, by one who was authorized to
discern God's inscriptions in the world. Indeed, this "terrible book" that
was the war so outshadowed Mather's Biblical text that he explicitly announced "a long war is the text which I am now going to insist upon" (C.
Mather 1978 [1699]:203). He would insist because, he acknowledged,
there were some who considered attempts to read the will of God in
worldly events presumptuous, even blasphemous.[30]

    The bulk of "Observable Things" enumerates ten overlapping lessons
the "wise" must draw from that terrible book written in blood. Echoing

his father, Mather argued that God had punished his chosen people in New England through appropriate instruments. Interpreting the bloody text, then, involved examining what relationships obtained between the colonists and the Indians such that the latter were God's chosen instruments of chastisement. Unlike Rowlandson—who embeds her consideration of what qualities made Indians the chosen scourge of God within the particularities of her experience and the character of her individual captors—Mather systematically examines the qualities of a typified Captive and Captor in order to understand the providential significance of their relationship.

To begin with, Mather returns to one of his favorite themes, noting several ways in which the colonists had become "Indianized." Like Swarton's narrative, "Observable Things" decries the settlers' dispersal into "unsettlements" without churches or ministers, "unsettlements" that corresponded in their disorderliness to the Indian habitations he preferred to call "rendezvous" or "kennels" rather than "towns."[31] He notes the colonists' lying, a trait (as we have seen in Rowlandson) associated with Satan, the great deceiver, as well as with Indians, known for their "treachery" and "inconstancy." He laments his people's insolence, another trait then commonly associated with Indians (as in Rowlandson's portrait of Wetamo). Finally, and most emphatically, he inveighs against the colonists' excessive indulgence toward their children, comparing it to the Indians' lack of proper family government—a persistent complaint of the English and French against people who refused to direct physical violence against their children. But Mather was less interested in enumerating Indian faults than in chastising the colonists for living like Indians—for transgressing the boundary between a godly, orderly, disciplined Self and a wild, untrustworthy, and insubordinate Other; or in a phrase that perhaps better captures the Puritan sense of self, for reverting to their natural, depraved selves, which Indians in their savagery exemplified.

Properly understood, then, the "Indian rod" employed by God served not only as a means of chastisement but as an exemplification of the forces of satanic disarray that were threatening English colonial social order. The colonists were susceptible to attack and capture by the French and Indians only because they had succumbed to wilderness temptations. Indeed, the English were even worse than Indians in two respects (and here Mather was echoing statements found in Swarton's and Dustan's narratives): Although the English possessed the true religion, they did not practice their religion as faithfully as the Indians observed their Catholic prayers, nor had they managed to convert the Indians as much as to corrupt them. The English were not only degenerating but were failing at the divine mission that justified Puritan expansion, that of spreading the Reformation throughout the world.

Degeneration was widespread, Mather insisted, noting that all ranks had been struck down by the "Indian rod": shepherds and magistrates; rich and poor; widows and orphans; young and old. He described vividly the sufferings all ranks had undergone because of their need for reformation—sufferings that in the case of women and children were exemplified by captivity. Mather's treatment of captivity, like the notion that Indians served as God's instruments of punishment, is familiar from Rowlandson's and Swarton's narratives; however, unlike Rowlandson, Mather strongly emphasized the vulnerability of his generalized Captive rather than any strength she gained from her wilderness trials.

Opposed to the Captive's vulnerability was the Captor's ferocious destructiveness. Indians were typified as carnivorous beasts and fearsome devils; as destroyers of home, family relationships, and family order; and as defilers, even devourers of the weak. Mather asked rhetorically:

> How many Women have been made a prey to those Brutish men, that are Skilful to Destroy? How many a Fearful Thing has been suffered by the Fearful Sex, from those men, that one would Fear as Devils rather than men? Let the Daughters of our Zion think with themselves, what it would be, for fierce Indians to break into their Houses, and brain their Husbands and their Children before their Eyes, and Lead them away a Long Journey into the Woods; and if they begin to fail and faint in the Journey, then for a Tawny Salvage to come with Hell fire in his Eyes, and cut 'em down with his Hatchet; or, if they could miraculously hold out, then for some Filthy and ugly Squaws to become their insolent Mistresses, and insolently to abuse 'em at their pleasure a thousand inexpressible ways; and, if they had any of their Sucking Infants with them, then to see those Tender Infants handled at such a rate, that they should beg of the Tygres, to dispatch 'em out of hand. Such things as these, I tell you, have often happened in this Lamentable War. (C. Mather 1978 [1699]:220–221)

As fearful daughters of Zion—or mothers of Zion, given Mather's emphasis on motherhood—female captives exemplified the vulnerability of the Puritan colonies in New England. Likened to the frail prey of destructive beasts, then to a weak and fearful victim of the Devil, the female Captive is helpless before the Indian destroyers of her home, family, and domestic order. In captivity all divinely sanctioned social roles are violated, accentuating the social disarray thought to be characteristic of the frontier. Like beasts, which live without social constraints; like the Devil, intent on the settlers' destruction; and like the frontier settlers themselves, the Indians showed little respect for the proper bonds joining husband and wife, parent and child, master and servant. They killed husbands before the eyes of their wives, and infants before the eyes of their mothers. These bonds broken, they carried off female captives into an inverted servitude. Once mistresses of their own households, the captives were now forced to serve masters and mistresses whom they considered their inferiors. Here they met with insolence and cruelty rather than with loving dominance; moreover, they were unable to protect their children.

Turning to the fate of captive children, Mather became even more distressed:

> Our Little Boys and Girls, even these Little Chickens, have been Seized by the Indian Vultures. Our Little Birds have been Spirited away by the Indian Devourers, and brought up, in a vile Slavery, till some of them have quite forgot their English Tongue, and their Christian Name, and their whole Relation. (C. Mather 1978 [1699]:222)

The fate of those "devoured" by the Indians as well as of those whom Indians had brutally killed, warned Mather didactically, should teach the young to be "serious, pious, orderly children, obedient unto your parents, conscientious to keep the Lord's Day, and afraid of committing any wickedness."[32] Their parents were expected to attend to the message as well: Only a renewed commitment to an authoritarian social order could preserve the colonists from utter destruction.

A master of Puritan rhetoric, Mather developed in these passages a compelling and authoritative typification of English vulnerability in a threatening New World. Although spiritual vulnerability was a standard theme of fast-day sermons, it is portrayed particularly vividly through this synthetic typification of captivity. Declaring a clerical monopoly over interpretation, and utilizing systematic oppositions in ethnicity, gender, and civility, Mather portrayed the English colonists as weak and innocent victims of the brutish demons who threatened to devour them.

Mather's typification of captivity is complex, developing three sets of symbolic oppositions between Indian predators and their English prey. One, the opposition between a vulnerable female Captive and her brutish male Captor, would come to figure as the dominant representation of captivity. To be sure, the two other oppositions employed by Mather had considerable rhetorical power. The opposition between a fearful female captive and her insolent and abusive mistress, as we have seen in Mary Rowlandson's narrative, portrays captivity as a violation of colonial patterns of domination· in terms of gender as well as ethnicity. And the opposition between "little chickens" and the "Indian vultures" who consume them encapsulates the colonial fear of fledgling Christian civility being consumed by the dark and demonic forces of the wild. After the publication of John Williams's captivity narrative in 1707, Cotton Mather's "little chickens" would come to be personified by none other than his own cousin Eunice Williams. And the selective tradition of captivity increasingly would foreground the opposition between a vulnerable colonial female and her savage male captor—an opposition that maintains and emotionally deploys male dominance over women at the same time as it reverses the ethnic power relations that were established through conquest.

"Observable Things" represents a decisive turn in the typification of captivity. Claiming a monopoly on the production of meaning, Mather defined "Indian captivity" primarily as divine punishment of a weak, degenerate society for its collective sins, not as a personal trial leading to renewed spiritual strength. Reading the text of captivity through his concern for social discipline and clerical authority, Mather spelled out its lesson as a call to moral reformation inspired by a fear of divine judgment and social chaos. In his reading, Indians represent the forces of disorder; captives, the colonists at their most vulnerable before Indian disorder—whether because they imitated it, were incorporated into it, or saw their own social order destroyed by it.

For Mary Rowlandson, vulnerability was the condition of renewed dependence upon God alone. Mather's interpretation of captivity, however, turned spiritual autobiography into jeremiad. The vulnerability of the captive served as an impetus to strengthen the established patterns of authority, thus buttressing the collective defense against the forces of lawlessness and anarchy, whether stemming from without or within.[33] Both in the spiritual autobiography and in Mather's typification, women are the exemplary captives; but for Mather it is women as weak and subject to the control of husbands and the clergy rather than women as regenerate sinners. This, then, was Indian captivity as read by Mather: not a journey of personal spiritual growth in a context removed from prior social relationships, but a threatening example of the violent consequences of succumbing to forces that attacked the established social hierarchy.

By definition, a hegemonic typification requires both abstraction and authority. In "Observable Things" Cotton Mather took his method of interpretation to an extreme, abstracting completely from the experience of any particular captive, absolutely polarizing Captive Self to Captivating Other, and claiming the authority to enforce his interpretation on the experience of all captives, and even of all colonists. Subsumed within the framework of "fearful things suffered by the fearful sex" are the particularities of Rowlandson's, Swarton's, and Dustan's experiences, the differences among their captors, and their varied responses to captivity. The complex identifications of Rowlandson with Wetamo and of Swarton with her mistress, Dustan's appropriation of her captor's tomahawk, Rowlandson's "removes," Swarton's survival skills, and Stockwell's very existence—all these are erased in a typification that allows the female captive only to fear, faint, fail, beg, or "miraculously hold out." Similarly, all motivations on the part of Indian captors, all hybrid identities, all kindnesses and favors are lost in a typification that allows male captors only to seize, devour, and wield their tomahawks, or female captors to be insolent and abusive.

To be sure, claiming authority to read a book "written in blood" is different from achieving that authority. Mather had one contemporary, in particular, who could speak with an even greater authority, for he was at once a redeemed captive and a clergyman. John Williams's The Redeemed Captive Returning to Zion (1707), published in the middle of the second intercolonial war (Queen Anne's War), would supplement Mather's interpretation of captivity with the voice of direct experience. It would take its place beside Rowlandson's Sovereignty and Goodness of God as one of the most well-known and influential of all Anglo-American captivity narratives.

## Redeemed and Unredeemed Captives:
## John and Eunice Williams

John Williams, the pastor of Deerfield, Massachusetts, was among more than one hundred captives seized from that town in 1704 by a force of some fifty Canadians and two hundred Algonquians and Iroquoians commanded by a French officer, Hertel de Rouville. At the time of his capture Williams had lived in Deerfield almost twenty years. He arrived there in 1686—three years after graduating from Harvard, four years after the town was successfully reestablished and fortified, and nine years after the captivity of Quentin Stockwell and his companions. Within a year of his arrival Williams married into New England's most prestigious family, taking as his bride Eunice Mather, the daughter of Increase's brother Eleazer of nearby Northampton. The Williams family, with all of Deerfield, generally had survived the first intercolonial war (King William's War) without undue hardship, despite the exposed position of the town. The devastating attack of 1704 came near the beginning of the second intercolonial war, late in February, when deep snows provided easy penetration of the town's poorly defended stockade. Snow and ice contributed to the captives' hardships on the three-hundred-mile march to Canada.[34]

In all, some fifty residents of Deerfield perished during the attack or on the journey to Canada. Of the eight Williams children five were captured, ranging between four and fifteen years of age. The eldest was away at college, and two were killed immediately—a six-year-old boy and an infant of six weeks. The children's nurse, an African slave named Parthena, was also killed. Near the beginning of the march to Canada, Eunice

Williams, weakened from recent childbirth, was killed, as was the family's "Negro man," Parthena's husband.[35] The captives were divided among a variety of Native groups that had participated, each for their own complex reasons, in the raid. Whereas Williams distinguished among two groups, "Indians" and "Macquas," recent scholarship (Haefeli and Sweeney 1995) has enumerated these as Western Abenakis, including Cowassucks, Pennacooks, Pigwackets, and more southerly Algonquian refugees; and three groups of sauvages domiciliés, or praying Indians. The latter three groups included Abenakis and refugee Pocumtucks, Norwottucks, and Sokokis from the Jesuit mission of St. Francis (now Odanak); Mohawks from the missions of Kahnawake (or Caughnawaga) and La Montagne (ancestral to today's Oka); and Hurons from the mission of Lorette (see Map 4.1). The minister was claimed by two Abenakis; his son Stephen, by a Pennacook sachem named Wattanummon. Williams's seven-year-old daughter Eunice was claimed by a Mohawk woman from Kahnawake, who, tradition attests, was inconsolable over the death of her daughter. Following Iroquois condolence practices, she acquired and adopted Eunice as a replacement.[36]

Although Williams expresses great grief over his "flock's being so far a flock of slaughter" (Williams 1976:50), and particularly over the death of his wife, The Redeemed Captive Returning to Zion does not dwell on his bereavement.[37] Neither does Williams focus on his own spiritual failings, but rather on the vulnerability of his flock before "Romish ravenous wolves" (71), an epithet that refers not to Indians but to the Jesuit priests of New France. The narrative is preoccupied with Williams's efforts to counter the spiritual seduction of the Jesuits, who successfully converted some of his congregation—including, for a time, his son Samuel. "All means were used to seduce poor souls" (73), Williams reported, noting instances of physical punishment, bribery, trickery, and threats to return the captives to the Indians. The minister tried through prayers and letters to counteract the Jesuits' "crafty designs to ensnare young ones" (76), but the Jesuits hampered his efforts by keeping him isolated from his family and congregation.

Williams eventually convinced Samuel to return to the fold, but his daughter Eunice remained lost to him. "The Mohawks would as soon part with their hearts as my child," Williams learned from the Jesuits (Williams 1976:66). He was permitted to see Eunice only twice, and during both visits he reminded her to pray and to remember her catechism and the Scriptures. When after some two and a half years of captivity Williams and about sixty of his flock were released from Canada—Williams in exchange for a French privateer known as "Baptiste"—Eunice was reportedly unable to speak English. Williams was forced to leave her behind, and he begged in his narrative for prayers "that this poor child, and so many others of our children who have been cast upon God from the womb and are now outcast ready to perish, might be gathered from their dispersions and receive sanctifying grace from God!" (67).

The loss of Eunice, which would haunt Williams for the rest of his life, became an emotionally compelling counterpoint to the main theme of his narrative. The Redeemed Captive develops most extensively the Jesuit threat to reformed Christianity, but it is with regard to captives among Indians that Williams expresses himself most fervently. He notes with distress the English captives he saw at the St. Francis mission, "they being in habit very much like Indians and in manner very much symbolizing with them" (Williams 1976:58–59). For children to lose not only their reformed religion but their English appearance and manners—their civility—was for them to revert completely to the natural state of depravity. Even worse was to forget the English language, at once a link to their English identity and a means of reading the Bible, so essential to maintaining a relationship to God unmediated by priests. Williams foresaw his own daughter's future when he was visited in his master's wigwam by "an English maid who was taken [in] the last war, who was dressed up in Indian apparel, could not speak one word of English, who said she could neither tell her own name [n]or the name of the place from where she was taken" (62). The memory of such captives must have intensified Williams's despair in leaving behind in Canada, in addition to his daughter, almost one hundred captives from Deerfield and elsewhere, "many of which are children, and of these not a few among the savages and having lost the English tongue, will be lost and turn savages in a little time unless something extraordinary prevent" (113).

Turning papist and turning savage: These are the twin nightmares expressed in The Redeemed Captive Returning to Zion. Despite Williams's best efforts to shepherd his flock, he lost four girls and one widow to the Jesuits, and his daughter Eunice and a girl named Joanna Kellogg to the Mohawks. Since the Mohawks were Catholic converts, this was a double loss: Both Eunice and Joanna were baptized as Catholics, married Mohawks, and reared children in Kahnawake. Despite repeated diplomatic efforts, both remained there, except for brief visits to their families in New England.[38] Joanna Kellogg's family was even more thoroughly affected by captivity than Eunice's, as several members became effectively bicultural, including Joseph, who worked as a translator and interpreter.[39] But of all the "lost captives," Eunice Williams would most haunt and fascinate New Englanders, not only because she was prominent in her father's narrative but also because she belonged to a leading Puritan family. Not a frontier child "bred ignorantly like Indians" but Cotton Mather's own cousin came to personify his "little chickens . . .

seized by Indian vultures, . . . little birds . . . spirited away by Indian devourers."

As witness to the twin threats of "popery" and "savagery" on the Puritan frontier, John Williams wrote a hybrid narrative that blends the genres of spiritual autobiography, providential history, and jeremiad. Though not as consistently compelling as Rowlandson's narrative, The Redeemed Captive Returning to Zion has outlived Mather's captivity narratives and rivaled Rowlandson's in popularity.[40] To the extent to which The Redeemed Captive is a spiritual autobiography, it is neither a confessional nor a search for correspondences between inward and outward experience, as was Rowlandson's. Considerably more abstract, Williams's narrative is less attuned to the captive's own failings, to variability among his captors, and to the concrete details of the ordeal (represented most vividly in the deceptively simple statement that "each night I wrung blood out of my stockings when I pulled them off") (Williams 1981:180). In the main, Williams's discussion of his spiritual state involves his struggle to achieve a "patient, quiet, humble resignation to the will of God," the state he encouraged as well in his family and flock. Williams reports the exemplary deaths of both his wife, "who never spoke any discontented word as to what had befallen us, but with suitable expressions justified God," and a captive named Mary Brooks, who could, "through the grace of God, cheerfully submit to the will of God" (Williams 1976:91, 48, 52).

Williams's own struggle to achieve a state of resignation was rather less successful than those of his wife or Mary Brooks. Like Rowlandson, he identifies with Job, quoting the same passage when attempting to reconcile himself and his family to their losses: "Naked came I out of my Mother's womb, and naked shall I return thither. The Lord gave and the Lord hath taken away, blessed be the name of the Lord" (Williams 1976:49). When offered a reunion with his children if he would convert to Catholicism, Williams examined his conscience to ascertain whether he "had by any action given encouragement for such a temptation" (74). His conscience was apparently clear, but separation from his children remained the heaviest burden of his captivity. He was especially sorely tried when he heard of his son's "fall" into Catholicism, an event that caused him to review his "afflictions and trials": "my wife and two children killed and many of my neighbors; and myself and so many of my children and friends in a popish captivity separated from our children, not capable to come to instruct them in the way they ought to go, and cunning crafty enemies using all their subtlety to insinuate into young ones such principles as would be pernicious" (104, 91). Like Mary Rowlandson, Williams compared his present situation with his former happiness, realizing that he and others had taken their blessings for granted: "I thought with myself how happy many others were, in that they had their children with them under all advantages to bring them up in the nurture and admonition of the Lord, while we were separated one from another and our children in great peril of embracing damnable doctrines" (91). This affliction, too, he turns to public use, exhorting his readers to profit from his difficulties: "Oh! That all parents who read this history would bless God for the advantages they have of educating their children and faithfully improve it!" (Williams 1981:208)

Separation from his children and his flock is the continuing theme of Williams's narrative, playing the role of removal in Rowlandson's account and of bereavement in Swarton's. But ever the pastor, Williams focuses resolutely outward, turning his personal struggles to public use. If Mary Rowlandson appears in her narrative as the isolated individual struggling to maintain her faith in the absence of husband, church, and community, John Williams appears as the representative of patriarchal order, desperately struggling against what he calls "popish rage and heathenish cruelty" (Williams 1976:77). Despite its title's invocation of captive Israel, The Redeemed Captive Returning to Zion presents its author less as a captive redeemed after undergoing spiritual trial than as an instrument of "God our supreme redeemer" (40).[41] The narrative itself was, in part, intended to further Williams's effort to redeem his remaining charges from Catholicism. That he was unsuccessful in Eunice's case underscored the vulnerability of the young to the combined French and Indian threat.

Williams's narrative falls uneasily within the genre of jeremiad, as it does within that of spiritual autobiography. It starts in the mode of the former, beginning not immediately with the Indian attack, as had Rowlandson's and subsequent narratives, but framing it with an interpretive generalization: "The history I am going to write proves that days of fasting and prayer, without reformation, will not avail to turn away the anger of God from a professing people" (Williams 1976:43). Unlike Cotton Mather, however, Williams is not forthcoming regarding the specific sins that called forth God's judgment. As a town with an established church, Deerfield did not fall into the category of degenerate frontier "unsettlements"; indeed, it appears in Williams's narrative as "God's sanctuary," from which he was carried into a "strange land" (46). Underscoring the imagery of Judæa capta, Williams reports that on the journey they were indeed told to "sing us one of Zion's songs" (Williams 1981:178). It is only at the climax of the narrative, when Williams struggles with his son's conversion to Catholicism, that Williams's diagnosis of his and his people's foremost sin becomes clear: They have failed to instill in their children a faith strong enough to resist the "trials and temptations" of captivity.

To the extent to which Williams's narrative is a jeremiad, then, it is in-
direct and muted compared to Cotton Mather's. It is as though God's
judgment is so harsh that it almost speaks for itself, requiring little "improvement." God's mercy in delivering Williams and his people, however, requires elaboration, lest Williams appear ungrateful or leave the
impression that God had abandoned his covenant with New England.
Thus, echoing the sermon he preached in Cotton Mather's pulpit upon
his return, "Reports of Divine Kindness,"[42] Williams offers his narrative
as

> a short account of some of those signal appearances of divine power and
> goodness for hoping it may serve to excite the praise, faith, and hope of all
> that love God, and may peculiarly serve to cherish a grateful spirit, and to
> render the impressions of God's mighty works indelible on my heart, and
> on those that with me have seen the wonders of the Lord and tasted of His
> salvation. (Williams 1976:40)

Interpreting Indians in the providential mode, Williams's presentation
is at once more abstract than Rowlandson's, more balanced than Cotton
Mather's, and more detached than either. For Williams, as for Swarton,
the main ordeal is not his captivity among Indians but his "popish captivity" in Canada. Like Rowlandson and Cotton Mather, Williams as-
sumes that Indians are naturally "cruel," "barbarous," and "bloodthirsty" (Williams 1976:46, 49), characterizations that, to his credit,
appear in the context of specific acts of violence. He is less interested in
documenting Indian savagery, which he takes for granted, than in the opportunity Indians provide to document God's "mercy in the midst of
judgment" (57). Williams's own masters appear as extraordinarily kind—
carrying his burdens, making him snowshoes, sharing the best of their
food. Even more striking was the solicitude shown toward Williams's
children, who were carried or pulled on sleds. Still, these masters lack
names, backgrounds, and motivations, and their kindness does not lead
Williams to question his typification of Indians as naturally cruel and
savage. Only through God's intercession, he states, could "such whose
tender mercies are cruelties" come to pity the captives. Like both Rowlandson and Mather, Williams interprets instances of tenderness as moments when "their savage cruel tempers were . . . overruled by God"
(54).

Given this interpretive framework, it is perhaps ironic that one example of Indian mercy was their religious tolerance on the march to Canada.
Williams's master gave him a portion of the Bible and allowed him to
meet in prayer and worship with other captives. One Sabbath when the
minister was allowed to preach to the English captives, he chose Lamen-

tations 1:18 for his text, a passage that reveals Williams's special concern for the young: "The Lord is righteous, for I have rebelled against his commandment. Hear, I pray you, all people, and behold my sorrow. My virgins and my young men are gone into captivity" (Williams 1976:51). Tolerance evaporated, however, upon their arrival at the St. Francis mission, when his master tried to force Williams to attend mass, cross himself, and kiss a crucifix. An Indian named Ruth instructed him, in English, to obey his master as Scripture enjoined, but Williams refused "to disobey the great God to obey any master." Ruth, the only Indian called by name in the entire narrative, is described as "a certain savagess taken prisoner in King Philip's War, who had lived at Mr. Buckley's at Wethersfield" (62). As a servant to that gentleman (probably a colleague of Williams's in the ministry), Ruth had often visited the Williams home. Somehow she had made her way to Canada and was now visiting the minister in his master's wigwam, trying to convert her former superior to the religion she had adopted. There could hardly be a better example of the fluidity of identities and statuses characteristic of mission villages—a fluidity as threatening to Williams as it was revitalizing to Native refugees.[43]

Williams successfully resisted Ruth's and his master's efforts to get him to cross himself and kiss the crucifix, convincing his master that he would rather suffer death or torture. But he was thrust into the church by physical force, where he observed "a great confusion instead of gospel order" (Williams 1976:61). From this point on, the narrative is dominated by Williams's confrontation with the religion he considered disorderly, idolatrous, and superstitious. The Jesuits become the significant Others against which Williams struggled to maintain his own identity and that of his flock, and his portrait of these Others is considerably more detailed and individuated than his portrait of his Indian captors. Although appalled by the French religion, Williams was impressed by French civility, praising especially Governor de Vaudreuil, who was "in all respects relating to my outward man courteous and charitable to admiration" (64). Outwardly Williams shared much with the French, and this basis of shared civility allowed their differences to be experienced and expressed much more sharply and specifically.

The otherness of the Indians remained the generalized otherness of savagery, expressed in terms of a series of negations: Those like Eunice, who "turned Indian," lost their English tongue, clothing, manner, and faith—that is, their identity as English, civilized, and sanctified. Williams enumerated the Jesuit threat in much more specific terms and mainly as a set of undesirable gains. To offer only a partial list, Williams opposed the Catholic interpretation of key passages of Scripture, the apostolic tradition, the idolatry of crucifix and rosary, the intercession of saints and the clergy, inequality among pastors and the authority of the pope, the observing of seven rather than two sacraments, the sacrifice of the Mass, the sacrament of extreme unction, and beliefs in transubstantiation and purgatory. The French, in other words, served Williams as a much more clearly defined Other than the Indians because of the shared traditions that underlay their differences.

If the otherness of Catholicism was more easily apprehended, the uncanny otherness of savagery remained more profoundly threatening. Although Eunice Williams "turned papist" as well as "savage," Williams, his family, and their friends consistently figured her situation as one of "captivity among the Indians." This was true long after it became clear that Eunice was not held at Kahnawake against her will. John Williams heard this directly from Eunice as well as from the chiefs of Kahnawake when he traveled to Canada in 1714, at the close of the second intercolonial war, as an official commissioner of a delegation to attempt to retrieve the captives. After a meeting with Eunice, then seventeen years old and married, he wrote that "she is yet obstinantly resolved to live and die here." Appealing to the chiefs, he was told by their speaker that "those taken by them were adopted into families, and not held as prisoners, but as children; and it was not their custom to compel any to return, but should leave them to their own liberty" (Demos 1994:116). When Williams died fifteen years later, he had neither seen Eunice again nor abandoned his regular prayers for her redemption. The sermon published after his death as a "memorial" reminded the fallen "children of godly parents" that God "invites even backsliding children to return," and urged such children to consider "from whence you are fallen . . . and turn again" (175).

Eunice would not "turn again," but she did return to New England to visit the Williams family. Travel and trade between Canada and New England resumed at the end of the second intercolonial war, and both acculturated captives and masters of redeemed captives, including one of John Williams's masters, paid visits to New England.[44] As surprising as this may seem from within the polarized typification of captivity, these visits were consistent with indigenous practices, in which adoption and hostage-exchange were used to establish enduring alliances between groups. Eunice—then known as Marguerite, A'ongote, or Gannenstenhawi—paid three visits to her English kin during the years between 1740 and 1744, accompanied by her Mohawk husband, Arosen, and their children. She and Arosen returned in 1761, near the end of the fourth intercolonial war, accompanied by her daughter and son-in-law (a prominent chief named Onnasategen) and one of her grandchildren.[45] Tradition recounts that Eunice and her family, wearing buckskin and moccasins, camped in the apple orchard of her brother, Rev. Stephen Williams, who wrote ambivalently on more than one occasion of a "joyfull, sorrowfull meeting" (Demos 1994:189). Eunice's visits to her brother were a sensation, attracting large crowds from surrounding communities as well as dignitaries such as the famous preacher Jonathan Edwards. Through Joseph Kellogg and other interpreters Stephen Williams attempted to arrange the permanent return of Eunice and her family, but in vain.

Perhaps Eunice's choice not to remain in New England had something to do with her continued status as an Other there. During her visit of 1741, coinciding with the height of the religious revival known as the Great Awakening, Eunice was present in the congregation during a revival sermon preached by her cousin, Rev. Solomon Williams. He pointed her out as a person who had been for a "long time in a miserable captivity, with a barbarous and heathen people." Praying for her deliverance from "those snares and thick-laid stratagems of the Devil to beguile and ruin poor souls," Williams constructed Eunice as exemplary of all those in the congregation who lived "in a state of slavery to sin" (Williams 1742:17–18, 26).[46] Almost four decades after Eunice's abduction, Solomon Williams still viewed her as captivated by the heathen and seduced by Satan. That a "child of the covenant" would remain by choice among the Catholic Mohawks of Kahnawake was simply unimaginable.

## Typification, Subordination, and the Limits of Hegemony

This chapter has traced an increasing abstraction of the captivity experience, an increasing typification of Indians, and an increasing polarization of Captor and Captive in the captivity narratives published during the quarter century after The Sovereignty and Goodness of God appeared in 1682. Although Rowlandson's narrative abstracts captivity from its nexus of political conflict and typifies Indians through dehumanizing epithets as well as providential hermeneutics, it is notable for the concreteness of its imagery, its concern with personal redemption, and its relatively individuated portraits of her Indian captors. The accounts of captivity published by Cotton Mather and John Williams present the Captive Self, the Captivating Other, and the experience of captivity in considerably more abstract and totalizing terms.

In clerical interpretations the captivity experience as a whole is read as a providential deliverance from subordination to diabolical and idolatrous forces. Neither the concrete details of captivity (as in Rowlandson's diary of her "removes") nor particular qualities of Indian captors (as in her contrasting portraits of Quanopin and Wetamo) are essential to establishing this interpretation. Each of the narratives considered in this chapter features at least one memorable image (Swarton's trail of blood, Williams's bloody socks, Dustan's bloody infant and tomahawk), and at least one captor who is somewhat more than a typification (Williams's Ruth, Swarton's English-bred mistress, Dustan's pious captor). But the interpretation of captivity that each narrative offers is largely independent of these details: It is a priori, and existed in some tension with the particulars of each captive's experience. This is particularly the case when the details involve resemblances between an Anglicized Captor and an Indianized Captive: The polarized typifications of Captor and Captive serve effectively to suppress this "middle ground."

As the representation of captivity became more abstract, it was joined more explicitly to orthodox representations of feminine vulnerability and subservience. Rowlandson's gender adds poignancy to her captivity, but one can imagine a male captive writing a similar spiritual autobiography, as John Bunyan had in another setting. But Cotton Mather's and John Williams's accounts treat the vulnerability of young or female captives as an instructive metaphor for the vulnerability of English civility, domesticity, and piety. Despite their differences, Hannah Swarton, Hannah Dustan, Samuel Williams, and Eunice Williams are used to personify spiritual degeneration and to illustrate the need for greater parental and clerical authority over women and children. Dustan's apparently anomalous case is especially revealing: Her decision to tomahawk her captors is attributed to her violated motherhood and fear of having to run naked through the gauntlet, and she is submitted to a particularly vigorous rebuke. And John Williams, like Quentin Stockwell, is an exception that proves the rule. Although all of the male captives are weakened on the march to Canada, it is less their vulnerability than their strength and endurance that is emphasized (spiritual strength approaching that of the martyr for Williams; survival through his own wit and the kindness of others for Stockwell).

The fear of "turning papist" and "turning savage" haunts each of these narratives except Stockwell's, which is largely preoccupied with remaining alive. Voiced most explicitly in John Williams's narrative and in Mather's figure of the "little chickens," this fear would seem to construct both the "papist" and the "savage" as a seductive, literally "captivating" object of desire. In the case of French Catholicism, this is explicitly acknowledged in Williams's narrative, and the minister goes to great lengths to confront systematically the arguments and strategies used by the Jesuits "to seduce poor souls." The attractions of savagery, on the other hand, required much less elaboration because they were naturalized. Viewed as the natural if degenerate state of humanity, savagery was always there to be "fallen" into, and it had to be vigorously resisted through the constraints of social order and spiritual discipline. In the absence of conformity to Biblical, paternal, and clerical authority, women and particularly children were vulnerable to both the destructive violence and the seductions of savagery—vulnerable to what Mather represented as being "seized," "spirited away," and "devoured."

Indian captors, then, are only sketchily drawn in the clerical narratives, for their savage characteristics are taken for granted and any departures from savagery are attributed to Providence. If English captives are figured as domesticated prey, their Indian captors are wild predators: wolves, tigers, vultures, dragons, or devils. The Indians' violence springs from their degraded nature rather than from any political grievance; their piety serves only to highlight, by counterexample, the spiritual degeneracy of the captives. The moments of dialogue in these narratives can hardly be called dialogical, for the captors' voices are only allowed to mimic those of the clerics (although an oppositional reading might detect a mocking tone). As in Rowlandson's narrative, the captor serves solely as an instrument of God to chastise, instruct, and convert the captive— and even fewer details are allowed (notably, Swarton's use of we, Mather's Indian family, and the displaced Ruth) that might supplement or subvert this typification.

The clerical typification of captivity is presented in its most abstract and totalizing form in Cotton Mather's "Observable Things." But of the captivity narratives of this period, it is The Redeemed Captive Returning to Zion that has proved the most enduring—perhaps less because of its central figure than because of the unredeemed captive at its margins. A fascinating if unsettling figure for her contemporaries, Eunice Williams over time would come to be understood less as an "unredeemed captive" than as a "white squaw"—a typification that bridged the gap between Captor and Captive, and that imagined, if ambivalently, an alternative social role for the adopted captive rather than a simple "fall." But it was not until Mary Jemison's narrative was published in the early nineteenth century that a transculturated female captive (also Iroquois) would gain something approximating her own voice (Namias 1993, Seaver 1992 [1824]).[47]

By the time Jemison's narrative was published in 1824, however, captivity had acquired more secular meanings—largely but not exclusively attached to male captives. Chapters 6 and 7 will examine alternatives to the clerical typification of captivity that emerged during the colonial era. The narratives of two Quaker captives—Jonathan Dickinson and Elizabeth Hanson—exemplify religious alternatives to the Puritan typification of captivity, whereas those of two more acculturated male captives—John Gyles and Peter Williamson—follow Quentin Stockwell in developing secular approaches to the experience Cotton Mather called "Indian captivity."

## Notes

1. Lepore 1998 offers an analysis of contesting accounts of Metacom's War, among them Mather's and Rowlandson's. On this and other works by Increase Mather, see also Hall 1988 and Slotkin 1973.

2. Mather 1977 [1684] is a facsimile of the entire Essay. For Stockwell's narrative, see pp. 39–58; also Mather 1981 [1684]. For Stockwell's experiences in Canada, see Coleman 1925, 1:132–135; 2:33.

3. Haefeli and Sweeney (1995:19, 25, passim) identify Stockwell's captors and provide an indispensable history of Pocumtuck's central role in Algonquian and Iroquoian history. Also see Melvoin 1989.

4. Baum (1993) compares Stockwell's secularism to the providential approach of Mary Rowlandson and another captive discussed in this chapter, John Williams.

5. The Synod's report, entitled "The Necessity of Reformation," is reprinted in Walker 1966:432–437. See also Levin 1978:70–74; Silverman 1984; and on declension, Canup 1990, Miller 1953, and Stout 1986.

6. In Europe the two earliest intercolonial wars were known as the War of the League of Augsburg, which ended in 1697 with the Peace of Ryswick, and the War of the Spanish Succession, which ended in 1713 with the Treaty of Utrecht. See Jennings 1975, 1984, and 1988; and Leach 1966 and 1973. Parkman 1983 (1895–97) is the classic nineteenth-century source and the object of Jennings's revisionism.

7. For captives in Canada, see Axtell 1985b, Baker 1897, Coleman 1925, Demos 1994, Haefeli and Sweeney 1995, Ulrich 1982, and Vaughan and Richter 1980.

8. Biographical sources on Cotton Mather include Breitwieser 1984, Levin 1978, Middlekauff 1971, and Silverman 1984.

9. On Judæa capta, see Kolodny 1984:12–28. Bercovitch (1972), Lowance (1980), Minter (1973), Ulrich (1982), and Vaughan and Clark (1981) discuss the Puritan use of Biblical types.

10. C. Mather 1977 [1702] is a modern, annotated edition; see also Mather 1981 [1702] for passages concerning captives. The most influential and representative of Mather's accounts of captivity are examined in this chapter; but others appear in his sermons and histories published between 1692 and 1714. See Washburn 1977–80, vols. 1, 3, and 4; and C. Mather 1714.

11. Some of these passages are reprinted in C. Mather 1981 [1702] and are analyzed by Ebersole (1995:62–72), who emphasizes Mather's intent to produce "morally rectifying" accounts of suffering and death. This is indisputable, but I would argue that an analysis of these accounts must not underestimate their morally horrifying effects. Subsequent collections of atrocity tales include such volumes as the anonymous Affecting History of the Dreadful Distresses of Frederick Manheim's Family . . . (1978 [1793]); Archibald Loudon's two-volume Selection of Some of the Most Interesting Narratives of Outrages Committed by the Indians in Their Wars with the White People (1978 [1808–11]); and John Frost's Heroic Women of the West: Comprising Thrilling Examples of Courage, Fortitude, Devotedness and Self-Sacrifice, Among the Pioneer Mothers of the Western Country (1978 [1854]). More-scholarly anthologies began to appear in the mid-nineteenth century, including multi-

ple editions of Samuel Gardner Drake's Indian Captivities (1978 [1839]) and Henry Rowe Schoolcraft's The American Indians (1978 [1851).

12. For details of Swarton's seizure from Fort Loyal, see Vaughan and Clark 1981:147–148; and Coleman 1925, 1:196–199, 204–208. The latter also surveys Canadian records on Hannah (or Joanna) Swarton and her family. On the heterogeneous, fluid, and hybrid groups called "Abenaki" by the English, see Haefeli and Sweeney 1995, Morrison 1984, and Calloway 1990, which offers a useful glossary (8–9, 301–306).

13. C. Mather 1977 [1697] is a facsimile of Humiliations; Orians 1970 includes a reprint of the sermon with commentary. C. Mather 1981 [1697]:147–157 is an annotated, modernized reprint of Swarton's narrative.

14. Kolodny interprets this passage as "suggestively an imitatio of Christ" (1984:25) as well as a sign of Swarton's vulnerability imprinted on the landscape.

15. For "inward" and "outward man," as well as "old" (unregenerated) and "new man," see OED 1971, 1:1710; and Bauman 1983:136, 152.

16. This reference is reminiscent of "sleeping oppressors" in Mather's third-person account of Hannah Dustan's captivity (C. Mather 1981 [1702]:153, 164).

17. Fitzpatrick (1991) also attributes Swarton's narrative to joint authorship.

18. Ebersole (1995:62–67) discusses fast-day observances and this sermon in particular. See also Bercovitch 1978, Elliott 1975, Miller 1953, and Stout 1986.

19. On the inability of Judæa capta to contain Dustan's response to captivity, see Kolodny 1984:12–28.

20. See Ulrich for the reference to Jael (1982:184–201) and an extensive discussion of Dustan, Swarton, and other female captives (1982:167–235).

21. This reference to Proverbs 12:10 was repeated in captivity narratives into the nineteenth century (Behen 1952:164–165) and has appeared in representations of alterity up to the present.

22. Judge Samuel Sewall reported the identity of Dustan's master in his diary (1973:372); see also Salisbury 1977:50.

23. Ramsey (1994), Stannard (1991), and others have questioned the accuracy of colonial accounts of infanticide, pointing out that like accounts of cannibalism, they are common in discourses that demonize an Other. This is undoubtedly true, but accounts such as this are consistent with the imperatives of a march in wartime and with the most well-informed ethnohistorical reconstructions of Algonquian cultures (e.g., Bragdon 1996).

24. See Ulrich 1982:184–201. The differential treatment of the Emerson sisters' two acts attests to the dehumanization of Indians, even children, during times of war.

25. In addition to Ulrich, see Burnham 1997:52–53 on Mather's attempt to control the potential subversiveness of female violence.

26. Although Cotton Mather refers to Dustan praying in captivity "like another Hannah" (1981 [1702]:163), there is no reference in the narrative to Dustan's finding God's word "comfortable"—that is, "spiritually strengthening" (OED 1971, 1:476).

27. C. Mather 1978 [1699] is a facsimile of Decennium Luctuosum; C. Mather 1981 [1702] is an annotated reprint of the version of the Dustan narrative included in Mather's Magnalia.

28. Dustan's tale has been included in numerous local histories and anthologies of "Indian atrocities," and Dustan is listed among the heroines in Notable American Women (James, James, and Boyer 1971). Dustan seems to emerge as a heroine as well in Ulrich's feminist account (Ulrich 1982), because unlike the Quaker captive Elizabeth Hanson, Dustan is neither meek nor vulnerable. Classical American literature, however, has treated Dustan more critically: Whittier, Thoreau, and Hawthorne all questioned the morality of her vengeance. See Arner 1973, Fiedler 1969, Ulrich 1982, and Whitford 1972.

29. Editions of Decennium Luctuosum include C. Mather 1978 and C. Mather 1913. C. Mather 1981 [1699]:135–144 includes annotated excerpts of Mather's brief references to particular captives in Decennium Luctuosum.

30. The increasingly strident call for clerical authority issued by ministers of the second and third generations is discussed in Stout 1986. For the Puritan reading of events as texts, see Clark 1979, Daly 1977, and Ebersole 1995:67–72; the latter discusses this sermon in particular. Ricoeur (1973), in a sense, secularizes the hermeneutic tradition of reading events as texts.

31. The word rendezvous occurs in the Dustan narrative, as quoted above. Elsewhere in Decennium Luctuosum Mather writes: "Truly the dark places of New England where the Indians had their unapproachable kennels were habitations of cruelty, and no words can sufficiently describe the cruelty undergone by our captives in those habitations" (C. Mather 1981 [1702]:139). See Canup 1990 for Mather's fear of Indianization.

32. Mather's warning to children foreshadows the didactic use of captivity narratives in literature produced for use in children's readers and Sunday school materials. See Derounian-Stodola and Levernier 1993:180–185; and Ebersole 1995:71–72, 180–185.

33. It is not coincidental that "Observable Things" dates from 1697, five years after the Salem witchcraft trials, in which Cotton Mather played a leading role. Persecution of Quakers was also intense during this period. Witches, Quakers, and Indians were seen as allied threats to the Puritan colonies. See Demos 1982, Erikson 1966, Karlsen 1987, Salisbury 1972, and Slotkin 1973.

34. For historical information on Deerfield see Demos 1994, Haefeli and Sweeney 1995, Leach 1966 and 1973, Melvoin 1989, Williams 1976 [1707], Parkman 1983 [1895–97], and Sheldon 1895–96.

35. For details regarding the Deerfield captives, see Coleman 1925, Demos 1994, Haefeli and Sweeney 1995, Williams 1976 [1707], and Williams 1981 [1707].

36. I have relied heavily on Haefeli and Sweeney's (1995) detailed account of the Native participants in the raid on Deerfield. Haefeli and Sweeney, like Demos (1995), draw on an unpublished biography of Eunice Williams written in 1842 for their accounts of Eunice's adoption, which are consistent both with Mohawk cultural practices and with the course of Eunice's life.

37. Williams 1978 contains reprints, in facsimile, of editions published in 1707 (the first), 1758 (the third), and 1853. The first and third editions also contain "Reports of Divine Mercy," the sermon Williams preached in Boston upon his return from captivity. Later editions contain additional documents and annotations regarding the Deerfield captives. Williams 1976 [1707], a modern, annotated edition, is reprinted with minor changes in Williams 1981 [1707].

38. Governor Dudley of Massachusetts sent his own son on a mission to Quebec to retrieve the captives in summer 1705. Also prominent in the redemption effort were relatives of captives, including John Sheldon and John Wells of Deerfield. These efforts secured the redemption of fifty-four captives in May 1706, in exchange for French prisoners held in New England. Demos (1994) chronicles various other efforts to redeem the Deerfield captives.

39. On the Kellogg family, see Coleman 1925, 2:97–102; Demos 1994; and Williams 1976 [1707]:136, n. 131. Several captives from New England (but not from Deerfield) became nuns, most notably Esther Wheelwright, who would become Mother Superior of the Ursuline convent in Quebec (Axtell 1985a:297–301).

40. Rowlandson's narrative appeared in ten editions during the colonial period, Williams's in six. Several times, in 1720 and in the 1770s, the two narratives were issued in close succession by the same publisher (see the Appendix). Clark (1976) and Baum (1993) compare Williams's narrative with Rowlandson's; Demos (1995:55–76) discusses the narrative in the context of Williams's other postcaptivity writings.

41. I am speaking figuratively here: Williams, more modest than Cotton Mather, would not explicitly claim this role for himself; and his Dedication to Joseph Dudley, Governor of Massachusetts, acknowledges that "heaven has honored you as the prime instrument in returning our captivity" (Williams 1981 [1707]:40).

42. See Ebersole 1995:72–76 and Demos 1994:55–76 for discussions of the four works Williams produced soon after his captivity. In addition to the narrative and sermon, they include a pastoral letter written from Canada, published in Cotton Mather's Good Fetch'd Out of Evil; and a jeremiad, God in the Camp.

43. Vaughan and Clark (1981:185) identify Ruth's master as probably the Rev. Gershorn Bulkeley. On mission villages and the syncretic Christianity of their inhabitants, see Axtell 1985b, Davis 1995, Demos 1994, Morrison 1984, Haefeli and Sweeney 1995, and Shoemaker 1995b.

44. For the visits of other captives' masters, see Demos 1994, and Haefeli and Sweeney 1995:3, 43–56.

45. One of Eunice's grandchildren, Eleazer Williams, grew to be an eccentric who claimed to be the Lost Dauphin, son of Louis XVI (Burger 1989). For additional information on Eunice Williams and her descendants see Demos 1994, Medlicott 1965, Melvoin 1989, Williams 1976 [1707], and Williams 1978.

46. The sermon is reprinted in Williams 1978 [1853]. See also Demos 1994:201–206.

47. Gherman (1975) considers Eunice Williams along with other so-called "white squaws"; see also Axtell 1975 and Namias 1993. For transculturation, see Hallowell 1963 and Pratt 1991.

# 6

# Captive Ethnographers, 1699–1736

The dominant Puritan typification of captivity gained its influence from both social and cultural sources: It bore the authority of those who articulated it—the clerical elite—as well as the hegemonic system of assumptions regarding savagery, civility, and gender embedded within it. To be sure, there are significant variations among the Puritan narratives: Rowlandson's concreteness and attention to her own spiritual state as mirrored in her mistress; Cotton Mather's abstractness and attention to the collective failings that had called forth God's wrath; Williams's preoccupation with the Jesuit and Indian threat to his congregation and children. But all offer a providential interpretation of captivity, one that typically sees God as chastising and delivering New England as his chosen people. This is true even of Rowlandson's spiritual autobiography, if the anonymous preface and the providential conclusion that frame her narrative are taken into account.

To assert control over the production of meaning, as Cotton Mather did so forcefully, is not necessarily to realize it. Even in asserting a clerical monopoly over the interpretation of captivity, Mather revealed the extent to which the authority of the clergy had waned in the late seventeenth century. Still, by controlling the press as well as the pulpit, the clergy was able to dominate the interpretation of captivity in New England print culture into the mid-eighteenth century. Mather repeated his typification of captivity in publications dating through 1714; and Rowlandson's and Williams's narratives were reissued in 1720 by a Boston bookseller, Samuel Phillips, who specialized in the works of the Mathers and other divines. Not until 1736—eight years after Mather's death, seven years after that of Williams—was an alternative perspective upon captivity published in New England. This was the narrative of John Gyles, who neither "turned savage" nor fully returned to the Puritan fold. Rather, Gyles used the knowledge he had gained during six years of captivity to serve the colonies as an interpreter and mediator in their dealings with

Eastern Abenakis. "Part horror story, part ethnography, part natural history, and part sermon," as Vaughan and Clark put it (1981:94), Gyles's hybrid narrative turns the selective tradition of captivity in a more secular direction without abandoning the familiar, still authoritative form of providential history.[1]

Outside of Puritan New England, two narratives by Quakers had already wrought significant changes upon the providential interpretation of captivity. The most prominent of these, Jonathan Dickinson's (1699), ranked with Rowlandson's and Williams's narratives as one of the most popular prose works published in the British colonies. Both Dickinson's narrative and the other Quaker narrative, by Elizabeth Hanson (1728), portray providential deliverances from captivity; but neither reads captivity as a divine punishment, offers a typological interpretation of events, or presents Indians as essentialized typifications. Spiritual autobiographies with a difference—by virtue of their pacifism, universalism, and quiet attentiveness—the Quaker narratives depart from the Puritan selective tradition in instructive ways.[2]

All three narratives considered in this chapter, especially that of John Gyles, temper providential hermeneutics with a more secular mode of interpretation that might be called proto-ethnographic. In analyzing these narratives, this chapter traces the initial stages of the transition from a premodern interpretation of captivity grounded in the epistemology of correspondences to a recognizably modern one grounded in an increasingly secular empiricism.[3]

### Shared Substance, Shared Light: The Dickinson and Hanson Narratives

From 1699 until the end of the colonial era, Philadelphia rivaled Boston as a site for the production of captivity narratives. There was such intense interest in the captivity of Quaker merchant Jonathan Dickinson and English missionary Robert Barrow that the Society of Friends rushed to acquire a press and a printer. Dickinson's narrative, the first work off the new press, attracted a wide audience in the colonies and abroad, where it appeared in illustrated Dutch and German editions as well as in English ones. Part spiritual autobiography, part adventure story, the narrative bore an appropriately hybrid title: God's Protecting Providence Man's Surest Help and Defence in Times of the Greatest Difficulty and Most Imminent Danger: Evidenced in the Remarkable Deliverance of Divers Persons, from the Devouring Waves of the Sea, and also from the More Cruelly Devouring Jawes of the Inhumane Canibals of Florida Amongst Whom They Suffered Shipwreck.[4] Although this title was probably not of the captive's own devising, providential "deliverance" from "devouring jaws" is indeed the dominant theme of Jonathan Dickinson's narrative.

A very different kind of captive from previous authors of captivity narratives, Jonathan Dickinson was a prosperous Jamaican planter and a trader in a wide assortment of commodities, including African slaves. He was shipwrecked off the notoriously treacherous southeastern coast of Florida in September 1696, while traveling from his plantation in Jamaica to Philadelphia with his entire household—his wife Mary, their infant son, and ten African slaves. They were accompanied by a male relative and by a distinguished missionary named Robert Barrow. Their ship, the Reformation, was loaded with a cargo of sugar, molasses, rum, meat, livestock, clothing, and other merchandise.

Upon their shipwreck south of Cape Canaveral, the Dickinson party and the ship's nine-member crew were captured by a group of coastal foragers known as Jeagas, who lived in the town of Jobe ("Hoe-Bay" in the narrative; see Map 3.1).[5] "Captured" is an accurate term given the dynamics of the interaction, but this was a capture that in the end amounted to a rescue: With the help of their captors, the Dickinson party survived their shipwreck and made it to safety. In other words, unlike the Puritan narratives, Dickinson's does not begin with a scene of colonial domesticity and civic order destroyed but rather with a shivering, desolate party finding its fate in the hands of Indians infamous for piracy and cannibalism.

The isolated inhabitants of Florida's southeastern coast—Jeagas, Tequestas, Guacatas, and the more powerful Ais—supplemented their diet of fish, shellfish, and plants by looting shipwrecked vessels.[6] Although the Spanish had generally friendly relations with these groups, English castaways could expect a hostile reception, as they were known to be participants in Charleston's Indian slave trade and frequent enemies of the Spanish.[7] It is probable that like the neighboring Calusas and Timucuas, southeastern coastal peoples sometimes sacrificed captives to their deities; but their reputation as "savage, heathen, Caribs" or cannibals was unwarranted.[8]

Dickinson's description of his first encounter with the Jeagas reveals both his style of interacting with his captors and his narrative's rhetorical style. Some eight hours after the castaways found shelter on shore two men approached,

> running fiercely and foaming at the mouth, having no weapons except their knives: and forthwith not making any stop; violently seized the two first of our men they met with, who were carrying corn from the vessel. . . . They used no violence, for the men resisted not, but taking them under the arm

brought them towards me. Their countenance was very furious and bloody.(1961 [1699]:28)

Dickinson persuaded his companions not to get their guns and kill these two men, "showing their inability to defend us from what would follow." He counseled the entire party to "put our trust in the Lord who was able to defend to the uttermost." When the men remained, looking upon them "with a wild, furious countenance," reports Dickinson, "I bethought myself to give them some tobacco and pipes, which they greedily snatched from me, and making a snuffing noise like a wild beast, turned their backs upon us and run away" (28).

When this pair had left, the castaways

> communed together and considered our condition, being amongst a barbarous people such as were generally accounted man-eaters, believing those two were gone to alarm their people. We sat ourselves down, expecting cruelty and hard death, except it should please the Almighty God to work wonderfully for our deliverance.

Knowing that the Spanish had some influence over the coastal Indians and that the English were despised, the party decided to represent themselves as Spaniards, delegating a Spanish-speaking mariner, Solomon Cressen, to speak for them. Meanwhile a group of Jeagas raided the shipwrecked vessel, while "their Casseekey (for so they call their king) with about thirty more came down to us in a furious manner, having a dismal aspect and foaming at the mouth." Shouting "Nickaleer," which the party came to understand as a derogatory term for "English," the Jeagas surrounded them, their knives drawn. "We stirred nor moved not," reported Dickinson, "but sat all or most of us very calm and still, some of us in a good frame of spirit, being freely given up to the will of God" (1961 [1699]:29–30).

Dickinson's description of this confrontation does not present an essentialized distinction between Indians and English (which in this setting includes the African slaves) but rather a behavioral one. He employs a language of similes and attributes, not metaphors. The Jeagas are described as being dominated by passion rather than reason: They run "fiercely," have a "wild, furious" countenance, and sound "like animals." The castaways, in contrast, were doing the opposite at the behest of Barrow and Dickinson: They were cultivating a state of peaceful and calm resignation, the "silent waiting upon God" that was characteristic of the Quaker sect.[9] The Jeagas, "ready to execute their bloody design," waited also, apparently for the orders of their cacique (chief).[10] "But," reported Dickinson, "on a sudden it pleased the Lord to work wonderfully for our preservation, and instantly all these savage men were struck dumb, and like men amazed the space of a quarter of an hour in which time their countenances fell, and they looked like another people" (1961 [1699]:30). Following this transformative silence—which, to judge from his description, struck Dickinson as similar to the trance-like state of "convincement" that gave the Quakers their name—the Jeagas turned their attention away from the castaways and toward their goods and clothing, the cacique confiscating their supply of Spanish coins. Thereafter, the English "perceived that the Casseekey's heart was tendered towards us"; he had "now become a defender of us from the rage of others" (31). For members of the Society of Friends there could hardly be a more dramatic example of the power of Friends to inspire others, through their example, to heed their own "inward light." Through the unmediated spiritual communication to which Quaker silence was dedicated, this would-be cannibal was transformed into a friend and protector.[11]

The Jobe cacique's response to Dickinson's party was exceptional, however, and the captives remained haunted by their captors' reputation for cannibalism. Their fear of "cruelly devouring jaws" was reinforced by the cacique, who warned them not to travel northward, toward the mission of Santa Lucía, where they hoped to come under Spanish protection. Instead, Dickinson understood from the cacique's signs, "We should have our throats and scalps cut and be shot, burnt and eaten" (1961 [1699]:32). In a decision they would later regret, Dickinson and his party discounted this warning, attributing it to the cacique's greedy desire to claim the captives for himself. Their skepticism regarding the cacique, however, failed to allay their fear of cannibalism: Hence, it seems, Dickinson's frequent description of Indians as "foaming at the mouth," with its evocation of an irrational, unrestrained appetite; hence certain captives' fear of fire, which they thought was being prepared to cook their flesh; hence the refusal to eat on the part of certain captives, who feared the Indians "would feed us to feed themselves" (35).

The typification of the Indians as treacherous cannibals was so strong that it led the captives to discount a friendly cacique's offer of information, and even led some to suspect malicious intentions behind the hospitable act of sharing food. Although Dickinson's wording usually seems to exclude him from the company of the fearful, when he summarizes the terrifying experience of captivity his metaphor also evokes cannibalism: "Thus would danger often appear unto us and almost swallow us up; but at times we should be set over it, having a secret hope that God would work our deliverance, having preserved us from so many perils" (1961 [1699]:36). Maintaining emotional control, rationality, and resignation vs. being swallowed up or devoured by an unrestrained, irrational Other:

These were the parameters within which Dickinson experienced (or at least expressed his experience of) captivity.

To be devoured or swallowed up is to be incorporated within an Other, transformed into an Other. This possibility, horrifying as it was, did not constitute Jonathan and Mary Dickinson's ultimate nightmare. They were most fearful for their six-month-old son—not so much that he would be physically devoured by their captors but that he would live to become one of them. Confessed Dickinson, "One thing did seem more grievous to me and my wife than any other thing. Which was that if it should so happen that we should be put to death, we feared that our child would be kept alive, and bred up as one of those people; when this thought did arise it wounded us deep" (1961 [1699]:59).

The fear that the Jeagas would adopt rather than kill the child was inspired, no doubt, by the solicitude (and probably, ritualized acceptance) the women had demonstrated toward him. When the captives were first taken to the town of Jobe the cacique's wife, "having a young child sucking at her breast, gave it to another woman, and would have my child; which my wife was very loath to suffer; but she would not be denied, took our child and suckled it at her breast, viewing and feeling it from top to toe; at length returned it to my wife" (34). Eventually Mary Dickinson became used to having Indian women nurse her child; indeed, Jonathan's narrative reports that when she had lost her own milk due to hunger and thirst, "we went a-begging at times to the Indian women to suckle our child; which they would seldom deny." The child thrived: He who "had been at Death's door from the time of his birth until we were cast away, began now to be cheerful, and have an appetite for food" (48). Mary Dickinson entered enough into the spirit of this intimate exchange to be willing to take an Indian child to her breast when asked, despite her lack of milk.[12] She received, in turn, a rare piece of fish.

The sharing of breast milk is by far the most benign interaction described in the narrative, and it contrasts markedly with both the captives' fear of cannibalism and with the trope, found often in Puritan narratives, of "sucking infants" being grabbed from mothers and dispatched by a tomahawk or dashed against a tree. But Mary Dickinson's initial aversion indicates that this intimate exchange was not without its threatening side: Breast-feeding, like cannibalism, involves the incorporation of the substance of another.[13] When this substance belongs not to a mother but to an Other, breast-feeding becomes a form of transformation and appropriation. Though feeding at the breast of Indian women strengthened the child and probably saved his life, it may have represented physically the threatening possibility that the child might "be bred up as one of those people." Mary and Jonathan Dickinson preferred that the child die.

Neither nightmare came to pass. The castaways were released by the cacique of Jobe and traveled north to the abandoned Jesuit mission of Santa Lucía.[14] Here, as predicted, they were captured by the local Guacatas, who as Dickinson put it, "rushed violently on us, rending and tearing those few clothes we had" (see Figure 6.1). Once again, however, the captives were preserved through a moment of silence and divine inspiration:

> After they had taken all from us but our lives, they began to talk one to another, vehemently foaming at mouth, like wild boars, and taking their bows and arrows with other weapons, cried out Nickaleer, Nickaleer. . . . But suddenly we perceived them to look about and listen, and then desisted to prosecute their bloody design. One of them took a pair of breeches and gave it to my wife.

This reprieve, however, was only temporary. Continued Dickinson, in one of the most intriguing passages of the narrative:

> We brought our great Bible and a large book of Robert Barclay's to this place. And being all stripped as naked as we were born, and endeavoring to hide our nakedness; these cannibals took the books, and tearing out the leaves would give each of us a leaf to cover us; which we took from them: at which time they would deride and smite us; and instantly another of them would snatch away what the other gave us, smiting and deriding us withal.
> . . . In this juncture it pleased God to tender the hearts of some of them towards us; especially the Casseekey his wife, and some of the chiefest amongst them, who were made instruments to intercede for us, and stop the rage of the multitude, who seemed not to be satisfied without our blood. (1961 [1699]:44)

At such a juncture a Puritan commentator might have referred to the Garden of Eden, but Dickinson refrains from any comparison of his and Mary's state to that of Adam and Eve. More salient for the Dickinsons, perhaps, was the former Quaker practice of "going naked as a sign." Up until the mid-1670s, when the practice was abandoned because of the hostility it engendered, both male and female Quakers would occasionally parade naked through the streets of England, employing their naked bodies to signify (ambiguously) either their own purity or the decadence of the crowd surrounding them. Quaker theologian Robert Barclay himself went naked through the streets of Aberdeen in 1672. That his followers, in this instance, tried to cover their bodies with the physical manifestation of Barclay's own words, as well as God's, suggests that they interpreted nakedness in this instance not as a sign of purity but as a sign

FIGURE 6.1   Jonathan Dickinson and his fellow captives stripped of their
clothing at St. Lucía. SOURCE: Ongelukkige Schipbreuk (Leiden, 1707). (Courtesy of
the Edward E. Ayer Collection, the Newberry Library, Chicago.)

of heightened vulnerability. After all, they were not controlling the signi-
fication process, and were naked before a naked audience they considered degenerate rather than an elaborately clothed audience they considered decadent. In this context clothing shifted its significance, becoming
a marker of civility, of rational control over the passions. Whereas in
Britain the meaning of the Friends' plain clothing and their sense of difference could be intensified by wearing no clothing at all, in Florida the
loss of clothing threatened or diminished their sense of difference from
those around them. How appropriate, then, to replace the clothing with
other signifiers of difference: the word of God and Barclay's exposition
on the "inward light" within each human being.[15]

   Despite the emphasis on maintaining markers of difference, Dickinson's narration of this episode, like the initial encounter with the Jeagas,
testifies to an essential commonality between captive and reputed cannibal. Although Dickinson's interpretation of deliverance through the intercession of Indian "instruments" is reminiscent of the Puritans, this is a
Providence that works through the "inward light," or Holy Spirit, and reveals itself in moments of silence. However bestial in outward appearance and behavior, however destructive of the markers of restraint and

rationality, Indians—like Quakers, like all human beings—were deemed capable of responding to the divine light within. In place of the almost relentless oppositional rhetoric of the Puritans there is evident in Dickinson's narrative a belief in the fundamental spiritual unity and perfectibility of all human beings.[16]

Only twice in his captivity narrative does Dickinson testify to the transformation of Indians through the workings of the "inward light." After the second episode, when he and his companions were under the protection of the cacique at Santa Lucía, they were subjected to the indigenous mode of seeking divine guidance. Dickinson describes his experiences in great detail, although he is only dimly aware of their significance. On the way to the Guacata town the captives were submitted to a gauntlet-like ordeal, some Indians striking or stoning them, others protecting them from these blows and deflecting arrows aimed at them. The gauntlet was followed by a council in which their mediator, Solomon Cressen, was interviewed. The captives were then dressed and displayed in Indian clothing, the women in raw deerskins, the men in straw breechcloths. "At length we heard a woman or two cry, according to their manner," reported Dickinson,

> and that very sorrowfully, one of which I took to be the Casseekey's wife which occasioned some of [us] to think that something extraordinary was to be done to us. We heard a strange sort of a noise which was not like unto a noise made by a man; but we could not understand what nor where it was; for sometimes it sounded to be in one part of the house, sometimes in another, to which we had an ear. And indeed our ears and eyes could perceive or hear nothing but what was strange and dismal; and death seemed [to have] surrounded us. (1961 [1699]:46)

The apprehensive captives finally ascertained that the noise was produced by the brewing of what the Spanish called "casseena"—which "when made, and cooled to sup, was in a conch-shell first carried to the Casseekey, who threw part of it on the ground, and the rest he drank up, and then would make a loud He-m; and afterwards the cup passed to the rest of the Caseekey's associates" (46–47). Most of the day was passed in "sipping, chatting and smoking," followed at night by drumming and singing: "a most hideous howling, very irksome to us" (47).

"Hideous howling" aside, this is an early and valuable description of the ceremonial drinking of the herbal stimulant known as black drink. Although Dickinson had little idea of what was going on, his detailed description allows us to infer that his fate was being determined by a council that had been purified, strengthened, and united by sharing black drink.[17] A Puritan captive, thinking he knew what he was experiencing, might have provided a vague account of devil worship; Dickinson, unsure of what was happening, reported his experience with a naive attentiveness that has earned him the respect of contemporary scholars. Swanton, for instance, cites Dickinson at length, calling him "one of our best informants regarding the ancient people of the east coast of Florida" (1952:132). It is, I believe, partly Dickinson's training in silent, patient watchfulness that enabled him to be a valuable informant regarding the daily and ceremonial life of his captors. It is also because in the absence of the Puritan's typological hermeneutics Dickinson was less inclined to foreclose description by rushing to interpretation.

This is not to say that Dickinson's narrative lacks an interpretive framework, only that the Quaker mode of interpretation is considerably more tentative and open than that of the Puritans. In Dickinson's narrative there is the concrete descriptiveness of Mary Rowlandson together with interpretive restraint and a more encompassing acknowledgment of commonality between Self and Other. Less preoccupied with himself than was Rowlandson (for he was less burdened by guilt, grief, and separation), and less inclined to interpret Others in his own terms, Dickinson gave an account of his experiences that in some ways anticipated ethnographic empiricism.[18]

The black drink ceremony is both the high point in Dickinson's description of his captors and the climax of his captivity. Following the ceremony Dickinson and the other captives—assuming they had been accepted as Spaniards—were turned over to the paramount Ais cacique, to whom other caciques paid tribute. In being handed over in this manner, as in the ritual itself, Dickinson's experience was similar to that of another southeastern captive earlier in the century, John Smith. After a precarious month at the paramount chief's town of Jece—where they feared their nationality would be exposed by other English castaways awaiting their fate—the captives were rescued by the Spanish, who were allies of England at the time. From that point on the tale is no longer a captivity narrative, but it remains one of severe hardship as the party makes its way to St. Augustine, Charleston, and finally Philadelphia.

On the journey homeward an incident occurred in St. Augustine that serves as a reminder that Quaker universalism could be severely limited in practice: Dickinson and his shipmaster inquired into the possibility of selling one slave each in order to buy necessities for the journey north. The local governor forbade the sale, but one of those who might have been sold, the shipmaster's "Negro Ben," had almost lost his life trying to save Dickinson's kinsman from freezing to death; all had suffered alongside their masters since the shipwreck. Like the majority of Quaker merchants of his day, Dickinson did not consider the buying, selling, or owning of slaves inconsistent with his religious beliefs. Although his narrative does not address this issue, Dickinson's praise for the orderliness of the Spanish missions through which he passed, combined with his participation in slavery, indicates that he approved of various involuntary means of submitting peoples considered savage to the influence of Christian civility—however much his narrative emphasizes the transformative power of exemplification and spiritual communication.[19]

To some extent the publication of Dickinson's narrative can be attributed to the fame of his companion Robert Barrow, who died in Philadelphia almost immediately after the party's arrival. Dickinson eulogized Barrow as

> having passed through great exercises in much patience; and in all the times of our greatest troubles was ready to counsel us to patience and to wait what the Lord our God would bring to pass. And he would often express that it was his belief, that our lives should be spared, not be lost in that wilderness and amongst those people who would have made a prey of us. (Dickinson 1961 [1699]:100)

It was likely one of Barrow's friends, a prominent member of the Philadelphia Meeting named Samuel Carpenter, who sponsored the publication of Dickinson's narrative and wrote an anonymous preface. Like the preface to Rowlandson's narrative, the preface by Carpenter attests to the veracity of the author and enumerates the works of Providence contained in the narrative.

Dickinson was soon to join Carpenter as one of the most prosperous and prominent residents of Philadelphia. Although he maintained two estates in Jamaica, Dickinson established two in Pennsylvania as well. He employed slave labor in both locations and continued to engage in the slave trade despite strong opposition from Quaker abolitionists in Pennsylvania.[20] He became an influential member of the Philadelphia Meeting and the legislative Assembly, and served a term as mayor of Philadelphia, where he had an unusually well-appointed home. His status in Pennsylvania may account in part for the republication of his narrative in at least three subsequent colonial editions (an English edition was published by Benjamin Franklin in 1735, another English edition in 1751, and a German edition in 1756).[21]

The second Quaker to leave an account of captivity among Indians lived a considerably more modest life. Elizabeth Meader Hanson lived with her husband, John, on an isolated farm in Dover township, New Hampshire (see Map 4.1). John was well acquainted with the danger of Indian attacks, as his paternal grandmother and an uncle had been killed in the first intercolonial war, and an aunt abducted by Indians was never heard from again. But as pacifists the Hanson family declined to take refuge in the garrison when Abenakis attacked the area in August 1724. This was during a period of uneasy peace between France and England, but Abenakis continued to be resentful of English trading practices and territorial expansion. Hostility had finally broken out into warfare in northern and western New England in 1723. Known as Lovewell's War, Lord Dummer's War, or Grey Lock's War, the conflict of 1723–27 remained a local affair. The French provided covert support for Abenaki warriors who mounted raids on exposed frontier towns. As in the first two intercolonial wars, the Abenaki forces included many refugees from New England displaced by previous wars.

An Eastern Abenaki war party attacked the Hanson home three days after Massachusetts forces had destroyed the Kennebec village of Norridgewock and killed, scalped, and mutilated Sebastien Rasles, a Jesuit priest as loved by Abenakis as he was despised by the English.[22] At the time of the attack John Hanson and his eldest daughter were at a Friends' Meeting. "They killed one child immediately as soon as they entered the door," relates Hanson, "thinking thereby to strike in us the greater terror and to make us more fearful of them" (1981 [1728]:231). In the very first paragraph Hanson has established her interpretive style: She characteristically offers an explanation for why her captors do what they do, even if these actions have come to be conventional in captivity narratives. Another child of four years of age was killed, who "continued screeching and crying very much in the fright, and the Indians, to ease themselves of the noise and to prevent the danger of a discovery that might arise from it, immediately before my face knocked its brains out." Again, a horrifying action, followed by a rational explanation of what motivated it. Hanson explains her own actions in a similarly understated way: "I bore this as well as I could, not daring to appear disturbed or show much uneasiness lest they should do the same to the other [child,] but should have been exceeding glad they had kept out of sight till we had been gone from our house." After mentioning dispassionately that the children were scalped, she (or her editor, for this is a more didactic voice) explains that scalping is "a practice common with these people," providing "testimony and evidence that they have killed so many" (232).[23]

Hanson, her two-week-old infant, three other children, and a servant girl were marched to Port Royal in Nova Scotia. Along the way Hanson was separated from two of the children and a servant. After five months among the Abenakis and one month among the French, Hanson's husband redeemed all but sixteen-year-old Sarah—this because "the affections they had for my daughter made them refuse all offers and terms of ransom" (1981 [1728]:242). Sarah's Abenaki mistress hoped that the girl would marry her son; but on the advice of a relative who made a second attempt to redeem her, Sarah instead accepted the marriage proposal of a

French Canadian militia captain. The couple remained in Canada but were not cut off entirely from Sarah's New England roots, as two of their children married descendants of captives from Deerfield.[24]

Some two years after her return from captivity Hanson was visited by a prominent Quaker preacher from England named Samuel Bownas. She was then a widow, for her husband had died on a second journey to Canada seeking Sarah's release. Likely Bownas was the anonymous "friend" who, as the title page states, took down Hanson's relation "from her own mouth" and published it, "almost in her own words," as God's Mercy Surmounting Man's Cruelty, Exemplified in the Captivity and Redemption of Elizabeth Hanson.[25] True to its title the narrative offers a providential interpretation, but unlike previous New England captives, Hanson does not present her difficulties as a punishment for individual or collective sins. In this narrative "man's cruelty" is not motivated by divine wrath but by human passion or deprivation. And "God's mercy" has a very human—often a feminine—face. Whereas Hanson's narrative is similar to Dickinson's in its emphasis on patient acceptance of God's will, it far exceeds the latter in its effort to understand and explain the motivations of her captors as human beings. As the opening passages indicate, the narrative almost entirely lacks oppositional typifications of Hanson's captors, even when they are harming her or her children. Instead, she employs what, borrowing Ricoeur's term, we might call a hermeneutics of empathy.[26]

Hunger, a primary concern of many captives, is the focal condition in Hanson's account. Hunger plagued captives and captors alike, and motivated both the vengeful cruelty of her master and the compassion of the Abenaki women, who showed Hanson how to supplement her failing breast milk with a gruel of walnut milk and corn meal. The bond Hanson established with Abenaki women—particularly with her master's wife, daughter, and mother-in-law—may have saved her child's life as well as her own. When her master, "naturally of a very hot and passionate temper," abused and threatened Hanson and her children, it was the women who protected them (1981 [1728]:238).

Weak from giving birth only two weeks before her captivity, Hanson initially found her master kind and considerate. He helped carry her baby and other burdens, and assisted her on steep portions of the trail, "in all of which he showed some humanity and civility more than I could have expected," commented Hanson conventionally, "for which privilege I was secretly thankful to God as the moving cause thereof" (233). But when "pinched with hunger," unsuccessful at hunting, and forced to boil and eat old beaverskin matchcoats, "the disappointment was so great that he could not forbear revenging it on us poor captives." Once, when her master violently threw food at Hanson, "his squaw and daughter broke out in a great crying," which made her "fear mischief was hatching against us." Hanson took refuge with her master's mother-in-law, who knew no English but signed to her that she should pray to God and prepare for death, as her master intended to kill her. "The poor old squaw was so very kind and tender that she would not leave me all that night but laid herself down at my feet, designing what she could to assuage her son-in-law's wrath, who had conceived evil against me chiefly, as I understood, because the want of victuals urged him to it" (1981 [1728]:236–237). The night passed without further incident, but her master repeated his threats on other occasions. Later, when her baby began to thrive on the walnut and corn milk, he "would often look upon it and say when it was fat enough, it should be killed, and he would eat it." Nevertheless, related Hanson, "I could not persuade myself that he intended to do as he pretended but only to aggravate and afflict me" (241).

Hanson was judging her master's intentions only from what she could surmise of his character and condition; but she was correct in assuming that an Abenaki would not cannibalize his captive—that is, unless he were to relinquish all claim to his status as a human being. As Hanson perceived, generosity was the supreme Abenaki virtue, and cannibalism was considered its opposite, the epitome of asocial, monstrous behavior.[27] On the other hand, as Hanson also surmised, captives who were not adopted could expect to be physically and verbally abused, especially in times of stress. Eventually the abuse reached a point at which Hanson seriously feared for her life. Her master, while lying sick in his wigwam, struck her son violently and without provocation. The boy "bore it with a wonderful patience, not so much as in the least complaining, so that the child's patience assuaged the barbarity of his hard heart, who, no doubt, would have carried his passion and resentment higher had the child cried." Soon afterward Hanson's master was back on his feet, intending, his wife and daughter warned, to kill Hanson and her son. Hanson went out to cut wood for the fire, hoping to pacify him by attending to her work, although she expected that the children would be killed "in this mad fit"—"having no other way but to cast my care upon God" (1981 [1728]:239). When she returned, she learned, to her relief, that her master had been suddenly struck with a dreadful pain, which he attributed to "the mischief he had done." She continued: "And after this he soon recovered but was not so passionate" (240).

This episode, the climax of the narrative, reveals clearly the great value Elizabeth Hanson placed on submission—so great that she left her young children alone to face possible death because in doing so she would be submitting both to her master and to God's will. Like Dickinson, Hanson met violent passion with quiet, patient submission, and like Dickinson she found that it could work to defuse a situation and transform an aggressor. Hanson is considerably more restrained than Dickinson, however, in attributing passion and irrationality to her captors. Perhaps this is largely because of their different circumstances; but Hanson describes moments of passion discretely and empirically—that is, as the response of her master, in particular, to provocations such as hunger and illness.

Similarly restrained and empirical are Hanson's efforts to understand and explain communal activities—for example, the return of the war party, which she understood as somewhat analogous to rituals in her own community. Upon arriving at "the Indian fort," she remembered, "many of the Indians came to visit us and, in their way, welcomed my master home and held a great rejoicing with dancing, firing guns, beating on hollow trees instead of drums, shouting, drinking, and feasting after their manner in much excess for several days together which, I suppose, in their thoughts was a kind of thanks to God put up for their safe return and good success" (1981 [1728]:236). This passage is remarkable for its author's obvious attempt to interpret Abenaki thoughts and actions by analogy to her own at the same time as she maintained an appreciation of difference (shown by her use of phrases such as "in their way," "after their manner," "I suppose in their thoughts," and "a kind of thanks"). In both its empathy (or universalism) and its tentativeness (or relativism), this description has a proto-ethnographic quality that is more sophisticated than Dickinson's, albeit less informative.

Although Hanson succeeded in making some sense of her captors' actions and in thinking the best of them, it was not easy for her to maintain equanimity. "While they were in their jollitry and mirth," she confessed, "my mind was greatly exercised. . . . I found it very hard to keep my mind as I ought under the resignation which is proper to be in under such afflictions and sore trials as at that time I suffered, in being under various fears and doubts concerning my children that were separated from me, which helped to add to and greatly increase my troubles" (236). The awkward syntax here seems to reflect her troubled state of mind, one she had not overcome years later when she dictated the narrative. After all, she was still separated from the daughter who remained in Canada as well as from the three family members she had lost in the attack or its aftermath. Hanson prays at the close of the narrative that "the Lord will enable me patiently to submit to His will in all things He is pleased to suffer to my lot while here" (243).

God's will but decidedly not a punishment, captivity was an affliction to be borne, like all others, through patience and attentiveness. With this approach to interpretation Hanson dictated a narrative that is less detailed than Rowlandson's or Dickinson's but more successful than either in according her captors, even her primary antagonist, human sentiments and struggles similar to her own. Oppositional typification—passion ver-

sus patience, carnality versus spirituality—gives way to sympathetic explanation; antipathy, to empathy.[28] In Hanson's spiritual autobiography,
published four decades after Rowlandson's, the captive becomes an interpreter of her captors rather than simply an interpreter of her experience.
This move toward the captive as interpreter and translator is furthered in
the narrative next published in New England—that of John Gyles.

## Manners and Customs:
## The Transculturated Captive

Memoirs of Odd Adventures, Strange Deliverances, &c. in the Captivity of John
Gyles, Esq., Commander of the Garrison on St. George's River, published in
1736, concerns a lengthy captivity of the preceding century, during the
first intercolonial war.[29] Gyles was about ten years of age when he was
abducted, in 1689, from the remote settlement of Pemaquid, Maine,
where his father served as chief justice (see Map 4.1). He spent nearly the
entire war in captivity, coming to maturity during his six years among
the Maliseets and three years as a servant to a French fur trader. Gyles
learned French and two Algonquian languages, Maliseet and Micmac,
during his captivity. After his release from captivity, he used his linguistic and ethnographic knowledge to establish a niche as a trader, interpreter, diplomat, and military officer on the Massachusetts frontier. Only
months after his release, in October 1698, and again in January 1699,
Gyles served as an interpreter and negotiator in conferences arranging
the return of other captives from what the colonists called the Eastern Indians.[30] Commissioned as a lieutenant in 1700, Gyles continued to serve
as an official interpreter for treaty conferences and prisoner exchanges
for several decades. In 1725 he became commander of a new garrison in
Maine, and he continued in the colonial service until he retired shortly
before his death, in 1754 or 1755. He had considerable influence among
Maliseets, Micmacs, and other Eastern Indians, one of whom stated, "We
look upon Capt. Gyles as a captain of the tribes in our parts" (Calloway
1991:222).

   A number of other captives had similar careers following their release,
including Joseph Bane (or Bean), who had been captured during the first
intercolonial war and who served with Gyles as an interpreter at treaty
conferences between Massachusetts and the Eastern Indians. Phineas
Stevens, a captive during Grey Lock's War, became an important military
captain, trader, and intermediary in New Hampshire. Several members of
the Kellogg family of Deerfield became influential translators and mediators upon their release from captivity. Joseph Kellogg was one of the foremost interpreters of the Mohawk language, a truckmaster (official Indian
trader), and a military captain. His company at Fort Dummer, Vermont in-

cluded Indians from Kahnawake and the Hudson River. Joseph's brother Martin and sister Rebecca were employed at the school for Mohawk children at Stockbridge. The colonial government turned to Gyles, Bean, Stevens, the Kelloggs, and others to help redeem and reintegrate other captives, maintain friendly relationships with Indian allies, and destroy those allied with the French. Indians often refused to treat with the colonists unless a captive-turned-mediator were present—an extension into colonial times of indigenous patterns of captivity and hostage-exchange.[31]

Unlike narratives written by captives who attempted to return to their previous lives as gentlewoman, goodwife, settler, minister, or merchant, Gyles's Memoirs expresses the perspective of a (partially) transculturated captive whose life was radically transformed by his experiences among Indians. Not yet, to be sure, would narratives appear by such "lost captives" as Eunice Williams and Joanna Kellogg, nor by their male counterparts, "renegades" such as Joseph Louis Gill, the son of two New England captives, who married an Abenaki woman from the St. Francis mission and served as a "white chief."[32] Tales by colonists who remained with their captors long enough to marry and rear children only began to appear in print in the early nineteenth century, when the popular accounts of Mary Jemison and John Tanner were published.[33] But Gyles's captivity narrative is the first written by a captive who continued to inhabit the middle ground between Indian and English worlds after his release from captivity.

As befits the product of such an individual, Gyles's Odd Adventures, Strange Deliverances, etc. is a hybrid narrative, one that encases the new wine of Enlightenment empiricism and "modern paganism" (Gay 1966) within the old wineskin of providential hermeneutics. Gyles's introduction states that the memoirs were compiled at the request of his second wife for the use of the family, "to excite in ourselves gratitude and thankfulness to God and in our offspring a due sense of their dependence on the Sovereign of the universe from the precariousness and vicissitudes of all sublunary enjoyments" (Gyles 1981 [1736]:94). True to form, the narrative offers a chronologically ordered account of Gyles's adventures among the Maliseets and French as well as sections on "Further Difficulties and Deliverances" and "Remarkable Events of Providence in the Deaths of Several Barbarous Indians." But Gyles, who educated himself in the classical tradition after returning from captivity, opens his narrative with a quotation not from Scripture but from Homer's Odyssey:

> Happier his lot who many sorrows past,
> Long laboring gains his natal shore at last.
>
> (94)

In comparing himself to Odysseus, Gyles not only calls attention to his own heroism and transformation during captivity but also places his account within the genre of the secular travel narrative rather than the spiritual autobiography (see Figure 6.2).

The conventional "adventures" and "deliverances" aside, the tantalizing "et cetera" of Gyles's title indicates where his interest really centers—that is, in the sections entitled "The First Winter's Hunting"; "Of the Manner of the St. John's Indians Living in the Summer" (on planting corn, gathering, and fishing); "Of Their Familiarity with and Frights from the Devil, etc." (on ritual and mythology); "A Description of Several Creatures Commonly Taken by the Indians on St. John's River" (on the beaver, wolverine, tortoise, and salmon); and "Of Their Feasting, etc." The latter section includes observations on the dog feast enjoyed prior to war; mourning rituals, including a feast to "wipe off tears"; marriage rituals; everyday feasts; and "A Digression Containing an Account of a Rape Committed by a Demon."[34] The digression turns out to be "an old story" about a beautiful girl "adorned with the precious jewel of an Indian education, so formed by nature and polished by art that they could not find for her a suitable consort." One day she was missing, and her parents finally found her swimming with a spirit who lived in the mountains above the river. Looking upon this spirit as their son-in-law, "(according to custom) they called upon him for moose, bear, or whatever creature they desired, and if they did but go to the waterside and signify their desire, the creature which they would have came swimming at them" (1981 [1736]:121–122). In a footnote Gyles compares the story to Europa's Rape, in which Zeus "captivates the maid" (122); but this is clearly an Algonquian tale about a woman's marriage to the "master of the game," whom a hunter must propitiate in order to be successful.[35]

Annotations and classical illusions are as characteristic of Gyles's narrative as Biblical quotations are of earlier narratives. The annotations often explain ethnographic or other details that Gyles deems likely to be unfamiliar to his audience: "A moose is a fine lofty creature"; "The tomahawk is a warlike club"; "A monoodah is an Indian bag"; "A virgin who has been educated to make monoodahs and birch dishes, to lace snowshoes, and make Indian shoes, to string wampum belts, sew birch canoes, and boil the kettle is esteemed as a lady of fine accomplishments"; "The Indian that takes and will keep a captive is accounted his master and the captive his property till he give or sell him to another" (1981 [1736]:99–121, nn. 14, 21, 26, 40, 41).

The voice of a translator and "ethnographic authority" (Clifford 1988b) pervades the body of the narrative, even when Gyles is discussing his own torture:

M E M O I R S

O F

O D D   A D V E N T U R E S,

Strange Deliverances, &c.

In the Captivity of

*J O H N   G Y L E S*, Efq;

Commander of the Garrifon on *St. George's River.*

---

Written by Himfelf.

---

*Forgetful Youth ! but know, the Power above*
*With eafe can fave each Objeć of his Love ;*
*Wide as his Will, extends his boundlefs Grace ;*
*Nor loft by Time, nor circumfcrib'd by Place.*
*Happier his Lot, who many forrows paft,*
*Long lab'ring gains his natal Shore at laft ;*
*Than who too fpeedy, haftes to end his Life*
*By fome Stern Ruffian,——*            Homer's Odyff.

---

*B O S T O N*, in *N. E.*

Printed and Sold by S. Kneeland and T. Green, in Queen-ftreet,
over againft the Prifon. Mdccxxxvi.

FIGURE 6.2  "Long-lab'ring gains his natal Shore at last": John Gyles's title page quoting Homer's Odyssey. SOURCE: Memoirs of Odd Adventures, Strange Deliverances, etc., in the Captivity of John Gyles (Boston, 1736). (Courtesy of the Edward E. Ayer Collection, the Newberry Library, Chicago.)

At home I had ever seen strangers treated with the utmost civility, and, being a stranger, I expected some kind treatment here. But soon found myself deceived . . . an old grimace-squaw took me by the hand and led me to the ring where the other squaws seized me by the hair of my head and by my hands and feet like so many furies, but my Indian master presently laid down a pledge and released me.

This is followed by a general explanation: "A captive among the Indians is exposed to all manners of abuse and to the utmost tortures unless his master or some of his master's relations lay down a ransom" (1981 [1736]:100–101). Similarly, Gyles's description of his brother's death by torture begins, "When any captives desert and are retaken, the Indians have a dance and at these dances torture the unhappy people who fall into their hands" (105).

Gyles demonstrated considerable initiative in ethnographic exploration. When a group of pagan Indians conducted a sweat lodge ceremony, Gyles expressed an "earnest desire" to view their "powwowing" (ceremonies) to an old woman who had been kind to him. Although the woman advised him that if he were discovered he would be killed or carried away by a "hairy man," Gyles resolved to observe the ceremony from outside the sweat lodge; he reported that he never saw their "hairy men or demons" (1981 [1736]:114). "Powwows" (shamans) were sometimes successful, Gyles believed, because "the devil was permitted to humor those unhappy wretches sometimes in some things" (115).

Satan was also behind Indian "fables," according to Gyles, who included two such myths in his book so "that it may further appear how much they were deluded or under the influence of Satan" (115). A more compelling reason, however, seems to be that the two myths spoke even more directly to his own experience—and his hopes—than did the myth of the woman captured by the master of the game. The first myth concerns a young boy who loses his way while hunting and suddenly finds himself in a beaver's house, where he remains until spring, when he "was turned out of the house and set upon a beaver dam and went home and related the affair to his friends at large" (116). The other myth, less benign, involves a boy "carried away by a large bird called a gulloua, who buildeth her nest on a high rock or mountain." As Gyles tells the story:

> A boy was hunting with his bow and arrow at the foot of a rocky mountain when the gulloua came diving through the air, grasped the boy in her talons, and though he was eight or ten years of age, she soared aloft and laid him in her nest, a prey of her young, where the boy lay constantly on his face but would look sometimes under his arms and saw two young ones with much fish and flesh in the nest and the old bird constantly bringing more, so that the young ones not touching him, the old one clawed him up and set him where she found him, who returned and related the odd event to his friends. (1981 [1736]:115–116)

The gulloua that preyed on the boy is none other than the giant cannibal bird pervasive in Algonquian mythology, the monster that the Wampanoags associated with European kidnappers. The Indians, Gyles wrote, showed him the monster's nest at the top of a mountain, and pointed out a large speckled bird somewhat like an eagle, saying "There is the bird, but he is now as a boy to a giant to what he was in former days" (116). In a footnote Gyles compares the bird to the harpies in Dryden's Virgil:

> When from the mountain tops, with hideous cry
> And clattering wings, the hungry harpies fly,
> They snatched—
> —And whether gods or birds obscene they were,
> Our vows for pardon and for peace prefer.
>
> (116)

The attention Gyles gave to this story suggests that it had more significance for him than would a mere devilish delusion. Rather than identify with Hebrew captives as had his Puritan predecessors, Gyles seems to have identified with mythical Indian boys who found themselves in alien surroundings but ultimately returned home to tell their stories to friends. One of them, the boy in the gulloua's nest, is even the same age as Gyles was at the time of his capture. Gyles's fear of not returning home, like Dickinson's, expressed itself in the language of cannibalism. But in Gyles's case the metaphor was not part of the European typification of savagery but was supplied by his captors themselves, perhaps in an effort to comfort the boy. At any rate, Gyles is a captive of a very different sort from those who heretofore had published accounts of their experiences: He is a captive who adopted his captors' language, learned their vision of the landscape, mastered their methods of hunting, and returned, like Odysseus, to tell the tale to his friends back home.[36]

Gyles survived the hardships of captivity and eventually emerged to tell his tale, it seems, because he fashioned a self that incorporated Algonquian languages, knowledge, and practices even as it remained oriented primarily to English interests and values. This flexible self-fashioning would seem to have reached its limit, however, when Gyles was sold to a French trader after his second master died. He admits that upon hearing this news, he broke down as he never had under torture. The narrative acquires a new, more sentimental voice: "'Sold! To a Frenchman!' I could say no more, went into the woods alone, and wept till I could scarce see or stand. The word sold, and that to a people of that persuasion which my dear mother so detested, and in her last words manifested so great fears of my falling into!" (1981 [1736]:125). Gyles resisted all efforts at conversion, recalling his mother's last words: "'Oh my dear child! If it were God's will, I had rather follow you to your grave, or never see you more in this world than you should be sold to a Jesuit, for a Jesuit will ruin you, body and soul" (99–100). Nevertheless—and here the ethnographic voice returns—Gyles admits finding some priests admirable and being as curious about Catholic ceremonies as he had been about Maliseet shamanism. When he heard that a Jesuit had been called to banish blackbirds from a field of wheat, for instance, Gyles told his fellow captives that he was "inclined to see the ceremony that I might rehearse it to the English" (127).

In its animosity toward the French and its providential mode of interpreting his deliverances, Gyles's narrative resembles those of John Williams and Hannah Swarton, and it is likely that these portions of the narrative are most influenced by what Derrida (1980) has called the "law of the genre."[37] More importantly, however, in its focus on practical knowledge of his captors and their environment Gyles's narrative takes the selective tradition of captivity much farther down the path already cleared by the Quaker captives: It reflects the pragmatic empiricism of a person who acquired an "Indian education" and found a way to turn it to use on his "natal shore."

## Notes

1. On Phillips see Franklin 1980:409–411; on publishing and print culture in New England see Burnham 1997, and Hall 1979 and 1988.

2. Dickinson's narrative was reprinted in England fourteen times between 1700 and 1868. Elizabeth Hanson's narrative was reprinted sixteen times in Samuel Gardner Drake's various anthologies of captivity narratives, which appeared between 1839 and 1872. See Andrews and Andrews 1961, Drake 1978 [1839], Derounian-Stodola and Levernier 1993:14, Mott 1947, and Vail 1949.

3. Ebersole (1995:88–97) analyzes these and other eighteenth-century narratives as indicating a breakdown of the providential interpretive framework. For another discussion of the captive as ethnographer, see Sayre 1997.

4. Dickinson 1977 [1699] is a facsimile of the first edition; 1961 [1699] is a modern edition with useful annotations and supplements by E. W. Andrews and C. M. Andrews, upon which I have relied heavily. The various colonial editions of Dickinson's narrative are listed in the Appendix.

5. The Jeagas were located north of the Tequestas and south of the Ais and Timucuas (Swanton 1946, map 1). They were probably subordinate to the Ais, the most powerful group in southeastern Florida, judging from the ability of the Ais cacique to confiscate goods salvaged from the shipwreck and to claim the captives (Swanton 1946:84–85, 141, 504, 649, passim; 1952:121–122, 132; Dickinson 1961:146–162; Hodge 1959, 1:30–32, 629; 2:733).

6. Ethnological and linguistic relationships are murky for southeastern Florida. Although not agricultural, the coastal peoples shared in various southeastern traits including chiefly privilege, the ceremonial use of black drink, and a summer ceremony somewhat resembling the Creek busk. Dickinson is our chief source for all of these. As Swanton (1946:762–765) indicates, we have little knowledge of the Ais, Tequesta, Jeaga, and Guacata languages, though they seem not to be related to Timucua. It is not possible to confirm Swanton's speculation that Calusa and the southeastern languages were Muskhogean (Swanton 1946:239;

Hudson 1976:23). A more recent discussion of the southeastern coastal peoples is provided by Wood (1989:51–56).

7. See Wood 1988 on the slave trade in Charleston, South Carolina.

8. Wood (1989:53) quotes Bishop Calderón's report of 1675. Dickinson himself is our primary source for the southeastern coastal peoples, and he never witnessed human sacrifice or cannibalism, although his party did hear from the Spaniards about the devouring of two Dutch castaways in one of the towns they passed through on their journey to St. Augustine. Swanton's one specific mention of cannibalism involves Europeans—specifically, the Spanish at Santa Lucía—as perpetrators rather than victims (Swanton 1946:134). For Calusan and Timucuan human sacrifice, see Swanton 1946:101, 649, 763; Swanton 1952:126–128; Hudson 1976:76–77; and Knowles 1940. Adair (1966 [1775]) denied that Calusas ate their victims, but there is archeological evidence of ritual cannibalism in an earlier period (Swanton 1946:195–196; Hodge 1959 [1907–10], 1:195). Knowles (1940) found conclusive evidence of ritual cannibalism in the Southeast only among the Caddoans, and speculates that it may have been instituted in retaliation for Spanish torture at the stake.

9. Bauman (1983:22) quotes from Robert Barclay's Apology, which the Dickinson party probably had with them during captivity. Bauman's work offers an excellent analysis of Quaker silence and its relationship to the dualistic self. Although Puritans shared the notion of the dualistic self, they generally failed to attribute a spiritual self to Indians, or considered it in thrall to Satan.

10. Cacique, Spanish for "captain," was the term used for their chiefs by Indian tribes who had come under Spanish influence.

11. There is a striking similarity between Dickinson's description of the Indians' transformation and Quaker accounts of their ministry in Britain: William Edmondson's audience in Ireland "were as people amazed"; Elizabeth Tomlinson "struck a great astonishment in the people." In contrast, an unsuccessful George Whitehead was stoned "in a furious manner" (Bauman 1983:68–70).

12. Slotkin, in a brief discussion of the Dickinson narrative, also characterizes the breast-feeding as an "intimate exchange" (Slotkin 1973:244); but otherwise my interpretation of Dickinson differs significantly from his. See also Schaffer's (n.d.) discussion of cannibalism and incorporation.

13. In a Native American context, the threatening side of breast-feeding is expressed in the Cherokee belief that infants may be transformed into witches by suckling substances other than breast milk (Fogelson 1975:121), and in Kwakiutl mythology, where babies at the breast might devour their mothers (Walens 1981:12). The Tupinamba of Brazil combined breast-feeding with cannibalism, smearing enemy blood on a nursing mother's nipples (Carneiro da Cunha n.d.).

14. Lewis and Loomie (1953) discuss Santa Lucía and other Spanish missions. Swanton identifies the Indians of St. Lucía as Guacata (1946:134, map 1).

15. The book of Barclay's mentioned in this passage would have been Apology for the True Christian Divinity (1678), the "major systematic exposition of Quaker belief and practice" at this time (Bauman 1983:24). On Barclay's employing nakedness as a sign, see Baltzell 1979:83. Bauman (1983) discusses the ambiguous meaning of nakedness as a sign, as well as the Quaker belief that God's word was continually being revealed.

16. On Quaker universalism, see Bauman 1983 and Stocking 1968b, 1973, and 1987. The latter considers the influence of Quaker and Evangelical principles regarding human unity upon nineteenth-century ethnologists.

17. Hudson (1976:226–229) discusses the black drink ceremony, reproduces a de Bry engraving of a Timucuan ceremony in which conch shells are prominent, and summarizes William Bartram's description of the drinking of black drink at a Creek council a century later. See also Hudson 1979. Since this ceremony occurred in the summer, it might have been part of the Green Corn ceremony, or busk, a time of forgiveness and reconciliation (R. D. Fogelson, personal communication; see Swanton 1932).

18. My argument with regard to Dickinson's Quaker empiricism corresponds in some respects with Robert K. Merton's classic discussion of the relationship between Puritanism and science in the seventeenth century (Merton 1970 [1938]; see also Kuhn 1970), and with Keith Thomas's analysis of the replacement of a providential worldview by scientific rationalism (Thomas 1971). However, like Baltzell (1979:95, 162–175), I find Quakers more predisposed than the authoritarian Puritans to empiricism. As Frederick B. Tolles wrote, "There was an intimate connection between the religious ethos characteristic of Quakerism and the demonstrable aptitude of Friends for scientific pursuits" (Tolles 1948:206).

19. For slavery and abolition among Quakers, see Nash and Soderlund 1991. For Guale missions, see Swanton 1946: 135–136 and 1952:110.

20. Dickinson and another wealthy Quaker merchant and slave trader, Isaac Norris, were primary targets of some of the earliest Quaker abolitionists (Andrews and Andrews 1961; Davis 1966:213–225; Nash 1968; Nash and Soderlund 1991; Tolles 1960).

21. See the Appendix.

22. The war of 1723–27 is discussed by Morrison (1984:185–193) and Calloway (1990:113–131; 1991).

23. This passage and others like it, which appear to be directed to an audience unfamiliar with frontier conditions, may reflect the influence of Hanson's English amanuensis, Samuel Bownas. Similarly, Dickinson's narrative may have been considerably influenced by Robert Barrow and Samuel Carpenter.

24. See Coleman 1925, 1:161–166; Vaughan and Clark 1981:229–230; and Ulrich 1982 for biographical information on Hanson.

25. Hanson 1987 is a facsimile reprint of the first American (1728) and English (1760) editions (see the Appendix). The latter, a more polished, embellished, somewhat distorted version, was published under Samuel Bownas's name. The American and English editions are close in content and structure, indicating that they are based on the same dictation. The 1728 edition was reprinted by Vaughan and Clark (Hanson 1981), and the 1760 edition was reprinted by VanDerBeets (Hanson 1973), together with some comparative passages from the second American edition (1754). VanDerBeets (1973) and Pearce (1947) compare the style and content of the American and English editions.

26. Ulrich's comparison of Rowlandson and Hanson emphasizes the latter's identification with her captors as human beings as well as her submissiveness, interpreted less in terms of religion and more in terms of gender than in my analy-

sis (Ulrich 1982:226–234). Ricoeur (1970, 1979) contrasts the hermeneutics of suspicion with the hermeneutics of empathy (or recollection).

27. For Abenaki views of cannibalism, see Morrison 1979, and Morrison 1984:67.

28. Here I borrow terms from Stocking (1968a), whose works and lectures have strongly influenced my thinking on proto-ethnography.

29. Gyles 1978 [1736] is a facsimile, the only modern edition to include an appendix detailing Gyles's activities after his captivity. Gyles 1973 and 1981 are annotated editions. Apart from brief discussions by Ebersole (1995:93–94) and by Vaughan and Clark (1981), there is little critical commentary on Gyles's narrative. VanDerBeets (1973) and Levernier and Cohen (1977) present the narrative primarily as anti-French propaganda. Trueman 1966 is a semifictional reconstruction of Gyles's captivity.

30. Calloway (1991:104–106) includes a reprint of the text of an agreement of 1698 for which Gyles ("Gills") served as an interpreter. The "Eastern Indians" included Abenakis, Passamaquoddies, Micmacs, and Maliseets (Calloway 1991:5). See Bock 1978, Calloway 1990 and 1991, Erikson 1978, Morrison 1989, and Prins 1996.

31. For biographical accounts of Gyles and other former captives who served the colonies, see Coleman 1925, Axtell 1985b:199–204, Calloway 1990 and 1991, and Morrison 1984. The latter stresses the limitations of colonial interpreters, who had to contend with significant differences in language and political authority among Indian groups. Although Slotkin (1973) is concerned with the emergence of Indianized frontier heroes, he does not consider Gyles.

32. On Gill, see Axtell 1975, Day 1981, and Calloway 1990 and 1991; and the captivity narrative of Susannah Willard Johnson (1978 [1796]), a New England captive adopted into Gill's Abenaki family.

33. Seaver 1992 [1824] is a modern edition of Jemison's narrative; Seaver 1978 [1856] is a facsimile of the fourth edition, annotated by Lewis Henry Morgan. Tanner 1994 [1830] has an introduction by Louise Erdrich but lacks the annotations of the original, edited by Edwin James; James 1978 [1830] is a facsimile of the first edition.

34. Prins (1996:120) discusses the dog feast as a ritual the Micmacs, Maliseets, and other Algonquians of the area (united in a political alliance known as the Wabanaki confederacy) may have adopted from Hurons in the mid-seventeenth century. The feast to "wipe off tears" was also probably adopted from Iroquoians.

35. For the Algonquian keeper of the game, see Brightman 1993 and Martin 1978.

36. Although Gyles's telling of Native American myths is unusual in a captivity narrative, a similar approach may have been taken in The Account of the Captivity of William Henry in 1755, published in 1766, which is known only through an extract published in.a London almanac (Henry 1978 [1768]; see also Vail 1949:570). Henry, an Ohio trader adopted by the Senecas, apparently conveyed in some detail lessons he claimed to have learned from the famous orator Canasatego. Henry not only outlined Iroquois principles of oratory and expressed admiration for their eloquence but also reproduced Canasatego's telling of an origin myth, complete with its political implications for Henry's time. Just as the Iro-

quois were almost destroyed by greed and quarreling, Canasatego told Henry, so too would be the French and English.

37. Gyles tells of being encouraged to publish his narrative not only by his wife but by others "for whose judgment I had a value." His account might have been edited and embellished by the chaplain of the garrison at which Gyles was stationed (Vaughan and Clark 1981:94). This would make the narrative all the more hybrid.

# 7

# Captivity and Colonial Structures of Feeling, 1744–1776

Between 1744 and 1748, after a hiatus of three decades, England and France once again were formally at war. During this third intercolonial war (known in the colonies as King George's War), most of the English captives taken to Canada were soldiers. But during the fourth intercolonial war (or French and Indian War), of 1754–61, and again during Pontiac's War (1763–64), substantial numbers of colonists also were taken captive. In the two decades between 1748 and 1767, a dozen new captivity narratives were published in the colonies—as many as had appeared in the half century between the publication of Rowlandson's narrative in 1682 and Gyles's in 1736.[1]

For the most part, the publication of captivity narratives continued to be centered in Boston and Philadelphia in the mid-eighteenth century, but narratives were also published in Germantown and Lancaster, Pennsylvania; New London and Hartford, Connecticut; and in New York. The most well known of all, Peter Williamson's French and Indian Cruelty, appeared in nine British editions beginning in 1757, before appearing at last in an American anthology in 1793 (Affecting History 1978, 1973). Several narratives published in Pennsylvania appeared in German, the language of many backcountry settlers, as well as in English. The authors of the mid-eighteenth-century narratives included, in addition to several soldiers and frontier settlers, fur traders, a military chaplain, and an African American slave. Geographically these captivities stretched from New York to Florida, but the majority were concentrated in western Pennsylvania, the scene of the most intense Anglo-French conflict. Although four women are included in this group, most mid-eighteenth-century captivity narratives were written by men.

The captives who published narratives of their experiences during the mid-eighteenth century were substantially more diverse than those con-

sidered in previous chapters. Their modes of interpretation were more diverse as well, grounded in what G. J. Barker-Benfield has called the "culture of sensibility" (1992).[2] To be sure, more than half of the mid-eighteenth-century narratives are to some degree spiritual autobiographies,
and if these are considered together with the numerous editions of the
Rowlandson, Williams, Dickinson, and Hanson narratives that were reissued during this period, the continuing salience of a providential interpretation of captivity is apparent.[3] Even so, the titles of the new narratives
often call to prospective readers' attention the "uncommon," "surprising," "entertaining," or "affecting" qualities of these narratives. Further-
more, as in the case of John Gyles's narrative, providential and more secular modes of interpretation are often interwoven in a single narrative.

Almost half of the mid-eighteenth-century authors discarded the providential framework altogether, presenting their accounts of captivity as
unadorned "facts" even as they attempted to arouse sympathetic feelings
of horror and pity in the reader. The more thoroughly secular narratives,
all deriving from the fourth intercolonial war, reflect the development in
the mid-eighteenth century of new "structures of feeling" (Williams
1997:128–135) grounded in the empiricism and moral philosophy of the
eighteenth century as well as in emergent American nationalism.

## Providence and Sentiment in the Mid-Eighteenth Century

Of the dozen captivity narratives first published in the mid-eighteenth
century, seven had significant spiritual dimensions. None of these attained the fame or influence of Rowlandson's, Williams's, or Dickinson's
accounts. But two narratives—William and Elizabeth Fleming's and
Robert Eastburn's—were printed five times or more in the colonies; and
Briton Hammon's narrative remains significant as the first African American autobiography. The following survey of these seven narratives indicates continuities in as well as attenuations of the providential interpretation of captivity.

The two narratives dating from the third intercolonial war, by
chaplain John Norton and soldier Nehemiah How, respectively, are
pious accounts of the capture of frontier forts by French and Indian
forces, followed by imprisonment in a Quebec prison rather than captivity among Indians. Norton's The Redeemed Captive (1748), like its
namesake, is an account of a Massachusetts minister attempting to care
for a flock in captivity. The title page includes Biblical references to
Hebrew captivities, but less predictably, these are juxtaposed to a
promotional reference to Norton's narrative as an "entertaining and
affecting" account. By 1748 the value of captivity narratives as senti-

mental literature was clearly appreciated even by those publishing providential interpretations.

Written in the form of a journal, John Norton's narrative commences a few days prior to his captivity. This unusual attention to the immediate historical context of the captivity allows Norton to support one of his major themes, French perfidy. On August 20, 1746, the commander of Fort Massachusetts, near Deerfield (see Map 4.1), surrendered to a French and Abenaki force under the command of General Vaudreuil on the condition that "the savages should have nothing to do with any of us" (Norton 1977 [1748]:9). Norton explains: "We knew that it was the manner of the Indians to abuse their prisoners, and sometimes to kill those that failed in traveling, and carrying packs, which we knew that some of our men could not do; and we thought it but little better for the General to deliver them to the Indians than it would be to abuse them himself" (11).

Norton's overriding theme of French complicity in Indian atrocities receives its strongest articulation early in the narrative, as he describes Abenakis scalping and dismembering the corpse of a dead English soldier. Following this, "a young Frenchman took one of the arms and flayed it, roasted the flesh, and offered some of it to Daniel Smeed, one of the prisoners, to eat, but he refused it." Norton continued, "The Frenchman dressed the skin of the arm (as we afterwards heard) and made a tobacco pouch of it" (10). Despite this example of what Cotton Mather called an "Indianized Frenchman," Norton remained considerably more fearful of "Frenchified Indians." When in violation of the terms of surrender most of the English—although not Norton—were turned over to the Abenakis, Norton's heart "was filled with sorrow, expecting that many of our weak and feeble people would fall by the merciless hands of the enemy" (12). He was somewhat comforted, however, upon witnessing various acts of kindness on the part of both French soldiers and Abenaki masters, who contrary to his expectations, carried captives who were too weak or injured to travel, relieved them of their packs, and provided them with horses and canoes. The French assisted a woman in giving birth to a daughter, who was christened Captivity Smeed by Norton, following a colonial naming practice dating back to the captivities of John Williams's time. Although Norton attributed French and Indian mercies to Providence, he also recorded that General Vaudreuil had promised to reward Indians who took good care of their captives.

In Canada Norton exchanged news with various English captives who had made their lives among the French. After receiving special treatment in Montreal, he was incarcerated in Quebec along with more than two hundred other English prisoners. When a shipload of English sailors introduced a deadly epidemic to the prison, Norton turned to the lamentations of Jeremiah, quoting, as had John Williams before him: "The Lord is righteous, for I have rebelled against his commandment. Hear as I pray for you, all people, and behold my sorrow. My virgins and my young men are gone into captivity" (31). But Norton did not attempt to name the sins for which the captives were suffering divine punishment; in this he resembled the Quaker captives more than his clerical predecessors.

The minister fell seriously ill himself, and from the point of his illness Norton's narrative is little more than a stark chronicle of seventy-three deaths, including, on May 25, 1747, that of "Mr. Nehemiah How, of No. 2, aged about fifty-six; taken at Great Meadow, October 11th, 1745" (39). Nehemiah How, a militia captain from Vermont, left his own account of captivity, completed at his death by "another hand" (perhaps that of Norton himself), which attested to How's character and to the belief "that he is gone from a captivity of sorrow on earth, to join in songs of everlasting joy among the ransomed of the Lord in the heavenly Zion" (How 1977 [1748]:22). A Narrative of the Captivity of Nehemiah How (1748), like Norton's Redeemed Captive, offers a providential interpretation of captivity.[4] The title page places How's captivity within the familiar framework of Israel's Babylonian captivity, quoting once again from Psalm 108: "How shall we sing the Lord's song in a strange land?" (see Figure 7.1). But for How, a captive of Abenakis from St. Francis mission, this Biblical quotation may have taken on special significance, for he was literally required to sing a ceremonial song during his captivity.

At the beginning of his narrative How reports having "committed my case to God, and prayed, that since it was his will to deliver me into the hands of these cruel men, I might find favour in their eyes: which request, God of his infinite mercy was pleased to grant; for they were generally kind to me while I was with them" (How 1977 [1748]:3). How acknowledges his captors' kindness despite his being required to dance, sing, and run the gauntlet; being threatened with death if he could walk no faster; and witnessing a dance around his companion "David Rugg's scalp," which was mounted atop a pole and "painted red, with the likeness of eyes and mouth on it" (6).

The alien and threatening nature of these captivity practices (which reflected the adoption of Iroquoian captivity rituals by the St. Francis Abenakis) were softened in How's case because he found a familiar face among his captors, that of one Pealtomy. After shaking How's hand and speaking with him, Pealtomy returned with Amrusus (Arosen), the Mohawk husband of Eunice Williams. "He asked me after his wife's relations," wrote How, "and showed a great deal of respect to me." Pealtomy tried to teach him the words he was expected to sing as he danced inside a ring of his captors. When How said he was unable to sing the words, Pealtomy "and the rest of the fort who could speak some English came to me, and bid me sing it in English, which was, 'I don't know where I go';

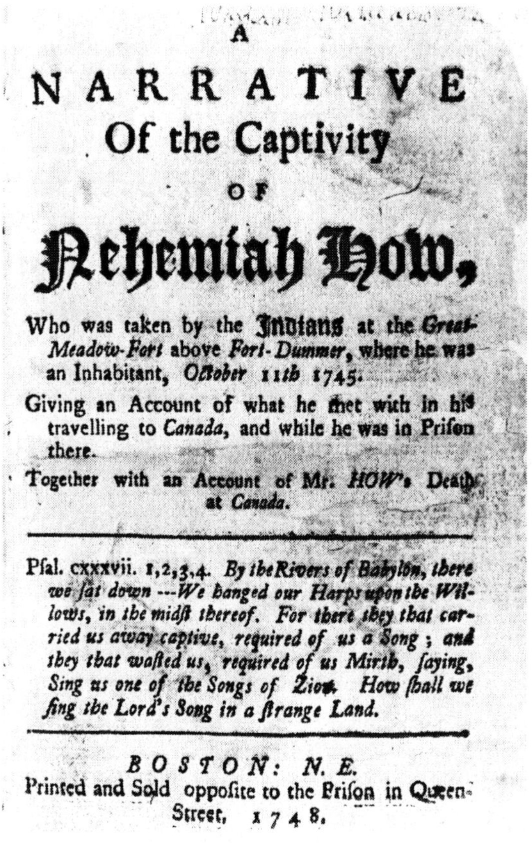

A

# NARRATIVE

## Of the Captivity

O F

## Nehemiah How,

Who was taken by the Indians at the Great-
Meadow-Fort above Fort-Dummer, where he was
an Inhabitant, October 11th 1745.

Giving an Account of what he met with in his
travelling to Canada, and while he was in Prison
there.

Together with an Account of Mr. HOW's Death
at Canada.

Pfal. cxxxvii. 1,2,3,4. By the Rivers of Babylon, there
we fat down ---We hanged our Harps upon the Wil-
lows, in the midst thereof. For there they that carried us away captive, required of us a Song ; and
they that wasted us, required of us Mirth, saying,
Sing us one of the Songs of Zion. How shall we
sing the Lord's Song in a strange Land.

BOSTON: N. E.
Printed and Sold opposite to the Prison in Queen-
Street, 1 7 4 8.

FIGURE 7.1 "They that carried us away captive, required of us a song":
Nehemiah How's title page, quoting Psalm 137. SOURCE: A Narrative of the
Captivity of Nehemiah How (Boston, 1748). (Courtesy of the Edward E. Ayer
Collection, the Newberry Library, Chicago.)

which I did, dancing round that ring three times" (7). After this ritual—
likely a request for the compassion of the bereaved women who had control over his life—How was led to a seat by the fire. There he was offered
rum by the French priest and bread and butter by an officer. How testifies
to the overall kindness of the French as well as the Indians, adding, "I desire to ascribe all the favours I have been the partaker of ever since my
captivity to the abundant grace and goodness of a bountiful God, as the
first cause" (12).

   In contrast to How's descriptions of Abenaki rituals, the records of his
incarceration in Quebec are preoccupied (like Norton's) with the arrival
and death of fellow prisoners. Although How calls his prison stay "a

very melancholy time," he does not note that the English captives' lives were in much greater danger in the French prison than in the Indian villages. How's own death closes the narrative, which was published in Boston by subscription. It is not difficult to imagine the market for his and Norton's narratives among the former captives, the relatives of the deceased, and the relatives of captives who, like Eunice Williams, remained in Canada.

The most fully developed and frequently published of the mid-eighteenth-century spiritual autobiographies was the work of Robert Eastburn, a blacksmith and fur trader who served as a deacon of the Philadelphia Presbyterian Meeting. A Faithful Narrative, of the Many Dangers and Sufferings, As Well As Wonderful Deliverances of Robert Eastburn (1758) recounts Eastburn's capture in 1756, en route to Oswego, New York, the only post on the Great Lakes not then held by the French (see Map 2.1). Eastburn's narrative is reminiscent of Rowlandson's in its personal interpretation of his afflictions; Cotton Mather's in his use of captivity to criticize English impiety and laxity; and Gyles's in his proto-ethnographic understanding of his captors' rituals (although Eastburn's interests were mainly confined to the warfare and adoption practices that affected him directly). Eastburn, like Gyles, was adopted during captivity, but he differed from Gyles in resisting transculturation and interpreting his transformative experience within a providential framework.

A captive of Catholic Mohawks, Eastburn was taken to Kahnawake, the Mohawk mission settlement that was home to Eunice Williams and numerous English captives. There he was saved from the gauntlet by a group of women who wished to send him two hundred miles upstream to be adopted into a bereaved family. Upon his arrival at the appointed town, Eastburn reported, "My father and mother that I had never seen before were waiting, and ordered me into an Indian house, where we were directed to sit down silent for a considerable time, the Indians appeared very sad, and my mother began to cry, and continued crying aloud for some time, and then dried up her tears, and received me for her son" (Eastburn 1973 [1758]:164).[5] Eastburn, who all along had refused to dance and sing for his captors on religious grounds, further displeased his Mohawk mother by refusing to go to Mass, and was banished to serve on a work crew. Although Eastburn was one of the few colonial captives to call his captors "my father and mother" rather than "master and mistress," he attributed his salvation not to his adopted status but to Providence. "I saw that God could make friends of cruel enemies," he reflected, "as He once turned the heart of angry Esau into love and tenderness" (164).

Eastburn eventually ended up as a servant in Montreal, first assisting a Black man in charge of digging a trench around the town, then a French smith in Kahnawake, and finally an English smith in Montreal. Throughout this time he searched unsuccessfully for a chance to escape, hoping to warn Oswego of an impending French attack. His own son was captured in the attack, leading Eastburn to fear that the boy had escaped being "delivered up a sacrifice to the Indian enemy, [only] to be instructed in popish principles, and employed in murdering their [English] countrymen" (169). To save his son from turning against his people and his faith, Eastburn petitioned General Vaudreuil to allow him to work with his son in Quebec. Eventually both were returned to Philadelphia via England and Boston, with about three hundred other prisoners. Like Mary Rowlandson and Hannah Swarton, Eastburn emerged from the experience spiritually transformed and grateful to God for his "temporal salvation," and more importantly, for "a soul-satisfying evidence of an eternal in the world to come." He expressed amazement at "what pains He had taken to wean me from an over-love of time things, and make me content that He should choose for me" (174–176).

Eastburn also offered his readers a jeremiad, pointing to French and Indian virtues in order to criticize his countrymen. "Our enemies seem to make a better use of a bad religion," he wrote, echoing Mather, "than we of a good one." He also noted the Indians' gratitude to God for victory ("an example this, worthy of imitation! an example which may make profane pretended Protestants blush"); the stoic virtues of French and Indian warriors alike ("I wish there was more of this hardness so necessary for war in our nation"); and French success at controlling Indian access to liquor (also "well worthy of imitation"). Echoing many other captives, he praised the harmony that obtained among Indian families and communities. "When I compared our manner of living with theirs," he concluded, "it made me fear that the righteous and jealous God (who is wont to make judgement begin at his own house first) was about to deliver us into their hands, to be severely punished for our departure from him" (156–157, 176). Cruel by nature but peaceful and pious in manner, Indians for Eastburn were doubly other: savage enemies to be conquered, but at the same time, virtuous models to be imitated. As in Mather, the two views were made consistent by the belief that in either guise Indians were the instruments of God's judgment. Although Eastburn had much greater personal experience among Indians than did Mather, his greater experience merely filled out the providential framework instead of transforming it.

In Eastburn's narrative the complex multiethnic texture of Canadian mission villages is readily apparent. During his stay in Kahnawake, this Pennsylvania Presbyterian acknowledged a Catholic Mohawk mother and father and worked as a servant to masters of French, English, and African descent. The latter, a man who spoke Mohawk as well as English and French, is not the first African American to appear in captivity literature: The slaves of John Williams, Jonathan Dickinson, and Dickinson's shipmaster all experienced captivity alongside their masters. But Black captives are relegated to the background in these narratives, often remaining unnamed. The publication of A Narrative of the Uncommon Sufferings and Surprizing Deliverance of Briton Hammon, A Negro Man—Servant to General Winslow, in 1760, broke this silence and anonymity, at least to a degree.[6]

The selective tradition of captivity offered an entryway into print culture for African Americans just as it had for women. The first published work by an African slave, Briton Hammon's Narrative may have been dictated to an amanuensis. It opens with a disclaimer reminiscent of the preface to Rowlandson's narrative:

> As my Capacities and Condition of Life are very low, it cannot be expected
> that I should make those Remarks on the sufferings I have met with, or the
> kind Providence of a good GOD for my Preservation, as one in a higher Station; but shall leave that to the Reader as he goes along, and so I shall only
> relate Matters of Fact as they occur to my Mind. (Hammon 1978 [1760]:3)

Just as Rowlandson's voice was characterized as the voice of experience rather than interpretation, and just as she was defined as inferior to her husband, so too Hammon is defined as inferior to his reader and capable only of relating "matters of fact" rather than providential interpretation. Nevertheless, Hammon does not actually offer unadorned "matters of fact" but rather a providential interpretation of his precarious passage from New England to Florida (where, like Dickinson, he was shipwrecked and captured by coastal Indians); Cuba (where he served the Governor, the Bishop, and spent years in a dungeon); London (where he traveled as a soldier and cook for the British navy); and finally back into the service of his "good master's" household in Boston.

Like his predecessors, Hammon presents his narrative as a demonstration "that I have been most grievously afflicted, and yet through the Divine Goodness, as miraculously preserved, and delivered out of many dangers; of which I desire to retain a grateful remembrance, as long as I live in the world" (14). He compares himself to Daniel delivered from the lion's den, characterizing his captors as bestial, barbarous, demonic savages. The captivity itself is a minor episode in Hammon's adventures, but it provides a framework within which his tale can be told. If it is a tale of forced and restricted movement, proper and improper servitude, and an exemplary Christian life, as it has been read by William Andrews (1986) and other critics,[7] Hammon's narrative does not differ in these respects from its predecessors. Read as the opening statement in African

American autobiography, Hammon's narrative is filled with silences and obsessed with the danger of freedom; but read as a continuation of the selective tradition of captivity, it illustrates the continued use of the providential interpretation of captivity to legitimate domestic power relations.

As a narrative of "uncommon sufferings" as well as a "surprising deliverance," Briton Hammon's account is also notable in constituting a "Negro servant" as a potential object for readers' sympathetic identification. Hammon's is among the first narratives to promise an account of a captive's "sufferings" as well as of "deliverances." Whereas the latter word had been featured in the title of captivity narratives since 1697 (in Cotton Mather's Humiliations Follow'd with Deliverances) and clearly indicates a providential hermeneutics, sufferings indicates the midcentury interest in cultivating the moral sense through evoking sympathy for the pain of others.[8] The titles of four midcentury narratives (including those by Robert Eastburn, William and Elizabeth Fleming, and Thomas Brown) feature "sufferings and deliverance"; and the five reissues of Mary Rowlandson's narrative published in the 1770s include a reference to "sufferings" in the title (see Figure 7.2).

The three remaining midcentury narratives that were couched (at least formally) in a providential framework were by German or Scotch-Irish settlers taken captive from the backwoods of Pennsylvania (see Map 3.1). This area bore the brunt of much of the violence during the fourth intercolonial war and was the site of acrimonious disputes between Quakers and other colonists regarding Indian policy.[9] The Journal of the Captivity of Jean Lowry and Her Children (Lowry 1978 [1760]) is reminiscent of John Williams's narrative in its detailed account of an Irish Calvinist's theological disputes with French Jesuits and military officers on such subjects as baptism, transubstantiation, the intercession of saints, and the infallibility of the Church. But Lowry's captivity itself is not interpreted in a providential light. "Poor me," Jean Lowry exclaims near the beginning of her narrative, capturing in one phrase the tone of the entire account. To point out her self-pity is not to minimize her hardships: A pregnant woman taken captive with two children after the death of her husband, Jean Lowry, like many other women in captivity, faced extremely trying circumstances. But her attitude toward her suffering is unprecedented in Anglo-American captivity narratives. Despite the anti-Catholic nature of the narrative, Lowry demonstrates little faith in the redemptive value of suffering, and recounts her experiences more in order to arouse her readers' sentiments than to express spiritual resignation.

The first and most popular of the Pennsylvania narratives was also providential in form alone. A Narrative of the sufferings and surprising deliverance of William and Elizabeth Fleming was published in six English and

A

# NARRATIVE

OF THE

Captivity, Sufferings, and Removes,

OF

## Mrs. *Mary Rowlandson,*

Who was taken Prifoner by the *Indians*, with feveral others ; and treated in the moſt barbarous and cruel Manner by thoſe vile *Savages :* With many other remarkable Events during her Travels.

*Written by her own Hand, for her private Uſe, and ſince made public at the earneſt Defire of ſome Friends, and for the Benefit of the Afflicted.*

BOSTON:
Re-printed and ſold by JOHN and THOMAS FLEET, at the *Bible* and *Heart,* Cornhill, 1800.

FIGURE 7.2    An armed Mary Rowlandson, a woodcut that first appeared in a 1773 edition of her narrative. SOURCE: Title page, A Narrative of the Captivity, Sufferings, and Removes of Mrs. Mary Rowlandson (Boston, 1800). (Courtesy of the Edward E. Ayer Collection, the Newberry Library, Chicago.)

three German editions in 1756. According to an unsigned introduction, the narrative was offered as an illustration of the sufferings of hundreds of backwoods settlers. In addition to its emphasis on the captives' "sufferings," the introduction departs significantly from previous narratives in presenting the Flemings' sufferings as an instructive example of the value of liberty. Unlike Rowlandson's and Hammon's captivity narratives, that of the Flemings does not serve the purpose of exploring the nature of orderly vs. inverted servitude. Nor does it, like Swarton's and

Hammon's narratives, present freedom as a dangerous and threatening state. Rather, this narrative suggests that servitude of all sorts is to be avoided—a reflection of pre-Revolutionary frontier attitudes.[10]

Another innovative feature of the Flemings' narrative is its nascent polyvocality. The narrative juxtaposes the voices of young William Fleming, his wife Elizabeth, and their primary captor, the Delaware war chief, Capt. Jacob. William Fleming begins, reporting that he had heard a warning that the Delawares and Shawnees were coming "with orders from the French who supplied them with ammunition, etc. to plunder, burn and destroy, everything of value they met with, and to scalp or captivate all that might be so unhappy as to fall into their hands" (Fleming 1978 [1756]:4). Although many who heard the warning "treated it as only the groundless surmises of the timorous, having too favourable an opinion of the friendly attachment of these Indians to this province," William took the threat seriously. He rushed home, but on the way he was captured by two Indians, one of whom turned out to be Capt. Jacob.[11] After grabbing his horse by the bridle, Fleming reported, Capt. Jacob "commanded me to alight, ... very complacently shook hands, and told me (for they could speak good English) I must go with them." Fleming's fear left him trembling and speechless, "which my enemies, savage as they were, took notice of, and endeavoured to encourage me, ... bidding me not to be afraid, for as I look young and lusty they would not hurt me"—provided, that is, he stood by them (5–6). After seeing a less fortunate captive bound, killed, and scalped, Fleming led his captors toward his house, which was then looted and burned. Capt. Jacob, explaining that they needed a woman to make bread, took Elizabeth captive. He treated her with respect and urged her not to be afraid.

Elizabeth Fleming's voice enters indirectly at this point: "My wife," reported Fleming, "emboldened by the familiarity of our masters, asked them several questions touching their reasons for using the English as they did, seeing they had always treated the Indians (particularly the Delawares and Shawnese) with the greatest friendship." She was told that General Braddock had not used them well in the recent battle at Fort Duquesne and had threatened to destroy all the Indians on the continent after defeating the French. Elizabeth asked what would become of the prisoners and learned that they would be given as kindred to Capt. Jacob's friends on the Ohio River. Her husband did not believe this, for he was told another story and "expected every moment to be sacrificed by them; yet so far as I could learn the French were to allow them a certain sum per scalp and for prisoners, if they were young, and fit for business." Fleming's captors went on to tell him "not to be afraid that they should abuse my wife, for they would not do it for fear of affronting their God (and pointed their hands toward heaven) for the man that affronts his God, will surely be killed when he goes out to war; this, continued they, is what makes the English have such bad luck" (15–16).

Despite these reassurances, the Flemings each sought and found an opportunity to escape, William joining a company searching for Capt. Jacob's party, Elizabeth losing her way in the woods. At this point Elizabeth introduces a sentimental voice into the narrative: "Let any one figure to themselves the melancholy of my condition; no husband to relieve me, or alleviate my grief! Yet how light, how trifling was all I now endured, to those hardships which soon after I was obliged to bear," she lamented (21). In truth Elizabeth Fleming suffered considerably less than many other female captives; but the narrative dwells upon her fear, vulnerability, and isolation, presenting her neither as sinful nor as an exemplary Christian but as an object of pity.

Elizabeth Fleming's complete isolation is new in the captivity literature, for previous female captives were generally too frightened to escape (Hannah Dustan being the notable exception). In an intriguing section of the narrative reminiscent of a rite of passage, Elizabeth describes hiding from the Indians in a desolate, burnt-out landscape, taking refuge in an oven, in a gum tree, and in fodder. Eventually discovered by several men she describes as "white," the disheveled Elizabeth, blackened with soot, was nearly killed by a "good man" startled by her strange appearance. She was saved by his companion, who cried out, "Hold, hold, she is a white woman by her voice" (27). This may be the first appearance in a captivity narrative of white in place of English as a marker of identity. Perhaps reflective of the mixed cultural background of Pennsylvania frontier settlers, this marker also indicates a developing sense of racial identification in the mid-eighteenth-century colonies.[12]

The Flemings' narrative bears a quotation from Psalm 3 on the title page ("I cried unto the Lord, and He heard me") and closes with the hymn "And Live We Yet By Power Divine?" It includes a reference to prayer and a comparison of Elizabeth's condition to Job's. But these spiritual references are little more than empty form. Captivity is presented in this narrative as an experience with political and emotional rather than spiritual significance. The political dimension is developed in William's voice, although his information derives in part from Elizabeth's more aggressive questioning of Capt. Jacob. Elizabeth's voice concentrates on the emotional dimension of captivity, depicting her as a weak and vulnerable victim in order to arouse the sentiments of pity and horror in the reader. Although in William's portion of the narrative Elizabeth appears more level-headed than he, and although she was clearly resourceful in assuring her own survival, she represents herself as a conventional romantic heroine. The Flemings' account exemplifies the split between male and female captives and the sentimentalism that became increasingly characteristic of captivity narratives, whether historical or fictional, in the second half of the eighteenth century.[13]

The third narrative set in backwoods Pennsylvania, The Narrative of Marie Le Roy and Barbara Leininger, was published in German and English editions by the German Printing Office in Philadelphia, possibly during Benjamin Franklin's tenure there.[14] Written in a mixture of the first- and third-person, this narrative was published "not in order to render our own sufferings and humble history famous, but rather in order to serve the inhabitants of this country, by making them acquainted with the names and circumstances of those prisoners whom me met, at the various places where we were, in the course of our captivity" (Le Roy and Leininger 1878 [1759]:410). Like Norton and How, these captives were concerned with documenting their place in local history and with bearing witness to the fate of their fellow captives. They catalog instances of kindness as well as cruelty, and to a greater degree than do the Flemings, testify to God's "gracious support in our weary captivity" (409).

God's support was especially welcome after Le Roy and Leininger escaped. "It is hard to describe the anxious fears of a poor woman under such circumstances," they wrote. Still, they tried:

> Even if we escaped the Indians, how would we ever succeed in passing through the wilderness, unacquainted with a single path or trail, without a guide, and helpless, half naked, broken down by more than three years of hard slavery, hungry and scarcely any food, the season wet and cold, and many rivers and streams to cross? (407–408)

In contrast to the Flemings' narrative, the difficulty of the captives' situation is invoked less for sentimental than for spiritual ends. "Under such circumstances," they continued, "to depend upon one's own sagacity would be the worst of follies. If one could not believe that there is a God, who helps and saves from death, one had better let running away alone" (408). Even after they thought they had reached the safety of Fort Pitt (the former Fort Duquesne), the women had difficulty convincing a group of English soldiers that they were English prisoners and not Indians. This case of mistaken identity, so similar to Elizabeth Fleming's, underscores the threat captivity posed to a European identity that was marked largely in terms of dress, adornment, language, and deportment.

The fragility of European identity in North America is a leitmotif of captivity literature, as we have seen previously in the tale of Eunice Williams. Whereas Marie Le Roy and Barbara Leininger quickly established their identities when challenged, Barbara's sister Regina Leininger became the Eunice Williams of backwoods Pennsylvania, the region's own symbol of transformed identity. Captured along with Barbara,

FIGURE 7.3   The Indians Delivering the English Captives to Colonel Bouquet, by Benjamin West. SOURCE: An Historical Account of the Expedition Against the Ohio Indians, by William Smith, 1765. (Courtesy of the Edward E. Ayer Collection, the Newberry Library, Chicago.)

Regina remained among her captors for eight years, until 1764, when she was among some two hundred captives the Delawares and Shawnees released reluctantly to Col. Henry Bouquet at the end of Pontiac's War (see Figure 7.3). An account by the historian of the expedition, Rev. William Smith, described the sorrow of the Indians,

> who delivered up their beloved captives with the utmost reluctance; shed torrents of tears over them, recommending them to the care and protection of the commanding officer. Their regard to them continued all the time they remained in camp. They visited them from day to day; and brought them what corn, skins, horses and other matters, they had bestowed on them, while in their families; accompanied with ... all the marks of the most tender affection. ([Smith] 1868 [1765]:76–77)

Many of the captives, like their Indian families, resisted repatriation. Regina herself, as the tale was remembered in Pennsylvania folklore, failed to recognize her German mother until the woman, at Col. Bouquet's suggestion, sang a lullaby she had sung to Regina as a child.[15] Others were bound in order to prevent their escape, leading William Smith to note, in a rare admission of English captivity practices, "It is no wonder that [the children] considered their new state in the light of a captivity, and parted from the savages with tears" ([Smith] 1868 [1765]:80).

Ever since the captivity of Eunice Williams, the attraction that life among Indians held for some captives had been a source of great soul-searching. As the interpretive framework that enabled John Williams to view this attraction as "backsliding" into savagery receded, colonial observers like William Smith began to view the attraction in terms of freedom and emotional attachment. Benjamin Franklin himself observed in a letter of 1753:

> When an Indian Child has been brought up among us, taught our language and habituated to our Customs, yet if he goes to see his relations and makes one Indian Ramble with them, there is no persuading him ever to return. [But] when white persons of either sex have been taken prisoners young by the Indians, and lived a while among them, though ransomed by their Friends, and treated with all imaginable tenderness to prevail with them to stay among the English, yet in a short Time they become disgusted with our manner of life, and the care and pains that are necessary to support it, and take the first good opportunity of escaping again into the Woods, from whence there is no reclaiming them. (Labaree and Wilcox 1959:481–482)

Cadwallader Colden, a mediator between New York and the Iroquois, made a similar observation, as did Hector de Crèvecoeur, the author of *Letters from an American Farmer*. No doubt they had experienced many a tearful scene, such as one held in Albany on June 23, 1724, when the sachems of Kahnawake gave up a captive to the Commissioners of Indian Affairs with the words:

> Brethren,
> You have hitherto with [great?] pains desired that the Indian Prisoner who was taken at Virginia by some of our People in 1722 should be released and sent home to this Native Country. The Squaw who has accepted of him as her adopted Son instead of her dead son is come with him in order to Deliver him unto you that he may go home. We conceive you are sensible what great affliction it must be for a mother to part with her Child but to Show our Regard for you we have prevailed on her to deliver him [up?] unto you and hope you may have Compassion on her.

The Commissioners responded:

> Brethren,
> We return you thanks for what you have effected at our Insistence but Especially the Squaw, who had accepted of him as her Son, we know it means a great Affliction for her to deliver him over to [us to be?] sent home. We shall give her a present to [dry her?] of her Tears. (Public Archives of Canada 1819, 76v–77)

Savages in tears as they released their captives; adopted White children finding Indian social bonds "singularly captivating," as Hector de Crèvecoeur put it (1957 [1782]:209); the same children viewing their repatriation as captivity: Clearly, repatriation scenes had great potential to destabilize the selective tradition of captivity. But these sentiments would not find their way into captivity narratives themselves until after the end of the colonial period. During the remainder of the colonial period the selective tradition of captivity would develop in quite the opposite direction.[16]

## Horrifying Matters of Fact: The Production of Savagery and Heroism

Briton Hammon was not the only mid-eighteenth-century captive to present his narrative as simple "matters of fact." *A Plain Narrative of the Uncommon Sufferings and Remarkable Deliverance of Thomas Brown*, also published in Boston in 1760, contains a disclaimer so similar to Hammon's that it reveals the formulaic nature of both. "As I am but a youth," Brown wrote,

> I shall not make those remarks on the difficulties I have met with, or the kind appearances of a good God for my preservation, as one of riper years might do; but shall leave that to the reader as he goes along, and shall only beg his prayers, that mercies and afflictions may be sanctified to me, and relate matters of fact as they occur to my mind. (Brown 1978 [1760])

Similarly, four other captives—all male—produced narratives in the decade following the fourth intercolonial war that offered "plain," secular interpretations of captivity. The narratives of Thomas Brown and these four captives (John Maylem, Charles Saunders, Isaac Hollister, and most notably, Peter Williamson) offer highly sensationalized descriptions of atrocities, including cannibalism, mutilation, and the threat of rape. Significantly, of these atrocities only rape was not attributed to the Captive Self as well as the Captivating Other. In fact, the only eyewitness accounts of cannibalism and some of the most gruesome examples of mutilation feature English protagonists.

Thomas Brown was a member of Major Robert Rogers's Corps of Rangers, a company of colonial soldiers who adopted what they viewed as Indian modes of warfare.[17] (Indeed, Brown's narrative refers to marching "Indian file," carrying a tomahawk and wearing snowshoes, and having taken a prisoner and "knocked him on the head.") Captured in 1757 while scouting outside of Fort William Henry, Brown saw a companion stripped, scalped, and beheaded. Brown, a lad of about seventeen years of age, met a different fate: He was kissed, his wounds were dressed, and he was marched to Canada. During his captivity, attests the crowded title page of his "plain narrative,"

> he was not only in constant Peril of his own Life: but had the Mortification of being an Eye-Witness of divers Tortures, and shocking Cruelties, that were practiced by the Indians on several English Prisoners;—one of whom he saw burnt to Death, another tied to a Tree and his Entrails draw out, &c.&c.

More notable than the already conventional torture scenes are the instances in which Brown, like John Gyles before him, demonstrates both a familiarity with Indian ways and the personal flexibility that came to be called "Yankee ingenuity." For example, wanting to get rid of the heavy sled he was required to pull, because he was too lame to draw it, Brown said that he "took three squaws on my sled, and pleasantly told them, I wished I was able to draw them: All this took with the Indians; they freed me of the sled, and gave it to the other prisoners; they stripped off all my clothes, and gave me a blanket. And the next morning, they cut off my hair and painted me" (Brown 1978 [1760]:14–15).

Despite this ritual of adoption, which also included tattooing his hand, stripping him, and forcing him to run the gauntlet, Brown continued to fear for his life, and he eventually ran away with a fellow captive, who died of starvation on the journey. "I sat down by him," reported Brown,

> and, at first, concluded to make a fire, as I had my gun, and eat his flesh, and if no relief came, to die with him; but, finally came to this resolution;—to cut off of his bones as much flesh as I could, and tie it up in a handkerchief, and so proceed as well as I could: Accordingly did so, and buried my companion on the day I left him. I got three frogs more the next day. Being weak and tired, about 9 o'clock I sat down; but could not eat my friend's flesh. I expected soon to die myself; and while I was commending my soul to God, I saw a partridge light just by me, which I thought was sent by Providence. (21)

Nevertheless, a tortuous path still lay ahead of Brown: He would serve two more stints as a captive and two more as a soldier before finally returning home.

Notwithstanding his providential rescue from starvation, Brown's narrative is essentially a war narrative preoccupied with bloodshed, torture, mutilation, and at least the contemplation of cannibalism. Similar in this respect, but less ethnographically detailed, is the Brief Narration of Isaac Hollister, a young captive adopted by the Senecas. Like Brown, Hollister managed to escape from captivity with a fellow captive, a Dutchman. Upon his deathbed his companion instructed Hollister that "if he died first, he would not have me afraid to eat of his flesh, for I am determined, says he, to eat of yours, if you should die before me." After the man died, Hollister followed his advice: "I went immediately about performing the disagreeable operation, and cut off 5 or 6 pounds of his legs and thighs" (Hollister 1978 [1767]:6). The implication is that unlike Brown, this captive forced himself to eat his companion's flesh.

In Thomas Brown's and Isaac Hollister's narratives of their captivity, cannibalism appears as a practical if disagreeable response to starvation. The butchering of their companions' bodies is described with horrifying simplicity, in passages that contrast greatly in tone to other captives' allegations of indigenous cannibalism. John Maylem's epic poem Gallic Perfidy (1978 [1758]), for example, maintains that he did not bother to cry for mercy:

> for Mercy who'd expect
> From Cannibals that gorge on Human Flesh,
> And swill, like Polypheme, the reeking Gore?
>                     (11–12)

Here and throughout the poem Maylem's classical analogies are not a means of understanding (as in John Gyles's comparison of the Abenaki gulloua to harpies), but a means of heightening the barbaric otherness of his captors and the gothic drama of his captivity. Maylem emerged from captivity bent on revenge:

> O Chief in War! of all (young) Albion's Force
> Invest me only with SUFFICIENT Power;
> I (yet a Boy) will play the Man, and chase
> The wily Savage from his secret Haunts;
> Not Alpine Mount shall thwart my rapid Course;
> I'll scale the Craggs, then, with impetuous Speed,
> Rush down the Steep, and scow'r along the Vale;
> Then on the Sea-Shore halt; and last, explore
> The green Meanders of eternal Wood!
>
> (15)

As Richard Slotkin (1973) and others have stressed,[18] for men like Maylem captivity served as an initiation not into Indian life but into the savagery they associated with the wilderness—a savagery they produced and appropriated in order to "chase the wily savage from his secret haunts" and claim his land. Like Mary Rowlandson and John Gyles, mid-century male captives emerged from their experience transformed; however, their transformation was not effected by either a spiritual trial or by transculturation but rather by engaging in (or against) acts they considered savage. Associated with cannibalism in the works of Brown, Hollister, and Maylem, savage otherness was signified by rape in two additional midcentury narratives, both involving the rescue of a captive heroine. In each of these narratives, intimations of sexual assault introduce a new, romantic dimension to the captivity tradition—one that would later be exploited by authors of explicitly fictional captivity narratives, such as Charles Brockden Brown (1984 [1787]) and James Fenimore Cooper (1983 [1826]).

By far the most significant of the two narratives alluding to rape is French and Indian Cruelty; Exemplified in the Life and Various Vicissitudes of Fortune, of Peter Williamson, a Disbanded Soldier, ... Containing a Particular Account of the Manners, Customs, and Dress, of the Savages (Williamson 1978 [1757]). Williamson's narrative has been the most popular of all captivity narratives, exceeding in number of editions and issues those of Mary Rowlandson, John Williams, and Jonathan Dickinson. Just as the three earlier narratives exemplify a variety of providential interpretations of captivity, so Peter Williamson's narrative exemplifies the secular mode of interpretation characteristic of the latter half of the eighteenth century.[19]

For this reason French and Indian Cruelty merits consideration in a survey of mid-eighteenth-century narratives even though it was not published in an American edition until it was anthologized in 1793.[20] (In Britain, in contrast, it appeared in at least nine editions and issues between 1757 and 1793. After 1793 the narrative was widely publicized in the United States as well.)[21]

The "life and various vicissitudes of fortune" recounted in Williamson's narrative are as follows: A Scot kidnapped as a boy and transported across the Atlantic, Williamson is sold as a servant to another Scot in Philadelphia. He becomes his "own master" at seventeen and marries seven years later, receiving from his father-in-law a tract of land on the Pennsylvania frontier (1978:8). He is captured not long afterward, in October 1754, probably by Delawares or Shawnees. After enduring a winter with the Indians, Williamson escapes, joins the British army, and participates in the rescue of another captive, Miss Long. Taken prisoner by the French, Williamson is sent to England and eventually discharged.

Following his release from prison the resourceful Williamson published his narrative, which fashions him, in sequence, as a tortured captive; an authority on Indian "manners, customs, and dress"; and a frontier hero. Like other male captives of the time, Williamson describes his work as a "plain, impartial, succinct narrative" containing only "matters of fact" (1). He protests too much, however: The language and plot of Williamson's narrative are anything but plain and impartial. His veracity was questioned in his own time,[22] and the epithets Williamson uses to characterize his captors are reminiscent of the inflated rhetoric of Cotton Mather. Williamson's Indians are "barbarous wretches," "bloodthirsty monsters," "infernal masters," "hellish miscreants": In other words, they are utterly alien beings who arouse terror, horror, and a desire for righteous vengeance in the Colonial Self.

Williamson provides abundant examples of "French chicanery and Indian cruelty," which range from his own torture at the stake to the secondhand tale of a wealthy trader who was scalped, roasted alive, and "for want of other food," made into an "Indian pudding" (10, 21). Although extreme, Williamson's representations of torture, mutilation, and cannibalism are well within the mid-eighteenth-century, selective tradition of captivity. Novel, however, is Williamson's juxtaposition of violence and sexuality, which first appears following his description of the scalping of a mother and child. "Inhuman and horrid as this was," he continued,

> it did not satiate them; for when they had murdered the poor woman, they acted with her in such a brutal manner, as decency, or the remembrance of the crime, will not permit me to mention; and this even, before the unhappy

husband; who, not being able to avoid the sight, and incapable of affording her the least relief, entreated them to put an end to his miserable being. (18)

Although Williamson leaves the nature of these indecencies to his readers' imagination, the very vagueness of his description in a book that is otherwise quite explicit, together with the references to insatiable appetites, crime, and the husband's misery are all suggestive of the sexual mutilation of the dead woman. Williamson's erotic references are somewhat more direct later in the narrative, after he escapes from captivity and joins an English regiment. While waiting for orders, he hears of the capture of an aristocratic young lady, Miss Long, and the formation of a rescue party led by her fiancé, Capt. James Crawford. The captain seeks out Williamson in particular, "as I had been so long among them, and pretty well acquainted with their manners and customs, and particularly their skulking places in the woods" (43). Williamson, bent on revenge, was delighted to lend his knowledge to the cause: "Never did I go on any enterprise with half that alacrity and cheerfulness I now went with this party. My wrongs and sufferings were too recent in my memory, to suffer me to hesitate a moment in taking an opportunity of being revenged to the utmost of my power" (44).

Crawford's party, Williamson wrote, defeated Miss Long's captors without difficulty, killing every man. "Great as our joy was, and flushed with success as we were at this sudden victory," Williamson's heart was ready to burst at the sight of the unhappy young lady: "For, oh! what breast, though of the brutal savage race we had just destroyed, could, without feeling the most exquisite grief and pain, behold in such infernal power, a lady in the bloom of youth, blessed with every female accomplishment that could set off the most exquisite beauty!" (45).

Having established the "savage breast" as capable of being moved by Miss Long's beauty—essential for constituting her as an object of their desire—Williamson paints a titillating scene of exposure and bondage:

Behold one nurtured in the most tender manner, and by the most indulgent parents, quite naked, and in the open woods, encircling with her alabaster arms and hands a cold rough tree, whereto she was bound with cords so straightly pulled, that the blood trickled from her fingers' ends! Her lovely tender body, and delicate limbs, cut, bruised, and torn with stones and boughs of trees as she had been dragged along, and all besmeared with blood!

After Miss Long was unbound and while she was recovering from her shock, "our men," recounts Williamson, "were busily employed in cutting, hacking, and scalping the dead Indians." Indeed, so desirous was every man to have a share in wreaking his revenge on them, that disputes happened among ourselves who should be the instruments of further showing it on their lifeless trunks, there not being enough for every man to have one wherewith to satiate himself: The Captain observing the animosity between us, on this occasion, ordered, that. the two divisions should cast lots for this bloody, though agreeable piece of work. (46)

Finally, having proven themselves just as insatiable in their appetite for mutilation as they considered their enemy to be, the party heads home-ward, carrying the rescued captive and fifty scalps. Miss Long recounts her brother's torture and death, reporting that while he was being abused she was stripped naked and treated in a "shocking manner." The next day she was to "perish in the like manner, after suffering worse, than even such a terrible death, the satisfying these diabolical miscreants in their brutal lust." Fortunately, concludes Williamson, "it pleased the Almighty to permit us to rescue her, and entirely extirpate this crew of devils!" (47–48)

Captive turned avenger, avenger turned publicist, Williamson recog-nized the ideological and commercial potential of situating the brutality of the captor and the vulnerability of the captive in a more explicitly sexual arena. Departing from the accumulated testimony of captives from Mary Rowlandson through Elizabeth Fleming regarding the sexual restraint of Indian warriors, Williamson constituted Miss Long into the helpless object of her captors' "brutal lust." Himself he fashioned into a knowledgeable avenger, one so transformed by his own captivity that he could turn the In-dians' savagery against them in defense of feminine purity. In splitting the vulnerability and transformability of the captive along gender lines (ex-tending an opposition already developed in the Flemings' narrative) Williamson fashioned typified male and female captives that brought him commercial success and would be copied extensively by others. For exam-ple, Charles Saunders's The Horrid Cruelty of the Indians (1763) reports that his fellow captive, a Miss York, was threatened by those "who took delight in accumulating horrors on distressed innocence," but was saved in the nick of time by a rescue party led by her fiancé (Saunders 1978 [1763]:12). Like Williamson, Saunders alludes to atrocities too horrible to specify. The typifications of the bound female captive and the rapacious Indian captor entered the selective tradition of captivity in the potent form of the unspo-ken—therefore unlimited—fantasy (see Figure 7.4).

Consistent with Williamson's presentation of himself as a knowledge-able, transculturated captive are the sections of his narrative devoted to what the title page advertises as "the manners, customs, and dress of the savages." The narrative's brief ethnographic section is embedded within Williamson's description of his captivity, following his tales of atrocity

FIGURE 7.4   Naked captives tied to a stake, from an anthology of captivity narratives first published in 1793. Modeled on Robert Vaughan's engraving for John Smith's *Generalle Historie of Virginia* (London, 1624), itself modeled on Theodor de Bry's engraving of John White's bucolic *Indians Dancing Around a Circle of Posts*, 1590. SOURCE: Frontispiece, *Affecting Distresses of Frederic Manheim's Family* (Philadelphia, 1800). (Courtesy of the Edward E. Ayer Collection, the Newberry Library, Chicago.)

and preceding the escape and rescue scenes. Besides describing Indian dress, adornment, and cuisine, Williamson remarks favorably on the chastity and constancy of Indian women, the bravery and fortitude of Indian men, and the decorum of councils when unsullied by liquor. He

notes approvingly their "love of liberty" and "affection to their relations," and suggests that "some other nations might be more happy, if, in
some instances, they copied them, and made wise conduct, courage, and
personal strength, the chief recommendations for war-captains, or
werowances, as they call them." Though he mentions Indian cruelty and
vindictiveness, and especially decries their "barbarous and extraordinary
manner" of putting the elderly to death,[23] the bulk of Williamson's criticism is directed at the French for using liquor and bounty payments to
induce the Indians to violence against the English. In this manner the
French, writes Williamson, "render themselves as obnoxious, cruel, and
barbarous, to a human mind, as the very savages themselves" (24–29).
The remainder of the narrative would seem to suggest that French and
Indian cruelty justifies similar savagery on the part of the British.

Williamson promoted himself as an ethnographic authority not only in
his narrative but also in his peacetime occupation as a tavern keeper in
Edinburgh. In front of his tavern stood a wooden Indian warrior; inside
was a display of spears, bows, arrows, and "Chief Jacob's nightcap"—
which, the label asserted, had been presented to Williamson by Benjamin
Franklin. Inside the tavern, "Indian Peter" (Williamson) would exhibit
himself in the dress of a "Delaware Indian Chief," lecture on Indian manners and customs, and demonstrate a "Mohawk war dance." The frontispiece of the fourth edition of French and Indian Cruelty shows
Williamson in his Delaware garb—the very clothes in which he chose to
be buried (see Figure 7.5). One of the original Indian "wannabes,"
Williamson not only exhibited himself to an eager public as the embodiment of Indian culture, but he also seems to have found his own self-
fashioning quite compelling.[24]

## Conclusion: The Selective Tradition of Captivity

This book began with the thesis that colonial captivity narratives comprise a hegemonic tradition, that is, "a version of the past which is intended to connect with and ratify the present," one in which "certain
meanings and practices are selected for emphasis and certain other
meanings and practices are neglected or excluded" (Williams
1977:115–116). I adopted the term typification to refer to the conventional
representations constructed in the captivity tradition, and I focused attention on the process through which the oppositional typifications of the
Captive Self and Captivating Other were constructed. I noted that the opposition between Captive Self and Captivating Other largely neglects
and excludes a complex convergence of indigenous and colonial captivity practices as well as significant moments of identification between
Self and Other. Having considered Peter Williamson's and other mid-

FIGURE 7.5    Mr. Peter Williamson in the Dress of a Delaware Indian, with His Tomahawk, Scalping Knife, Etc. SOURCE: Frontispiece in French and Indian Cruelty, by Peter Williamson (London, 1759). (Courtesy of the Edward E. Ayer Collection, the Newberry Library, Chicago.)

eighteenth-century narratives, we can now also see that as the selective tradition of captivity developed it expressed and helped to shape distinctive structures of feeling. These changed over time as dramatically as did their associated modes of interpretation.

Rather than begin with Mary Rowlandson's narrative like most studies of captivity narratives, I chose to begin with what the selective tradition excludes: the captivity of Native Americans by Europeans. Tisquantum, Pocahontas, Kalicho, Arnaaq, and Nutaaq stand for countless anonymous Indian captives abducted as tokens of otherness, objects of knowledge, and instruments of conquest. We dwelt in particular on Pocahontas, whose place in American historical memory rests not on her status as a captive of the English but on her rescue of an English captive, John Smith. The most famous of all English captives among Indians, Smith was the first to write a sentimental rescue tale fashioning himself as a hero. Unlike Williamson's narrative, Smith's is concrete and complex, attesting to his detailed and particularized knowledge of his Powhatan captors.

Similarly concrete is Mary Rowlandson's spiritual autobiography, although it is equally notable for the decontextualization of her captivity from political contestation. We noted Rowlandson's attentiveness to the particularities of her captors and to the details of her experiences, a concreteness lacking in subsequent, more abstract clerical renderings of captivity. The most enduring of the clerical accounts, John Williams's Redeemed Captive, portrays a vulnerable family and flock facing the twin threats of Catholicism and savagery: one a comprehensible otherness described with a high degree of specificity, the other an opaque, abstract state of depravity and cruelty. The opposition between Indian depravity and colonial vulnerability is heightened in the clerical accounts, especially Cotton Mather's, through typifying Indian captors as male and their captives as female. In other words, in the clerical typification of captivity a vulnerable female Captive, far removed from the paternalistic order of home, church, and town, finds herself in the power of a male Captor unrestrained in his brutality. This formulation, of course, lends itself to the construction of righteous vengeance—expressed first in the figure of Hannah Dustan. Later, in the works of Peter Williamson and his successors, vengeance is more thoroughly gendered, and a male frontier hero emerges as the third typification in a constellation of captivity.[25]

Other captives besides Mary Rowlandson offered concrete and particularistic representations of captivity; among them were Jonathan Dickinson, on account of his Quaker attentiveness and interpretive restraint, and John Gyles, because of his familiarity with Abenaki "manners and customs." In Dickinson's narrative, cannibalism is the major preoccupation—an emblem both of the Indians' unrestrained appetites and the captives' vulnerability to degeneration. But Dickinson finds even presumed cannibals capable of being transformed through the workings of the holy spirit, and his narrative in the end confirms the common humanity of his captors. In Gyles's narrative, in contrast, it is not the Captor but the Captive Self who, like Odysseus, is transformed. Of all the captivity narratives published during the colonial period, Gyles's is most situated in the middle ground between cultures.

Dickinson's and Gyles's narratives add nuance to a process of typification that would otherwise appear as a linear progression from the more concrete to the more abstract, the more particularistic to the more conventional, the more gender-neutral to the more gender-coded. By the mid-eighteenth century, however, Indian Captors were largely typified Others. Nehemiah How's encounter with Eunice Williams's husband, Arosen, like William and Elizabeth Fleming's with Capt. Jacob, is an unusual example of specificity. The most influential narrative of the mid-eighteenth century, Peter Williamson's, offers not only more typified captors but also more typified captives, splitting the two along gender lines into a vulnerable, pitiable victim and an avenger whose brutality mimics and is justified by that attributed to his savage antagonists.

There is a considerable gap between Peter Williamson's self-fashioning through articulating the experience of captivity and that of Mary Rowlandson seventy-five years previously. Their narratives may be taken as expressing not only two different modes of interpretation—providential and secular—but also two different structures of feeling. Although typifications of the Captivating Other are central to each, the Self produced through a complex mixture of opposition to and identification with that Other is of a very different quality in the two narratives. Rowlandson, interpreting her captivity as a spiritual trial, expresses in her narrative a search for humility and resignation to God's will. She views her captors as instruments of God, but describes several individuals in some detail—especially her "mistress" Wetamo, with whom she identifies to the extent that she attributes the same sin, that of pride, to both herself and her mistress. If Rowlandson's narrative embodies what might be called a contemplative structure of feeling centered on humility, Williamson's embodies a heroic one centered on vengeance. He describes his captors almost entirely in terms of abstract typifications, as embodying a set of "manners and customs" that are largely horrifying. Unlike Rowlandson, however, he appropriates aspects of the savagery that he attributes to the Indians.

The interplay between the two processes we have followed closely in this book—oppositional typification, on the one hand, and transformative identification, on the other—is complex and varied. Although the selective tradition of captivity emphasizes the first and neglects or excludes the latter, we have seen moments of identification or transformation in nearly all of the colonial captivity narratives. In such moments the opposition between Captive Self and Captivating Other is resisted, and the captivating quality of the Other is acknowledged. The middle ground in which Self meets Other was to become increasingly salient for European Americans after Independence, as they set about differentiating themselves not only from Native Americans and African Americans but also from Europeans. The narratives of adopted captives published in the nineteenth century were, among other things, explorations of the flexibility of transplanted identities.[26]

As we have seen, captivity narratives published during the fourth intercolonial war increasingly focused on freedom and self-reliance and reflected a fascination with ambiguous cultural identities. Although only two new captivity narratives were published in the colonies between 1763 and 1776, there was a dramatic resurgence of interest during that period in Mary Rowlandson's and John Williams's narratives.[27] The Redeemed Captive Returning to Zion was reissued three times during the 1770s; and A Narrative of the Captivity, Sufferings, and Removes of Mary Rowlandson appeared five times (the first editions since 1720). The Rowlandson editions departed from earlier colonial editions not only in their secularized title but in featuring illustrations. Some of these illustrations remain close to the text (see Figures 4.3 and 4.4); but on the title page of the 1773 edition, Rowlandson is not "standing amazed" during the attack but is defending her home with a musket (see Figure 7.2). As Greg Sieminski (1990) has noted, this illustration re-frames Rowlandson as a Revolutionary heroine. In Revolutionary discourse the British were criticized for failing to protect the colonists against Indians, and this illustration portrays colonial militancy and self-reliance. That the colonist was a woman underscored both the severity of the threat and the upheaval it demanded in power relations.

The selective tradition of captivity continued to develop during successive wars of nationalist expansion. Even as the nation became less vulnerable to Indian opposition, the typifications of the vulnerable female captive threatened by a brutal male captor remained potent justifications for aggression against, displacement of, and domination over Indians. Novelists and historians emphasized captivity in their constructions of a romantic and heroic past. Historical monuments memorialized female captives (see Figures 1.1 and 5.3), and school and Sunday school texts told the tales of Hannah Swarton, John Williams, Regina Leininger, and others (see Figure 5.2). Captivity was featured in such mass entertainment venues as dime novels, Wild West shows, and motion pictures. Just as the clerical typification carried the authority of the Puritan elite, subsequent representations of captivity carried the authority of local and na-

FIGURE 7.6    Philip, King of Mount Hope, by Paul Revere, 1772. Engraving
published a century after Metacom's death, modeled on Thomas Verelst's
portraits of "Sa Ga Yeath Qua Pieth Tow" and "Ho Nee Yeath Taw No Row," two
Mohawk visitors to London, 1710. SOURCE: The Entertaining History of King
Philip's War, by Benjamin Church (Newport, R.I., 1772). (Courtesy of the Edward
E. Ayer Collection, the Newberry Library, Chicago.)

tional historians, school and church publication boards, representative
government, and the mass media.[28]

The hegemonic typifications of the Captive Self and Captivating Other
have not remained unchallenged, however. Among the most notable
challenges are representations of adopted captives, whether in the visual
form of Benjamin West's engraving (see Figure 7.3) or the literary form of
narratives such as Mary Jemison's (Seaver 1992 [1838]), the circulation of
which has rivaled that of Rowlandson's, Williams's, Dickinson's, and
Williamson's narratives. Another significant development was the representation of Indians as personifications of freedom, eloquence, and other
democratic virtues. By 1772 even Metacom could be presented as a romantic hero, by none other than Paul Revere (see Figure 7.6). Metacom,
Pontiac, and other former antagonists joined Pocahontas as characters in
countless romantic fictions and dramas in the early to mid-nineteenth
century. To be sure, romantic portrayals of Pocahontas and Metacom can

hardly be considered counter-hegemonic, for they presented both figures as tragic victims of an inevitable historical process.[29] But Mary Jemison—who like Eunice Williams, chose to remain with and bear children among her Iroquois captors—is not as easily incorporated into dominant understandings of the superiority of European civility to Indian savagery.

More fully counter-hegemonic are Native Americans' representations of themselves as Captives. Although few of these survive from the colonial period (the Wampanoag cannibal bird is an exception), Native American authors in the nineteenth and twentieth centuries have countered the hegemonic tradition of captivity with accounts of being captured as prisoners of war, impounded on reservations, forcibly enrolled in boarding school, and forcibly removed from their families.[30] The extent to which the selective tradition of captivity excludes the experiences of Native American captives will become fully apparent only when indigenous captivity narratives are given the same degree of scholarly attention that has been accorded to colonial captivity narratives. I close this book with the hope that it will inspire further research that broadens our understanding of the "Indian captivity narrative" as an indigenous as well as a colonial American genre.

## Notes

1. Modern secondary sources on the third and fourth intercolonial wars include Jennings 1988; Leach 1966, 1973, and 1986; Peckham 1964; Richter 1992; and White 1991. The fourth intercolonial war began in 1754, two years before the start of the Seven Years' War (1756–63) in Europe.

2. Ebersole (1995:98–109) offers a valuable analysis of the emergence of a "culture of sensibility" together with sentimental reading practices. A concern with the senses, sentiments, and affections united Newton, Locke, Hume, Rousseau, Adam Smith, the Scottish moral philosophers, John Wesley, and the participants in the Great Awakening in the American colonies.

3. See the Appendix for mid-eighteenth-century editions of previously published narratives. In emphasizing the continued significance of a providential interpretive framework in the mid-eighteenth century, I differ with Levernier and Cohen (1977), Pearce (1947), and VanDerBeets (1984), all of whom see mid-eighteenth-century narratives primarily as vehicles of anti-Indian, anti-French propaganda. Slotkin (1973) considers eighteenth-century captivity narratives only sketchily, seeing war narratives as the characteristic genre of the century. In general, the captivity narratives of the mid-eighteenth century have received considerably less scholarly scrutiny than their Puritan and Quaker predecessors, but see also Calloway 1983 and 1992, Sekora 1993, and Ebersole 1995. The latter discusses the attenuation of providential hermenuetics and the "mixed" nature of many mid-eighteenth-century narratives (88–97).

4. No modern edition exists for many of the narratives discussed in this chapter; but see Calloway 1992 for a reprint of How's narrative as well as a number of related accounts that were not published during the colonial era.

5. Eastburn's narrative is included in an anthology edited by VanDerBeets (1973), from which I quote. Eastburn 1977 [1758] is a facsimile edition.

6. Andrews (1986) discusses the erasure of a Black voice in Hammon's narrative, as well as Hammon's claim that he lacked interpretive competence (the latter is discussed also in Sekora 1993). In 1784 the spiritual autobiography of a second Black captive, John Marrant (Aldridge 1973 [1788]), was published in London; the first American edition appeared in 1820. Marrant's tale of his captivity among Cherokees in 1769 became one of the most widely disseminated captivity narratives of all time.

7. Other commentators on Hammon's narrative include Burnham (1997), Foster (1979), and Sekora (1993). The latter is particularly notable for examining the close relationship between Hammon's narrative and Thomas Brown's, also published in 1760, and for reading Hammon's narrative as not only "expand[ing] the scope of the captivity tale, but at the same time [creating] the terms of possibility for the slave narrative" (Sekora 1993:103).

8. Recent analyses of sentiment and sympathy in captivity narratives and (fictional) romances include Armstrong and Tennenhouse 1992, Burnham 1997, Castiglia 1996, and Ebersole 1995.

9. Bauman (1971) discusses disputes regarding Indian policy in Pennsylvania.

10. The Appendix lists the various editions of the Flemings' narrative. The Flemings' focus on freedom is consistent with the transition from the Puritan concern with order to the Yankee concern with liberty that Bushman (1967) finds in colonial Connecticut.

11. Capt. Jacob (or Jacobs) was noted for his role in the defeat of General Braddock at Fort Duquesne, which initiated the fourth intercolonial war. Soon after the events recounted in the Flemings' narrative, Capt. Jacob and his family were killed in a British attack (Hodge 1959 [1907–10], 2:627).

12. See G. E. Thomas 1975, and Alden T. Vaughan 1982, on the development of racialized identities in the North American colonies. Other sources on colonial American identity include Canny and Pagden 1987, Canup 1990, and Zuckerman 1977.

13. Namias 1993 focuses on the differentiated representation of male and female captives.

14. Franklin might also have been involved in printing the first English edition of the Flemings' narrative. Le Roy and Leininger 1878 [1759], from which I quote, is an English translation of the German edition, which the Garland series reproduces (Le Roy and Leininger 1978 [1759]). Not considered here is another Pennsylvania narrative that was published only in a German almanac (Urssenbacher 1978 [1762]).

15. See Derounian-Stodola and Levernier (1993:114–115; 204, n. 7) for the publication history of Regina Leininger's story, which dates to a German version published in 1766 by a Lutheran clergyman, Melchior Mühlenberg, in a periodical named Hallische Nachrichten. Levernier and Cohen (1977) excerpt a version from Francis Parkman (1851). In 1856 Reuben Weiser published a quasi-fictional version based on the 1765 account and on the recollections of his grandmother, the daughter-in-law of the famous translator and negotiator Conrad Weiser

(Weiser 1978 [1860]). In Weiser's version, the captive's name is given as "Regina Hartman." Keehn (1991) is a well-researched fictional account for young adults.

16. For a more extensive discussion of captives who resisted repatriation, see Axtell 1975. For Col. Bouquet, see also Ewing 1956 and Slotkin 1973.

17. Another member of Rogers's Rangers, Major Israel Putnam, was the subject of a popular captivity narrative published after the Revolutionary War (Humphreys 1978 [1788]); see also Ebersole (1995:160–164). Rogers himself published a journal, a romantic play called Ponteach, and other writings on North America. Much like Peter Williamson, Rogers fashioned himself into a transculturated expert on Indians (Slotkin 1973).

18. Slotkin (1973) calls this initiation into savagery "regeneration through violence." See also Pearce (1952a, 1957, 1969), commenting on Melville's "metaphysics of Indian-hating." Taussig (1987) has explored a similar appropriation of savagery in another colonial context.

19. This is not to say that Providence is absent from the narrative—for Williamson was a devout Presbyterian—but that religious references are incidental rather than fundamental to the narrative.

20. Affecting History of the Dreadful Distresses of Frederic Manheim's Family (1973 [1793]; 1978 [1793]) contains an abridged version of Williamson's narrative. For its frontispiece, see Figure 7.4.

21. The Appendix lists the editions of French and Indian Cruelty published through 1776. Williamson 1978 includes several editions of the narrative; I quote from the first edition. It also includes two fictional imitations published in London (Thomson 1978 [1761] and Gatenby 1978 [1784]); see Grace 1978 [1764] for another fictional imitation. Another mid-eighteenth-century narrative published only in Britain, by Gamaliel Smethurst (1978 [1774]), lacked the influence of Williamson's but has some of the same distinctive features: an escape from captivity, an emphasis on "simple truths," and "remarks on the customs and manners of the savages."

22. In part this is because three years prior to the publication of French and Indian Cruelty an entirely fictional work by Edward Kimber appeared, which like Williamson's narrative included captivity among Indians as one of several reversals of fortune (Kimber 1978 [1754]). Kimber's hero also was kidnapped as a boy and transported to America. See Ebersole 1995:109–128.

23. Charles Saunders's narrative gives a more sympathetic account of senilicide, noting that the practice, though cruel, was thought to "free them [the elderly] from pain and save them from becoming troublesome to society" (1978 [1763]:14–17).

24. Nolan 1964 provides information on Williamson's life. Deloria's Playing Indian (1998) is the most recent and comprehensive discussion of Indian "wannabes."

25. The male frontier hero, exemplified by Daniel Boone and memorialized in The Rescue (see Figure 1.1), is largely a development of the late eighteenth and nineteenth centuries. See Burnham 1997, Castiglia 1996, and Namias 1993, and especially Slotkin 1973.

26. For discussions of Mary Jemison, John Tanner, and other adopted or transculturated captives, see Axtell 1975, Derounian-Stodola and Levernier 1993,

Drinnon 1972, Fierst 1986 and 1996, Heard 1973, Kolodny 1984, Namias 1992, and 1993, and Scheckel 1998.

27. The Appendix lists narratives published between 1763 and 1766, including two new colonial narratives (by William Henry (and Isaac Hollister) and one published only in London (by Gamaliel Smethurst).

28. For broad overviews of post-Revolutionary developments in the selective tradition of captivity, see Derounian-Stodola and Levernier 1993, Levernier and Cohen 1977, and VanDerBeets 1971, 1972a, 1972b, 1973, and 1984. Of the most recent books on captivity narratives, Burnham 1997, Castiglia 1996, Ebersole 1995, Namias 1993, and Scheckel 1998 all consider the relationship among gender, race, and nation in captivity narratives. Namias focuses on historical captivities; Burnham, Castiglia, Ebersole also consider fiction; Ebersole also discusses cinema; and Scheckel also discusses drama.

29. For Pocahontas as a romantic figure, see Tilton 1994:58–92 and Scheckel 1998. For Metacom, see Crosby 1988, McMullen 1994, and Swan 1959; and especially Lepore 1998:191–226. Although less prominent in romantic portrayals, Wetamo has been memorialized (usually as "Weetamoo") in local place-names, a famous yacht, and at least one nineteenth-century illustration of her drowning (reproduced in Some Events 1934:22). Weinstein (1986, 1994; Weinstein-Farson 1989) and Calloway (1992) indicate the fallacy of the romantic view of Metacom and Wetamo as the last of a vanishing race; see also O'Brien n.d.

30. Krupat 1994 is a good introduction to Native American autobiographical narratives, many of which include references to captivity as I have defined it. Strong n.d.b. considers the captivity accounts in Simmons 1942 and Zitkala 1976 [1900], and in a novel by Sherman Alexie (1996).

# Appendix:
# Bibliography of British and British
# Colonial Captivity Narratives, 1682–1776

This list includes all known editions of historically based captivity narratives that appeared in Britain and the British colonies between 1682 and 1776 with two notable exceptions: It includes German-language narratives published in Pennsylvania, but excludes fictional narratives (i.e., those of Henry Grace, Edward Kimber, and John Thomson) and accounts published in periodicals or almanacs (i.e., those of John Smith, Abraham Urssenbacher, and the anonymous Adventure of a Young English Officer). The list reflects the author's research in the Newberry Library's Edward E. Ayer Collection, as well as bibliographies by Derounian-Stodola and Levernier (1993), Newberry Library (1912), Salisbury (1997), Smith (1928), Vail (1949), Vaughan (1983), Vaughan and Clark (1981), and Washburn [1977]. Boldface type indicates the first edition of a narrative.

1682

| | |
|---|---|
| Mary Rowlandson | The Soveraignty & Goodness of God, Together, with the Faithfulness of His Promises Displayed; Being a Narrative of the Captivity and Restauration of Mrs. Mary Rowlandson . . . . Boston: [Samuel Green, Jr.] for John Ratcliffe and John Griffin. A ghost edition, bound with Joseph Rowlandson's The Possibility of God's Forsaking a People, That Have Been Visibly Near and Dear to Him, Together with the Misery of a People Thus Forsaken. |
| Mary Rowlandson | The Soveraignty & Goodness of God . . . . 2d ed. Cambridge, Mass.: Samuel Green, Sr. |
| Mary Rowlandson | The Soveraignty & Goodness of God . . . . 3d ed. Cambridge, Mass.: Samuel Green, Sr. |
| Mary Rowlandson | A True History of the Captivity and Restoration of Mrs. Mary Rowlandson, a Minister's Wife in New-England; Wherein Is Set Forth, the Cruel and Inhumane Usage She Underwent Amongst the Heathens . . . . 4th ed. London: Joseph Poole. |

1684
Quentin Stockwell

"Quintin Stockwell's Relation of His Captivity and Redemption." In Increase Mather, An Essay for the Recording of Illustrious Providences, Wherein an Account Is Given of Many Remarkable and Very Memorable Events, Which Have Happened in this Last Age; Especially in New-England. Boston: Samuel Green [Jr.] for Joseph Browning.

1697
Hannah Dustan

"Narrative of a Notable Deliverance from Captivity." In Cotton Mather, Humiliations Follow'd with Deliverances, A Brief Discourse on the Matter and Method of that Humiliation which Would Be an Hopeful Symptom of Our Deliverance from Calamity, Accompanied and Accommodated With a Narrative, of a Notable Deliverance Lately Received By Some English Captives, from the Hands of Cruel Indians; And Some Improvement of that Narrative, Whereto Is Added a Narrative of Hannah Swarton . . . . Boston: B. Green and J. Allen, for Samuel Phillips.

Hannah Swarton

"A Narrative of Hannah Swarton Containing Wonderful Passages Relating to Her Captivity and Deliverance." In Cotton Mather, Humiliations Follow'd with Deliverances, . . . Whereto Is Added a Narrative of Hannah Swarton, Containing a Great Many Wonderful Passages, Relating to Her Captivity and Deliverance. Boston: B. Green and J. Allen, for Samuel Phillips.

1699
Jonathan Dickinson

God's Protecting Providence Man's Surest Help and Defence in the Times of the Greatest Difficulty and Most Imminent Danger: Evidenced in the Remarkable Deliverance of Divers Persons, from the Devouring Waves of the Sea . . . and also from the More Cruelly Devouring Jawes of the Inhumane Canibals of Florida . . . . Philadelphia: Reiner Jansen.

Hannah Dustan

"A Notable Exploit; Wherein Dux Fæmina Facti." Revised version. In Cotton Mather, Decennium Luctuosum: An History of Remarkable Occurrences in the Long War, Which New-England Hath Had with the Indian Salvages, from the Year, 1688, to the Year, 1698. Boston: B. Green and J. Allen, for Samuel Phillips.

1700
Jonathan Dickinson

God's Protecting Providence . . . . 2d ed. London: T. Sowle. 2 printings.

1701
Jonathan Dickinson       God's Protecting Providence . . . . 3d ed. London.

1702
Hannah Dustan            "A Notable Exploit; Wherein Dux Fæmina Facti." Ex-
                         panded version. In Cotton Mather, Magnalia Christi
                         Americana, Book Seven. London: Thomas Parkhurst.

Hannah Swarton           "A Narrative of Hannah Swarton . . . ." Revised ver-
                         sion. In Cotton Mather, Magnalia Christi Americana,
                         Book Six. London: Thomas Parkhurst.

1707
John Williams            The Redeemed Captive, Returning to Zion: or, A Faithful
                         History of Remarkable Occurences in the Captivity and
                         Deliverance of Mr. John Williams, Minister of the Gospel
                         in Deerfield . . . . Boston: Bartholomew Green, for
                         Samuel Phillips.

1720
Jonathan Dickinson       God's Protecting Providence . . . . 3d ed., reprint. Lon-
                         don: J. Sowle.

Mary Rowlandson          The Soveraignty & Goodness of God . . . . 5th ed. Boston:
                         T. Fleet, for Samuel Phillips.

John Williams            The Redeemed Captive . . . . 2d ed. Boston: T. Fleet, for
                         Samuel Phillips.

1728
Elizabeth Hanson         God's Mercy Surmounting Man's Cruelty, Exemplified in
                         the Captivity and Redemption of Elizabeth Hanson.
                         Philadelphia: Samuel Keimer.

1734
Jonathan Dickinson       God's Protecting Providence . . . . 3d ed., reprint. Lon-
                         don: for A. Betteforth and C. Hitch.

[1735]
Jonathan Dickinson       God's Protecting Providence . . . . 2d ed., reprint.
                         Philadelphia: Benjamin Franklin. [A ghost edition,
                         known only through an advertisement.]

1736
John Gyles               Memoirs of Odd Adventures, Strange Deliverances, etc.
                         in the Captivity of John Gyles, Esq., Commander of the
                         Garrison on St. George's River; Written By Himself.
                         Boston: S. Kneeland and T. Green.

1748
Nehemiah How             A Narrative of the Captivity of Nehemiah How, Who Was
                         Taken By the Indians At the Great-Meadow Fort Above
                         Fort Dummer, Where He Was an Inhabitant, October
                         11th, 1745 . . . . Boston: printed for the author. 2 print-
                         ings.

| | |
|---|---|
| John Norton | The Redeemed Captive, Being a Narrative of the Taking & Carrying into Captivity the Reverend Mr. John Norton, When Fort-Massachusetts Surrendered to a Large Body of French and Indians, August 20th, 1746. Boston: [Gamaliel Rogers and Daniel Fowle.] 2 printings. |
| John Norton | The Redeemed Captive . . . . Boston: S. Kneeland. |

1751

| | |
|---|---|
| Jonathan Dickinson | God's Protecting Providence . . . . 4th ed. Philadelphia: William Bradford. |

1754

| | |
|---|---|
| Elizabeth Hanson | God's Mercy Surmounting Man's Cruelty . . . . 2d ed. Philadelphia: James Chattin. |

1756

| | |
|---|---|
| Jonathan Dickinson | Jonathan Dickinsons erstaunliche Geschichte von dem Schiffbruche . . . . Germantown, Pa.: Christopher Saur. |
| William Fleming and Elizabeth Fleming | A Narrative of the Sufferings and Surprising Deliverance of William and Elizabeth Fleming, Who Were Taken Captive By Capt. Jacob, Commander of the Indians, Who Lately Made an Excursion on the Inhabitants of the Great-Cove, Near Conecoehieg, in Pennsylvania, As Related By Themselves. Philadelphia: printed for the authors [by Franklin and Hall?], [1756]. 3 printings. |
| William Fleming and Elizabeth Fleming | A Full and Authentic Narrative . . . . Lancaster, Pa.: William Dunlap. |
| William Fleming and Elizabeth Fleming | A Narrative of the Sufferings and Surprising Deliverance of William and Elizabeth Fleming . . . ; a Narrative Necessary to Be Read By All Who Are Going on the Expedition, As Well As Every British Subject; Wherein It Fully Appears, that the Barbarities of the Indians Is Owing To the French, and Chiefly Their Priests. New York: J. Parker and W. Weyman. |
| William Fleming and Elizabeth Fleming | A Narrative . . . . Boston: Green and Russell. |
| William Fleming and Elizabeth Fleming | Eine Erzehlung von den Trübsalen und der wunderbahren Befreyung so geschehen an William Fleming und dessen Weib Elisabeth . . . . Lancaster, Pa.: W. Douglas; Germantown, Pa.: Christopher Saur. 3 printings. |

1757

| | |
|---|---|
| Peter Williamson | French and Indian Cruelty; Exemplified in the Life and Various Vicissitudes of Fortune, of Peter Williamson, a |

Disbanded Soldier: Containing a Particular Account of the Manners, Customs, and Dress of the Savages . . . . York, England: N. Nickson.

1758

Robert Eastburn — A Faithful Narrative, of the Many Dangers and Sufferings, As Well As Wonderful Deliverances of Robert Eastburn, During His Late Captivity Among the Indians . . . . Philadelphia: William Dunlap.

Robert Eastburn — A Faithful Narrative . . . . 2d ed. Boston: Green and Russell.

John Maylem — Gallic Perfidy: A Poem. Illustrated. Boston: Benjamin Mecom.

John Williams — The Redeemed Captive . . . . 3d ed. Appendix by Rev. [Stephen] Williams and Rev. [Thomas] Prince. Boston: S. Kneeland.

Peter Williamson — French and Indian Cruelty . . . . 2d ed. York, England: J. Jackson.

Peter Williamson — French and Indian Cruelty . . . . 3d ed. Glasgow: J. Bryce and D. Paterson, for the author.

1759

Jonathan Dickinson — God's Protecting Providence . . . . 4th ed., reprint. London: Luke Hinde.

Marie Le Roy and Barbara Leininger — The Narrative of Marie Le Roy and Barbara Leininger, Who Spent Three and One Half Years As Prisoners Among the Indians, and Arrived Safely in the City on the Sixth of May . . . ; Written and Printed As Dictated By Them. Philadelphia: German Printing Office [by Benjamin Franklin or P. Miller and L. Weiss].

Marie Le Roy and Barbara Leininger — Die Erzehlungen von Maria Le Roy und Barbara Leininger . . . . Philadelphia: Deutsche Buchdruckerei [German Printing Office].

Peter Williamson — French and Indian Cruelty . . . . 4th ed. Illustrated. London: R. Griffiths, for the author.

1760

Thomas Brown — A Plain Narrativ[e] of the Uncommon Sufferings and Remarkable Deliverance of Thomas Brown, of Charlestown, in New-England . . . . Boston: Fowle & Draper. 3 printings.

Briton Hammon — A Narrative of the Uncommon Sufferings, and Surprising Deliverance of Briton Hammon, a Negro Man,—Servant to General Winslow. Boston: Green and Russell.

Elizabeth Hanson — An Account of the Captivity of Elizabeth Hanson, Now or Late of Kachecky, in New England, . . . Taken in Substance from Her Own Mouth, by Samuel Bownas. 3d ed. London: Samuel Clark.

Jean Lowry — A Journal of the Captivity of Jean Lowry and Her Children, Giving an Account of Her Being Taken By the Indians, the 1st of April 1756, from Pennsylvania, with an Account of the Hardship She Suffered, etc. Philadelphia: William Bradford.

1762
Peter Williamson — French and Indian Cruelty . . . . 5th ed., revised. Edinburgh: printed for the author.

1763
Charles Saunders — The Horrid Cruelty of the Indians, Exemplified in the Life of Charles Saunders, Late of Charles-Town, in South Carolina, Giving an Accurate and Concise Account of His Captivity and Unheard of Sufferings Among the Indians. Birmingham: T. Warren, Jr.

1766
William Henry — Account of the Captivity of William Henry in 1755, and of His Residence Among the Senneka Indians Six Years and Seven Months Till He Made His Escape from Them. Boston, 1766. [A ghost book, known only through an abstract in The London Chronicle, vol. 23, nos. 1798–1799 (June 23–25, 1768).]

Peter Williamson — French and Indian Cruelty . . . . 6th ed. Edinburgh.
Peter Williamson — French and Indian Cruelty . . . . 7th ed. Dublin: Adams and Ryder, for the author.

[1767]
Isaac Hollister — A Brief Narration of the Captivity of Isaac Hollister, Who Was Taken By the Indians, Anno Domini, 1763. New London, Conn.: [Timothy Green].

Isaac Hollister — A Brief Narration . . . . Hartford, Conn.: Knight and Sexton. [1767–69?]

1770
Mary Rowlandson — A Narrative of the Captivity, Sufferings, and Removes of Mrs. Mary Rowlandson, Who Was Taken Prisoner By the Indians with Several Others, and Treated in the Most Barbarous and Cruel Manner By These Vile Savages . . . . 6th ed. Illustrated. Boston: N. Coverly.

Mary Rowlandson — A Narrative of the Captivity, Sufferings, and Removes of Mrs. Mary Rowlandson . . . . 6th ed. Illustrated. Boston: Z. Fowle.

1771
Mary Rowlandson           A Narrative of the Captivity, Sufferings, and Removes of
                          Mrs. Mary Rowlandson . . . . 7th ed. Illustrated.
                          Boston: N. Coverly.

[1772]
Jonathan Dickinson        God's Protecting Providence . . . . 5th ed. London: Mary
                          Hinde.

1773
Mary Rowlandson           A Narrative of the Captivity, Sufferings, and Removes of
                          Mrs. Mary Rowlandson . . . . 8th ed. Illustrated.
                          Boston: John Bowle.

Mary Rowlandson           A Narrative of the Captivity, Sufferings, and Removes of
                          Mrs. Mary Rowlandson . . . . 8th ed. Illustrated. New
                          London, Conn.: Timothy Green.

John Williams             The Redeemed Captive . . . . 4th ed. New London,
                          Conn.: Timothy Green [1773].

1774
Smethurst, Gamaliel       A Narrative of an Extraordinary Escape Out of the Hands
                          of the Indians, in the Gulph of St. Lawrence; Interspersed
                          With a Description of the Coast, and Remarks on the Cus-
                          toms and Manners of the Savages There. London [1774].

John Williams             The Redeemed Captive . . . . 5th ed. Boston: John Bowle.
1776
John Williams             The Redeemed Captive . . . . 5th ed., reprint. New Lon-
                          don, Conn.: Timothy Green.

# References

Abler, Thomas S. 1980. "Iroquois Cannibalism: Fact, Not Fiction." Ethnohistory 27:309–316.

_____. 1992. "Scalping, Torture, Cannibalism, and Rape: An Ethnohistorical Analysis of Conflicting Values in War." Anthropologica 34:3–20.

Abler, Thomas S., and Michael H. Logan. 1988. "The Florescence and Demise of Iroquoian Cannibalism: Human Sacrifice and Malinowski's Hypothesis." Man in the Northeast 35:1–26.

Abu-Lughod, Lila. 1990. "The Romance of Resistance: Tracing Transformation of Power Through Bedouin Women." American Ethnologist 17:41–55.

Ackerknecht, Erwin H. 1944. "White Indians: Psychological and Physiological Peculiarities of White Children Abducted and Reared By North American Indians." Bulletin of the History of Medicine 15:15–36.

Adair, John. 1966 [1775]. The History of the American Indians . . . . New York: Argonaut Press.

"Adventure of a Young English Officer Among the Abenakee Savages." 1978 [1767]. In Bickerstaff's Boston Almanack, for the Year of Our Lord 1768. Facsimile. Garland Library of Narratives of North American Indian Captivities, comp. Wilcomb E. Washburn, vol. 9. New York: Garland.

Affecting History of the Dreadful Distresses of Frederic Manheim's Family . . . . 1973 [1793]. In Held Captive By Indians: Selected Narratives, 1642–1836, ed. Richard VanDerBeets. Knoxville: University of Tennessee Press.

Affecting History of the Dreadful Distresses of Frederic Manheim's Family . . . . 1978 [1793]. Facsimile. Garland Library of Narratives of North American Indian Captivities, comp. Wilcomb E. Washburn, vol. 21. New York: Garland.

Aldridge, William. 1973 [1788]. A Narrative of the Lord's Wonderful Dealings with John Marrant, a Black Born in New York . . . . In Held Captive By Indians, ed. Richard VanDerBeets. Knoxville: University of Tennessee Press.

Alexie, Sherman. 1996. Indian Killer. New York: Atlantic Monthly Press.

Anderson, Benedict. 1983. Imagined Communities: Reflections on the Origin and Spread of Nationalism. London and New York: Verso.

Anderson, Virginia DeJohn. 1994. "King Philip's Herds: Indians, Colonists, and the Problem of Livestock in Early New England." William and Mary Quarterly, 3d ser., 51:601–624.

Andrews, Evangeline Walker, and Charles McLean Andrews, eds. 1961. Jonathan Dickinson's Journal; or God's Protecting Providence. New Haven: Yale University Press.

Andrews, William L. 1986. To Tell a Free Story: The First Century of Afro-American Autobiography, 1760–1865. Urbana and Chicago: University of Illinois Press.

Arens, W. 1979. The Man-Eating Myth. New York and Oxford: Oxford University Press.

Armstrong, Nancy, and Leonard Tennenhouse. 1992. "The American Origins of the English Novel." American Literary History 4:386–410.

Arner, Robert. 1973. "The Story of Hannah Duston: Cotton Mather to Thoreau." American Transcendental Quarterly 18:19–23.

Asad, Talal. 1986. "The Concept of Cultural Translation in British Social Anthropology." In Writing Culture: The Politics and Poetics of Ethnography, ed. James Clifford and George Marcus. Berkeley: University of California Press.

Axtell, James. 1975. "The White Indians of Colonial America." William and Mary Quarterly, 3d ser., 32:55–88. Reprinted in Axtell, The European and the Indian, 1981. Revision in Axtell, The Invasion Within, 1985.

––––––. 1981. The European and the Indian: Essays in the Ethnohistory of Colonial North America. New York and Oxford: Oxford University Press.

––––––. 1985a. "The English Apostates." In The Invasion Within.

––––––. 1985b. The Invasion Within: The Contest of Cultures in Colonial North America. New York and Oxford: Oxford University Press.

––––––. 1988. After Columbus: Essays in the Ethnohistory of Colonial North America. New York and Oxford: Oxford University Press.

Axtell, James, and William C. Sturtevant. 1980. "The Unkindest Cut, or, Who Invented Scalping." William and Mary Quarterly, 3d ser., 37:451–472. Reprinted in Axtell, The European and the Indian.

Baker, Charlotte Alice. 1897. True Stories of New England Captives Carried to Canada During the Old French and Indian Wars. Deerfield, Mass.: A. E. Hall.

Baker, Charlotte Alice, and Emma L. Coleman, eds. 1925. Epitaphs in the Old Burying-Ground at Deerfield, Massachusetts. Deerfield, Mass.: Pocumtuck Valley Memorial Association.

Baltzell, E. Digby. 1979. Puritan Boston and Quaker Philadelphia. Boston: Beacon Press.

Barbeau, C. Marius. 1950. "Indian Captivities." Proceedings of the American Philosophical Society 94:522–548.

Barbour, Phillip L. 1964. The Three Worlds of Captain John Smith. Boston: Houghton Mifflin.

––––––. 1970. Pocahontas and Her World. Boston: Houghton Mifflin.

Barbour, Phillip L., ed. 1986. The Complete Works of Captain John Smith (1580–1631). 3 vols. Chapel Hill: University of North Carolina Press.

Barclay, Robert. 1678. An Apology for the True Christian Divinity. . . . [Aberdeen?]. Early English Books, 1641–1700; 268:1. Ann Arbor: University Microfilms, 1968.

Barker-Benfield, G. J. 1992. The Culture of Sensibility: Sex and Society in Eighteenth-Century Britain. Chicago: University of Chicago Press.

Barnett, Louise K. 1975. The Ignoble Savage: American Literary Racism, 1790–1890. Westport, Conn.: Greenwood.

Baron, Donna Keith, J. Edward Hood, and Holly V. Izard. 1996. "They Were Here All Along: The Native American Presence in Lower-Central New England in the Eighteenth and Nineteenth Centuries," William and Mary Quarterly, 3d ser., 53:561–586.

Barth, John. 1980 [1960]. The Sot-weed Factor. Rev. ed. Toronto and New York: Bantam Books.

Basso, Keith H. 1979. Portraits of "The Whiteman." Cambridge: Cambridge University Press.

Baum, Rosalie Murphy. 1993. "John Williams's Captivity Narrative: A Consideration of Normative Ethnicity." In A Mixed Race: Ethnicity in Early America, ed. Frank Shuffleton. New York and Oxford: Oxford University Press.

Bauman, Richard. 1971. For the Reputation of Truth: Politics, Religion, and Conflict Among the Pennsylvania Quakers, 1750–1800. Baltimore: Johns Hopkins University Press.

_____. 1983. Let Your Words Be Few: Symbolism of Speaking and Silence Among Seventeenth-Century Quakers. Cambridge: Cambridge University Press.

Beauchamp, William M. 1975 [1907]. Civil, Religious, and Mourning Councils and Ceremonies of Adoption of the New York Indians. Bulletin 113, New York State Museum. Reprint. Albany: State Education Department, State University of New York.

Behen, Dorothy Forbis. 1952. "The Captivity Story in American Literature, 1577–1826: An Examination of Written Reports in English, Authentic and Fictitious, of the Experiences of the White Men Captured By the Indians North of Mexico." Ph.D. diss., University of Chicago.

Bercovitch, Sacvan. 1978. The American Jeremiad. Madison: University of Wisconsin Press.

Bercovitch, Sacvan, ed. 1972. Typology and Early American Literature. Amherst: University of Massachusetts Press.

Berkhofer, Robert F., Jr. 1978. The White Man's Indian: Images of the American Indian from Columbus to the Present. New York: Alfred A. Knopf.

_____. 1988. "White Conceptions of Indians." In History of Indian-White Relations, ed. Wilcomb E. Washburn. Vol. 4, Handbook of North American Indians, gen. ed. William C. Sturtevant. Washington, D.C.: Smithsonian Institution Press.

Best, George. 1938 [1578]. A True Discourse of the Late Voyages of Discoverie, for the Finding of a Passage to Cathaya, by the Northwest, under the Conduct of Martin Frobisher General. In The Three Voyages of Martin Frobisher, vol. 1, ed. Vilhjalmur Stefansson. London: Argonaut.

Bock, Philip K. 1978. "Micmac." In Northeast, ed. Bruce Trigger. Vol. 15, Handbook of North American Indians, gen. ed. William C. Sturtevant. Washington, D.C.: Smithsonian Institution Press.

Boon, James A. 1982. Other Tribes, Other Scribes: Symbolic Anthropology in the Comparative Study of Cultures, Histories, Religions, and Texts. Cambridge: Cambridge University Press.

Bourdieu, Pierre. 1977. Outline of a Theory of Practice. Trans. Richard Nice. Cambridge: Cambridge University Press.

Bradford, William. 1953. Of Plymouth Plantation, 1620–1647. Ed. Samuel Eliot Morison. New York: Knopf.

Bragdon, Kathleen. 1996. Native People of Southern New England, 1500–1650. Norman: University of Oklahoma Press.

Braroe, Niels Winther. 1975. Indian and White: Self-Image and Interaction in a Canadian Plains Community. Stanford: Stanford University Press.

Brasser, T. J. 1971. "The Coastal Algonkians: People of the First Frontiers." In North American Indians in Historical Perspective, eds. Eleanor Burke Leacock and Nancy Oestereich Lurie. New York: Random House.

Breitwieser, Mitchell Robert. 1984. Cotton Mather and Benjamin Franklin: The Price of Representative Personality. Cambridge: Cambridge University Press.

_____. 1990. American Puritanism and the Defense of Mourning: Religion, Grief, and Ethnology in Mary Rowlandson's Captivity Narrative. Madison: University of Wisconsin Press.

Brightman, Robert. 1993. Grateful Prey: Rock Cree Human-Animal Relationships. Berkeley: University of California Press.

Brindenbaugh, Carl. 1980. Jamestown, 1544–1699. New York and Oxford: Oxford University Press.

Brow, James. 1996. Demons and Development: The Struggle for Community in a Sri Lankan Village. Tucson: University of Arizona Press.

Brown, Charles Brockden. 1984 [1787]. Edgar Huntly; or, Memoirs of a Sleep-Walker. Bicentennial Edition. Kent, Ohio: Kent State University Press.

Brown, Thomas. 1978 [1760]. A Plain Narrative of the Uncommon Sufferings and Remarkable Deliverance of Thomas Brown of Charlestown, in New England . . . . Facsimile. Garland Library of Narratives of North American Indian Captivities, comp. Wilcomb E. Washburn, vol. 8. New York: Garland.

Bucher, Bernadette. 1981. Icon and Conquest: A Structural Analysis of the Illustrations of deBry's Great Voyages. Trans. Basia Miller Gulati. Chicago and London: University of Chicago Press.

Burger, Geoffrey E. 1989. "Eleazer Williams: Elitism and Multiple Identity on Two Frontiers." In Being and Becoming Indian: Biographical Studies of North American Frontiers, ed. James Clifton. Chicago: Dorsey Press.

Burnham, Michelle. 1997. Captivity and Sentiment: Cultural Exchange in American Literature, 1682–1861. Hanover, N.H.: University Press of New England, for Dartmouth College.

Bushman, Richard L. 1967. From Puritan to Yankee: Character and the Social Order in Connecticut, 1690–1765. Cambridge, Mass.: Harvard University Press.

Butler, Judith P. 1987. Subjects of Desire: Hegelian Reflections in Twentieth-Century France. New York: Columbia University Press.

Caldwell, Patricia. 1983. The Puritan Conversion Narrative: The Beginnings of American Expression. Cambridge: Cambridge University Press.

Calloway, Colin G. 1983. "An Uncertain Destiny: Indian Captivities on the Upper Connecticut River." Journal of American Studies 17:189–210.

_____. 1990. The Western Abenakis of Vermont, 1600–1800: War, Migration, and the Survival of an Indian People. Norman: University of Oklahoma Press.

Calloway, Colin G., ed. 1991. Dawnland Encounters: Indians and Europeans in Northern New England. Hanover, N.H.: University Press of New England.

_____. 1992. North Country Captives: Selected Narratives of Indian Captivity from Vermont and New Hampshire. Hanover, N.H.: University Press of New England.

_____. 1997. After King Philip's War: Presence and Persistence in Indian New England. Hanover, N.H.: University Press of New England, for Dartmouth College.

Campisi, Jack. 1991. The Mashpee Indians: Tribe on Trial. Syracuse, N.Y.: Syracuse University Press.

Canny, Nicholas. 1973. "The Ideology of English Colonization: From Ireland to America." William and Mary Quarterly, 3d ser., 30:575–598.

Canny, Nicholas, and Anthony Pagden, eds. 1987. Colonial Identity in the Atlantic World, 1500–1800. Princeton, N.J.: Princeton University Press.

Canup, John. 1990. Out of the Wilderness: The Emergence of an American Identity in Colonial New England. Middletown, Conn.: Wesleyan University Press.

Carneiro da Cunha, Manuela. n.d. "Cannibalism, Memory, and Time Among the Tupinamba." Department of Anthropology seminar series, University of Chicago, June 4, 1990.

Carroll, Lorrayne. 1996. "'My Outward Man': The Curious Case of Hannah Swarton." Early American Literature 31:45–73.

Castiglia, Christopher. 1996. Bound and Determined: Captivity, Culture-Crossing, and White Womanhood from Mary Rowlandson to Patty Hearst. Chicago: University of Chicago Press.

Ceci, Lynn. 1975. "Fish Fertilizer: A Native North American Practice?" Science 188 (April 4):26–30.

_____. 1986. "The Anthropology of Shell Beads: Subsistence, Systems, and Symbols. In Proceedings of the 1986 Shell Bead Conference, ed. Charles F. Hayes. Research Records No. 20. Rochester, N.Y.: Research Division, Rochester Museum and Science Center.

_____. 1990. "Squanto and the Pilgrims: On Planting Corn 'in the Manner of the Indians'." In The Invented Indian: Cultural Fictions and Government Policies, ed. James A. Clifton. New Brunswick, N.J.: Transaction.

Chambers, Ross. 1991. Room for Maneuver: Reading (the) Oppositional (in) Narrative. Chicago: University of Chicago Press.

Chandler, Nahum D. 1996. "The Figure of the X: An Elaboration of the Du Boisian Autobiographical Example." In Displacement, Diaspora, and Geographies of Identity, eds. Smadar Lavie and Ted Swedenburg. Durham, N.C.: Duke University Press.

_____. 1997. "The Problem of Purity: A Study in the Early Work of W.E.B. Du Bois. Ph.D. diss., University of Chicago.

Chapin, Howard M. 1931. Sachems of the Narragansetts. Providence: Rhode Island Historical Society.

Cheshire, Neil, Tony Waldron, Alison Quinn, and David Quinn. 1980. "Frobisher's Eskimos in England," Archivaria 10:23–50.

Cheyfitz, Eric. 1997. The Poetics of Imperialism: Translation and Colonization from "The Tempest" to Tarzan. 2d edition. Philadelphia: University of Pennsylvania Press.

Church, Benjamin. 1865 [1716]. The History of King Philip's War. Reprint of Church, The Entertaining History. Ed. Henry Martyn Dexter. Boston: John Kimball Wiggin.

_____. 1975 [1716]. Diary of King Philip's War. Eds. Alan Simpson and Mary Simpson. Chester, Conn.: Pequot Press, for the Little Compton Historical Society.

_____. 1978 [1716]. The Entertaining History of Philip's War. Reprinted in So Dreadfull a Judgment: Puritan Responses to King Philip's War, 1676–1677, eds. Richard Slotkin and James K. Folsom. Middletown, Conn.: Wesleyan University Press.

Clark, Edward W. 1976. "Introduction." In The Redeemed Captive, by John Williams, ed. Edward W. Clark. Amherst: University of Massachusetts Press.

Clark, Michael. 1979. "The Crucified Phrase: Sign and Desire in Puritan Semiology." Early American Literature 13:278–293.

Clifford, James. 1988a. "Identity in Mashpee." In The Predicament of Culture.

_____. 1988b. The Predicament of Culture: Twentieth-Century Ethnography, Literature, and Art. Cambridge, Mass.: Harvard University Press.

_____. 1997. Routes: Travel and Translation in the Late Twentieth Century. Cambridge, Mass.: Harvard University Press.

Clifford, James, and George Marcus, eds. 1986. Writing Culture: The Politics and Poetics of Ethnography. Berkeley: University of California Press.

Clifton, James A., ed. 1990. The Invented Indian: Cultural Fictions and Government Policies. New Brunswick, N.J.: Transaction.

Cohn, Bernard. 1983. "Representing Authority in Victorian India." In The Invention of Tradition, eds. Eric Hobsbawm and Terence Ranger. Cambridge: Cambridge University Press.

_____. 1985. "The Command of Language and the Language of Command." In Subaltern Studies, vol. 4, ed. Ranajit Guha. Delhi: Oxford University Press.

_____. 1996. Colonialism and Its Forms of Knowledge: The British in India. Princeton, N.J.: Princeton University Press.

Coleman, Emma Lewis. 1925. New England Captives Carried to Canada Between 1677 and 1760 During the French and Indian Wars. 2 vols. Portland, Maine: Southworth.

Comaroff, John, and Jean Comaroff. 1992. Ethnography and the Historical Imagination. Boulder, Colo.: Westview.

Conkey, Laura E., Ethel Boissevain, and Ives Goddard. 1978. "Indians of Southern New England and Long Island: Late Period." In Northeast, ed. Bruce Trigger. Vol. 15, Handbook of North American Indians, gen. ed. William C. Sturtevant. Washington, D.C.: Smithsonian Institution Press.

Connecticut Historical Society (Hoadly Memorial). 1932. Collections. Hartford, Conn.

Cook, Edward M., Jr. 1976. The Fathers of the Towns: Leadership and Community Structure in Eighteenth-Century New England. Baltimore: Johns Hopkins University Press.

Cook, Sherburne F. 1973a. "Interracial Warfare and Population Decline Among the New England Indians." Ethnohistory 20:1–24.

_____. 1973b. "The Significance of Disease in the Extinction of the New England Indians." Human Biology 45:485–508.

_____. 1976. The Indian Population of New England in the Seventeenth Century. University of California Publications in Anthropology, vol. 12. Berkeley: University of California Press.

Cooper, James Fenimore. 1983 [1826]. The Last of the Mohicans: A Narrative of 1757. Eds. James A. Sappenfield and E. N. Feltskog. Albany: State University of New York Press.

Crèvecoeur, Hector St.-Jean de. 1957 [1792]. Letters from an American Farmer. New York: Dutton.

Crosby, Alfred W. 1978. "'God . . . would destroy them, and give their country to another people . . . .'" American Heritage 29 (6):38–43.

Crosby, Constance. 1988. "From Myth to History, or Why King Philip's Ghost Walks Abroad." In The Recovery of Meaning: Historical Archaeology in the Eastern United States, eds. Mark P. Leone and Parker B. Potter. Washington, D.C.: Smithsonian Institution Press.

Daly, Robert. 1977. "Puritan Poetics: The World, The Flesh, and God." Early American Literature 12:136–162.

Damas, David, ed. 1984. Arctic. Vol. 5, Handbook of North American Indians, gen. ed. William C. Sturtevant. Washington, D.C.: Smithsonian Institution Press.

Davis, David Brion. 1966. The Problem of Slavery in Western Culture. Ithaca, N.Y.: Cornell University Press.

Davis, Margaret H. 1992. "Mary White Rowlandson's Self-Fashioning as Puritan Goodwife." Early American Literature 27:49–60.

Davis, Natalie Zemon. 1995. New Worlds: Marie de l'Incarnation. In Women on the Margins: Three Seventeenth-Century Lives. Cambridge, Mass.: Harvard University Press.

Day, Gordon M. 1981. The Identity of the Saint Francis Indians. National Museums of Canada, National Museum of Man, Mercury Series, no. 71. Ottawa: Canadian Ethnology Service.

Deane, Charles, ed. 1866. A True Relation of Virginia, By Captain John Smith. Boston.

Dearborn, Mary V. 1986. Pocahontas's Daughters: Gender and Ethnicity in American Culture. New York and Oxford: Oxford University Press.

Deloria, Philip. 1998. Playing Indian. New Haven: Yale University Press.

Demos, John. 1970. A Little Commonwealth: Family Life in Plymouth Colony. London and New York: Oxford University Press.

_____. 1982. Entertaining Satan: Witchcraft and the Culture of Early New England. London and New York: Oxford University Press.

_____. 1994. The Unredeemed Captive: A Family Story from Early America. New York: Alfred A. Knopf.

Denning, Michael. 1986. "'The Special American Conditions': Marxism and American Studies." American Quarterly 38:356–380.

_____. 1987. Mechanic Accents: Dime Novels and Working-Class Culture in America. London and New York: Verso.

Derounian, Kathryn Zabelle. 1987. "Puritan Orthodoxy and the 'Survivor Syndrome' in Mary Rowlandson's Captivity Narrative." Early American Literature 22:82–93.

_____. 1988. "The Publication, Promotion, and Distribution of Mary Rowlandson's Indian Captivity Narrative in the Seventeenth Century." Early American Literature 23:239–261.

Derounian-Stodola, Kathryn Zabelle, and James Arthur Levernier. 1993. The Indian Captivity Narrative, 1550–1900. Twayne's U.S. Authors Series, no. 622. New York: Twayne and Maxwell Macmillan International; Toronto: Maxwell Macmillan Canada.

Derrida, Jacques. 1980. "The Law of the Genre." In Glyph. Baltimore: Johns Hopkins University Press.

Dickason, Olive Patricia. 1984. The Myth of the Savage, and the Beginnings of French Colonialism in the Americas. Edmonton: University of Alberta Press.

Dickinson, Jonathan. 1961 [1699]. Jonathan Dickinson's Journal; or God's Protecting Providence . . . . Eds. Evangeline Walker Andrews and Charles McLean Andrews. New Haven: Yale University Press.

———. 1977 [1699]. God's Protecting Providence. . . . Facsimile. Garland Library of Narratives of North American Indian Captivities, comp. Wilcomb E. Washburn, vol. 4. New York: Garland.

Diebold, Robert K. 1972. "A Critical Edition of Mrs. Mary Rowlandson's Captivity Narrative." Ph.D. diss., Yale University.

Dodding, Edward. 1979 [1577]. "Doctor Dodding's report of the sickness and death of the man at Bristol which Capt. Furbisher brought from the Northwest." Ms., Public Record Office, London SP12/118. Trans. N. Cheshire and T. Waldron. In Newfoundland from Fishery to Colony: Northwest Passage Searches, vol. 4: New American World: A Documentary History of North America to 1612, ed. David B. Quinn. New York: Arno Press.

Domínguez, Virginia R. 1986. White by Definition: Social Classification in Creole Louisiana. New Brunswick, N.J.: Rutgers University Press.

Downing, David. 1980–81. "'Streams of Scripture Comfort': Mary Rowlandson's Typological Use of the Bible." Early American Literature 15:252–259.

Drake, James. 1995. "Symbol of a Failed Strategy: The Sassamon Trial, Political Culture, and the Outbreak of King Philip's War." American Indian Culture and Research Journal 19:111–141.

———. 1997. "Restraining Atrocity: The Conduct of King Philip's War." New England Quarterly 70:33–56.

Drake, Samuel Gardner. 1832. Indian Biography. Boston.

———. 1834. The Book of the Indians of North America. Boston.

———. 1880. The Aboriginal Races of North America. 15th ed. New York.

———. 1978 [1839]. Indian Captivities. Facsimile. Garland Library of Narratives of North American Indian Captivities, comp. Wilcomb E. Washburn, vol. 55. New York: Garland.

Drimmer, Frederick, ed. 1985 [1961]. Captured By the Indians: Fifteen Firsthand Accounts, 1750–1870. New York: Dover, 1985. Reprint of Scalps and Tomahawks: Narratives of Indian Captivity.

Drinnon, Richard. 1972. White Savage: The Case of John Dunn Hunter. New York: Schocken.

———. 1980. Facing West: The Metaphysics of Indian-Hating and Empire Building. Minneapolis: University of Minnesota Press.

Dunn, Mary Maples. 1980. "Saints and Sinners: Congregational and Quaker Women in the Early Colonial Period." In Women in American Religion, ed. Janet Wilson James. Philadelphia: University of Pennsylvania Press.

Eastburn, Robert. 1973 [1758]. A Faithful Narrative of the Many Dangers and Sufferings, As Well As Wonderful Deliverances of Robert Eastburn . . . . In Held Captive By Indians: Selected Narratives, 1642–1836, ed. Richard VanDerBeets. Knoxville: University of Tennessee Press.

_____. 1977 [1758]. A Faithful Narrative . . . . Facsimile. Garland Library of Narratives of North American Indian Captivities, vol. 8, comp. Wilcomb E. Washburn. New York: Garland.

Ebersole, Gary L. 1995. Captured By Texts: Puritan to Postmodern Images of Indian Captivity. Charlottesville and London: University Press of Virginia.

Elliott, Emory. 1975. Power and the Pulpit in Puritan New England. Princeton, N.J.: Princeton University Press.

Erickson, Vincent O. 1978. "Maliseet-Passamaquoddy." In Northeast, ed. Bruce Trigger. Vol. 15, Handbook of North American Indians, gen. ed. William C. Sturtevant. Washington, D.C.: Smithsonian Institution Press.

Erikson, Kai. 1966. Wayward Puritans: A Study in the Sociology of Deviance. New York: Wiley and Sons.

Ewing, William S. 1956. "Indian Captives Released By Colonel Bouquet." Western Pennsylvania Historical Magazine 39:187–203.

Fabian, Johannes. 1983. Time and the Other: How Anthropology Makes Its Object. New York: Columbia University Press.

Fausz, J. Frederick. 1977. "The Powhatan Uprising of 1622: A Historical Study of Ethnocentrism and Cultural Conflict." Ph.D. diss., College of William and Mary.

_____. 1981. "Opechancanough: Indian Resistance Leader." In Struggle and Survival in Colonial North America, eds. David G. Sweet and Gary B. Nash. Berkeley: University of California Press.

Feest, Christian F. 1966. "Powhatan: A Study in Political Organization." Wiener Völkerkundliche Mitteilungen 13:69–83.

_____. 1978a. "North Carolina Algonquians." In Northeast, ed. Bruce Trigger. Vol. 15, Handbook of North American Indians, gen. ed. William C. Sturtevant. Washington, D.C.: Smithsonian Institution Press.

_____. 1978b. "Virginia Algonquians." In Northeast, ed. Bruce Trigger. Vol. 15, Handbook of North American Indians, gen. ed. William C. Sturtevant. Washington, D.C.: Smithsonian Institution Press.

_____. 1987. "Pride and Prejudice: The Pocahontas Myth and the Pamunkey." European Review of Native American Studies 1(1):5–12. Reprinted in The Invented Indian: Cultural Fictions and Government Policies, ed. James Clifton. New Brunswick, N.J.: Transaction, 1990.

_____. 1990. The Powhatan Tribes. New York and Philadelphia: Chelsea House.

Feest, Christian F., ed. 1987. Indians and Europe. Aachen: Herodot/Rader-Verlag.

Fenton, William N. 1971. "The Iroquois in History." In North American Indians in Historical Perspective, eds. Eleanor Burke Leacock and Nancy Oestereich Lurie. New York: Random House.

_____. 1978. "Northern Iroquoian Culture Patterns." In Northeast, ed. Bruce Trigger. Vol. 15, Handbook of North American Indians, gen. ed. William C. Sturtevant. Washington, D.C.: Smithsonian Institution Press.

_____. 1985. "Structure, Continuity, and Change in the Process of Iroquois Treaty Making." In The History and Culture of Iroquois Diplomacy, eds. Francis Jennings, William N. Fenton, Mary A. Druke, and David R. Miller. Syracuse, N.Y.: Syracuse University Press.

Fiedler, Leslie A. 1969. The Return of the Vanishing American. New York: Stein and Day.

_____. 1988. "The Indian in Literature in English." In History of Indian-White Relations, ed. Wilcomb Washburn. Vol. 4, Handbook of North American Indians, gen. ed. William C. Sturtevant. Washington, D.C.: Smithsonian Institution Press.

Fierst, John T. 1986. "Return to 'Civilization': John Tanner's Troubled Years at Sault Ste. Marie." Minnesota History 50:23–36.

_____. 1996. "Strange Eloquence: Another Look at The Captivity and Adventures of John Tanner." In Reading Beyond Words: Contexts for Native History, eds. Jennifer S. H. Brown and Elizabeth Vibert. Peterborough, Ont., and Orchard Park, N.Y.: Broadview.

Fitzhugh, William, ed. 1985. Cultures in Contact: The Impact of European Contacts on Native American Cultural Institutions, A.D. 1000–1800. Washington, D.C.: Smithsonian Institution Press.

Fitzpatrick, Tara. 1991. "The Figure of Captivity: The Cultural Work of the Puritan Captivity Narrative." American Literary History 3:1–26.

Flannery, Regina. 1939. An Analysis of Coastal Algonquian Culture. Catholic University of America, Anthropological Series, vol. 7. Washington, D.C.

Fleming, William. 1978 [1756]. A Narrative of the Sufferings and Surprizing Deliverance of William and Elizabeth Fleming . . . . Facsimile. Garland Library of Narratives of North American Indian Captivities, vol. 8., comp. Wilcomb E. Washburn. New York: Garland.

Fogelson, Raymond D. 1971. "The Cherokee Ballgame Cycle: An Ethnographer's View." Ethnomusicology 15:327–38.

_____. 1974. "On the Varieties of Indian History." Journal of Ethnic Studies 2:105–112.

_____. 1975. "An Analysis of Cherokee Sorcery and Witchcraft." In Four Centuries of Southern Indians, ed. Charles M. Hudson. Athens: University of Georgia Press.

_____. 1977. "Cherokee Notions of Power." In The Anthropology of Power, eds. Raymond D. Fogelson and Richard N. Adams. New York: Academic Press.

_____. 1980. "Windigo Goes South: Stoneclad Among the Cherokees." In Manlike Monsters on Trial, eds. M. M. Halpin and M. M. Ames. Vancouver: University of British Columbia Press.

_____. 1982. "The Anthropology of the Self: Some Retrospects and Prospects." In Psychosocial Theories of the Self, ed. Benjamin Lee. New York: Plenum Press.

_____. 1985. "Interpretations of the American Indian Psyche: Some Historical Notes." In Social Contexts of American Ethnology, 1840–1984, ed. June Helm. 1984 Proceedings of the American Ethnological Society. Washington, D.C.: American Anthropological Association.

_____. 1987. "The History of the Study of North American Indian Religions." In Encyclopedia of Religion, ed. Mircea Eliade. New York: Macmillan and Free Press.

_____. 1989. "The Ethnohistory of Events and Nonevents." Ethnohistory 36:133–147.

_____. 1990. "On the 'Petticoat Government' of the Eighteenth-Century Chero-kee." In Personality and the Cultural Construction of Society, eds. David K. Jordan and Marc J. Swartz. Tuscaloosa: University of Alabama Press.

Foreman, Carolyn Thomas. 1943. Indians Abroad, 1493–1938. Norman: University of Oklahoma Press.

Foster, Frances Smith. 1979. Witnessing Slavery: The Development of Antebellum Slave Narratives. Westport, Conn.: Greenwood.

Foucault, Michel. 1965. Madness and Civilization: A History of Insanity in the Age of Reason. New York: Random House.

_____. 1973. The Order of Things: An Archeology of the Human Sciences. New York: Vintage.

_____. 1978. History of Sexuality, vol. 1. Trans. Michael Hurley. New York: Pantheon.

_____. 1979. Discipline and Punish: The Birth of The Prison. Trans. Alan Sheridan. New York: Random House.

_____. 1980. Power/Knowledge: Selected Interviews and Other Writings, 1972–1977. Ed. and trans. Colin Gordon. New York: Pantheon.

Franklin, Benjamin V. 1980. Boston Printers, Publishers, and Booksellers, 1640–1800. Boston: G. K. Hall.

Friederici, Georg. 1985 [1907]. "Scalping in America." In Smithsonian Institution Annual Report for 1906. Reprinted in Scalping and Torture: Warfare Practices Among North American Indians, comp. W. G. Spittal. Oshweken, Ont.: Iroqrafts.

Frost, John. 1978 [1854]. Heroic Women of the West: Comprising Thrilling Examples of Courage, Fortitude, Devotedness, and Self-Sacrifice, Among the Pioneer Mothers of the Western Country. Facsimile. Garland Library of Narratives of North American Indian Captivities, comp. Wilcomb E. Washburn, vol. 66. New York: Garland.

Fuller, Thomas. 1662. The History of the Worthies of England . . . . London: [John Grismond and William Godbid].

Gatenby, William. 1978 [1784]. A Full and Particular Account of the Sufferings of William Gatenby. Facsimile. Garland Library of Narratives of North American Indian Captivities, comp. Wilcomb E. Washburn, vol. 9. New York: Garland.

Gay, Peter. 1966. The Enlightenment: An Interpretation; The Rise of Modern Paganism. New York: Vintage Books.

Gearing, Frederick O. 1958. "The Structural Poses of 18th Century Cherokee Villages." American Anthropologist, n.s., 60:1148–1157.

_____. 1962. Priests and Warriors: Social Structures for Cherokee Politics in the Eighteenth Century. American Anthropological Society Memoir 93. Washington, D.C.: American Anthropological Association.

Gerard, William R. 1904. "The Tapahanek Dialect of Virginia." American Anthropologist, n.s., 9:87–112.

Gherman, Dawn Lander. 1975. "From Parlour to Tepee: The White Squaw on the American Frontier." Ph.D. diss., University of Massachusetts.

Gleach, Frederic W. 1994. "Pocahontas and Captain John Smith Revisited." In Actes du vingt-cinquième congrès des algonquinistes, ed. William Cowan. Ottawa, Ont.: Carleton University.

_____. 1996. "Controlled Speculation: Interpreting the Saga of Pocahontas and Captain John Smith." In Reading Beyond Words: Contexts for Native History, eds. Jennifer S. H. Brown and Elizabeth Vibert. Petersborough, Ont.: Broadview Press.

_____. 1997. Powhatan's World and Colonial Virginia: A Conflict of Cultures. Lincoln: University of Nebraska Press.

Goddard, Ives. 1978. "Eastern Algonquian Languages." In Northeast, ed. Bruce Trigger. Vol. 15, Handbook of North American Indians, gen. ed. William C. Sturtevant. Washington, D.C.: Smithsonian Institution Press.

_____. 1984. "Agreskwe, a Northern Iroquoian Deity." In Extending the Rafters: Interdisciplinary Approaches to Iroquoian Studies, eds. Michael K. Foster, Jack Campisi, and Marianne Mithun. Albany: State University of New York Press.

Goddard, Ives, and Kathleen Bragdon, eds. and trans. 1988. Native Writings in Massachusett. Philadelphia: American Philosophical Society.

Goody, Jack. 1977. The Domestication of the Savage Mind. Cambridge: Cambridge University Press.

Gookin, Daniel. 1972 [1836]. "Historical Account of the Doings and Sufferings of the Christian Indians in New England, in the Years 1675, 1676, 1677." Transactions and Collections of the American Antiquarian Society [Archaeologia Americana] 2:42–34. Reprint. New York: Arno.

Grace, Henry. 1978 [1764]. The History of the Life and Sufferings of Henry Grace . . . Being a Narrative of the Hardships He Underwent During Several Years Captivity Among the Savages in North America . . . in Which Is Introduced an Account of the Several Customs and Manners of the Different Nations of Indians. Facsimile. Garland Library of Narratives of North American Indian Captivities, vol. 10, comp. Wilcomb E. Washburn. New York: Garland.

Gramsci, Antonio. 1972. Selections from the Prison Notebooks. Eds. Quintin Hoare and Geoffrey Nowell Smith. New York: International Publishers.

Green, Rayna D. 1975. "The Pocahontas Perplex: The Image of Indian Women in American Culture." Massachusetts Review 16:698–714.

_____. 1988. "The Indian in Popular American Culture." In History of Indian-White Relations, ed. Wilcomb Washburn. Vol. 4, Handbook of North American Indians, gen. ed. William C. Sturtevant. Washington, D.C.: Smithsonian Institution Press.

Greenblatt, Stephen J. 1976. "Learning to Curse: Aspects of Linguistic Colonialism in the Sixteenth Century." In First Images of America, vol. 2, eds. Fredi Chiapelli, Michael J. B. Allen, and Robert L. Benson. Berkeley: University of California Press.

_____. 1980. Renaissance Self-Fashioning: From More to Shakespeare. Chicago: University of Chicago Press.

_____. 1988. Shakespearean Negotiations. Berkeley and Los Angeles: University of California Press.

_____. 1991. Marvelous Possessions: The Wonder of the New World. Chicago: University of Chicago Press.

Greene, David L. 1985. "New Light on Mary Rowlandson." Early American Literature 20:25–38.

Grumet, Robert. 1980. "Sunksquaws, Shamans, and Tradeswomen: Middle Atlantic Coastal Algonkian Women During the 17th and 18th Centuries." In Women and Colonization: Anthropological Perspectives, eds. Mona Etienne and Eleanor Leacock. New York: Praeger Scientific.

Gyles, John. 1973 [1736]. Memoirs of Odd Adventures, Strange Deliverances etc. in the Captivity of John Gyles, Esq. . . . . In Held Captive By Indians: Selected Narratives, 1642–1836, ed. Richard VanDerBeets. Knoxville: University of Tennessee Press.

_____. 1978 [1736]. Memoirs of Odd Adventures . . . . Facsimile. Garland Library of Narratives of North American Indian Captivities, vol. 6, comp. Wilcomb E. Washburn. New York: Garland.

_____. 1981 [1736]. Memoirs of Odd Adventures . . . . In Puritans Among the Indians: Accounts of Captivity and Redemption, 1676–1724, eds. Alden T. Vaughan and Edward W. Clark. Cambridge, Mass.: Harvard University Press.

Haefeli, Evan, and Kevin Sweeney. 1995. "Revisiting the Redeemed Captive: New Perspectives on the 1704 Attack on Deerfield." William and Mary Quarterly, 3d ser., 52:3–46. Reprinted in After King Philip's War: Presence and Persistence in Indian New England, ed. Colin G. Calloway. Hanover, N.H.: University Press of New England, for Dartmouth College, 1997.

Hall, Christopher. 1938 [1598–1600]. "The First Voyage of M. Martin Frobisher." In The Three Voyages of Martin Frobisher, vol. 1, ed. Vilhjalmur Stefansson. Also in Newfoundland from Fishery to Colony, ed. David B. Quinn. New York: Arno Press, 1979.

Hall, David. 1979. "The World of Print and Collective Mentality in Seventeenth-Century New England." In New Directions in American Intellectual History, eds. John Higham and Paul K. Conkin. Baltimore: Johns Hopkins University Press.

_____. 1988. The Last American Puritan: The Life of Increase Mather, 1639–1723. Middletown, Conn.: Wesleyan University Press.

Hallowell, A. Irving. 1926. "Bear Ceremonialism in the Northern Hemisphere." American Anthropologist, n.s., 28:1–175.

_____. 1963. "American Indians, White and Black: The Phenomenon of Transculturation." Current Anthropology 4:519–531. Reprinted in Contributions to Anthropology: Selected Papers of A. Irving Hallowell, eds. Raymond D. Fogelson, Fred Eggan, Melford E. Spiro, George W. Stocking, A.F.C. Wallace, and Wilcomb E. Washburn. Chicago: University of Chicago Press.

_____. 1976 [1960]. "Ojibwa Ontology, Behavior, and World View." In Contributions to Anthropology: Selected Papers of A. Irving Hallowell, eds. Raymond D. Fogelson, Fred Eggan, Melford E. Spiro, George W. Stocking, A.F.C. Wallace, and Wilcomb E. Washburn. Chicago: University of Chicago Press.

Hambrick-Stowe, Charles E. 1982. The Practice of Piety: Puritan Devotional Disciplines in Seventeenth-Century New England. Chapel Hill: University of North Carolina Press.

Hamell, George R. 1983. "Trading in Metaphors: The Magic of Beads." In Proceedings of the 1982 Glass Trade Bead Conference, ed. Charles F. Hayes. Research Records No. 16. Rochester, N.Y.: Rochester Musuem and Science Center, Research Division.

_____. 1987. "Mythical Realities and European Contact in the Northeast During the Sixteenth and Seventeenth Centuries." Man in the Northeast 33:63–87.

Hammon, Briton. 1978 [1760]. A Narrative of the Uncommon Sufferings and Surprising Deliverance of Briton Hammon,—Servant to General Winslow. Facsimile. Garland Library of Narratives of North American Indian Captivities, comp. Wilcomb E. Washburn, vol. 8. New York: Garland.

Handler, Richard. 1988. Nationalism and the Politics of Culture in Quebec. Madison: University of Wisconsin Press.

Hanson, Alan. 1989. "The Making of the Maori: Culture Invention and Its Logic." American Anthropologist, n.s., 91:890–902.

Hanson, Elizabeth. 1973 [1760]. An Account of the Captivity of Elizabeth Hanson . . . . In Held Captive By Indians: Selected Narratives, 1642–1836, ed. Richard VanDerBeets. Knoxville: University of Tennessee Press.

_____. 1977 [1728]. God's Mercy Surmounting Man's Cruelty . . . . Facsimile. Garland Library of Narratives of North American Indian Captivities, vol. 6, comp. Wilcomb E. Washburn. New York: Garland.

_____. 1977 [1760]. An Account of the Captivity of Elizabeth Hanson . . . . Garland Library of Narratives of North American Indian Captivities, vol. 6, comp. Wilcomb E. Washburn. New York: Garland.

_____. 1981 [1728]. God's Mercy Surmounting Man's Cruelty . . . . In Puritans Among the Indians: Accounts of Captivity and Redemption, 1676–1724, eds. Alden T. Vaughan and Edward W. Clark. Cambridge, Mass.: Harvard University Press.

Heard, J. Norman. 1973. White into Red: A Study of the Assimilation of White Persons Captured By Indians. Metuchen, N.J.: Scarecrow Press.

Heath, Dwight B., ed. 1963 [1622]. A Journal of the Pilgrims at Plymouth. Reprint of Mourt's Relation. New York: Corinth Books.

Hegel, G.W.F. 1964 [1807]. The Phenomenology of Mind. Trans. J. B. Baillie. New York: Humanities Press.

Hemming, John. 1978. Red Gold: The Conquest of the Brazilian Indians, 1500–1760. Cambridge, Mass.: Harvard University Press.

Henwood, Dawn. 1997. "Mary Rowlandson and the Psalms: The Textuality of Survival." Early American Literature 32:169–186.

Henry, William. 1978 [1768]. "Account of the Captivity of William Henry . . . ." Facsimile of abstract in the London Chronicle. Garland Library of Narratives of North American Indian Captivities, comp. Wilcomb E. Washburn, vol. 10. New York: Garland.

Hirsch, E. D., Jr. 1987. Cultural Literacy: What Every American Needs to Know. Boston: Houghton Mifflin Company.

Hobsbawm, Eric, and Terence Ranger, eds. 1983. The Invention of Tradition. Cambridge: Cambridge University Press.

Hodge, Frederick Webb, ed. 1959 [1907–10]. Handbook of American Indians North of Mexico. Bureau of American Ethnology, Bulletin 30. 2 vols. Reprint. New York: Pageant Books.

Hollister, Isaac. 1978 [1767]. A Brief Narration of the Captivity of Isaac Hollister . . . . Facsimile. Garland Library of Narratives of North American Indian Captivities, vol. 10, comp. Wilcomb E. Washburn. New York: Garland.

How, Nehemiah. 1977 [1748]. A Narrative of the Captivity of Nehemiah How . . . . Facsimile. Garland Library of Narratives of North American Indian Captivities, vol. 6, comp. Wilcomb E. Washburn. New York: Garland.

_____. 1992 [1748]. A Narrative of the Captivity of Nehemiah How . . . . In North Country Captives: Selected Narratives of Indian Captivity from Vermont and New Hampshire, ed. Colin G. Calloway. Hanover, N.H.: University Press of New England.

Hubbell, Jay B. 1957. "The Smith–Pocahontas Story in Literature." Virginia Magazine of History and Biography 65:275–300.

Hudson, Charles M. 1976. The Southeastern Indians. Knoxville: University of Tennessee Press.

Hudson, Charles M., ed. 1979. Black Drink: A Native American Tea. Athens: University of Georgia Press.

Hulme, Peter. 1992. Colonial Encounters: Europe and the Native Caribbean, 1492–1797. Reprint ed. London: Routledge.

Hultkrantz, Ake. 1953. Conceptions of the Soul Among North American Indians: A Study in Religous Ethnology. Ethnographical Museum of Sweden, Monograph Series, Publication No. 1. Stockholm.

Hulton, Paul. 1984. America 1585: The Complete Drawings of John White. Chapel Hill: University of North Carolina Press; London, U.K.: British Museum Publications.

Humins, John H. 1987. "Squanto and Massasoit: A Struggle for Power." New England Quarterly 60:54–70.

Humphreys, David. 1978 [1788]. An Essay on the Life of the Honorable Major-General Israel Putnam . . . . Facsimile. Garland Library of Narratives of North American Indian Captivities, vol. 19, comp. Wilcomb E. Washburn. New York: Garland.

Jaenen, Cornelius J. 1976. Friend and Foe: Aspects of French-Amerindian Cultural Contact in the Sixteenth and Seventeenth Centuries. New York: Columbia University Press.

Jakobson, Roman. 1960. "Linguistics and Poetics." In Style in Language, ed. Thomas Sebeok. Cambridge: Massachusetts Institute of Technology Press.

James, Edwin, ed. 1978 [1830]. A Narrative of the Captivity and Adventures of John Tanner. Facsimile. Garland Library of Narratives of North American Indian Captivities, vol. 46, comp. Wilcomb E. Washburn. New York: Garland.

James, Edward T., Janet Wilson James, and Paul Boyer, eds. 1971. Notable American Women, 1607–1950. 3 vols. Cambridge, Mass.: Harvard University Press.

Jennings, Francis. 1975. The Invasion of America: Colonialism and the Cant of Conquest. New York: W. W. Norton.

_____. 1984. The Ambiguous Iroquois Empire: The Covenant Chain Confederation of Indian Tribes with English Colonies from Its Beginnings to the Lancaster Treaty of 1744. New York: W. W. Norton.

_____. 1988. Empire of Fortune: Crowns, Colonies, and Tribes in the Seven Years War in America. New York: W. W. Norton.

Jewett, Robert, and John Shelton Lawrence. 1977. The American Monomyth. New York: Anchor Press/Doubleday.

Johnson, Richard R. 1977. "The Search for a Usable Indian: An Aspect of the Defense of Colonial New England." Journal of American History 64:623–651.

Johnson, Susannah Willard. 1978. A Narrative of the Captivity of Mrs. Johnson . . . . Facsimile of 1796, 1797, and 1814 editions. Garland Library of Narratives of North American Indian Captivities, vol. 23, comp. Wilcomb E. Washburn. New York: Garland.

Jones, James Athearn. 1830. Traditions of the North American Indians. 3 vols. London: Henry Colburn and Richard Bentley.

Jordan, Winthrop D. 1969. White Over Black: American Attitudes Toward the Negro, 1550–1812. New York: W. W. Norton.

Kapchan, Deborah, and Pauline Turner Strong, eds. 1999. Theorizing the Hybrid. Special issue, Journal of American Folklore, no. 445. In press.

Karlsen, Carol F. 1987. The Devil in the Shape of a Woman: Witchcraft in Colonial New England. New York: W. W. Norton.

Karp, Ivan, and Steven Lavine, eds. 1991. Exhibiting Cultures: The Poetics and Politics of Museum Display. Washington, D.C.: Smithsonian Institution Press.

Kasson, Joy S. 1990. Marble Queens and Captives: Women in Nineteenth-Century American Sculpture. New Haven: Yale University Press.

Kawashima, Yasuhide. 1969. "Legal Origins of the Indian Reservation in Colonial Massachusetts." American Journal of Legal History 13:42–56.

_____. 1989. "Indian Servitude in the Northeast." In History of Indian-White Relations, ed. Wilcomb Washburn. Vol. 4, Handbook of North American Indians, gen. ed. William C. Sturtevant. Washington, D.C.: Smithsonian Institution Press.

Keehn, Sally M. 1991. I am Regina. New York: Bantam Doubleday Dell.

Kemp, William B. 1984. "Baffinland Eskimo." In Arctic, ed. David Damas. Vol. 5, Handbook of North American Indians, gen. ed. William C. Sturtevant. Washington, D.C.: Smithsonian Institution Press.

Kibbey, Ann. 1986. The Interpretation of Material Shapes in Puritanism: A Study of Rhetoric, Prejudice, and Violence. Cambridge: Cambridge University Press.

Kimber, Edward. 1978 [1754]. The History of the Life and Adventures of Mr. Anderson. Facsimile. Garland Library of Narratives of North American Indian Captivities, comp. Wilcomb E. Washburn, vol. 7. New York: Garland.

Knowles, Nathaniel. 1940. "The Torture of Captives By Indians of Eastern North America." Proceedings of the American Philosophical Society 82:151–225.

Koehler, Lyle. 1979. "Red-White Power Relations and Justice in the Courts of Seventeenth-Century New England." American Indian Culture and Research Journal 3:1–31.

_____. 1980. A Search for Power: The "Weaker Sex" in Seventeenth-Century New England. Urbana: University of Illinois Press.

Kolodny, Annette. 1981. "Turning the Lens on 'The Panther Captivity': A Feminist Excercise in Practical Criticism." In Writing and Sexual Difference. Special Issue, Critical Inquiry 8:329–345.

_____. 1984. The Land Before Her: Fantasy and Experience of the American Frontiers, 1630–1860. Chapel Hill: University of North Carolina Press.

_____. 1993. "Among the Indians: The Uses of Captivity." New York Times Book Review. Reprinted in Women's Studies Quarterly 3–4:184–95.

Krech, Shepard, III. 1991. "The State of Ethnohistory." Annual Review of Anthropology 20:345–375.

Kroeber, A. L., and Clifton B. Kroeber. 1962. "Olive Oatman's First Account of Her Captivity Among the Mohave." California Historical Society Quarterly 41:309–317.

Krupat, Arnold, ed. 1994. Native American Autobiography: An Anthology. Madison: University of Wisconsin Press.

Kuhn, Thomas S. 1970. The Structure of Scientific Revolutions. 2d ed. Chicago: University of Chicago Press.

Kupperman, Karen Ordahl. 1977. "English Perceptions of Treachery, 1583–1640: The Case of the American 'Savages'." The Historical Journal 20:263–287.

_____. 1980. Settling with the Indians: The Meeting of English and Indian Cultures in America, 1580–1649. Totowa, N.J.: Rowman and Littlefield.

_____. 1984. Roanoke: The Abandoned Colony. Totowa, N.J.: Rowman and Allanheld.

_____. 1988. Captain John Smith: A Collection of His Writings. Chapel Hill: University of North Carolina Press.

Labaree, Leonard W., and William B. Wilcox, eds. 1959. The Papers of Benjamin Franklin, vol. 4. New Haven: Yale University Press.

Lang, Amy Schrager. 1990. "Introduction to 'A True History of the Captivity and Restoration of Mrs. Mary Rowlandson.'" In Jouneys in New Worlds: Early American Women's Narratives, ed. William L. Andrews. Madison: University of Wisconsin Press.

Lauber, Almon Wheeler. 1970 [1913]. "Indian Slavery in Colonial Times Within the Present Limits of the United States." Columbia University Studies in History, Economics, and Public Law 54:253–604. Reprint. Williamstown, Mass.: Corner House.

Lawrence, D. H. 1964 [1923]. Studies in Classic American Literature. New York: Viking.

Leach, Douglas E. 1958. Flintlock and Tomahawk: New England in King Philip's War. New York: Macmillan.

_____. 1961. "The 'Whens' of Mary Rowlandson's Captivity." New England Quarterly 34:352–363.

_____. 1966. The Northern Colonial Frontier, 1607–1763. New York: Holt, Rinehart, and Winston.

_____. 1973. Arms for Empire: A Military History of the British Colonies in North America, 1607–1763. New York: Macmillan.

_____. 1986. Roots of Conflict: British Armed Forces and Colonial Americans, 1677–1763. Chapel Hill: University of North Carolina Press.

Lears, T. J. Jackson. 1985. "The Concept of Cultural Hegemony: Problems and Possibilities." American Historical Review 90:567–593.

Lepore, Jill. 1994. "Dead Men Tell No Tales: John Sassamon and the Fatal Consequences of Literacy," American Quarterly 46:479–512.

_____. 1998. The Name of War: King Philip's War and the Origins of American Identity. New York: Knopf.

Le Roy, Marie, and Barbara Leininger. 1878 [1759]. "The Narrative of Marie Le Roy and Barbara Leininger." Pennsylvania Archives, 2d ser., 7:401–412. Harrisburg, Pa.

_____. 1978 [1759]. Die Erzehlungen von Maria Le Roy und Barbara Leininger . . . . Facsimile. Garland Library of Narratives of North American Indian Captivities, vol. 8, comp. Wilcomb E. Washburn. New York: Garland.

Levernier, James A. 1975. "Indian Captivity Narratives: Their Functions and Forms." Ph.D. diss., University of Pennsylvania.

Levernier, James A., and Hennig Cohen, eds. 1977. The Indians and Their Captives. Westport, Conn.: Greenwood.

Levin, David. 1978. Cotton Mather: The Young Life of the Lord's Remembrancer, 1663–1703. Cambridge, Mass.: Harvard University Press.

Lewis, Clifford M., and Albert J. Loomie. 1953. The Spanish Jesuit Mission in Virginia, 1570–1572. Chapel Hill: University of North Carolina Press.

Lincoln, Charles H. 1966 [1913]. Narratives of the Indian Wars, 1675–1699. New York: Charles Scribner's Sons. Reprint, New York: Barnes and Noble.

Linnekin, Jocelyn. 1991. "Cultural Invention and the Dilemma of Authenticity." American Anthropologist, n.s., 91:446–449.

Lipps, Julius. 1966. The Savage Hits Back. Hyde Park, N.Y.: University Books.

Logan, Lisa. 1993. "Mary Rowlandson's Captivity and the 'Place' of the Woman Subject." Early American Literature 28:255–277.

Lok, Michael. 1938 [1867]. Michael Lok's Account of the First Voyage. In The Three Voyages of Martin Frobisher, vol. 1, ed. Vilhjalmur Stefansson. London: Argonaut.

Loudon, Archibald. 1978 [1808–11]. A Selection, of Some of the Most Interesting Narratives, of Outrages, Committed By the Indians, in Their Wars, with the White People; Also, an Account of Their Manners, Customs, Discipline and Encampments, Treatment of Prisoners, Etc. . . . . 2 vols. Facsimiles. Garland Library of Narratives of North American Indian Captivities, comp. Wilcomb E. Washburn, vols. 29–30. New York: Garland.

Lowance, Mason I., Jr. 1980. The Language of Canaan: Metaphor and Symbol in New England from the Puritans to the Transcendentalists. Cambridge, Mass.: Harvard University Press.

[Lowry, Jean]. 1978 [1760]. A Journal of the Captivity of Jean Lowry and Her Children . . . . Facsimile. Garland Library of Narratives of North American Indian Captivities, comp. Wilcomb E. Washburn, vol. 8. New York: Garland.

McBride, Kevin. 1994. "The Source and Mother of the Fur Trade: Native Dutch Relations in Eastern New Netherland." In Enduring Traditions: The Native Peoples of New England, ed. Laurie Weinstein. Westport, Conn.: Bergin & Garvey.

McMullen, Ann. 1994. "'The Heart Interest': Native Americans at Mount Hope and the King Philip Museum." In Passionate Hobby: Rudolf Frederick Haffenreffer and the King Philip Museum, ed. Shepard Krech. Bristol, R.I.: Haffenreffer Museum of Anthropology, Brown University; Seattle: University of Washington Press.

McNickle, D'Arcy. 1978 [1936] The Surrounded. Albuquerque: University of New Mexico Press.

_____. 1978. Wind from an Enemy Sky. Albuquerque: University of New Mexico Press.

_____. 1992. The Hawk Is Hungry, and Other Stories. Ed. Birgit Hans. Tucson: University of Arizona Press.

Marsden, Michael T., and Nachbar, Jack G. 1988. "The Indian in the Movies." In History of Indian-White Relations, ed. Wilcomb E. Washburn. Vol. 4, Handbook of North American Indians, gen. ed. William C. Sturtevant. Washington, D.C.: Smithsonian Institution Press.

Martin, Calvin. 1978. The Keeper of the Game: Indian-Animal Relationships and the Fur Trade. Berkeley: University of California Press.

Martin, Calvin, ed. 1987. The American Indian and the Problem of History. Oxford: Oxford University Press.

Masson, Margaret W. 1976. "The Typology of the Female as a Model for the Regenerate: Puritan Preaching, 1690–1730." Signs 2:304–315.

Mather, Cotton. 1702. Magnalia Christi Americana; or, The Ecclesiastical History of New-England . . . . 7 vols. London.

_____. 1714. Duodecennium Luctuosum. Boston.

_____. 1913 [1699]. Decennium Luctuosum. In Narratives of the Indian Wars, 1675–1699, ed. Charles H. Lincoln. New York: Charles Scribner's Sons, 1913. Reprint ed., New York: Barnes and Noble, 1966.

_____. 1977 [1697]. Humiliations Follow'd with Deliverances . . . . Facsimile. Garland Library of Narratives of North American Indian Captivities, vol. 1, comp. Wilcomb E. Washburn. New York: Garland.

_____. 1977 [1702]. Magnalia Christi Americana . . . . Annotated ed., vols. 1–2. Ed. Kenneth B. Murdock. Cambridge, Mass.: Harvard University Press.

_____. 1978 [1699]. Decennium Luctuosum. Facsimile. Garland Library of Narratives of North American Indian Captivities, vol. 3, comp. Wilcomb E. Washburn. New York: Garland.

_____. 1981 [1697]. Humiliations Follow'd with Deliverances . . . . Excerpted in Puritans Among the Indians: Accounts of Captivity and Redemption, 1676–1724, eds. Alden T. Vaughan and Edward W. Clark. Cambridge, Mass.: Harvard University Press.

_____. 1981 [1699]. Decennium Luctuosum. Excerpted in Puritans Among the Indians: Accounts of Captivity and Redemption, 1676–1724, eds. Alden T. Vaughan and Edward W. Clark. Cambridge, Mass.: Harvard University Press.

_____. 1981 [1702]. Magnalia Christi Americana. Excerpted in Puritans Among the Indians: Accounts of Captivity and Redemption, 1676–1724, eds. Alden T. Vaughan and Edward W. Clark. Cambridge, Mass.: Harvard University Press.

Mather, Increase. 1977 [1684]. An Essay for the Recording of Illustrious Providences . . . . Facsimile. Garland Library of Narratives of North American Indian Captivities, vol. 2, comp. Wilcomb E. Washburn. New York: Garland.

_____. 1978 [1676]. A Brief History of the War with the Indians in New-England. In So Dreadfull a Judgment: Puritan Responses to King Philip's War, 1676–1677, eds. Richard Slotkin and James K. Folsom. Middletown, Conn.: Wesleyan University Press.

_____. 1981 [1684]. An Essay for the Recording of Illustrious Providences . . . . Excerpted in Puritans Among the Indians: Accounts of Captivity and Redemption, 1676–1724, eds. Alden T. Vaughan and Edward W. Clark. Cambridge, Mass.: Harvard University Press.

Mauss, Marcel. 1954 [1925]. The Gift: Forms and Functions of Exchange in Archaic Societies. Trans. Ian Cunnison. New York: Norton.

Maylem, John. 1978 [1758]. Gallic Perfidy: A Poem. Facsimile. Garland Library of Narratives of North American Indian Captivities, vol. 8, comp. Wilcomb E. Washburn. New York: Garland.

Medlicott, Alexander, Jr. 1965. "Return to the Land of Light: A Plea to an Unredeemed Captive." New England Quarterly 38:202–216.

Melvoin, Richard. 1989. New England Outpost: War and Society in Colonial Deerfield. New York: W. W. Norton.

Merton, Robert K. 1970 [1938]. Science, Technology, and Society in Seventeenth-Century England. New York: H. Fertig.

Middlekauff, Robert. 1971. The Mathers: Three Generations of Puritan Intellectuals, 1596–1728. New York: Oxford University Press.

Miller, Christopher L., and George R. Hamell. 1986. "A New Perspective on Indian-White Contact: Cultural Symbols and Colonial Trade." Journal of American History 73:311–328.

Miller, Perry. 1939. The New England Mind: The Seventeenth Century. Cambridge, Mass.: Harvard University Press.

_____. 1953. The New England Mind: From Colony to Province. Cambridge, Mass.: Harvard University Press.

Minter, David L. 1973. "By Dens of Lions: Notes on Stylization in Early Puritan Captivity Narratives." American Literature 45:335–347.

Mooney, James. 1907. "The Powhatan Confederacy, Past and Present." American Anthropologist, n.s., 9:129–152.

Moran, Gerald F. 1980. "'Sisters' in Christ: Women and the Church in Seventeenth-Century New England." In Women in American Religion, ed. Janet Wilson James. Philadelphia: University of Pennsylvania Press.

Morgan, Edmund S. 1966. The Puritan Family: Religion and Domestic Relations in Seventeenth-Century New England. Rev. ed. New York: Harper and Row.

_____. 1975. American Slavery, American Freedom: The Ordeal of Colonial Virginia. New York: Norton.

Morrison, Kenneth M. 1979. "Towards a History of Intimate Encounters: Algonkian Folklore, Jesuit Missionaries, and Kiwakwe, the Cannibal Giant." American Indian Culture and Research Journal 3(4):51–80.

_____. 1984. The Embattled Northeast: The Elusive Ideal of Alliance in Abenaki-Euramerican Relations. Berkeley: University of California Press.

Morse, Jarvis M. 1935. "John Smith and His Critics: A Chapter in Colonial Historiography." Journal of Southern History 1:123–137.

Mossiker, Frances. 1976. Pocahontas: The Life and the Legend. New York: Alfred A. Knopf.

Mott, Frank Luther. 1947. Golden Multitudes: The Story of Best Sellers in the United States. New York: Macmillan.

Muldoon, James. "The Indian as Irishman." Essex Institute Historical Collections 111:267–289.

Mullaney, Stephen. 1983. "Strange Things, Gross Terms, Curious Customs: The Rehearsal of Cultures in the Late Renaissance." Representations 3:40–67.

Murdock, Kenneth B. 1942. "William Hubbard and the Providential Interpretation of History." Proceedings of the American Antiquarian Society 52:15–37.

_____. 1949. Literature and Theology in Colonial New England. Cambridge, Mass.: Harvard University Press.

_____. 1955. "Clio in the Wilderness: History and Biography in Puritan New England." New England Quarterly 34:221–238. Revised in Early American Literature 6 (1971):201–222.

Namias, June. 1992. "Introduction." In A Narrative of the Life of Mrs. Mary Jemison. Ed. June Namias. Norman: University of Oklahoma Press.

_____. 1993. White Captives: Gender and Ethnicity on the American Frontier. Chapel Hill: University of North Carolina Press.

Nanepashemet. 1993. "It Smells Fishy to Me: An Argument Supporting the Use of Fish Fertilizer By the Native People of Southern New England." In Algonkians of New England: Past and Present, ed. Peter Benes. The Dublin Seminar for New England Folklife Annual Proceedings for 1991. Boston: Boston University.

Nash, Gary B. 1968. Quakers and Politics: Pennsylvania, 1681–1726. Princeton, N.J.: Princeton University Press.

_____. 1972. "The Image of the Indian in the Southern Colonial Mind." William and Mary Quarterly, 3d ser., 29:197–230.

Nash, Gary B., and Jean R. Soderlund. 1991. Freedom By Degrees: Emancipation in Pennsylvania and Its Aftermath. New York and Oxford: Oxford University Press.

Nash, Roderick. 1982. Wilderness and the American Mind. 3d ed. New Haven: Yale University Press.

Newberry Library. 1912. Narratives of Captivity Among the Indians of North America: A List of Books and Manuscripts on This Subject in the Edward E. Ayer Collection. Chicago: Newberry Library.

Nolan, J. Bennett. 1964. "Peter Williamson in America: A Colonial Odyssey." Pennsylvania History 31:22–29.

Norton, John. 1977 [1748]. The Redeemed Captive. . . . Facsimile. Garland Library of Narratives of North American Indian Captivities, vol. 6, comp. Wilcomb E. Washburn. New York: Garland.

Norton, Mary Beth. 1996. Founding Mothers and Fathers: Gendered Power and the Forming of American Society. New York: Knopf.

Obeyesekere, Ganath. 1992a. The Apotheosis of Captain Cook: European Mythmaking in the Pacific. Princeton, N.J.: Princeton University Press.

_____. 1992b. "'British Cannibals': Contemplation of an Event in the Death and Resurrection of James Cook, Explorer." Critical Inquiry 18 (summer):630–654.

O'Brien, Jean. 1997. Dispossession by Degrees: Indian Land and Identity in Natick, Massachusetts. Cambridge: Cambridge University Press.

_____. n.d. "On Events and Nonevents: 'Vanishing' Indians in Nineteenth-Century New England." In Native North American Cultures, Histories, and Representations, eds. Sergei Kan and Pauline Turner Strong. Lincoln: University of Nebraska Press. Forthcoming.

O'Gorman, Edmundo. 1961. The Invention of America: An Inquiry into the Historical Nature of the New World and the Meaning of Its History. Bloomington: Indiana University Press.

Orians, Harrison, ed. 1970. Days of Humiliation, Times of Affliction and Disaster: Nine Sermons for Restoring Favor with an Angry God, 1696–1727. Gainesville, Fla.: Scholar's Facsimile and Reprints.

Ortiz, Alfonso. 1972. "Ritual Drama and the Pueblo World View." In New Perspectives on the Pueblos, ed. Alfonso Ortiz. Albuquerque: University of New Mexico Press.

_____. 1977. "Some Concerns Central to the Writing of 'Indian' History." Indian Historian 10 (winter):17–22.

Oxford English Dictionary. 1971. Compact Edition, 2 vols. Glasgow and New York: Oxford University Press.

Parkman, Francis. 1851. History of the Conspiracy of Pontiac and the War of the North American Tribes Against the English Colonies After the Conquest of Canada. Boston: C. C. Little and J. Brown.

_____. 1983 [1895–97]. France and England in North America. Ed. David Levin. Abridged. Library of America. New York: Viking.

Pearce, Roy Harvey. 1947. "The Significances of the Captivity Narratives." American Literature 19:1–20.

_____. 1952. "Melville's Indian-Hater: A Note on the Meaning of the Confidence-Man." Publications of the Modern Language Association 67:942–948.

_____. 1957. "The Metaphysics of Indian-Hating." Ethnohistory 4 (winter):27–40.

_____. 1965. Savagism and Civilization: A Study of the Indian and the American Mind. [Rev. ed. of The Savages of America, 1953.] Baltimore: Johns Hopkins University Press.

_____. 1969. "The Metaphysics of Indian-Hating: Leatherstocking Unmasked." In Historicism Once More: Problems and Occasions for the American Scholar. Princeton: Princeton University Press.

_____. 1974. "From the History of Ideas to Ethnohistory." Journal of Ethnic Studies 2:86–92.

Peckham, Howard Henry. 1964. The Colonial Wars, 1689–1762. Chicago: University of Chicago Press.

Peckham, Howard Henry, ed. 1954. Captured By Indians: True Tales of Pioneer Survivors. New Brunswick, N.J.: Rutgers University Press.

Pennington, Loren E. 1966. Hakluytus Posthumus: Samuel Purchas and the Promotion of English Overseas Expansion. Emporia State Research Studies 14 (3). Emporia: Kansas State Teachers College.

Perdue, Theda. 1979. Slavery and the Evolution of Cherokee Society, 1540–1866. Knoxville: University of Tennessee Press.

Peterson, Jacqueline, and Jennifer S. H. Brown, eds. 1985. The New Peoples: Being and Becoming Métis in North America. Winnipeg: University of Manitoba Press.

Plane, Ann Marie. 1996. "Putting a Face on Colonization: Factionalism and Gender Politics in the Life History of Awashunkes, the 'Squaw Sachem' of Saconet." In Northeastern Indian Lives, 1632–1816, ed. Robert S. Grumet. Amherst: University of Massachusetts Press.

Porterfield, Amanda. 1992. Female Piety in Puritan New England: The Emergence of Religious Humanism. New York and Oxford: Oxford University Press.

Potter, Stephen R. 1989. "Early English Effects on Virginia Algonquian Exchange and Tribute in the Tidewater Potomac." In Powhatan's Mantle: Indians in the Colonial Southeast, eds. Peter H. Wood, Gregory A. Waselkov, and M. Thomas Hatley. Lincoln: University of Nebraska Press.

Pratt, Mary Louise. 1986. "Fieldwork in Common Places." In Writing Culture: The Poetics and Politics of Ethnography, eds. James Clifford and George F. Marcus. Berkeley: University of California Press.

_____. 1992. Imperial Eyes: Travel Writing and Transculturation. London: Routledge.

Prins, Harald E. L. 1996. The Mi'kmaq: Resistance, Accommodation, and Cultural Survival. Case Studies in Cultural Anthropology, ed. George and Louise Spindler. Fort Worth, Tex.: Harcourt Brace College Publishers.

Public Archives of Canada. 1819. Federal Archives Division, Indian Records, Record Group 10. Ottawa. Microfilm Collection, Newberry Library, Chicago.

Pulsifer, David, and Nathaniel B. Shurtleff, eds. 1855–1861. Records of the Colony of New Plymouth in New England. Boston.

Pulsipher, Jenny Hale. 1996. "Massacre at Hurtleberry Hill: Christian Indians and English Authority in Metacom's War." William and Mary Quarterly, 3d ser., 53:459–486.

Purchas, Samuel. 1617. Purchas His Pilgrimage. 3d ed. London.

Purchas, Samuel. 1625. Hakluytus Posthumus; or Purchas His Pilgrimes. 20 vols. Glasgow: James MacLehose.

Quinn, David B. 1955. The Roanoke Voyages, 1584–1590. 2 vols. Hakluyt Society Publications, 2d ser., vols. 104–105. London.

Radin, Paul, ed. 1940. An Indian Captivity (1789–1822): John Tanner's Narrative. San Francisco: Work Projects Administration.

Ramsey, Colin. 1994. "Cannibalism and Infant Killing: A System of 'Demoning' Motifs in Indian Captivity Narratives." Clio 24:55–69.

Rhode Island Historical Society. 1835. Collections. Providence, R.I.: John Miller.

_____. 1970. Rhode Island Land Evidences, Abstracts. Reprint. Providence, R.I.

Richter, Daniel K. 1983. "War and Culture: The Iroquois Experience." William and Mary Quarterly, 3d ser., 40:528–559.

_____. 1992. The Ordeal of the Longhouse: The Peoples of the Iroquois League in the Era of European Colonization. Chapel Hill: University of North Carolina Press.

Richter, Daniel K., and James Merrell, eds. 1987. Beyond the Covenant Chain: The Iroquois and Their Neighbors in Indian North America, 1600–1800. Syracuse, N.Y.: Syracuse University Press.

Ricoeur, Paul. 1970. Freud and Philosophy: An Essay on Interpretation. Trans. Denis Savage. New Haven: Yale University Press.

_____. 1973. "The Model of the Text: Meaningful Action Considered as a Text." Social Research 38:529–562. Reprinted in Interpretive Social Science: A Reader, eds. Paul Rabinow and William M. Sullivan. Berkeley: University of California Press, 1979.

_____. 1979. "Psychoanalysis and the Movement of Contemporary Culture." In Interpretive Social Science: A Reader, eds. Paul Rabinow and William M. Sullivan. Berkeley: University of California Press.

Robertson, Karen. 1996. "Pocahontas at the Masque." Signs: Journal of Women in Culture and Society 21:551–583.

Rountree, Helen. 1989. The Powhatan Indians of Virginia: Their Traditional Culture. Norman: University of Oklahoma Press.

Rowlandson, Mary. 1975 [1682]. The Narrative of the Captivity and Restoration of Mrs. Mary Rowlandson. Reprint. Ed. Robert Diebold. Lancaster, Mass.: Lancaster Bicentennial Commission.

_____. 1977 [1682]. A True History of the Captivity and Restoration of Mary Rowlandson . . . . 4th ed. (London). Facsimile. Garland Library of Narratives of North American Indian Captivities, vol. 1, comp. Wilcomb E. Washburn. New York: Garland.

_____. 1978 [1682]. The Sovereignty and Goodness of God . . . . In So Dreadfull a Judgment: Puritan Responses to King Philip's War, 1676–1677, eds. Richard Slotkin and James K. Folsom. Middletown, Conn.: Wesleyan University Press.

_____. 1981 [1682]. The Sovereignty and Goodness of God . . . . In Puritans among the Indians: Accounts of Captivity and Redemption, 1676–1724, eds. Alden T. Vaughan and Edward W. Clark. Cambridge, Mass.: Harvard University Press.

_____. 1990 [1682]. A True History of the Captivity and Restoration of Mrs. Mary Rowlandson. 4th ed. (London). Ed. Amy Schrager Lang. In Journeys in New Worlds: Early American Women's Narratives, ed. William L. Andrews. Madison: University of Wisconsin Press.

_____. 1997 [1682]. The Sovereignty and Goodness of God By Mary Rowlandson, with Related Documents. Ed. Neal Salisbury. Boston: Bedford Books.

Sahlins, Marshall. 1968. Tribesmen. Englewood Cliffs, N.J.: Prentice-Hall.

_____. 1981. Historical Metaphors and Mythical Realities. Ann Arbor: University of Michigan Press.

_____. 1983. "Raw Women, Cooked Men, and Other 'Great Things' of the Fiji Islands." In The Ethnography of Cannibalism, eds. Paula Brown and Donald Tuzin. Society of Psychological Anthropology Special Publication. Washington, D.C.: American Anthropological Association.

_____. 1985. Islands of History. Chicago: University of Chicago Press.

_____. 1996. How "Natives" Think: About Captain Cook, For Example. Chicago: University of Chicago Press.

Said, Edward W. 1978. Orientalism. New York: Random House.

Sainsbury, John A. 1975. "Indian Labor in Early Rhode Island." New England Quarterly 48:378–393.

Salisbury, Neal. 1972. "The Conquest of the 'Savage': Puritans, Puritan Missionaries, and Indians, 1620–1680." Ph.D. diss., University of California, Los Angeles.

_____. 1974. "Red Puritans: The 'Praying Indians' of Massachusetts Bay and John Eliot." William and Mary Quarterly, 3d ser., 31:27–54.

_____. 1981. "Squanto: Last of the Patuxets." In Struggle and Survival in Colonial America, eds. David G. Sweet and Gary B. Nash. Berkeley: University of California Press.

_____. 1982. Manitou and Providence: Indians, Europeans, and the Making of New England, 1500–1643. Oxford: Oxford University Press.

_____. 1987. "Social Relationships on a Moving Frontier: Natives and Settlers in Southern New England, 1638–1675." Man in the Northeast 33:89–99.

Salisbury, Neal, ed. 1997. The Sovereignty and Goodness of God By Mary Rowlandson, with Related Documents. Boston: Bedford Books.

Salwen, Bert. 1978. "Indians of Southern New England and Long Island: Early Period." In Northeast, ed. Bruce Trigger. Vol. 15, Handbook of North American Indians, gen. ed. William C. Sturtevant. Washington, D.C.: Smithsonian Institution Press.

Samuels, David William. 1999. "The Whole and the Sum of the Parts, Or, How Cookie and His Cupcakes Told the Story of Apache History in San Carlos." In Theorizing the Hybrid, eds. Deborah Kapchan and Pauline Turner Strong. Special issue, Journal of American Folklore, no. 445. In press.

Sanders, Ronald. 1978. Lost Tribes and Promised Lands: The Origins of American Racism. Boston: Little, Brown.

Saunders, Charles. 1978 [1763]. The Horrid Cruelty of the Indians . . . . Facsimile. Garland Library of Narratives of North American Indian Captivities, vol. 10, comp. Wilcomb E. Washburn. New York: Garland.

Sayre, Gordon M. 1997. Les Sauvages Américains: Representations of Native Americans in French and English Colonial Literature. Chapel Hill: University of North Carolina Press.

Schaffer, Kay. n.d. "Whose Cannibalism?: Consumption, Incorporation and the Colonial Body." In Culture and Colonialism, ed. Maíre Ní Flauthúin. Galway: Galway University Press. Forthcoming.

Scheckel, Susan. 1998. Race and Nationalism in Nineteenth-Century American Culture. Princeton: Princeton University Press.

Schoolcraft, Henry Rowe. 1978 [1851]. The American Indians: Their History, Condition, and Prospects. Facsimile. Garland Library of Narratives of North American Indian Captivities, vol. 60, comp. Wilcomb E. Washburn. New York: Garland.

Schutz, Alfred. 1964. Studies in Social Theory, ed. Arvid Brodelsen. Vol. 2, Collected Papers, ed. Maurice Natanson. Hague: M. Nijhoff.

_____. 1973. The Problem of Social Reality, ed. Maurice Natanson. 4th ed. Vol. 1, Collected Papers, ed. Maurice Natanson. Hague: M. Nijhoff.

Seaver, James Everett. 1978. A Narrative of the Life of Mrs. Mary Jemison. 4th ed. Facsimile of 1824 and 1856 editions. Garland Library of Narratives of North American Indian Captivities, vol. 41, comp. Wilcomb E. Washburn. New York: Garland.

_____. 1992 [1824]. A Narrative of the Life of Mrs. Mary Jemison. With an introduction and annotations by June Namias. Norman: University of Oklahoma Press.

Seelye, John. 1977. Prophetic Waters: The River in American Life and Literature. New York: Oxford University Press.

Sekora, John. 1993. "Red, White, and Black: Indian Captivities, Colonial Printers, and the Early African-American Narrative." In A Mixed Race: Ethnicity in Early America, ed. Frank Shuffleton. New York and Oxford: Oxford University Press.

Settle, Dionyse. 1979 [1577]. "A true reporte of Capteine Frobisher his last voyage into the West and Northwest regions." In New American World: A Documentary History of North America to 1612, vol. 4, Newfoundland from Fishery to Colony: Northwest Passage Searches, ed. David B. Quinn. New York: Arno Press.

Sewall, Samuel. 1973. The Diary of Samuel Sewall, 1674–1729. Ed. M. Halsey Thomas. 2 vols. New York: Farrar, Straus and Giroux.

Sewell, David R. 1993. "'So Unstable and Like Mad Men They Were': Language and Interpretation in American Captivity Narratives." In A Mixed Race: Ethnicity in Early America, ed. Frank Shuffleton. New York and Oxford: Oxford University Press.

Shea, Daniel. 1968. Spiritual Autobiography in Early America. Princeton: Princeton University Press.

Sheehan, Bernard W. 1980. Savagism and Civility: Indians and Englishmen in Colonial Virginia. Cambridge: Cambridge University Press.

Sheldon, George. 1895–96. A History of Deerfield, Massachusetts . . . with a Special Study of the Indian Wars in the Connecticut Valley. 2 vols. Deerfield, Mass.: E. A. Hall.

Shoemaker, Nancy. 1995a. "Introduction." In Negotiators of Change: Historical Perspectives on Native American Women, ed. Nancy Shoemaker. New York: Routledge.

_____. 1995b. "Kateri Tekakwitha's Tortuous Path to Sainthood." In Negotiators of Change: Historical Perspectives on Native American Women, ed. Nancy Shoemaker. New York: Routledge.

Shuffleton, Frank. 1976. "Indian Devils and the Pilgrim Fathers: Sqaunto, Hobomok, and the English Conception of Indian Religion." New England Quarterly 49:108–116.

Sieminski, Greg. 1990. "The Puritan Captivity Narrative and the Politics of the American Revolution." American Quarterly 42:35–56.

Silverman, Kenneth. 1984. The Life and Times of Cotton Mather. New York: Harper and Row.

Simmons, Leo W., ed. 1942. Sun Chief: The Autobiography of a Hopi Indian. New Haven: Yale University Press.

Simmons, William S. 1970. Cautantowwit's House: An Indian Burial Ground on the Island of Conanicut in Narragansett Bay. Providence, R.I.: Brown University Press.

_____. 1976. "Southern New England Shamanism: An Ethnographic Reconstruction." In Papers of the Seventh Algonquian Conference, 1975, William Cowan, ed. Ottawa, Ont.: Carleton University.

_____. 1978. "Narragansett." In Northeast, ed. Bruce Trigger. Vol. 15, Handbook of North American Indians, gen. ed. William C. Sturtevant. Washington, D.C.: Smithsonian Institution Press.

_____. 1979. "Conversion from Indian to Puritan." New England Quarterly 52:197–218.

_____. 1986. Spirit of the New England Tribes: Indian History and Folklore, 1620–1984. Hanover, N.H.: University Press of New England.

Simmons, William S., and George F. Aubin. 1975. "Narragansett Kinship." Man in the Northeast 9:21–31.

Slotkin, Richard. 1973. Regeneration Through Violence: The Mythology of the American Frontier, 1600–1800. Middletown, Conn.: Wesleyan University Press.

Slotkin, Richard, and James K. Folsom, eds. 1978. So Dreadfull a Judgment: Puritan Responses to King Philip's War, 1676–1677. Middletown, Conn.: Wesleyan University Press.

Smethurst, Gamaliel. 1978 [1774]. A Narrative of an Extraordinary Escape out of the Hands of the Indians, in the Gulph of St. Lawrence; Interspersed with a Description of the Coast, and Remarks on the Customs and Manners of the Savages There. Facsimile. Garland Library of Narratives of North American Indian Captivities, comp. Wilcomb E. Washburn, vol. 10. New York: Garland.

Smith, Bradford. 1953. Captain John Smith: His Life and Legend. Philadelphia: Lippincott.

Smith, Clara. 1928. Supplement to Narratives of Captivity Among the Indians of North America: A List of Books and Manuscripts on This Subject in the Edward E. Ayer Collection. Chicago: Newberry Library.

Smith, John. 1986. The Complete Works of Captain John Smith (1580–1631). 3 vols. Ed. Philip L. Barbour. Chapel Hill: University of North Carolina Press.

_____. 1986 [1608]. A True Relation of Such Occurrences and Accidents of Noate as Hath Hapned in Virginia. In Complete Works, vol. 1.

_____. 1986 [1612]. A Map of Virginia, with a Description of the Country, the Commodities, People, Government and Religion . . . . In Complete Works, vol. 1.

_____. 1986 [1624]. The Generall Historie of Virginia, New-England, and the Summer Isles . . . . In Complete Works, vol. 2.

_____. 1986 [1630]. The True Travels . . . . In Complete Works, vol. 3.

Smith, Marian W. 1951. "American Indian Warfare." Transactions of the New York Academy of Science, 2d ser., 12:348–365.

[Smith, William.] 1868 [1765]. Historical Account of General Bouquet's Expedition Against the Ohio Indians in 1764. [Reprint, with additions, of An Historical Account of the Expedition Against the Ohio Indians (Philadelphia).] Ed. Francis Parkman. Cincinnati, Ohio.

Smith-Rosenberg, Carroll. 1993. "Subject Female: Authorizing American Identity." American Literary History 5:481–511.

Snell, William Robert. 1972. "Indian Slavery in Colonial South Carolina, 1671–1795." Ph.D. diss., University of Alabama.

Snyderman, George S. 1948. "Behind the Tree of Peace: A Sociological Analysis of Iroquois Warfare." Pennsylvania Archaeologist 18 (3–4):3–93.

Some Indian Events of New England. 1934. Boston: State Street Trust Co.

Sommer, Doris. 1991. Foundational Fictions: The National Romances of Latin America. Berkeley: University of California Press.

Speck, Frank G. 1919. "The Functions of Wampum Among the Eastern Algonkian." Memoirs of the American Anthropological Association 6:3–71.

_____. 1928. "Territorial Subdivisions and Boundaries of the Wampanoag, Massachusett, and Nauset Indians." Indian Notes and Monographs 44.

_____. 1945. The Celestial Bear Comes Down to Earth. Reading Public Museum and Art Gallery, Scientific Publications, no. 7. Reading, Pa.

Spelman, Henry. 1910 [1613?]. Relation of Virginia. In Travels and Works of Captain John Smith, vol. 1, eds. Edward Arber and Arthur G. Bradley. Edinburgh: John Grant.

Spiess, Arthur E., and Bruce D. Spiess. 1987. "New England Pandemic of 1616–1622: Causes and Archaeological Implication." Man in the Northeast 34:71–83.

Stallybrass, Peter, and Allon White. 1986. The Politics and Poetics of Transgression. Ithaca, N.Y.: Cornell University Press.

Stanford, Ann. 1976. "Mary Rowlandson's Journey to Redemption." Ariel 7:27–37.

Stannard, David E. 1991. "Recounting the Fables of Infanticide and the Functions of Political Myth." Journal of American Studies 25.

Starna, William A., and Ralph Watkins. 1991. "Northern Iroquoian Slavery." Ethnohistory 38:34–57.

Stefansson, Vilhjalmur, ed. 1938. The Three Voyages of Martin Frobisher: From Original Text by George Best, 1578. 2 vols. London: Argonaut.

Stewart, Kathleen. 1996. A Space by the Side of the Road: Cultural Poetics in an 'Other' America. Princeton, N.J.: Princeton University Press.

Stocking, George W., Jr. 1968a. "Empathy and Antipathy in the Heart of Darkness." Journal of the History of the Behavioral Sciences 4:189–194.

———. 1968b. Race, Culture, and Evolution: Essays in the History of Anthropology. New York: Free Press.

———. 1973. "From Chronology to Ethnology: James Cowles Prichard and British Anthropology, 1800–1850." In Researches into the Physical History of Man, by James Cowles Prichard, ed. George W Stocking, Jr. Chicago: University of Chicago Press.

———. 1987. Victorian Anthropology. New York: Free Press.

———. 1992. The Ethnographer's Magic and Other Essays in the History of Anthropology. Madison: University of Wisconsin Press.

Stocking, George W., Jr., ed. 1985. Objects and Others: Essays on Museums and Material Culture. Vol. 3, History of Anthropology. Madison: University of Wisconsin Press.

———. 1991. Colonial Situations: Essays in the Contextualization of Anthropological Knowledge. Vol. 7, History of Anthropology. Madison: University of Wisconsin Press.

Stout, Harry S. 1986. The New England Soul: Preaching and Religious Culture in Colonial New England. New York and Oxford: Oxford University Press.

Strong, Pauline Turner. 1986. "Fathoming the Primitive: Australian Aborigines in Four Explorers' Journals, 1697–1845." In Travel Literature, Ethnography, and Ethnohistory, ed. Caroline Brettell. Special issue. Ethnohistory 33:175–194.

———. 1992a. "Captive Selves, Captivating Others: The Practice and Representation of Captivity Across the British-Amerindian Frontier, 1575–1775." Ph.D. diss., University of Chicago.

———. 1992b. "Captivity in White and Red: Convergent Practice and Colonial Representation on the British-Amerindian Frontier, 1606–1736." In Crossing Cultures: Essays in the Displacement of Western Civilization, ed. Daniel A. Segal. Tucson: University of Arizona Press.

———. 1992c. "Review of American Puritanism and the Defense of Mourning: Religion, Grief, and Ethnology in Mary Rowlandson's Captivity Narrative, by Mitchell Robert Breitwieser." Ethnohistory 39:355–357.

———. 1994. "Review of The Invented Indian: Cultural Fictions and Government Policies, ed. James A. Clifton." American Ethnologist 21:1052–1053.

———. 1995. "The Search for Otherness." In Invisible America: Unearthing Our Hidden History, eds. Mark P. Leone and Neil Asher Silberman. New York: Henry Holt and Company.

———. 1996a. "Animated Indians: Critique and Contradiction in Commodified Children's Culture." Cultural Anthropology 11:405–424.

———. 1996b. "Feminist Theory and the Invasion of the Heart in North America." In Native American Women's Responses to Christianity, eds. Michael Harkin and Sergei Kan. Special issue. Ethnohistory 43:683–712.

———. 1997. "Exclusive Labels: Indexing the National 'We' in Commemorative and Oppositional Exhibitions." Museum Anthropology 21(1):42–56.

———. n.d.a. "Captivity, Adoption, and Slavery." In Blackwell Companion to Native American History, eds. Philip J. Deloria and Neal Salisbury. Blackwell Publishers. Forthcoming.

———. n.d.b. "'To Forget Their Tongue, Their Name, and Their Whole Relation': The Contest of Kinship in North America." In Relative Values: New Directions in Kinship Study, eds. Sarah Franklin and Susan McKinnon. University of California Press. Forthcoming.

Strong, Pauline Turner, and Barrik Van Winkle. 1996. "'Indian Blood': Reflections on the Reckoning and Refiguring of Native North American Identity." Cultural Anthropology 11:547–576.

Sturtevant, William C. 1976. "First Visual Images of Native America." In First Images of America, vol. 1, eds. Fredi Chiapelli, Michael J. B. Allen, and Robert L. Benson. Berkeley: University of California Press.

Sturtevant, William C., and David B. Quinn. 1987. "This New Prey: Eskimos in Europe in 1567, 1576, and 1577." In Indians and Europe, ed. Christian F. Feest. Aachen: Herodot/Rader-Verlag.

Swagerty, William Royce. 1981. "Beyond Bimini: Indian Responses to European Incursions in the Spanish Borderlands, 1513–1600." Ph.D. diss., University of California, Santa Barbara.

Swan, Bradford. 1959. An Indian's an Indian, or the Several Sources of Paul Revere's Engraved Portrait of King Philip. Providence: Rhode Island Society of Colonial Wars.

Swanton, John R. 1926. "Notes on the Mental Assimilation of Races." Journal of the Washington Academy of Sciences 16:493–502.

———. 1932. "The Green Corn Dance." Chronicles of Oklahoma 10:170–195.

———. 1946. The Indians of the Southeastern United States. Bureau of American Ethnology Bulletin 137. Washington, D.C.: Government Printing Office.

———. 1952. The Indian Tribes of North America. Bureau of American Ethnology Bulletin 145. Washington, D.C.: Government Printing Office.

Sweet, David G., and Gary B. Nash, eds. 1981. Struggle and Survival in Colonial America. Berkeley: University of California Press.

Tanner, John. 1994 [1830]. The Falcon: A Narrative of the Captivity and Adventures of John Tanner During Thirty Years Residence Among the Indians in the Interior of North America. Introduction by Louise Erdrich. New York: Penguin.

Taussig, Michael. 1980. The Devil and Commodity Fetishism in South America. Chapel Hill: University of North Carolina Press.

———. 1987. Shamanism, Colonialism, and the Wild Man: A Study in Terror and Healing. Chicago: University of Chicago Press.

———. 1993. Mimesis and Alterity. New York: Routledge.

Thomas, G. E. 1975. "Puritans, Indians, and the Concept of Race." New England Quarterly 48:3–27.

Thomas, Keith. 1971. Religion and the Decline of Magic. New York: Scribner.

Thomson, John. 1978 [1761]. The Travels and Surprising Adventures of John Thomson, Who Was Taken, and Carried to America, and Sold for a Slave There; How He Was Taken Captive By the Savages . . . and His Return to Scotland. Garland Library of Narratives of North American Indian Captivities, comp. Wilcomb E. Washburn, vol. 9. New York: Garland.

Tilton, Robert S. 1994. Pocahontas: The Evolution of an American Narrative. Cambridge: Cambridge University Press.

Todorov, Tzvetan. 1982. The Conquest of America: The Question of the Other. Trans. Richard Howard. New York: Harper and Row.

Tolles, Frederick B. 1948. Meeting House and Counting House: The Quaker Merchants of Colonial Philadelphia, 1682–1763. Chapel Hill: University of North Carolina Press.

_____. 1960. Quakers and the Atlantic Culture. New York: Macmillan.

Tompkins, Jane. 1985. Sensational Designs: The Cultural Work of American Fiction, 1790–1860. New York: Oxford University Press.

Tooker, Elisabeth. 1978. "The League of the Iroquois: Its History, Politics, and Ritual." In Northeast, ed. Bruce Trigger. Vol. 15, Handbook of North American Indians, gen. ed. William C. Sturtevant. Washington, D.C.: Smithsonian Institution Press.

Toulouse, Teresa A. 1992a. "Mary Rowlandson and the 'Rhetoric of Ambiguity.'" Studies in Puritan American Spirituality 3:21–52.

_____. 1992b. "'My Own Credit': Strategies of (E)Valuation in Mary Rowlandson's Captivity Narrative." American Literature 64:655–676.

Trigger, Bruce. 1969. The Huron: Farmers of the North. New York: Holt, Rinehart, and Winston.

_____. 1976. The Children of Aataentsic: A History of the Huron People to 1660. 2 vols. Montreal: McGill-Queen's University Press.

_____. 1978. "Cultural Unity and Diversity." In Northeast, ed. Bruce Trigger. Vol. 15, Handbook of North American Indians, gen. ed. William C. Sturtevant. Washington, D.C.: Smithsonian Institution Press.

_____. 1985. Natives and Newcomers: Canada's "Heroic Age" Reconsidered. Montreal: McGill-Queen's University Press.

Trigger, Bruce, ed. 1978. Northeast. Volume 15, Handbook of North American Indians, gen. ed. William C. Sturtevant. Washington, D.C.: Smithsonian Institution Press.

Trigger, Bruce, and James F. Pendergast. 1978. "Saint Lawrence Iroquoians." In Northeast, ed. Bruce Trigger. Vol. 15, Handbook of North American Indians, gen. ed. William C. Sturtevant. Washington, D.C.: Smithsonian Institution Press.

Trueman, Stuart. 1966. The Ordeal of John Gyles: Being an Account of His Odd Adventures, Strange Deliverances etc. As a Slave of the Maliseets. Toronto: McClelland and Stewart.

Turner, E. Randolph III. 1985. "Socio-Political Organization Within the Powhatan Chiefdom and the Effects of European Contact, A.D. 1607–1646." In Cultures in Contact: The Impact of European Contacts on Native American Cultural Institutions, A.D. 1000–1800, ed. William Fitzhugh. Washington, D.C.: Smithsonian Institution Press.

Turner, Victor. 1967. "Betwixt and Between: The Liminal Period in Rites de Passage." In The Forest of Symbols: Aspects of Ndembu Ritual. Ithaca: Cornell University Press.

Ulrich, Laurel Thatcher. 1980. "Virtuous Women Found: New England Ministerial Literature, 1668–1735." In Women in American Religion, ed. Janet Wilson James. Philadelphia: University of Pennsylvania Press.

_____. 1982. Good Wives: Image and Reality in the Lives of Women in Northern New England, 1650–1750. New York: Alfred A. Knopf.

Underhill, John. 1837 [1638]. Newes from America. Reprint. Collections of the Massachusetts Historical Society, 3d ser., vol. 6.

Updike, Daniel B. 1937. Richard Smith: First English Settler of the Narragansett Country, Rhode Island. Boston: Merrymount.

[Urssenbacher, Abraham.] 1978 [1762]. "Erzehlung Eines unter den Indianern Gewesener Gefangenen." Facsimile reprint of extract from Neu-eingerichteter Amerikanischer Geschichts- und Haus-Calender. Garland Library of Narratives of North American Indian Captivities, comp. Wilcomb E. Washburn, vol. 8. New York: Garland.

Vail, R.W.G. 1949. The Voice of the Old Frontier. Philadelphia: University of Pennsylvania Press.

VanDerBeets, Richard. 1971. "A Surfeit of Style: The Indian Captivity Narrative as Penny Dreadful." Research Studies 39:296–307. Reprinted in VanDerBeets, The Indian Captivity Narrative, 1984.

_____. 1972a. "'A Thirst for Empire': The Indian Captivity Narrative as Propaganda." Research Studies 40:207–215. Reprinted in VanDerBeets, The Indian Captivity Narrative, 1984.

_____. 1972b. "The Indian Captivity Narrative as Ritual." American Literature 43:548–562. Reprinted in VanDerBeets, The Indian Captivity Narrative, 1984.

_____. 1984. The Indian Captivity Narrative: An American Genre. Lanham, Md.: University Press of America.

VanDerBeets, Richard, ed. 1973. Held Captive By Indians: Selected Narratives, 1642–1836. Knoxville: University of Tennessee Press.

Van Gennep, Arnold. 1960 [1908]. The Rites of Passage. Trans. Monika B. Vizedom and Gabrielle L. Caffee. Chicago: University of Chicago Press.

Vaughan, Alden T. 1979. New England Frontier: Puritans and Indians, 1620–1675. Rev. ed. New York and London: W. W. Norton.

_____. 1982. "From White Man to Redskin: Changing Anglo-American Perceptions of the American Indian." American Historical Reivew 87:917–953.

_____. 1983. Narratives of North American Indian Captivity: A Selective Bibliography. Garland Reference Library of the Humanities, vol. 370. New York: Garland.

Vaughan, Alden T., and Edward W. Clark, eds. 1981. Puritans Among the Indians: Accounts of Captivity and Redemption, 1676–1724. Cambridge, Mass.: Harvard University Press.

Vaughan, Alden T., and Daniel K. Richter. 1980. "Crossing the Cultural Divide: Indians and New Englanders, 1605–1763." Proceedings of the American Antiquarian Society 90(1).

Visweswaran, Kamala. 1997. "Histories of Feminist Ethnography." Annual Review of Anthropology 26:591–621.

Wagner, Roy. 1975. The Invention of Culture. Englewood Cliffs, N.J.: Prentice-Hall.

Walens, Stanley. 1981. Feasting with Cannibals: An Essay on Kwakiutl Cosmology. Princeton: Princeton University Press.

Walker, Williston, ed. 1966. The Creeds and Platforms of Congregationalism. Boston: Pilgrim Press.

Wallace, A.F.C. 1969. The Death and Rebirth of the Seneca. New York: Alfred A. Knopf.

Washburn, Wilcomb E. [1977]. Narratives of North American Indian Captivities. Catalog and index for Garland Library of Narratives of North American Indian Captivities, selected and arranged by Wilcomb E. Washburn. New York: Garland.

Washburn, Wilcomb E. 1978. "Seventeenth-Century Indian Wars." In Northeast, ed. Bruce Trigger. Vol. 15, Handbook of North American Indians, gen. ed. William C. Sturtevant. Washington, D.C.: Smithsonian Institution Press.

_____. 1983. "Introduction." In Narratives of North American Indian Captivity: A Selective Bibliography, ed. Alden T. Vaughan. Garland Reference Library of the Humanities, vol. 370. New York: Garland.

Washburn, Wilcomb E., comp. 1977–80. The Garland Library of Narratives of North American Indian Captivities. 111 volumes. New York: Garland.

Washburn, Wilcomb E., ed. 1988. History of Indian-White Relations. Volume 4, Handbook of North American Indians, gen. ed. William C. Sturtevant. Washington, D.C.: Smithsonian Institution Press.

Watkins, Owen C. 1972. The Puritan Experience: Studies in Spiritual Autobiography. London: Routledge and Paul.

Weber, Max. 1949 [1904]. "'Objectivity' in Social Science and Social Policy." In The Methodology of the Social Sciences, eds. E. Shils and H. Finch. New York: Free Press.

_____. 1968. Economy and Society: An Outline of Interpretive Sociology. Eds. Guenther Roth and Claus Wittich. Berkeley: University of California Press.

_____. 1977. Critique of Stammler. Trans. Guy Oakes. New York: Free Press.

Weinstein, Laurie. 1986. "'We're Still Living on Our Traditional Homeland': The Wampanoag Legacy in New England." In Strategies for Survival: American Indians in the Eastern United States, ed. Frank W. Porter III. Westport, Conn.: Greenwood.

Weinstein, Laurie, ed. 1994. Enduring Traditions: The Native Peoples of New England. Westport, Conn.: Bergin and Garvey.

Weinstein-Farson, Laurie. 1989. The Wampanoag. Indians of North America, ed. Frank W. Porter III. New York and Philadelphia: Chelsea House.

Weiser, Reuben. 1978 [1860]. Regina, the German Captive; or, True Piety Among the Lowly. 3d ed. Facsimile. Garland Library of Narratives of North American Indian Captivities, vol. 69, comp. Wilcomb E. Washburn. New York: Garland.

White, Hayden. 1976. "The Noble Savage Theme as Fetish." In First Images of America, vol. 1, eds. Fredi Chiapelli, Michael J. B. Allen, and Robert L. Benson. Berkeley: University of California Press.

White, Richard. 1991. The Middle Ground: Indians, Empires, and Republics in the Great Lakes Region, 1650–1815. Cambridge: Cambridge University Press.

Whitford, Kathryn. 1972. "Hannah Dustin: The Judgment of History." Essex Institute Historical Collections, 108:304–325.

Williams, John. 1976 [1707]. The Redeemed Captive. Ed. Edward W. Clark. Amherst: University of Massachusetts Press.

———. 1978. The Redeemed Captive. . . . Facsimiles of the 1707, 1758, and 1853 editions. Garland Library of Narratives of North American Indian Captivities, comp. Wilcomb E. Washburn, vol. 5. New York: Garland.

———. 1981 [1707]. The Redeemed Captive. . . . In Puritans Among the Indians: Accounts of Captivity and Redemption, 1676–1724, eds. Alden T. Vaughan and Edward W. Clark. Cambridge, Mass.: Harvard University Press.

Williams, Raymond. 1977. Marxism and Literature. Oxford and New York: Oxford University Press.

Williams, Roger. 1973 [1643]. A Key into the Language of America. Eds. John J. Teunissen and Evelyn J. Hinz. Detroit: Wayne State University Press.

Williams, Solomon. 1742. A Sermon Preach'd at Mansfield, Aug. 4, 1741. Boston.

Williamson, Peter. 1978. French and Indian Cruelty. . . . Facsimile of the 1757, 1758, and 1796 editions. Garland Library of Narratives of North American Indian Captivities, vol. 9, comp. Wilcomb E. Washburn. New York: Garland.

Willison, George F. 1945. Saints and Strangers. New York: Reynal and Hitchcock.

Wood, Peter H. 1988. "Indian Servitude in the Southeast." In History of Indian-White Relations, ed. Wilcomb Washburn. Vol. 4, Handbook of North American Indians, gen. ed. William C. Sturtevant. Washington, D.C.: Smithsonian Institution Press.

———. 1989. "The Changing Population of the Colonial South: An Overview By Race and Region, 1685–1790." In Powhatan's Mantle: Indians in the Colonial Southeast, eds. Peter H. Wood, Gregory A. Waselkov, and M. Thomas Hatley. Lincoln: University of Nebraska Press.

Woodward, Grace Steele. 1976. Pocahontas. Reprint. Norman: University of Oklahoma Press.

Young, Philip. 1962. "The Mother of Us All." Kenyon Review 24:391–441.

Zitkala Sa. 1976 [1900]. "The School Days of an Indian Girl; An Indian Teacher Among Indians." Atlantic Monthly. Reprinted in American Indian Stories. Glorieta, N.M.: Rio Grande Press.

Zolla, Elemire. 1973. The Writer and the Shaman. New York: Harcourt, Brace, Jovanovich.

Zuckerman, Michael. 1977. "The Fabrication of Identity in Early America." William and Mary Quarterly, 3d ser., 34:183–214.

# Index